JESSE LIBERTY'S
from scratch
PROGRAMMING SERIES

Microsoft® SQL™ Server 2000 Database Development

from scratch

Rob Hawthorne

que®

201 West 103rd Street,
Indianapolis, Indiana 46290

Associate Publisher
Dean Miller

Acquisitions Editor
Michelle Newcomb

Development Editor
Marla Reece-Hall

Managing Editor
Thomas F. Hayes

Project Editor
Tonya Simpson

Copy Editors
Cindy Fields
Megan Wade

Indexer
Kelly Castell

Proofreader
Benjamin Berg

Technical Editors
Jim Cooper
Adil Rehan

Team Coordinator
Cindy Teeters

Media Developer
Jay Payne

Interior Designer
Sandra Schroeder

Cover Designer
Maureen McCarty

Production
Steve Geiselman
Brad Lenser
Heather Miller

Overview

Table of Contents

About the Author

Rob Hawthorne currently works for KPMG Consulting, based in Wellington, New Zealand, for the eIntegration division. This allows him to work closely with the eStrategy and Process division, also of KPMG Consulting. Prior to this Rob worked for Advantage Group Limited within their E-Commerce division, developing real applications for real business people.

You can find more information about KPMG Consulting at `http://www.kpmgconsulting.com/` and Advantage Group at `http://www.advantagegroup.co.nz/`.

Rob has a degree from the University of Otago, `http://www.otago.ac.nz`, (the best university in the world!), where he graduated with a double major in information science and management (specializing in operations management).

Furthering his education is a high priority to Rob, and he has gained MCP and MCSD status from Microsoft. He is planning for further qualifications from Microsoft, but this book has kept him quite busy for the last few weeks!

Rob lives in Wellington, New Zealand (see `http://www.wellingtonnz.com/`), with his loving wife and wonderful kids. Outside of work, Rob enjoys seeing the beautiful countryside of New Zealand on a mountain bike.

New Zealand offers wonderful scenery from rugged mountains to calm lakes to fantastic sun-drenched beaches. New Zealand has no poisonous snakes, spiders, or anything really dangerous (except maybe a Weta or two, but they aren't even poisonous!). And the skiing and snowboarding are great! Where in the world can a person find greener pastures than in New Zealand? As Rob would say, "Man, I love this country!" See `http://www.purenz.com/` for more information.

As you can see, Rob is very proud of his country. New Zealand is home of the mighty All Blacks, and although we didn't win the World Cup last time, we still retain the America's Cup!

Dedication

I would like to dedicate this book to Daphne Skinner, my mum. Mum provided me with the support, courage, and desire to succeed not only with this book, but also many other aspects of my life.

Unfortunately, mum, you didn't get a chance to see the book published; you passed away in June during the writing of the book. But I know, mum, that you are watching and listening, and this is my way of saying thank you. You have given me so much.

So thank you for your love and kindness and all the support, courage, and guidance you have given me, especially to achieve this mammoth task.

You will be in my heart always.

Acknowledgments

I would like to thank many, many people for the help, support, and encouragement that they have shown me while I have been writing this book.

First, I would like to thank the team at Que Publishing; they have been fantastic. But most notably have been

Holly Allender, for giving me the opportunity to have a go at writing the book. Without Holly, this would not have been possible. Thank you, Holly.

Adil Rehan and Jim Cooper, for giving me the guidance I needed when I went a little off track. Guys, your technical expertise has helped keep me on track. Thank you, Jim and Adil.

Michelle Newcomb, for her patience and understanding. Things had been a little trying while writing the book, but Michelle, you have been great; even with my inane questions you were always patient and willing to help. Thank you, Michelle.

Marla Reece-Hall, for her wonderful school-marm attitude. You have been firm but extremely fair. Thank you, Marla, for all your help and wonderful advice.

Tonya Simpson, for keeping a Kiwi on track and within the boundaries I needed to be and actually getting this book onto shelves. Tonya, you have, like Michelle and Marla, made this book possible, thank you.

Next I would like to thank the professors at Otago University for drumming into my thick head the core concepts that made this book (and my career) possible:

Dr Stephen MacDonell, Dr Geoff Kennedy, Dave Campbell, and Dr Richard Pascoe. You guys really kick-started my career and my keen interest in software development. Thank you, guys!

Next I would like to thank people from work for understanding the pressure of writing a book, but most notably I would like to thank Tony Stewart, Paddy Payne, and the Evolve team for their quiet encouragement and understanding. Thank you, guys.

Kim Tunzelman for all her hard work. Without you, Kim, we wouldn't have all the wonderful spy names that we have. Kim, you were great, thank you.

Jillian Key for the awesome graphics work. Without you, Jillian, we would not have the fantastic graphics for our Spy Net Web site. You have been great.

Finally, I would like to thank my wife and kids for their patience and support. Guys, I really love and appreciate you! And yes Jacob, Daddy will be able to read you two stories every night now. Thank you, son, for being so patient.

Although I have said thank you to these people, the words "thank you" do not seem enough to express the gratitude that I feel toward each and every one of you. You have all been wonderful, and without each of you I would not have been able to achieve so much.

I hope I have the chance to work with each of you again in the near future.

Rob Hawthorne

Tell Us What You Think!

As the reader of this book, *you* are our most important critic and commentator. We value your opinion and want to know what we're doing right, what we could do better, what areas you'd like to see us publish in, and any other words of wisdom you're willing to pass our way.

As an associate publisher for Que, I welcome your comments. You can fax, email, or write me directly to let me know what you did or didn't like about this book—as well as what we can do to make our books stronger.

Please note that I cannot help you with technical problems related to the topic of this book, and that due to the high volume of mail I receive, I might not be able to reply to every message.

When you write, please be sure to include this book's title and author as well as your name and phone or fax number. I will carefully review your comments and share them with the author and editors who worked on the book.

Fax: 317-581-4666

Email: quefeedback@macmillanusa.com

Mail: Dean Miller
         Que
         201 West 103rd Street
         Indianapolis, IN 46290 USA

Introduction

This book is different from any other book written on SQL Server 2000 *ever*. Here's the difference: Other software development books start by teaching you simple skills that build in difficulty, adding skill upon skill as you go. When you've learned all the skills, the books then demonstrate what you can do—a sample program.

This book does not start with programming technique—though it does contain database theory, it starts with a project. We begin by analyzing and designing the requirements for the project, and then we implement that design. Development skills are taught in the context of implementation; first you understand what you are trying to accomplish, and then you learn the skills needed to get the job done.

Who Should Use This Book?

This book is definitely for you if you are

- A software developer who wants to increase your skills and learn about database management.
- A Microsoft Access developer who wants to develop larger applications.
- A Web designer (HTML) coder who wants to begin writing applications that are dynamic and database-driven.
- A C or C++ programmer or a programmer in another language who wants to make the transition to database development and management.
- New to database development or software development in general and want to gain knowledge to advance in your career or gain job satisfaction.

<table>
<tr><td>how tŏŏ
prō nouns' it</td><td>"SQL" can be pronounced in one of two ways. You can say *S.Q.L.* by sounding out each letter. However, the more common way, especially when describing SQL Server 2000, is to pronounce it *see-quill*.</td></tr>
</table>

The *syntax* of the language (what words you use) is not difficult. It is more like English than nearly any other computer language. However, rather than focus on the syntax of the language, you should focus on the *semantics* (what you are trying to say) of the language.

 Syntax is the proper use of terms and punctuation. This can be likened to English grammar, meaning the structure of a sentence.

 Semantics is the meaning and purpose of the code. This can be likened to the concept you are trying to communicate. For example, when explaining an idea, you use not only your voice (or words), but also your hands or drawings.

Conventions Used in This Book

The following are some of the unique features in this series.

 Geek Speak—An icon in the margin indicates the use of a new term. New terms will appear in the paragraph in *italics*.

<table>
<tr><td>how tŏŏ
prō nouns' it</td><td>**How To Pronounce It**—You'll see an icon set in the margin next to a box that contains a technical term and how it should be pronounced. For example, "cin is pronounced *see-in*, and cout is pronounced *see-out*."</td></tr>
</table>

 An icon in the margin indicates code that can be entered, compiled, and run.

EXCURSION

Excursions

Excursions are short diversions from the main topic being discussed, and they offer an opportunity to flesh out your understanding of a topic.

With a book of this type, a topic might be discussed in multiple places as a result of when and where we add functionality during application development. To help make this all clear, we've included a Concept Web that provides a graphical representation of how all the programming concepts relate to one another. You'll find it on the inside front cover of this book.

Notes offer comments and asides about the topic at hand, as well as full explanations of certain concepts.

 Tips provide great shortcuts and hints on how to develop in SQL Server 2000 more effectively.

 Warnings help you avoid the pitfalls of programming and making mistakes that will make your life miserable.

In addition, you'll find various typographic conventions throughout this book:

- Commands, variables, and other code appear in text in a special `computer font`.
- In this book, I build on existing listings as we examine code further. When I add new sections to existing code, you'll spot it in **`bold computer font`**.
- Commands and such that you type appear in **`bold computer font`**.
- Placeholders in syntax descriptions appear in an *`italic computer font`* typeface. This indicates that you will replace the placeholder with the actual filename, parameter, or other element that it represents.

Breaking the Code

In some instances, when you look at a code listing, you'll notice that some lines of code have been broken in two and that the line numbers have letters. For example, see lines 10 and 10a:

```
10:  SELECT Column1, Column2, Column3, Column4
10a: FROM Table1 WHERE Column1 = 512
```

Here I've broken up a single line of code because it was too long to fit on a single line within the page. The code is still valid and can be typed in just as you find it (without the line numbers, of course).

The letter *a* is a signal to you that normally I'd combine these two lines into one. If this were one long line, it would look like this:

```
10: SELECT Column1, Column2, Column3, Column4 FROM Table1 WHERE Column1 = 512
```

In many cases, I must make coding adjustments to break the line and still have legal code. For example

```
10: SELECT @MyVar = 'A string value in the variable for demonstration'
```

To break this line of code, I must end the SELECT statement and add a new one on the subsequent line:

```
10: SELECT @MyVar = 'A string value in the variable '
10a:SELECT @MyVar = @MyVar + 'for demonstration'
```

Again, the resulting code is legal; it is just not how I might otherwise have written it. (Don't worry about the meaning of any of this code; it is all explained in the text of the book).

What to Expect

This book has been designed to give you hands-on experience with SQL Server 2000. We are going to build an application from scratch, beginning from the analysis and design phase right through to the design and implementation of the user interface.

You will gain skills and knowledge in the language of SQL Server 2000, and the many and varied tools offered by SQL Server 2000.

This book is not intended to be the "be all and end all" of SQL Server 2000 books. That is the purpose of such technical resources as Microsoft Developer Network (MSDN). The book guides you through the steps of creating and managing a total database application. It offers you, with examples, the skills to administer and maintain the application.

In Appendix B, "Installation Tips for SQL Server 2000," you will find installation instructions for SQL Server 2000 on a Windows 98 platform. Installation tips and guides for other configurations are also covered.

SQL Server 2000 Editions

SQL Server 2000 comes in three main editions and three minor (or cut-down) versions.

Personal Edition is designed for installations on Windows 98, NT 4.0 Workstation, and Windows 2000 Professional. Personal Edition enables these operating systems to have an application database that can be optimized for a disconnected or mobile user. It also enables small application development on a single-user machine. This suits our needs very well and will allow us to explore the tools of SQL Server 2000 without getting bogged down in a *multiuser* environment.

Multiuser means having more than one user at a time connected to your application. Users can all be performing the same tasks, different tasks, or even be idle but still connected. When designing an application, it is important to think about whether your application will need to support multiple users.

Another edition of SQL Server 2000 is *Standard Edition*. This is mainly used for a single developer or a small team of developers to connect and develop rich functionality for a client, without the overhead of the Enterprise Edition.

The total SQL Server 2000 package comes in the *Enterprise Edition*. This edition is designed for full enterprisewide deployment of SQL Server 2000. It enables *fail-over clustering* of SQL Server 2000 servers, which can process hundreds of thousands of rows of information and support hundreds of simultaneous users. Implementing this would be a little extreme and outside the scope of this book.

Fail-over clustering enables to you to have multiple SQL Servers to back each other up in the event of an emergency or planned down time. If one server becomes unavailable, the other server or servers will take over the processing. This means that you can have high availability of your application.

The three minor editions of SQL Server 2000 are mentioned next because they might be useful to you in the near future.

Developer Edition is for developers when deploying full-scale SQL Server 2000 applications. The Developer Edition has all the features and benefits of Enterprise Edition but is only licensed for use as a development and test platform; it cannot be used as an enterprisewide solution.

Desktop Engine is the .exe (or re-distributable) of the SQL Server 2000 underlying database engine. This enables single developers to distribute their applications with a SQL Server 2000 database engine, but does not provide all the rich functionality provided in other editions. This enables a developer to build a front end in Microsoft Visual Basic (VB) or any other tool with SQL Server 2000 as the underlying database.

CE Edition is used, of course, for the Windows CE device's operating system. It allows for the storage and retrieval of information and can be used to synchronize with SQL Server 2000 when you get back to the office.

What Are We Actually Going To Do?

We will achieve the following that will stand you in good stead for developing a robust application:

- Develop the necessary skills and tools to effectively develop a working database application—the Spy Net application.
- Establish some professional guidelines based on industry standards that you will be able to take advantage of.

- Use the mathematical skills, especially Set Theory, that you learned in school.
- Provide you with a reference for further study.
- Build a foundation to further develop your skills in SQL Server 2000 management.
- Guide you through the installation of SQL Server 2000 on a Windows 98 platform.

Yes, SQL Server 2000 will run on a Windows 2000 platform, but why don't I have you install SQL Server 2000 on a Windows 2000 machine? Well, generally you won't notice any difference in the way SQL Server 2000 works on either Windows 98 or 2000. Now, that's not to say that there aren't differences, but most of them are minor enough for us not to concern ourselves with.

When writing this book I had to write for the lowest common denominator (which is Windows 98 for SQL Server 2000). Aren't I nice to you Windows 98 fans out there? Wherever possible, I have noted the minor differences between SQL Server 2000 Personal Edition running on a Windows 2000 machine compared to a Windows 98 machine, just so I can try to alleviate any issues you might have.

However, all you really need to know is that some screens might appear slightly differently depending on whether you're running Windows 98 or 2000 (or even NT 4.0), but you still will be able to build the application and continue with the project without any issues.

So let's take a brief look at the system requirements for SQL Server 2000.

Hardware and Software Configurations

Let's take a look at the hardware and software requirements for SQL Server 2000. Although this is not complicated, it will let you know instantly whether you can install the CD!

First we will take a look at the hardware requirements, and then progress onto the software requirements, outlining the base requirements for the different installations of SQL Server 2000 that we can have.

What Hardware Do I Need for this Type of Installation?

We cover the hardware and software requirements for SQL Server 2000 in this section. (The installation guide with detailed instructions on how to install SQL Server 2000 is in Appendix B.) Microsoft lists the following as the basic hardware requirements for SQL Server 2000:

- Minimum processor speed of 166 MHz.

- The Enterprise Edition requires 64MB of memory (RAM); all other versions require 32MB of memory.

- For a full installation of SQL Server 2000 you need 180MB of hard drive space.

- For a typical installation of SQL Server 2000 you need 170MB of hard drive space.

- For a minimum installation of SQL Server 2000 you need 65MB of hard drive space

- If you install the additional Analysis Services software, you will need a further 50MB of hard drive space. Note that this is an optional feature to install.

- If you install the additional English Query software, you will need a further 40MB of hard drive space. Note that this is an optional feature to install.

Although Microsoft recommends a minimum CPU speed of 166MHz, I actually installed the Personal Edition of SQL Server 2000 on a Windows 98 machine with 32MB of RAM, a 1GB hard drive, and a Pentium 75MHz processor.

Microsoft has made the application so that it will install on your operating system's minimum requirements (except the hard drive space required and RAM), not a minimum requirement of the application. So even old die-hard PC users like myself who have not upgraded their machines in a long time (bad boy, I know) can still run the latest software. Microsoft, I applaud you.

What About Other Installations?

This hardware requirement guide generally covers most installations of SQL Server 2000; however, the Enterprise Edition is slightly different in that it requires more RAM for a base installation, as previously noted.

If you want to install Enterprise Edition on a cluster of enterprisewide machines, you are limited to 64GB of RAM and 32 CPUs on a Microsoft Windows 2000 Data-Center operating system. Although this might sound excessive, many organizations require a large amount of hardware like this to ensure that their applications are available 24 hours a day, 7 days a week. With a large hardware network, fail-over (or fail-safe) measures can be implemented.

This concludes the hardware requirements for the deployment of SQL Server 2000 on your chosen platform. We need to look at the software requirements and verify that you have the basic requirements so that we can get this installation under way and get developing. So without further adieu, I bring you...

Software Requirements for SQL Server 2000

Okay, so I know what type of hardware I need, but what about software?

We have decided that the only installation we need to concern ourselves with is the installation of SQL Server 2000 Personal Edition. However, because this book is a comprehensive SQL Server 2000 reference book, it would be wise to mention the software requirements for each operating system that supports SQL Server 2000.

Windows 98 Requirements

Microsoft Windows 98 will support an installation of SQL Server 2000 Personal Edition and Desktop Edition. Windows 98 requires the installation of

- Internet Explorer 5.0 (at a minimum). And that's it! Your release of Windows 98 will depend on whether you have Internet Explorer 5 installed. Open your browser, select Help, and then About Internet Explorer to easily verify this. You will see a dialog box similar to that shown in Figure 1.

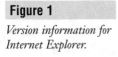

Figure 1

Version information for Internet Explorer.

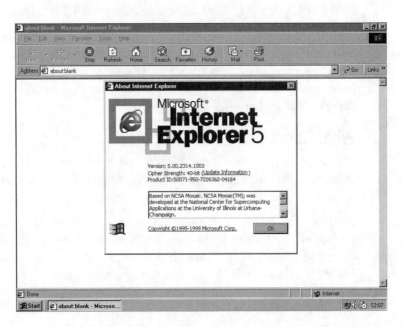

If you do not have Internet Explorer 5.0 installed it can be downloaded from the Microsoft site. Search for Internet Explorer under downloads within the Microsoft site, or at `http://www.microsoft.com/ie/`.

Two main reasons why Internet Explorer 5.0 (or greater) must be installed are for the Microsoft Management Console (MMC) and to view the Hypertext Markup

Language (HTML) help files that come with SQL Server 2000. A minimum installation of Internet Explorer is fine (there is no need for all the fancy add-ons). Internet Explorer does not have to be your default browser, either.

Windows NT 4.0 Workstation and Windows 2000 Professional Requirements

Windows NT 4.0 Workstation requires the installation of the following:

- Internet Explorer 5.0 (at a minimum)
- Service Pack 4 (or later)

The operating system (after SP 4 and IE 5 have been installed) will enable the installation of SQL Server 2000 Personal Edition, Desktop Edition, and Developer Edition. Windows 2000 Professional will support the same installations of SQL Server 2000 as Windows NT 4.0.

Windows NT 4.0 Server and Windows 2000 Server Requirements

If you have the opportunity to practice a server installation, grab it with both hands! Server deployment of SQL Server 2000 offers you the most flexibility. Server deployment allows for many more concurrent users and, as mentioned previously, cluster support.

Windows NT Server 4.0 and Windows NT Server 4.0 Enterprise Edition support SQL Server 2000 Enterprise Edition, Standard Edition, Personal Edition, Developer Edition, and Desktop Edition.

Windows NT 4.0 Server requires the installation of

- Internet Explorer 5.0 (at a minimum)
- Service Pack 4 (or later)

 Note   Windows NT 4.0 Server Enterprise Edition requires the installation of Service Pack 5.0 (or later) as well as Internet Explorer 5.

Windows 2000 Data-Center, Windows 2000 Advanced Server, and Windows 2000 Server support the same installations of SQL Server 2000 as NT 4.0 Server. However, because Windows 2000 is the latest operating system from Microsoft, no software updates are needed at this stage.

Windows CE Installation

So far the only requirements for Windows CE are the Windows CE operating system. Because the version of SQL Server 2000 that runs on CE is designed to capture data, connect, and then download to Enterprise Edition or Standard Edition, the requirements are kept to a minimum.

Next Steps

If you and I were to work together and if I were your mentor, I would teach you the basics of SQL Server 2000 with a hands-on approach by building an application together. Most people (myself included) learn best by doing rather than by explanation. Building an application together would give you not only an introduction to the tools of SQL Server 2000, but also allow you to take control and learn in your own way.

That is exactly how this book works: We'll sit down together and write a program, and along the way I'll teach you what you need to know. From the very first page, we will focus on understanding the problem we are trying to solve and designing a solution, rather than on the syntax of the language.

You are probably thinking what a marathon that was. You should be in my shoes!

In Chapter 1 we will look at what our business problem is, what solution we propose, and how to use SQL Server 2000 to achieve that business solution. We will set up the connection to our instance name of SQL Server 2000 that we have just installed (see Appendix B, "Installation Tips for SQL Server 2000," for information).

So sit back, relax, and enjoy the ride as we explore the world of databases.

Chapter 1

Taking Spy Net from Idea to SQL Server Database

"So what is it I am going to build from scratch in SQL Server 2000?" you may well ask. Well, instead of answering the question directly, I will give you some background (a case study of sorts) about the idea for the application and build up your knowledge of the requirements for the conceptual design phase and the beginning point for developing any new database application.

Requirements are the stated objectives upon which you and the client agree. The application must perform these requirements at a minimum to ensure success of the application.

After I introduce you to the *client* and the objectives for our application, we then put together our data model with the relationships between the tables.

When you're done with the groundwork in this chapter, you'll be ready to install and configure SQL Server and connect to it for the first time. If you've already done part or all of this, you should check your settings against the settings we'll be using for our project. These are listed with the installation instructions in Appendix B, "Installing and Configuring SQL Server 2000."

A Case Study for Spy Net Limited

You are the program director of Spy Net Limited (a fictitious company in no way related to persons living or dead or companies registered or not).

Spy Net Ltd. is an organization much like any other organization, except that Spy Net manages the resourcing of spies on assignments rather than the purchasing and selling of goods.

Recently the activity of the "bad guys" has grown into such a frenzy that you have had real trouble in managing your spies and the current assignments they are working on. So, having the brilliant and capable mind that you have, you decide to research the problem to see whether a solution is available to you.

After some extensive (and I might say, very dedicated) research, you find a book—not just any book, but a complete guide on how to build a spy database from scratch. Isn't that a coincidence?

Okay, so although the case study is fictional, even a little outrageous, the problem we are trying to solve is not. We are faced with an everyday problem (the same as our clients are): so much information to record and so few resources available to manage and implement it.

An Overview of the SQL Spy Net Application

SQL Spy Net is a fictional, but useful, database that enables you to gain the knowledge required to learn a whole range of SQL Server 2000 skills. SQL Spy Net is a *relational* database (see the section "Using Relational Theory to Model Spy Net's Application," later in this chapter) that captures information about spies and their activities and also information about bad guys and their dastardly plans to take over the world.

SQL Spy Net describes real-world objects and the objects' interaction with one another.

 Capture refers to the capability to retain data after a user has entered the information. For example, when you place an order at the grocery store, the clerk captures your order by entering it into the system.

 The term *object* is used very loosely throughout the computer world, but it is usually a computer representation of something we can either see or touch—for example, a person. You can think of objects as parts or characteristics of a database—either the whole database itself or individual tables—that you can test, manipulate, or respond to.

SQL Spy Net also gives the user (you and your team of administrators) the ability to enter and maintain mission-critical data and report on the data. An example of such information is a list of the spies who are not currently working on any assignments or those who have too many assignments.

However, because you do not want everybody viewing or editing your information, you must also implement security into your model to limit access to the application and the sensitive data it contains. Who knows, spies' lives might be depending on it!

In spite of this, you should not limit the application to a single user. Instead, the SQL Spy Net application will conform to three basic principles: *scalability*, *availability*, and *maintainability*.

The terms *scalability*, *availability*, and *maintainability* all refer to the capability of an application to be enhanced, available, and preserved in an effective working state.

 Scalability is concerned with how much additional load can be placed on the application without degrading performance. In other words, is your code written to grow with your company and the number of users you'll have in the future?

 Availability is concerned with the user's ability to gain access to the data. It can also refer to the capability of an application to be available to its users (also called *uptime*). As a DBA, you're likely to hear requests for 24-hour, 7-day access, or the nearest thing to it.

 Maintainability is concerned with the ongoing maintenance of SQL Server 2000 and the application. It can include the ease of performing backups and other administrative tasks.

To begin with, we should think about some of the types of information we want to capture in SQL Spy Net.

Determining What the Application Should Do

Obviously, we want to gather information regarding spies, but what type of information? Do we need their names? Their dates of birth? How should a spy relate to a bad guy?

We will build some common data capture functions into our application, including addresses, dates of birth, and alias names of both spies and bad guys.

Currently on our books, we have about 20 active spies and 10 of the world's most notorious bad guys. We need to hold this information in a way that enables us to get at it quickly and is easy to maintain.

Our application should also enable us to view a history of activities by both parties. This functionality will allow us to assess the highs and lows of activities during the year, permitting us to effectively re-source spies at certain times of the year.

Similar to most other companies, we also need to stay on a budget, so we must watch our salaries and expenses.

Tracking and analyzing trends and financials extends our base model into a management tool. Given this functionality, we will be able to analyze trends. Therefore, when our application is in a stage of maturity, we can provide a graphing facility to plot the trends.

The analysis process is very brief in this book because the topic is SQL Server 2000, not analyzing requirements. However, we will try to adhere to the *Microsoft Solutions Framework (MSF)* model. The main thing to keep in mind is to get a clear picture of what you want in the way of reports out of your database and what information you have available to input.

The *Microsoft Solutions Framework (MSF)* model is a process designed by Microsoft to assist in application development and deployment. It is a very large topic and includes processes on the roles that each member of the team performs and guidelines for helping you get your projects in on time and within budget. More detailed information can be found on Microsoft's Web site, at `http://www.microsoft.com/msf/`.

What Are We Going to Achieve?

So, we have the following reasons for building the SQL Spy Net database:

- To effectively manage spy information
- To effectively allocate resources to an assignment
- To report on current spy activity
- To thwart all evil plans hatched by bad guys so we can promote world peace

Now we have a clear definition of what we are going to achieve: a scalable, secure, and reliable database application that will make entry and retrieval of sensitive information a simple and easy process.

EXCURSION
Measuring Our Success

It is important not only for us to have clear achievable goals, but also for our goals to be clear enough for our clients as well. We must be able to measure what we claim we can do. How else will our clients be able to actively assess the usefulness of the application?

Next, we need to look at how we will achieve this.

Modeling the SQL Spy Net Application

As we already discussed in the preceding section, we are going to develop an application that allows us to track the spies for whom we are responsible and the fervent activity of the bad guys.

We have already set some objectives we want to achieve. It pays to remember these objectives when developing the system, not so we can systematically check every single line of code, but just to have them playing in the back of our minds so we don't defeat one purpose for the benefit of another. When a section (or module) is complete, it can be measured against the set objectives.

> **EXCURSION**
> *Creating Your Data Ruler*
>
> Objectives, which are agreed on by you and the client, must be *measurable*. This enables us to effectively assess the success of the stated objectives, as already mentioned. This, in turn, enables us to learn from the project, and when it comes time for *scoping* a new project, we will be able to do so with a little more accuracy.

Scoping is the process of defining the boundaries of the project. Within scope, we state the objectives on which we and the client agree and what we are actually going to achieve within the given timeframe.

Designing the Spy Net Tables

Now that we have some detail about the application's functionality, we need to see how objects in the real world become virtual objects and how those objects (*entities*) relate to each other. We also must decide which details (*properties*) we want to include on each person or object.

An *entity* is something that can be modeled on a real-world object, usually a table. One example of an entity is a person.

Each person has *properties* or *attributes*, which include his or her name, status, address, and (most important) just whose side that person is on!

To summarize, we have the following details to keep track of:

- Spies—Names, addresses (including international region), statuses, and salaries
- Bad guys—Names,addresses (including international region), statuses, and aliases
- Activities—Type of activity, spy and bad guy involved, who won, and when

With the real-world objects and our goals in mind, we can start thinking of the *entity relationship diagram (ERD)* for our application. It is obvious that we need to capture information about our spies, so we might need a spy table. This could also apply for the bad guys as well. This process is known as *data modeling*.

Data modeling is the process of portraying how the application works and the data flows and how the tables and elements of the application are linked. A variety of tools can be used, including data-flow diagrams (DFDs), state-transition diagrams (STDs), and entity relationship diagrams (ERDs).

Entity Relationship Diagram (ERD) is a core concept to effective database development. The ERD allows us to design our application, either on paper or with a tool such as EasyCase (which is the tool I am using), before we try to implement a model within our database. An ERD has virtual objects that are representations of real-life objects, and it defines the relationships between each of these objects. For example, our ERD will define the relationships between spies and bad guys.

With ERD design, it is essential not to get bogged down in the relationships, the fields required in tables, and so on. The more important part of the process is the thought that goes into the design of the application. After all, nothing is set in stone, and we can always revisit our design in the future.

Using Relational Theory to Model Spy Net's Application

Basic relational theory is actually quite simple when you get the hang of it. It enables you to specify the particular relationship that two entities have with each other. In some applications, these relationships can look very complex, but if you break an application down, you will begin to see the flow of the application—just by looking at how the relationships are defined.

EXCURSION

Theory and Revolution

As I mentioned in the preceding section, a database is made up of entities and properties, which usually take the form of rows and columns in a table, respectively.

Keep in mind that true relational theory uses other terms for each of these concepts and has a more academic focus. However, I'll bet you didn't buy this book for a college course, so we'll stick to what you need to know to put the SQL Spy Net application together. I recommend, though, that if you're going to do more with database design (and as a DBA you will), you should learn all you can about relational theory.

So, relational theory defines *relationships* between entities, but this still does not explain what it is. Relational theory is really only a way of storing and looking at data.

It defines how data looks and relates to other similar data sets. It is based on mathematical set theory, and I bet you thought you would never use that skill again when you left school!

A *relationship* is a virtual data link or connection that derives from a real-world connection. For example, each spy is a person and each bad guy is a person, so we can create a relationship between spies and bad guys. Relationships take one of three forms: one-to-one, one-to-many, and many-to-many. We will look at how to determine which one to use by looking at real-world relationships in just a couple more paragraphs.

Probably one of the best ways of describing how relational theory works is to actually start applying it to our project. First, let's start with the entities and attributes in our database, and then we'll see how they relate to each other.

A spy is a person (object) that has some attributes that we can represent: surname, first name, date of birth, and so on. If we were to model a spy, it would look similar to Figure 1.1.

Figure 1.1

Modeling our spy entity.

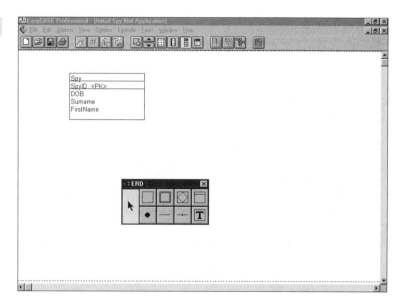

Who else do we have involved in our application? Like a spy, a bad guy entity has certain attributes that can be modeled (in this case, a very similar set of attributes). If we were to model a bad guy, it would look similar to Figure 1.2.

The next step is to figure out the relationship between a spy and a bad guy. Probably one of the most obvious relationships is the fact that a spy battles a bad guy and vice versa. One spy can battle many bad guys (either at once or over a period of time), and the same can be said for a bad guy. They can battle many, one, or no spies, either at once or over a period of time.

Figure 1.2

Modeling our bad guy entity.

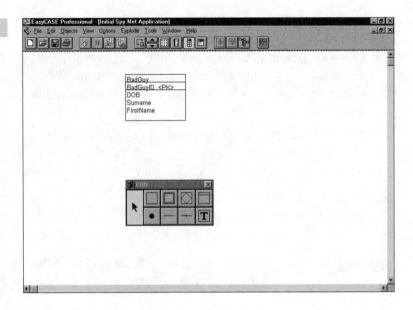

EXCURSION

Deciding Which Type of Relationship Should Be Implemented Between Two Entities

When thinking about relationships between entities, you must ask certain questions to help you determine the type of relationship you will define.

You should ask yourself, "Can one row in entity 'A' (spies) be matched to more than one row in entity 'B' (bad guys)? And conversely, can one row in entity 'B' be matched to more than one row in entity 'A'?"

If you answer no to both questions, the type of relationship will be a one-to-one (notated as 1-1).

If you answer no to one question and yes to the other, the relationship will be a one-to-many (1-N).

If you answer yes to both, the relationship will be a many-to-many (N-M).

Based on our excursion's questions, we get a many-to-many relationship between our spy and bad guy entities.

If you were to draw this type of relationship, it would look similar to Figure 1.3.

And there we have it, the initial part of our diagram drawn. From here, we will refine the diagram and look at some of the intricacies of data modeling.

Figure 1.3

Drawing the many-to-many relationship between our two entities.

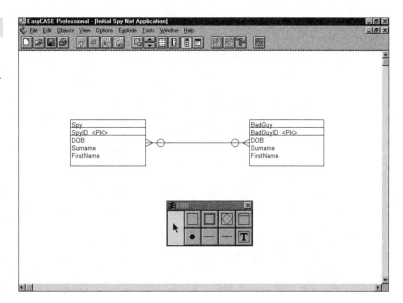

Sorting Objects into Tables

We now have two tables in our diagram, but aren't they really the same thing? They are both people who share very similar attributes (name, date of birth, addresses, and aliases). The only real difference between them is the team or side they work for. Given this, should they actually be separate tables, or should they be combined into one with only some minor attribute differences?

EXCURSION

Getting Comfortable with Design

Database design can be a very subjective process. What I decide is a correct model might not be what you decide is a correct model. For example, with the previous problem, do we make the spies and bad guys one table, or do we model them separately? The biggest benefit of combining them into one is we can update the data for both in a single place, but the drawback is that the model then must distinguish a difference between the two.

Obviously, for this application, I have already made the decision for you, so you're stuck! When you're ready to create a database on your own, you should consider the aspects we cover here and in Chapter 3, "Making Virtual Spies—Creating Spy Net in SQL Server 2000" look through other options. In fact, after you finish this book, you might re-create SQL Spy Net on your own using a different design with the same goals and information and compare the result when you look up information.

But as I have learned, anyone can gain knowledge from what others have done. I find that 10 or 20 lines of code are worth a whole chapter for understanding some concepts. You might find that looking at others' code (MSDN produced by Microsoft is an invaluable developer resource) or database design aids your understanding. Most people enjoy taking the time out to explain an idea or concept. One thing I have learned is don't be afraid to ask!

Many relational database concepts are easily and freely available to you. With an installation of SQL Server 2000, you can install some sample databases (Pubs or Northwind). These are fully functional relational databases that have plenty of examples you can learn from, and they give you the chance to play with a real live database that will not impact on anyone.

So, do not be afraid to ask questions (even if they do sound dumb); look for available resources; and most of all, have fun!

If we decided to combine similar tables into a single table, we would reduce levels of complexity in the application and make the structure flatter (*denormalization*). However, this would have some side effects we might not want. In Chapter 3, "Making Virtual Spies—Creating Spy Net in SQL Server 2000", we'll see how normalization affects the way we design the database and the side effects we might incur.

What you need to know for now, though, is that my philosophy of database design includes keeping one of those side effects—having *nulls* in the database—to an absolute minimum, though you must ensure that the trade-off to not having nulls is *not* to have *data redundancy*.

Null is a special value in relational theory and databases. It has no specific value. It is not equal to an empty string ("") or even zero. Therefore, a less-than (<), greater-than (>), or equal sign (=) can't be used to compare it to any other value, including another null value.

Redundant data is data that is repeated more than once in any application. It is very inefficient to store the same details in two or more places because it is hard to maintain and is costly in storage space.

Using Subtypes to Future-Proof Spy Net

To help us reduce nulls, we should use *subtypes*. These enable us to design the application to not only reduce nulls, but also to give us the greatest flexibility for future expansion.

If you have done any object-oriented programming you probably are familiar with the concept of subtyping and inheritance. Basically, a *subtype* enables us to take the properties (attributes) of a given item (such as a table) and derive a new item that has all the attributes from the first item; this is known as inheritance. We can even add some new attributes.

The parent entity (in the previous definition) is the *super-type*. This is the one from which the subtype is derived. For example, a person is a super-type and a spy is a subtype because a spy has some attributes that were inherited from the Person table.

After our application has been deployed, we can simply add to the application by creating another child (subtype) of the super-type. For example, given a super-type Person, we could create an Employee subtype. This is still technically a person, but with some slight differences from the Person type—for example, Salary Rate. It also enables it to inherit all the attributes from its parent, such as the Name attribute.

We will change our ERD from having two separate entities—which repeat the same attributes—to having three entities, in which our Spy and BadGuy entities inherit their attributes from a Person entity. Our new ERD will look similar to Figure 1.4.

As you can see, with this model we can achieve at least one of our stated objectives simply. This model enables the application to be scalable without large coding changes. We can, at any given time, expand the model to include new types of people. This also reduces some of the problems we faced with our earlier model.

Figure 1.4

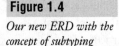

*Our new ERD with the
concept of subtyping
applied to our diagram.*

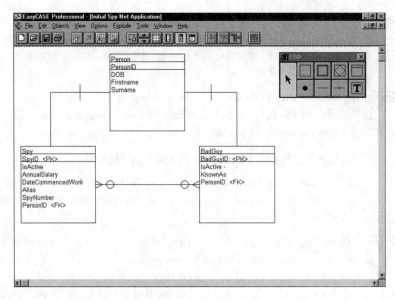

Building Relationships Between Enemies

Notice in the preceding section that "persons" in general and spy/bad guys have a
natural relationship. The programming equivalent of the *relationship* between the
super-type and the subtype is one of the ways you can "connect" data objects to help
ensure *referential integrity*.

You use database features such as a *primary key* and a *foreign key* to link data that has a
relationship (and to some extent lock them together) to enforce rules that protect
data integrity.

A primary key is an attribute in a table that uniquely identifies each row. For example, we could think of our Social Security numbers as being a primary key.
Everyone's number is different, so it uniquely identifies each of us.

A *foreign key* is the primary key of the table to which you want to link. For example,
our employers use our Social Security numbers (which are the primary keys of the
Employee table as a foreign key) to link the taxes we pay. Therefore, our Salary table
becomes linked to the Employee table through our Social Security number.

Referential integrity is the process of ensuring that our data is consistent. For example,
we cannot insert a row into our Salary table unless there's a row in our Person table.

Now, as we gather information for SQL Spy Net or any other database, we look for the natural relationships. For example, we could put all the information about a spy into one large table, including identification number, name, address, salary, status, and so on. But what if we need to alter tax information for everyone and we have 20,000 spies rather than 20? We'd have to run a *query* that would affect all 20,000 rows. Whereas if we categorize information into separate tables and connect the information using relationships, with the use of primary and foreign keys, we need to make the data change in only one place.

Queries enable you to update, delete, and retrieve information from the database. They use special commands for achieving this. They are useful because they can be dynamic or predefined. More about queries is covered in Chapter 3, "Making Virtual Spies—Creating Spy Net in SQL Server 2000".

Everything within a relational database must be uniquely identifiable. The table names must be unique. For example, you cannot have two Spy tables. Similarly, you cannot have two rows of information that are exactly the same.

To do this, we introduce the primary key. This enables us to specify that a column within a table is unique and the data contained will never be repeated. For example, given the following rows of information, in Figure 1.5, the first column (SocialSecurityNo) would be unique. Therefore, this obviously would be the column that would have the primary key defined on it.

Figure 1.5

Identifying a primary key for a table.

SocialSecurityNo	Surname	FirstName	DOB
123456	Bloggs	Joe	1/12/72
654321	Hendrix	James	1/12/72
742356	Hawthorne	Rob	1/12/72
564231	Hawthorne	Mike	1/12/72
654124	Happy	Joe	1/12/72
124561	Happy	Smile	1/12/72

This is fine, but how do we relate our first table to another table? This is where we introduce foreign keys. These are the primary keys from other tables that you want your table to contain a reference to. For example, in Figure 1.6, table A has a primary key defined (denoted by the little key); so does table B.

But also notice that within table B is the column from table A that has the primary key defined. This allows us to specify that table B is linked (related) to table A through the foreign key.

By placing the primary key of table A into table B, we have created our one-to-many relationship. In other words, a single row in table A can relate to one or more rows in table B. This relationship is signified by the line drawn between these to tables with the key end of the line pointing to the primary key.

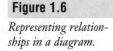

Figure 1.6

Representing relation-ships in a diagram.

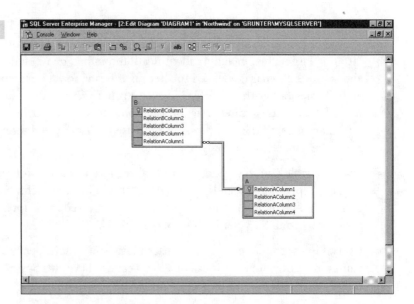

To see which side of a relationship is the many side within SQL Server 2000, look for the infinity symbol (∞) at the end of the relationship line.

Refining Our Relationship Between the Spy and Person Tables

When we first drew our ERD, we defined the relationship between the Spy and BadGuy tables as being many-to-many. Even though this type of relationship is perfectly valid when we are initially data modeling, it cannot be implemented in a relational database.

Confused? I was also at first. When I was first introduced to relational theory and database design, I could not understand why we would have a relationship that could never be implemented.

However, as was explained to me (and now to you), relational theory is purely mathematical in basis. This type of relationship suits our needs very well when we are designing applications because it prevents us from being tied down with implementation issues and allows us to focus on the whole picture. We can then refine the model at a later stage (as we are doing now) to suit the limitations of the technology.

The reason the many-to-many relationship cannot be implemented directly is that we cannot know how many rows of one table will ever directly relate to how many rows in another table, and vice versa. If we tried to implement this sort of model, we would have two tables with repeating rows, and this would break the rules of *normalization*.

Although our database (and in fact all relational databases) cannot support this type of relationship, we need to define a way that we can. This is where we introduce the *associative* (or *junction*) table.

 An *associative table* is a table that is created only to remove the complex many-to-many relationship that two existing tables might have. This effectively changes the relationship from one many-to-many to two one-to-many relationships. The associative table contains a reference to the other two tables through their primary keys (so the primary keys become foreign keys in the associative table).

An associative table is just that, it associates two or more tables together. It enables us to split a complex many-to-many relationship into two one-to-many relationships.

For our Spy/BadGuy example, we would introduce a new associative table called Activity. The Activity table would keep track of the Spy and the BadGuy that have battled and who the winner was.

The diagram in Figure 1.7 shows the new ERD that has been created between the two (now three) tables.

Figure 1.7

Breaking up the many-to-many relationship with an associative entity.

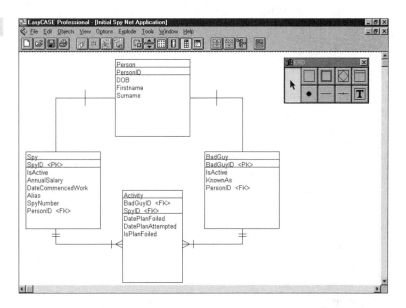

 Note

Notice the primary key of the Activity table? This is called a *concatenated* primary key. This type of key is actually a primary key made up of the two foreign keys of the other tables.

And this is where we will leave relation theory and our application design for now. There is much more to do, but I have given you enough to get started. In Chapter 3, where we revisit our design, you will be able to easily see the intricacies of the design.

Taking a Broad Overview of Spy Net

The application is the glue that holds all the skills together. Without the application, the book would just be a pile of examples.

The application we will build pieces the sections of the book together so you can experience the thrill of developing your first SQL Server 2000 application from scratch.

By the end of the book, the application will be fully functional (it will meet all the client's objectives), and you will have a code library you will be able to refer to later. We are even going to implement a nice Web front end to our database in Chapter 12, "Designing a Front End to Support Our SQLSpyNet Database" so that you can have an even broader range of skills!

You could use the application as a sort of strategy game a little later. You and a friend could practice giving your spies and bad guys assignments and score based on how many successes or failures you each have.

You could adapt the schema to use it for recording employee—or person-like—information and jobs on which they have worked. This would then become a time-recording application.

You could even start up your own spy organization and implement our design into your organization! Whatever your choice, you will still finish with an application you can be proud of. After all, you took the time to build it yourself!

Next, we need to build and deploy our application. To do this, we must establish a connection to our SQL Server 2000 installation. If you haven't installed SQL Server 2000 already, or you installed it but it's not connected yet, go through the steps in Appendix B.

Some of you eager beavers might already have SQL Server 2000 installed and running. Maybe you've even connected to SQL Server 2000 already. To get this application to work properly, though, your installation and connection configurations are important, especially if you're running SQL Server 2000 on Windows NT or Windows 2000. Refer to Appendix B to make sure you have the correct connection and configuration settings.

Summary

We now have the basic requirements for our client's business needs and the design for our application. This has opened up the world of SQL Server 2000, and you should go ahead and explore through Enterprise Manager (once you have of course established a connection by following the guide in Appendix B). Just remember, don't save any changes unless you are really sure that you want to!

Next Steps

In Chapter 2, "Exploring the Tools of SQL Server 2000," we look at the core development and management tools that come with SQL Server 2000. In fact, if you have already installed SQL Server 2000 and configured it by the notes in Appendix B, you have actually just experienced using at least one of the tools—Enterprise Manager. In Chapter 2, you'll see some of the other tools you'll be using throughout the book.

Then, in Chapter 3, we'll turn our "paper" spies and bad guys into SQL Server 2000 objects with additional configuration settings and some actual database building.

So come and join me as we experience the thrill of designing, developing, and deploying an application in SQL Server 2000.

Chapter 2

The Tools of SQL Server 2000 for Managing an Instance

SQL Server 2000 is a rich and powerful database management system. In addition, the user interface is both friendly and intuitive and allows beginners to SQL Server 2000 the chance to learn the features of the tool without being bogged down writing code.

The interface is very much like standard Windows-type interfaces, with menu bars, icons, tree-view controls, radio buttons, and so on. This familiarity enables someone who has never seen the application before to pick up the basic tasks fairly quickly.

The next few sections briefly introduce you to the tools of SQL Server 2000 and discuss the main functions and benefits of each.

Although we won't actually develop anything further for our application in this chapter, it is really important for us to get familiar with the tools of SQL Server 2000. This not only aids you in developing your application quickly, but will also cement your knowledge in SQL Server 2000.

Our application is going to use two of the tools that we discuss in this chapter extensively—let's see if you can guess what they are! These tools are the real keys to SQL Server 2000 and will give you greater flexibility (understanding what the different ways are of performing certain tasks) when developing the application.

Don't worry too much about all the functionality of the tools; you will learn more as you go through the book and your knowledge expands.

Exploring Database Objects with Enterprise Manager

Enterprise Manager is a *snap-in* of the Microsoft Management Console (MMC) that forms a large part of the Windows network server management tools. You have already had some experience with Enterprise Manager when you created the connection to your instance of SQL Server 2000.

A *snap-in* is a component that runs inside the MMC. Snap-ins cannot run by themselves; they must be contained within the MMC.

Different snap-ins are available for adding extra management applications. For example, MMC supports not only SQL Server 2000, but also Internet Information Server (IIS) and Microsoft Transaction Server (MTS), as well as a host of other application snap-ins.

SQL Server Enterprise Manager is the main control application for managing, creating, and maintaining databases. It offers an MMC-like interface, so the learning curve is greatly reduced if you are familiar with Internet Information Server.

The Graphical User Interface (GUI) tools within Enterprise Manager will allow you to back up your database, implement a scheduled task, create and manage user accounts, and draw database diagrams.

Enterprise Manager for SQL Server 2000 offers a tree-view control that expands to display the databases that are installed on the instance of SQL Server 2000 that you are running. You can visually see databases and the objects within a database, including tables, stored procedures, users, and so on.

With a few simple mouse-clicks, you can drill down into the individual objects for each database and get detailed information; for example, you can get the permissions for a table, script a stored procedure, and delete or rename a view. Figure 2.1 shows a list and tree of objects in the Enterprise Manager.

Enterprise Manager enables you to quickly and easily see the activity and objects within your instance of SQL Server 2000. You can effortlessly administer scheduled tasks and other database management functions, including (but not limited to) managing security logins for the server, importing and exporting data, and setting up database replication.

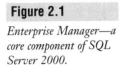

Figure 2.1

Enterprise Manager—a core component of SQL Server 2000.

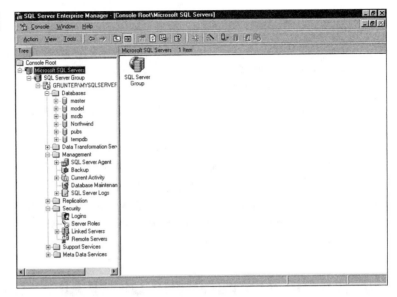

Why You're Sure to Love Enterprise Manager

Enterprise Manager is a central location where you can totally manage the instance of SQL Server 2000 that you have installed. Most of the additional tools of SQL Server 2000 (discussed in this chapter) can be launched from Enterprise Manager, including the Import and Export wizard and Query Analyzer.

As already stated, the ease of use will allow you to come to grips with the basic ins and outs of SQL Server 2000 quickly and will offer you full control over the instance. You can perform administrative, design, and database creation tasks.

Even if you do not know where the commands are located for a particular task, Enterprise Manger has numerous wizards available that will assist you in your day-to-day maintenance tasks.

Enterprise Manager is customizable. You can change the default icon statuses (like Windows Explorer), display hidden or system objects, and make changes to the way the instance of SQL Server 2000 is configured when you click on it (prompt for login, start the server, and so on) .

How This Tool Fits into Our SQL Spy Net Application

Because Enterprise Manager is the central location for SQL Server 2000, you will need to master the tool to effectively administer and maintain the SQL Spy Net application.

Because Enterprise Manager allows us to perform both simple and complex tasks, we will use Enterprise Manager to create our application database and build the first three tables through the user interface. This will demonstrate the ease of creating a database and tables through Enterprise Manager. You also will get to build some of the tables through code (using Query Analyzer) in Chapter 3.

We will also use Enterprise Manager to define the relationships between the first three tables we build. This will show you how easy it is to create a database schema. Later in the application's development, we will create tasks that are scheduled to happen at a given time in Chapter 11. These tasks can be set up to perform database backups, import and export data, or even send emails to users. Talk about flexible!

So as you can see, Enterprise Manager does mean a lot to our application. It offers you the flexibility to learn about the tool, as well as enhancing your knowledge about database maintenance.

Getting the Answers with Query Analyzer

With Query Analyzer, you can enter Transact-SQL statements directly against a database. This allows you to perform `Select` statements against a table, execute a stored procedure, or create a `View` through Transact-SQL. Do not worry about these statement names; we examine what each of these means in Chapters 4 and 5.

However, this is not all that Query Analyzer provides. You also have the ability to view the results of the query you performed in grid or text form. In grid form, you can save the results as a comma-delimited list, which is great if you want to export the results and create a graph against the data by importing it into a statistical package such as Excel.

Query Analyzer enables you to create an *execution plan* for your Transact-SQL statement. This means that a query that is performing poorly can be analyzed, and resource-intensive sections of the query can be optimized without losing the much-needed results of the query.

 An *execution plan* offers information on how SQL Server 2000 retrieves the results of a query by using tables and indexes. The results can appear in three ways: graphically, textually, or in a concise textual format.

There is also an Index Tuning Wizard that analyzes the indexes used in a query and decides whether adding more indexes to the tables referenced will improve performance.

An ***index*** is like an index in a book. It allows SQL Server 2000 to quickly and easily navigate to a row in a table if an index is defined. By default, a primary key has a *unique* (no other row can be like this row) index defined.

There is also a Transact-SQL syntax checker (almost like a compiler) that will verify your syntax before executing a statement. This enables you to find syntactical errors before execution.

One of the cool new features of Query Analyzer in SQL Server 2000 is the tree-view control. Although the tree-view control might not be new to Enterprise Manager, it is to Query Analyzer and goes by the name Object Browser. This control has been added to the Query Analyzer interface and, although a small thing, is a very big thing to developers.

Enterprise Manager makes it simple to view not only the databases on a particular server/instance, but also the tables, views, stored procedures, users, and so on for a given database. Figure 2.2 shows the new Object Browser in Query Analyzer.

EXCURSION

Why Is the New Object Browser in Query Analyzer So Great?

There have been many times when I have been using Query Analyzer to perform Transact-SQL tasks and had to switch continuously back and forth between Query Analyzer and Enterprise Manager to view the names of database objects so I could write queries that accessed them. The need for this has now been completely eliminated.

When you have to work in an environment where you do not have access to the new SQL Server 2000 tools, living without the new Object Browser is very difficult.

Figure 2.2

Object Browser within Query Analyzer—a new feature of SQL Server 2000.

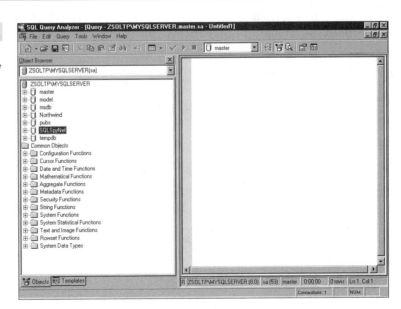

However, Microsoft has gone one step further for developers and, in my opinion, this is fantastic! To generate a basic query for a table, you only need to right-click and choose from the list Select, Insert, Update, or Delete. The resulting window that pops up has the basic code written for you, with data types defined (for those queries that need it). If you have ever written a `Select` statement before that required you to access multiple columns, or an `Update` statement but did not know all the data types, you will really appreciate this feature. Check it out in Figure 2.3.

Figure 2.3

A sample script file that can be generated.

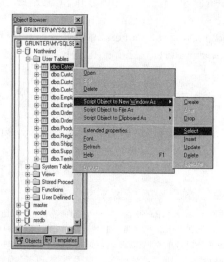

But wait, there's more; there are also some basic templates that Microsoft has included to enhance the interface that little bit more.

There are basic templates for Create Database, Create Table, Create Stored Procedure, and many more. By initially selecting the Templates tab on the Object Browser, you will be given a list of current templates. Then by right-clicking and selecting these items from the menu, you will be presented with an outline for executing the statement, and all you have to do is fill in the blanks. Talk about programming by example! Figure 2.4 shows the Create Database template in action.

Finally, you also have the ability to modify these templates to suit your own needs. This means that you can create custom templates for repetitive tasks that you perform as a DBA, or you can tailor the ones that are supplied with SQL Server 2000 to suit your organization.

These are not all the functions available in Query Analyzer. As your experience with the product grows, so will your knowledge and expertise with the tool. You will find more functions that will further suit your needs.

Figure 2.4

Another sample script file that can be generated.

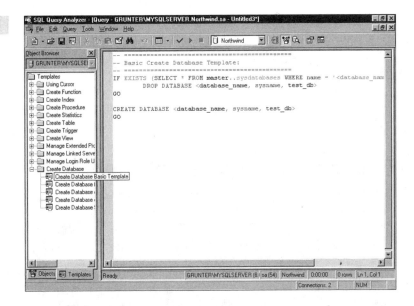

What You Can Do with Query Analyzer

Query Analyzer is a very flexible tool. With Query Analyzer, you can do almost as much as you can through Enterprise Manager, although you must write the code to perform the same tasks. This means that you get an understanding of the layout, form, and structure of Transact-SQL, as well as becoming a proficient DBA.

With Query Analyzer, you can compile the Transact-SQL that you want to execute before executing it. This means that you can ensure the code is syntactically correct before submitting it to the database. The code window for Query Analyzer is color-coded to allow you to easily see keywords and special SQL Server 2000 functions. These colors are fully customizable, so you can create your own color scheme.

When submitting a query through Query Analyzer, you can check the execution of the query with the execution plan tool to ensure that it is effectively using the indexes and resources available.

Probably the last main benefit to using Query Analyzer is that if the interface fails for some unknown reason (a `.dll` fails to register correctly and so on), you can still perform your DBA tasks if you are familiar with Query Analyzer.

Using This Tool for the SQL Spy Net Application

Query Analyzer will be used intensely throughout the development of our SQL Spy Net application. Not only will we be using Enterprise Manager to create our database and three base tables, we also will be using Query Analyzer to develop the remainder of the tables, as well as test Transact-SQL statements to ensure they perform correctly.

We will use Query Analyzer to learn Transact-SQL statements (refer to Chapters 3 and 4) and to build most of our stored procedures that our application will use.

As you can see, Query Analyzer is a very flexible product. It has tools within it, making it a very diverse and effective development/management tool.

Tracking Code Crimes with Profiler

Profiler? You might be wondering, "Isn't that some sort of police criminal expert?" In real life maybe, but in SQL Server 2000...no, not really. Profiler does help you track down your coding resource hogs, though. It enables you to create a *trace file* for Transact-SQL statements that have been sent to SQL Server 2000.

 Trace files capture the events that are executed on a server so you can view them or replay them later. You can save the trace file for use later, or you can step through the events that were fired and manually re-create them.

"Where do I find Profiler?" you might ask. Profiler can be launched from one of two places:

- First, within Enterprise Manager, select Tools, SQL Profiler from the drop-down menu.
- It can be launched on its own from your Start menu group. Select Start, Programs, Microsoft SQL Server (or whatever your SQL Server group is called), and then select Profiler.

The Profiler is especially useful when you want to see the Transact-SQL statements being sent to a database from a client application. The trace allows you to see the stored procedures being called, the parameters being passed, the views being run, and the users logging in to the database through the application's interface. Figure 2.5 shows Profiler in action.

The Profiler will allow you to monitor the Transact-SQL statements so that complex or slow performing queries can be isolated and modified to allow for faster execution. It can also be used to monitor the application to check that resources are being utilized properly.

Once again, the ease of the GUI allows even inexperienced users to create a trace and to easily diagnose problems.

Figure 2.5

A profile for SQL Server 2000 in action.

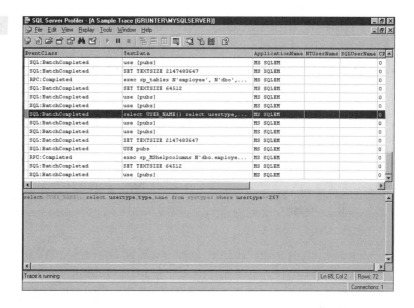

When You'll Use Profiler

Profiler will allow you to pinpoint application problems.

EXCURSION

Using Profiler for Real-World SQL Server Upgrades

Recently, I had to upgrade a SQL Server from version 6.5 to version 7.0. The client had an old Visual Basic interface (written by a third party) and no source code available for the client application. I used Profiler to trace the Transact-SQL statements that were sent to the database to ensure that the upgrade to SQL Server version 7.0 would go smoothly.

Profiler offers a lot of flexibility in being able to get an overview of what is happening on the server as well as pinpoint problems. You can save the trace file to disk for later use. You can narrow your trace to individual users or machines, or you can expand your trace so you can see everything that is happening on the whole server.

Warning

You must be careful when saving and replaying trace files, especially against a production database. Because the Transact-SQL statements have already been executed, you might be causing the same update to happen twice! As you can imagine, this could be disastrous on a live database.

Profiling and the SQL Spy Net Application

So, when will we use the Profiler to track down our spies and their secret codes? Possibly never! We are going to write such effective, solid code that we will not have any errors in the code whatsoever. (Wow, look at the pig flying past the window! We'll use Profiler in Chapter 13.)

With all the best intentions in the world, we cannot guarantee that our code will always be bug-free. I have never seen an application that was 100 percent bug-free. And anybody who told me that they had an application that was either only had a one-line-of-code application or hadn't tested things as thoroughly as he or she thought. The Profiler will allow you to trace any errors in the code or just give us application-wide tracing, so we can see what sort of performance we are getting out of our SQL Server.

Profiler offers many benefits when it is used effectively. We will not need to use it unless we have an error that we cannot easily trace or we want to monitor the server's activities. But it is handy to know that the resource is available for us when we need it.

Importing and Exporting Data the Easy Way

The Import and Export data icon within the Start Menu Group of SQL Server will launch the Data Transformation Services (DTS) Wizard.

Like SQL Profiler, the DTS Import/Export Wizard can be launched from one of two places.

- Within Enterprise Manager, select Tools, Data Transformation Services, and then select either Import or Export from the drop-down menu.
- Launch it on its own from your Start menu group. Select Start, Programs, Microsoft SQL Server (or whatever your SQL Server group is called), and then select Import and Export Data.

The DTS Import/Export Wizard will allow you to import or export to or from your SQL Server 2000 database using either ODBC or OLE-DB native providers (see Figure 2.6).

Figure 2.6

The DTS Import/Export Wizard for SQL Server 2000 in action.

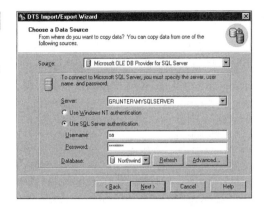

The DTS Import/Export Wizard enables you to communicate with many heterogeneous data sources, including the following:

- Databases including, but not limited to
    - Oracle
    - Microsoft Access
    - IBM's DB2
    - SQL Server
- Spreadsheets
- Text files

The functionality is very easy to use because the steps in the wizard guide you the whole way through the process.

Not only will the DTS Import/Export Wizard allow you to import and export data, but you can also import *whole* database tables when importing from another database. This enables you to import both the data from another database and the structure (column names, data types, and so on) of the tables.

When you have completed the DTS Import/Export Wizard, you can specify whether the task is run immediately or set to run at a given time.

Delaying the task to run at a given time is handy if the server is under a heavy load or you receive a regular feed of data from a provider. You can then set up the DTS package to run when the new information arrives, reducing the amount of "hands-on" work you have to do.

Why You Should Use DTS

DTS provides a nice and easy interface to import or export data into or from any SQL Server 2000 database.

DTS supports importing and exporting to many heterogeneous data sources, as we covered earlier. The wizard functionality of DTS makes it easy for us to determine the data source that we are going to either export to or from.

DTS is very flexible because it allows us to execute the package immediately, or we can schedule it to occur at some later time. We also can save the package. This allows us to edit the package that DTS uses to import the data, providing us with the flexibility to change the package to suit our business needs.

With this sort of flexibility, we can write custom scripts, send emails, roll back changes, set up scheduled tasks, and many other tasks. These contribute to alter the way the data is imported or exported, giving us not only full control over the database with SQL Server 2000 tools but also the way the data is sent from or received into the server.

Generating SQL Spy Net Data with DTS

To show you how the DTS Import/Export Wizard works, we will create an Excel spreadsheet of spy names, bad guy's details, and many of our other tables and then import the new data into our application. We will save the DTS script and view the resulting package within Enterprise Manager. However, you are going to have wait until Chapter 14 before we do anything cool with the DTS Import/Export Wizard.

DTS also offers us the ability to import data from other spy organizations when our operations expand. So we can migrate the data from legacy systems (mainframes) into a brand-new SQL Server 2000 database, giving us the best spy operations around.

Checking Out SQL Server 2000's Other Tools

So far we have covered only a few of the SQL Server 2000 tools of the trade. As a full database management system, SQL Server 2000 offers you many other tools with which to configure and manage your instances of SQL Server 2000. Although these tools are very important to SQL Server 2000 and DBAs, we are not going to cover them in depth in this book. There is enough to write about already!

Instead, I list here some brief details on the tools so that you can further research them and their uses and enjoy the benefit of enhancing your DBA knowledge further. You can also get a quick look at some of these tools for troubleshooting in Appendix C.

2

- Server Network Utility enables you to configure and modify the network libraries on which SQL Server 2000 listens to requests.

- Client Network Utility enables you to configure the network libraries that the client uses to connect to SQL Server 2000.

- Service Manager is a neat little utility that allows you to start, pause, and stop the individual services of SQL Server 2000. You can do this for each instance of SQL Server 2000 that you have installed on the server or any other instance of SQL Server 2000 on the network. You can manipulate the following services through Service Manager:

  - *SQL Server Service*—The service that starts the database server on your machine. Without this running, nobody will be able to connect to your instance of SQL Server 2000.

  - *SQL Server Agent Service*—The service that starts all the administrative tasks that run within your instance of SQL Server 2000 (a task that is scheduled to run at a certain time, for example).

  - *Microsoft Search Service*—This service only runs under Windows NT and 2000 and provides a service for the full-text search engine.

  - *MSDTC Service*—The service manager for distributed transactions.

- Analysis Services enables you to build data warehouses that are used for data analysis, so the users' queries do not affect the performance of the live database.

- English Query is another SQL Server 2000 add-on that allows users to send English-like language questions to the database. This enables many users to query the database without having to know any SQL.

Summary

In this chapter, we have looked at some of the main components of SQL Server 2000. As you can see, the range of tools for SQL Server 2000 is quite diverse and offers many degrees of functionality. These tools enable a DBA full control over the database, data, and server without being tied down with large code statements.

Most administrative tasks can be performed easily through the interfaces.

Although this chapter has only briefly introduced you to the workings of the tools of SQL Server 2000, you will become more familiar with each of the main tools as we work through the project in the next few chapters.

Next Steps

In the next chapter, we are going to create our SQLSpyNet database—not just through Enterprise Manager, which we have used, but also through Query Analyzer. So you will get a chance to get your hands really dirty with the core development tools of SQL Server 2000!

In this chapter

- *Playing Program Director (Sys Admin) for SpyNet*
- *Creating the SQL Spy Net Application Database*
- *Using the Data Definition Language (DDL) to Create Databases and Objects*
- *Bringing Our Data Model and Database Together*

Chapter 3

Making Virtual Spies—Creating Spy Net in SQL Server 2000

Ladies and gentlemen, this is it! The moment that we (well, I) have been waiting for. In this chapter things are really going to begin rocking. We will create the SQL Spy Net application database and our application tables. We will discuss important database concepts such as normalization and integrity. We also will finish drawing our entity relationship diagram (ERD) and complete the analysis of our application.

But first we must tidy up a couple of administration tasks. We must make sure SQL Server's installation settings are tailored for our project.

This combination makes for a bit of a long chapter, but these two segments, moving from diagram to database, go hand in hand. Along the way, I give you several tidbits of information on relational theory and good design practices—the "why" behind the option selections. You might want to review these asides when you create your next project.

Playing Program Director (Sys Admin) for SpyNet

First things first. Let's ensure our application (and SQL Server 2000) are secure. We will also get a brief introduction to user administration.

Because I am not psychic, I do not know what you set your sa password to, but I assume that you either did not supply one at all or that you used something like password.

sa stands for System Administrator. This gives you god-like control over SQL Server 2000. This user account can do anything it wants to the instance of SQL Server 2000 or the databases inside the instance. So be careful—that's a lot of rope to hang yourself with!

Even if you didn't set the password to either of these, the practice of changing your password will assist in your understanding of SQL Server 2000's security and show you how to change passwords, especially when users forget theirs, as they inevitably will!

By now I assume you've either followed the instructions in Appendix B, "Installing and Configuring SQL Server 2000," or you've gotten SQL Server up and running on your own. It's crucial that you follow the same configurations for connecting to SQL Server, and it's a good idea to check all your settings against those I've walked you through in Appendix B.

So, if you're operating on Windows NT or 2000, be sure you're using the sa account rather than the administrator account. If your administrator doesn't want you monkeying around with SQL Server on a network, reconsider installing Personal Edition on a standalone machine, as I've done for this book.

Setting the sa Password

If you do not have Enterprise Manager running, start the application now.

1. Navigate your way through the tree-view control in Enterprise Manager. You will find a folder called Security. This folder holds information relevant to the security of SQL Server 2000, including database logins (such as sa), server roles (such as System Administrators), and linked and remote servers (which allow you to link to other servers).

   Within the Security folder you will see the Logins icon.

2. Click the Logins icon, and you will see the logins defined for this instance (and all the databases) of SQL Server 2000. If your screen is like mine, you will only see the sa login, as shown in Figure 3.1.

   Double-click the sa login icon now. You will see a screen similar to that shown in Figure 3.2.

Figure 3.1

Logins defined in your instance of SQL Server 2000.

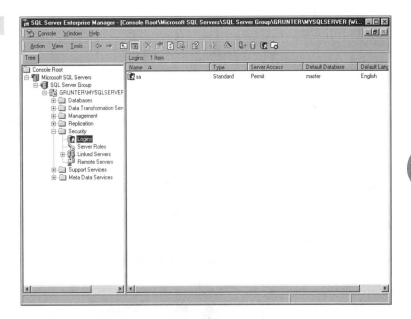

Figure 3.2

Details for the sa *login.*

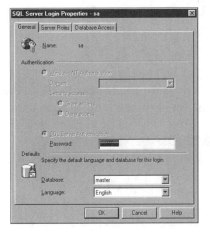

3. Type your new password into the dialog box (make it something that you will remember but not that others can easily guess) and click Apply or OK. The system will automatically ask you to verify the password change that you have just implemented.

The only catch to changing your password is that you must edit the server registration properties that you use.

4. Click the SQL Server 2000 instance (under the server group that you created in Appendix B), right-click and choose Edit SQL Server Registration Properties. You will be presented with a dialog box similar to the initial registration screen. This appears in Figure 3.3.

Figure 3.3

Edit SQL Server Registration properties.

5. After you enter the new password and click OK, SQL Server 2000 will ask if you want to change the connection information, as shown in Figure 3.4.

Figure 3.4

Confirm active server connection changes.

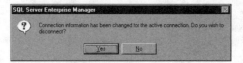

6. After you have answered yes, SQL Server 2000 will update the connection information to use when you use one of the client tools to connect to SQL Server 2000.

 When SQL Server 2000 attempts to update your connection information, it disconnects the current connection that you have to the server, and then reconnects for you.

If you have any session-specific information set, for example the way to handle NULLs, this information might be lost. Therefore, when SQL Server 2000 reconnects, just check that your configuration options are still set.

Okay that's about it, a nice and easy process. For your users, however, you would not need to change the connection information, only their passwords.

The second administration task that we must perform—and this is quite important—is to ensure that the configuration options of the model database in SQL Server 2000 are set to best suit our needs.

 The *model* database is a system database from which SQL Server 2000 uses to copy your new databases. SQL Server 2000 has several system databases, such as master and tempdb.

Configuring the Model Database to Meet Our SQL Spy Net Application Requirements

The model database has some basic configuration options that are copied when you create a new database, either through Enterprise Manager (using the user interface) or Query Analyzer (using Transact-SQL).

1. After SQL Server 2000 reconnects for you, drill through Enterprise Manager and locate the model database. We will check and alter where necessary the configuration settings of the model database to ensure we get the best settings to suit our needs when creating a new database.

2. With the model database selected, right-click the database and choose Properties. You will see a window similar to that shown in Figure 3.5. This screen provides a basic summary of the model database settings.

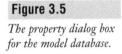

Figure 3.5

The property dialog box for the model database.

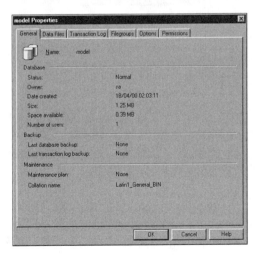

Note

In most scenarios you would not need to alter these options except the initial space allocated option. On the whole, the defaults of SQL Server 2000 are normally fine.

We must ensure the following options are set for each tab; we will approach this in three stages:

- Storage space allocation
- Configuring the options for the model database
- Who can do what—checking out the permissions

I'll break up the process into smaller chunks to give you more information on the options you're setting on each tab and why.

File Space

First we will check the basic storage space allocation for this database and any copied databases.

Click the data files tab; you will see a screen similar to that shown in Figure 3.6.

Figure 3.6

Data files configuration settings.

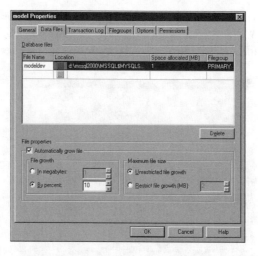

This is the storage allocation for the data files that your database will contain. As you can see, in this configuration I have my data files for the database stored on the D drive. This is because disk I/O (input/output) is one of the largest bottlenecks in any application development.

EXCURSION

Watching Out for Bottlenecks

Although disk drives have gotten bigger and the access slightly faster, the same basic method for accessing data has remained virtually unchanged for more than 20 years!

For a database to request data from a disk, a single head (like the arm of a record player) scans the disk for information. You can imagine if you have 200 concurrent users that the job of that single head is enormous. It must retrieve data, update data, and maintain storage information at a rate fast enough to support all those users. So the best thing we can possibly do is split the load.

One of the best methods for achieving this is through a *RAID* array configuration, called Data Striping (RAID 0).

 Redundant Array of Independent Disks (RAID) is a system of having multiple disks (called an array) to give better performance, reliability, more storage, and at a lower cost. RAID also has a fault-tolerance capability built in, which is actually one of the biggest factors to using RAID. It is available on RAID systems 0 through to 5.

Although RAID is not part of SQL Server 2000, it is actually a hardware configuration; the RAID levels 0, 1, and 5 are generally used with SQL Server 2000 and can affect the performance of SQL Server 2000.

Unfortunately, a RAID configuration is not an option on Windows 95 or 98 platforms.

This allows many disks to perform many tasks at the same time and all to be in sync with each other.

But if you are like me and this option is not available, what do you do? If you have multiple physical disks, you can split the data, transaction logs, and the program files across many disks. Unfortunately, if you don't have multiple disks you cannot implement this sort of option, but "hey them's the breaks."

To ensure that we do not run out of disk space, we manipulate some of the properties in the window. Make sure the Automatically Grow File option is selected and the File Growth Setting is configured to 10%.

Okay, I've done it, but what does it mean? The Automatically Grow File option specifies to SQL Server 2000 that when the data file reaches its upper limit of 5MB it needs to increase the file size by 10% (500KB).

Alternatively, we could use the Increase File Size by Megabytes option, but the problem with this option is that it can run out of disk space very early on, or there might not be enough file size increase later. For example, when the data file increases to 5MB, the system automatically increases it to 6MB. But if we only have 6MB left on disk, an error is returned.

In the second scenario, when our data file is 300MB in size, increasing it by 1MB will not give us enough of a growth in storage. If it is set to 10%, that is 30MB, which can tide us over for a while.

We also have the ability to set the maximum size of the data file, effectively allowing us to limit its growth to a set size. If we leave the unrestricted file growth option set, the data file will grow until we run out of disk space. However, if we know that our database will never grow too large or we want to put limits on its size, we can specify that the data file never be allowed to grow larger than a whole number of megabytes.

What are the other options on the screen for?

- The filename is the name that SQL Server 2000 uses internally to refer to the data storage area. The space allocated is the initial total space allocated for the data file to grow. If, like my configuration, yours is set to 1MB, you need to bump this up to 5MB. You can achieve this by clicking in the field and typing the new size that you want to allocate.

- The filegroup property is the filegroup to which the data file belongs. When a database is created the default filegroup of PRIMARY is created. The primary data file is added to this group along with any other data files that are not specifically assigned to any other filegroups.

The primary filegroup also contains all the system tables. We increased the initial size to ensure that the filegroup does not run out of disk space. If this happens, no new entries can be added to the system tables, and an error will be returned. This means you won't be able to create any new users, tables, stored procedures, and so on; and that is very fatal to any application!

The Transaction Log

Next we need to check the transaction log settings. Click the Transaction Log tab. As you see in Figure 3.7, the screen is similar to the data files screen, including options that are similar.

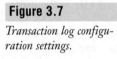

Figure 3.7

Transaction log configuration settings.

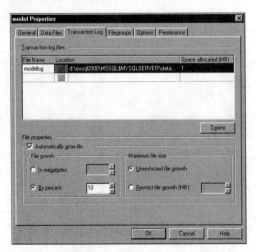

The only difference here is that you do not specify a filegroup to which the transaction log belongs. Once again we are going to change the space-allocated size to 5MB.

Let's stop here and explain the data file and transaction logs. When you or your team inserts data into your database, it is written to the data file, which is physically stored on disk. This is what makes a database different from a C++ or similar application; we can *persist* the data.

Persisting data—With a C++ or VB application the data is held in memory. Therefore, the data is available only while the application is running. With a database the data is written to disk, allowing you to reuse it any time you want, hence you persevere (or persist) the state of the data.

The transaction log keeps a record of all changes made to the data in the database. This allows us to undo a change (*rollback* is the technical term; more about this in Chapter 8) if we need to. Generally your transaction logs will not grow too large, but this depends on the individual system's circumstances.

Filegroups

Now that you understand the changes we made, let's take a look at the next tab, Filegroups, as shown in Figure 3.8.

Figure 3.8

The Filegroups tab settings.

Earlier we talked about the Primary filegroup, which contains all the system tables and any other tables that are not assigned to other filegroups. What does this allows us to do? You can have all your system tables defined into one filegroup (Primary) so that they can reside on one disk by specifying that a particular data file belongs to the filegroup.

Although we can specify the following settings for our SQL Spy Net database (which we will build shortly), we cannot enforce these changes for the model database. If we made these the default specifications for the model database, whenever we create a new database the filegroup specifications would be copied also, and we would end up overwriting our data in our data files. Not a very good idea!

To prevent this from happening, SQL Server 2000 will not allow you to create new data files, transaction logs, or filegroups on the model database or any other system databases.

We can then have all our user tables defined into another filegroup so that they can reside on a separate disk. We can also have some user tables defined into one filegroup and others defined into another filegroup. This enables us to segregate our data files, thus increasing performance for our application.

How do we achieve this? We need to specify a filegroup as being the default. This means that whenever a table is created it is stored in the default filegroup. If a group is not specified as being the default, all tables will be stored in the Primary filegroup.

To remove a filegroup, you only need to select it and click Delete.

To delete (drop) a filegroup, all data files that reference that group must be assigned to another group or removed. You will not be able to drop a filegroup unless all the data files have been removed.

Setting the Options for Our Model Database

The Options tab, shown in Figure 3.9, allows us to configure database-level operations that can make a dramatic difference to how the application behaves.

The first setting that we have for the Options tab is the Access setting. This allows us to specify who can access the database. The following changes can be made to this:

- Restrict Access allows us to specify that only certain database roles have access to the model database. This can be important to set if you want to prevent any users other than those in these roles from being able to modify the database settings. The Single User option means that only one user can access the database at any given time. Do not select this option; we do not need to restrict access at this stage.

- Read-Only stops the data and the system objects from being able to be altered. Nothing in the database can be altered until the Read-Only setting has been removed. Do not set the database to be read-only. We need the databases that are created from the model to be editable.

Figure 3.9

The Options tab settings for the model database.

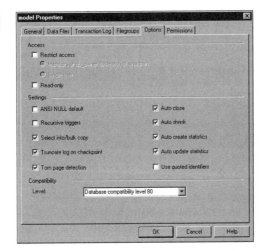

3

The second setting on the Options tab, the Settings group, allows us to specify the behavior of our database application.

- ANSI NULL Default allows you to specify whether a column in a table will be NULL or NOT NULL by default. When this option is checked, the ANSI SQL-92 standard is used, which means that a NULL is assumed. However, this isn't SQL Server 2000's default, and this option should remain unchanged. Also, I believe in reducing NULLs out of our database as much as we can, and this option will assist in achieving this. Make sure this option is not enabled. We will take a look at NULLs again shortly.

- The Recursive Triggers option allows triggers to fire recursively (the capability of a trigger to call itself). We will not be using recursive triggers immediately; so do not enable this option at this stage.

- The Select Into/Bulk Copy option allows us to perform a copy of a database table's data and structure without logging it in the transaction log. Why would you do this? To insert data into a table the transaction is logged in the transaction log, so that you can rollback the transaction. When you use the Select Into statement, the transaction is not written to the transaction log, so the copy of the data and the table is much faster. The database does not keep track of the changes; the only issue is that you cannot rollback the changes. We might need this statement in our application database, so we will leave this option enabled (check the option if it is not already checked).

- Truncate Log on Checkpoint allows SQL Server 2000 to reduce the size of the transaction log at some given point in time. This option prevents the transaction log from growing exponentially and thus prevents it from filling the disk. Ensure this option is enabled; it will save some difficulties about log sizes for the immediate future.

- Torn Page Detection allows SQL Server 2000 to locate incomplete pages. When data is stored on disk it is written into a page. A page is 8KB in size, and disk I/O operations are performed using a 512-byte sector. So we get one database page on 16 disk sectors. When a sector is complete, a switch (a bit operator which is a 1 or 0) is set to indicate that the sector is complete for a page. If, in the process of storing data on the sector a power outage occurs, then the switch will not be set and SQL Server 2000 will detect that the sector was not written correctly. In other words, SQL Server 2000 will detect the torn page. It is best to leave this option enabled so SQL Server 2000 can detect corrupt data pages.

- Auto Close specifies that the database will be shut down and all stray processes tidied up when the last user exits the database. This is especially useful for desktop editions of SQL Server 2000 (and is the default) because it allows the database to be manipulated as though it were any other file in the file system. This allows for copying, packaging, and mailing. It is not the default for other editions of SQL Server 2000 because the overhead of closing and reopening the database automatically when a user connects or disconnects is very costly. While deploying on a desktop version of SQL Server 2000 we will leave this option selected. This will help us to preserve resources on our PCs.

- Auto Shrink allows SQL Server 2000 to shrink the data files and the transaction logs periodically. The files are shrunk only when they contain more than 25% of unused space. Like Auto Close, this is turned on by default for desktop edition databases and not for any other editions of SQL Server 2000. To prevent running out of disk space, ensure this option is turned on.

- Auto Create Statistics allows SQL Server 2000 to improve query performance. The built-in query optimizer will be able to use the statistics for best evaluating how to execute a query. This is the default option (turned on) for all editions of SQL Server 2000. You can turn this option off and build the statistics manually, but it really is easier to allow SQL Server 2000 to handle this task. Because the default is to have this option enabled, and I am all for making our jobs easier, ensure that it is turned on.

- Auto Update Statistics specifies to SQL Server 2000 to update the statistics that it uses. This option improves performance for queries because the query optimizer will be able to best evaluate how to execute a query with up-to-date statistics. Once again this option can be turned off so you can build the statistics manually. Ensure this option is enabled to gain the best performance from our queries.

- Use Quoted Identifiers allows you to define object names with double quotes (""). This is useful if you have object names that do not follow the Transact-SQL rules or includes keywords. When this option is turned on and you are referring to an exact value (literal) you must use single quotes ('). By default this option is off because it is not good practice to use keywords for object names. We will discuss this a little later when creating our first table. One thing to note though is if you do have an object name that does not follow the rules, you can reference this with square brackets ([]). These brackets can be used whether this option is set or not. Because it is desirable not to use invalid object names in a database, ensure this option is not enabled. As an aside, some ODBC drivers do not interpret the double quotes as we would like them to, so it is better not to use this option.

 We will take a look at naming conventions and reserved words when we create our first tables in the "What Can We Call Our Columns?" excursion a little later in this chapter.

The final option that we are able to specify for the model database, and of course subsequent databases, is the compatibility levels of the database.

- The Level option allows us to specify whether our database will be compatible with previous versions of SQL Server. The main effect this has is on a few Transact-SQL statements and on some internal processing of NULLs, namely CONCAT NULL YIELDS NULL. When setting to versions earlier than version 7.0 this option is ignored, so when a string is appended to a NULL, the value of the string is returned rather than a NULL.

 Watch out for the section "Preventing NULLs in Our SQL Spy Net Application" later in the chapter for more riveting information about NULLs.

The main benefit to setting the compatibility level to a version earlier than 8.0 (2000) is for planned upgrades. This means that a database written in a previous version can be slowly upgraded to ensure that no compatibility issues are between the syntax of the earlier Transact-SQL statements and the requirements of the newer version.

Even if a database is set to earlier compatibility than the current version, the database will still gain all the performance benefits of the newer tools, making upgrades a simple and easy process. Way cool!

Because we are building our application from scratch, ensure the compatibility level is set to Database Compatibility Level 80.

Let's look at each section of the CONCAT NULL YIELDS NULL statement individually. CONCAT is short for concatenate, which means to append two things together. A NULL is a special value that we have discussed earlier, which is like nothing but is not equal to either zero or an empty string. YIELDS is the product of an equation.

Once again I will use an example to demonstrate the concept behind the statement. If we have a string variable with a value of MyString and we try to append (or concat) this to another string variable with the value of NULL, the product (or yield) will be NULL. The formula is as follows: MyString + NULL = NULL)

Permissions

The last tab available is the Permissions tab. With this we can specify the default permissions for the actions that a user or role (similar to a group in NT) can perform on our database. As you can see in Figure 3.10, the only permissions you can alter are for the Public role, which we take a more in-depth look at in Chapter 9.

Figure 3.10

Permissions that a user or group can perform.

If you do not specify what rights or permissions a user or role has at this level then the default is no permission. So the Public role will not be able to create tables, views, or stored procedures or to perform backups and so on.

Whose Database Is It, Anyway?

Why is the Public role the only one shown? We haven't created any other users or roles yet. We will implement some security in Chapter 9, but SQL Server 2000 has a default role called Public. This role cannot be removed from the instance of SQL Server 2000, but the permissions for this role can be modified.

We do not specify users in the model database because users are relevant to each database. So when the model database is copied we do not need any users it might contain.

What about the **sa** login—why doesn't it show in the list? The **sa** login is actually a member of the Public role, but it is also a member of a special role called db_owner.

This means that **sa** will have all the Public role's permissions, as well as all the permissions of the db_owner role. db_owner is a system role that doesn't allow us to alter the permissions for it. This is to prevent us from accidentally locking ourselves out of our own database.

For our application database and subsequent databases, we are better off leaving the default security settings intact for the model database.

We do not want to create problems for ourselves before we even begin! Because our users will be created later (in Chapter 9), if we modify the security now we might have problems ensuring the users have correct permissions and access.

And so, ladies and gentleman, this concludes our preliminary setup options for our databases that we create in SQL Server 2000. Next, we are going to create the SQL Spy Net application database and turn our plan into an application. So, put in your favorite spy-movie soundtrack, take a stretch if you need to, and let's get on with it!

Creating the SQL Spy Net Application Database

As in most tasks within SQL Server 2000, there are many different ways to achieve the same thing. You can use a nice user interface or you can enter Transact-SQL directly against the database.

Even most of the configuration options for the model database that we just went through can be set using Transact-SQL!

What methods are available to create a database in SQL Server 2000? Listed here are the three basic methods you can use to create a database:

- Run the Database Creation Wizard, which is contained in Enterprise Manager. This is a simple wizard that allows you to enter the parameters that you require to model your database on. Although using the wizard is an effective and simple way to create an application database, as a DBA you usually will use one of the two following methods because they are a little quicker. For this reason we will not cover the creation of a database through the wizard.

- Using the UI in Enterprise Manager to create a database. This is done by selecting the New Database option from the pop-up menu when you right-click the database folder within Enterprise Manager. This is the most common way of creating a database in SQL Server 2000, probably because of the friendly user interface you are provided. We will initially create our application database with this method.

- Enter the CREATE DATABASE Transact-SQL statement directly into Query Analyzer. This is by far the most difficult to remember (I always have trouble remembering the exact syntax), but it gives you the most flexibility and is probably the preferred way for most DBAs. The reason? The knowledge is cross-transferable. Even if you move to another database management system (heaven forbid), you will know the basic structure of the statement.

As you can see, the ability to create a database quickly and easily (by all levels of users) is well catered for in SQL Server 2000.

Using Enterprise Manager to Create Our Application Database

In this section we will develop the database through the user interface in Enterprise Manager. Unfortunately though, I am going to make an assumption about the PC on which you are running SQL Server 2000.

I am assuming that you do not have multiple hard drives. On the PC that I am using I have three separate hard drives, but not everybody will have the same configuration, so we will go with the lowest common denominator. However, if you do have the ability to specify different drives for the data and transaction logs, feel free to do so (this was discussed in the section "Configuring the Model Database to Meet Our SQL Spy Net Application Requirements," earlier in this chapter).

Well, let's get down to business!

If you do not have Enterprise Manager running, start the application now. Drill through the tree-view control and locate the Databases folder. If you right-click the Databases folder you will be presented with a pop-up menu similar to that shown in Figure 3.11. Select the New Database option.

Figure 3.11

The create a new data-base command in Enterprise Manager.

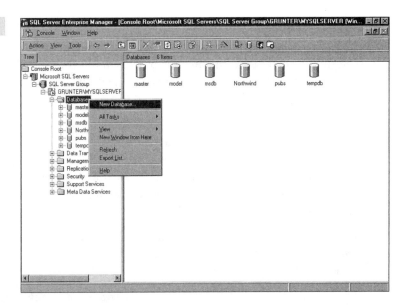

The next screen collects some basic information in regard to the creation of a database. We are going to call our database SQLSpyNet. This is the name that SQL Server 2000 will use to recognize our application database. You could name your database something else, but throughout the rest of the book I will refer to the SQLSpyNet naming convention, so it will be easier if you use this name. The new screen will look similar to that shown in Figure 3.12.

Figure 3.12

The Create New Database Properties dialog screen.

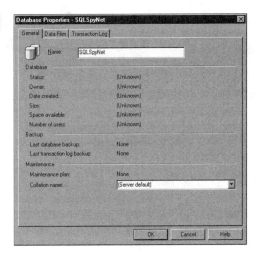

The General Tab

The General tab is relatively limited in the actions that you can perform. Other than entering the database name the only other action is the collation name. This is used to set the type of locale configuration that the database will have. You only need to alter this if your database will talk to a computer that has a different locale setting than your server (your PC) has.

The *locale* refers to the way the characters on your computer are displayed and stored. The locale is set for your machine when the operating system is installed. Different countries and languages use different locale settings so that unique characters to their language can be displayed. For example, the U.S. English character set uses the *Latin1_General* locale.

Because we are developing our application from scratch and currently do not have a requirement to communicate with other databases, we shall leave the database default to the server's settings.

Notice that the screen has two other tabs: the tabs for configuring the data files and the transaction logs. If you have a quick look, you will see they imitate the settings (except the filenames) that we adjusted in the section, "Configuring the Model Database to Meet Our SQL Spy Net Application Requirements."

Click OK now, and SQL Server 2000 will create your first database for you! Simple, isn't it?

Note If you don't see your new database in the Databases folder, right-click and select Refresh.

The Properties Tab

Now select the SQLSpyNet database, right-click, and choose the Properties option. You will be presented with a screen similar to the one that we saw in Figure 3.9. Click the Options tab and you will see the screen shown in Figure 3.13.

We are going to check that the options that we set in the model database are reflected in our new database. If the settings are correct they should mirror the settings in Figure 3.13. When you are happy with the settings, click OK.

If you explore in the new database (namely the Tables, Views, and Stored Procedures folders), you will see that some database objects have already been created. These are the system objects that SQL Server 2000 uses to keep track of the objects contained in our database. For example, if you open the Tables folder you will see a list of system tables.

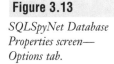

Figure 3.13

SQLSpyNet Database Properties screen— Options tab.

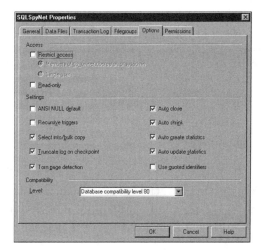

If you do not see the system tables, you will need to alter the registration properties of Enterprise Manager. You can do this by selecting the ServerName\InstanceName icon, right-clicking, and then selecting Edit SQL Server Registration Properties; you will see the registration dialog window.

When the dialog window starts, ensure the Show System Databases and System Objects box is selected. Click OK.

For more information, see the section "Configuring SQL Server 2000" in Appendix B or "Setting the sa Password," earlier in this chapter.

These system tables contain information about the schema of the database, for example the names of tables, views, and stored procedures (in the sysobjects table), the names, size, type of columns within tables (the syscolumns table), and the names and access of the users (the sysusers table). This allows SQL Server 2000 to track not only the tables, views, and stored procedures, but also the users and many other objects defined in our database.

Well, that is about all we have to do with our database so far. We can now delete (drop) the database. "What?!?" I hear you cry.

We know how to develop a database through the nice UI that Enterprise Manager provides, so let's learn how to do this through Transact-SQL code.

For the rest of the application development we are going to use a mixture of Transact-SQL code (my preference) and the UI in Enterprise Manager. However, we will not repeat tasks as we have done in this section. Instead, we will implement our changes and move to the next task, or else we will never get our application up and running!

Dropping Spies Like Flies

First, though, we need to drop the SQLSpyNet database that we just created.

Start Query Analyzer through the start menu group or by selecting Tools from the menu bar in Enterprise Manager and selecting the SQL Server Query Analyzer option. Then enter the code in Listing 3.1 into the Transact-SQL window, as shown in Figure 3.14.

Figure 3.14

Removing our database by using code in the Query Analyzer window.

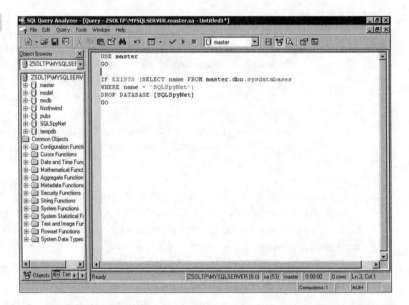

Listing 3.1—Deleting Our SQLSpyNet Database Using Transact-SQL Code

```
1: USE master
2: GO
3: IF EXISTS (SELECT name FROM master.dbo.sysdatabases
3a:WHERE name = 'SQLSpyNet')
4: DROP DATABASE [SQLSpyNet]
5: GO
```

After you have entered the code in the window, click the Green Triangle in the toolbar, or use the hotkeys Alt+X to run the code.

After the code has finished running you will see two statements of confirmation that the task has completed. They will be similar to these:

```
1: Deleting database file
   ➥'c:\mssql2000\MSSQL$MYSQLSERVER\data\SQLSpyNet_Log.LDF'.
2: Deleting database file
   ➥'c:\mssql2000\MSSQL$MYSQLSERVER\data\SQLSpyNet_Data.MDF'.
```

Tip   Save these file paths because you will need them later when we re-create the database.

This confirms that the data file and the transaction log have been deleted.

Note   If you did not name your database SQLSpyNet, enter the name you chose in place of SQLSpyNet.

Analysis

The meaning of the code is relatively simple. The first two lines of code (1 and 2) ensure that this statement is being fired from the master database. All database manipulation such as DROP and CREATE should be fired from the master database.

The third two lines (3 and 3a) check the existence of your database within our instance of SQL Server 2000; this is called a control-of-flow statement, and there will be more on this in Chapter 4.

The fourth line of code actually performs the database drop, and the fifth line executes the two former statements consecutively.

Do not worry about the SELECT statement or the WHERE criteria; I explain this in more detail in Chapter 4.

If you now refresh your Databases folder in either Enterprise Manger or Query Analyzer (through the Object Browser; refer to Chapter 2), you will see that the SQLSpyNet database has gone!

There we go; so far we have created and deleted a database by using two of the tools available in SQL Server 2000. We will now re-create the SQLSpyNet database through Transact-SQL code; so don't close down Query Analyzer yet!

Using the Data Definition Language (DDL) to Create Databases and Objects

With the new features of Query Analyzer, getting the basic outline of the common database objects that you need to create is very easy. With a couple of mouse clicks and some fill-in-the-gaps programming, you can have a database created in only a couple of moments.

The important part of this process though is what to put in the gaps. Understanding how a CREATE DATABASE statement is built is just as important (if not more) than just entering the code.

In this section we will go through the CREATE DATABASE statement rather than use the templates that SQL Server 2000 provides.

First though we need to clarify a couple of points about SQL. As I said earlier, SQL is a standard language for manipulating data and databases. It is based on mathematical set theory. But two distinct parts exist to SQL—the Data Definition Language (DDL) and the Data Manipulation Language (DML).

DDL is used to create database objects and define how the data will look in the database. For example, through the DDL we can not only create databases, tables, views and so on, but we can also delete them (as in the previous example). It is easy to spot the DDL because the SQL statement usually begins with CREATE, ALTER, or DROP.

DML is used to manipulate the data within a database. For example, through the DML we cannot only insert new rows of data but we can also delete them (as in the previous example). It is easy to spot the DML because the SQL statement usually begins with SELECT, INSERT, UPDATE, or DELETE.

With this in mind, if you look at the Transact-SQL statement that we entered to delete our database, you will see that it is a mixture of DDL and DML. The DROP statement in line 4 is DDL and the SELECT statement in line 3 is DML.

We now have an idea of what DDL and DML are. Let us create our SQLSpyNet database (once again) with a Transact-SQL DDL statement and really get this show on the road!

The CREATE DATABASE statement is a complex beast and has many parameters that you can specify. Because of the limitations of this book (namely size!), we are only going to cover the options that are the most relevant to us. The code in Listing 3.2 will re-create our SQLSpyNet database for us.

Listing 3.2—Creating Our SQLSpyNet Database Through Transact-SQL Code

```
1:USE master
2:GO
3:CREATE DATABASE SQLSpyNet
3a:ON PRIMARY (NAME = 'SQLSpyNet_Data',
3b:FILENAME =
3c:'x:\SQLSpyNet_Data.MDF',
3d:SIZE = 5MB,
3e:FILEGROWTH = 10%)
4: LOG ON (NAME = 'SQLSpyNet_Log',
4a:FILENAME =
4b:'x:\SQLSpyNet_Log.LDF',
4c:SIZE = 5MB,
4d:FILEGROWTH = 10%)
5:GO
```

You will need to replace the x:\ with the path on which you would like to create the data file and transaction log.

> **Tip**
>
> To get the file path that your previous database used, copy the file paths that you saved earlier. If you didn't save them, you will need to enter them where the x:\ is.

After you have entered the file paths you can run the code. SQL Server 2000 will return at least two messages similar to the following:

```
1: The CREATE DATABASE process is allocating 5.00 MB on disk 'SQLSpyNet_Data'.
2: The CREATE DATABASE process is allocating 5.00 MB on disk 'SQLSpyNet_Log'.
```

Analysis

Let's examine the code that you have entered.

- Line 1 specifies to Query Analyzer that it switch to the master database.
- Line 2 forces the execution of the code in line 1. Use the GO command whenever you would like code to be fired immediately instead of waiting until the whole block is executed. This is a unique feature of all versions of SQL Server. Some other RDBMSs use a semicolon (;) to execute a block of code immediately. Through different options we can change this, but we don't really need to unless using code from another RDBMS.
- Line 3 is the actual DDL that creates the database. The only parameter required is the database name. We could create a database by only specifying a name. Unfortunately though, this does not allow us enough flexibility.

- Line 3a specifies the filegroup (PRIMARY, the default) that will be used and the data filename. The bracket denotes the beginning of the data file parameters. The NAME = allows you to set the name that SQL Server 2000 will use to refer to the data file for this database.

- Lines 3b and 3c specify the location of the data file.

- Lines 3d and 3e specify the initial size of the data file and the size by which it grows. If you leave off the % sign, the file growth size will be in MBs (the default). The end bracket denotes the end of the data file parameters.

- Line 4 specifies the transaction log parameters. The bracket denotes the beginning of the transaction log parameters. The NAME = allows you to set the name that SQL Server 2000 will use to refer to the transaction log for this database.

- Lines 4a, 4b, 4c and 4d—These parameters are the same as they are for the data file (see previous).

- Line 5 executes the previous Transact-SQL block from the last GO statement; that is, everything from CREATE DATABASE down.

If you now refresh your Databases folder in Enterprise Manager or Object Browser in Query Analyzer, you will see the SQLSpyNet database. Now I am sure a smart person like yourself found that easy, didn't you?

Just perform a quick check on your newly created database (by looking at the database properties, remember? If not look at "The Properties Tab," earlier in this chapter.), and make sure the options for the database fit our needs that we specified earlier. If you find any discrepancies, make the necessary changes.

As I mentioned earlier, we can specify many other parameters when creating a database through Transact-SQL code. We can specify that the database is for data loading only, the collation to be used, and the filegroups that the database will use. As you can see, developing a database through Transact-SQL code is very flexible but definitely a little harder than using the UI through Enterprise Manager.

We will now briefly look at tables and discuss some more database concepts.

Building Tables for Our Spies

Tables are the key to all databases. They enable us to store related information for retrieval at a later stage. Without tables we would not be able to store and retrieve the information that is so critical to our databases, so we wouldn't have a database!

A table will allow us to store a spy's name, address, date of birth, and so on, but we can also store the activities that our spies are involved in.

Tables can be related to each other, unrelated, or only used on a temporary basis. They are very flexible, and a well-designed table will help to ensure that information is stored accurately and concisely.

Three main types of tables are used within SQL Server 2000:

- User-defined tables—Developers who want to store user-defined information (such as a spy's details) within a table create these. They are easily identifiable in SQL Server 2000 Enterprise Manager because their type is defined as User. Within the Object Browser in Query Analyzer, they are listed in a separate folder named User, under the main Tables folder.

- System tables—These are used by the internal workings of SQL Server 2000 to manage the database objects. They are characteristically identifiable by the "sys" naming convention; for example, sysobjects. This table contains a list of database objects within a database.

- Temporary tables—As the name suggests, these tables are created only on a temporary basis. They are characterized by the hash (#) symbol in front of their names. Different types of temporary tables have different levels of scope.

This gives you a brief overview of the tables that are available in SQL Server 2000. We will work with them more as we develop the SQL Spy Net application further.

But why have tables? Tables are modeled on real-world objects (people, spies, bad guys) and events (activities). We have already seen this with the ERD we partially designed earlier, in Chapter 1.

But tables that are not related provide us with few benefits. We might as well have a data file on a single PC! Defining a relationship between our tables is the key to having an effective and informative data store.

We can implement relationships between tables that model the relationships in a real-world scenario. For example, a spy can battle a bad guy to prevent world domination. We can then model and implement this relationship in our database to represent what happens when a spy battles a bad guy.

 Note

Of course, all this spy business might not seem too practical when you're ready to work with a real-world client, unless you're working for military intelligence! But, everything we discuss here applies to business relationships such as sales-people to customers, customer address information, and dates and items in sales data, for example. But then, you'll have the rest of your career to create good ol' boring sales records, so enjoy the fun while you can. I'll let you decide who the "bad guys" are in your world.

Relationships also help us enforce integrity of our data. After we define a relationship, through primary and foreign keys, we can specify that in the table that has the foreign key (the child), it can only contain a row of data if a value exists in the parent table (we will prove this after we have built our tables).

This prevents us from entering a spy in our Spy table without them first existing in the Person table.

Revisiting the Analysis of the SQL Spy Net Application

So far in our application development we have decided to implement the Spy table and the BadGuy table as subtypes of a person table. We have also implemented the Activity table as an associative table between the Spy and BadGuy tables.

Well what about the rest of the application? Because as I stated earlier, this book is about SQL Server 2000 not analyzing requirements, I will give you the rest of the ERD without boring you too much about the details. However, I will endeavor to explain the ERD, as shown in Figure 3.15, so you have an overview of the application.

Figure 3.15

Final ERD of the SQLSpyNet database.

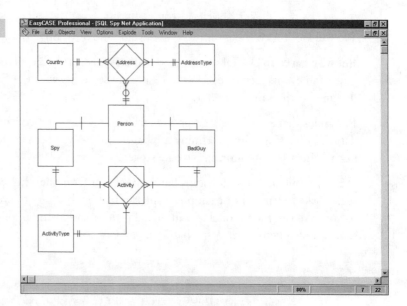

As you can see, the ERD for the whole application is relatively simple. It contains only a few tables. We have defined the spies and the bad guys to be subtypes of the person entity.

As discussed earlier (in Chapter 1), this allows us the greatest flexibility for adding to our application. If we need an employee entity, creating an employee subtype is a simple process of creating an employee subtype.

The important factor to note is how the bad guys and the spies relate to each other. A spy is only given an assignment if a bad guy is wrecking havoc on the world, so this is their relationship.

In a lifetime, a spy can be involved in foiling one or more bad guy's plans, and a bad guy can be involved in one or more dastardly deeds. So we have a many-to-many relationship.

Because this cannot be implemented in a relational database, we need an associative entity. So we introduce the Activity entity. This keeps track of the bad guys that a spy has fought, as well as the plans that they have foiled.

The ActivityType entity allows us to enter a list of evil plans that the bad guys hatch. These plans could include (and most probably will) taking over the world! They could wreck havoc and generally cause a disturbance among the citizens.

The Address entity is only used to track the addresses of a person. Because it is possible for a person to have more than one address, we have broken it out into another table, thus reducing repeating rows in our person table and enabling our data model (ERD) to conform to 1NF.

1NF is First Normal Form, which is the first level of normalization (see the Excursion "1NF, 2NF, 3NF, 4!"). Basically, a table must not contain a list of values in any single column (that is, a comma-delimited list of values), and there must be no repeating groups.

1NF, 2NF, 3NF, 4!

Normalization is derived from the study of relational theory and was developed by E.F. Codd, the father of relational theory. It is the process of arranging tables and data within our database to reduce dependencies and inefficient structures as much as possible.

Normalization is linear in nature (each rule is applied after another rule is complete) and is used to define the best database structure that you can possibly achieve.

Six normal forms, or stages, are defined in the process of normalization. As mentioned, the rules of normalization are linear; therefore, the second rule depends on the first rule, the third rule depends on the second, and so on.

3NF is the level that most developers take their database applications to when normalizing their databases. Why? Most developers find that that third normal is sufficient to meet the requirements of the application and ensure data consistency.

Note By removing repeating rows from our Person table, we have ensured that our table now conforms to First Normal Form (1NF).

As I referred to earlier, defining a data model is not the same for everybody, and having said this, this model will not suit some people. They might look at the model and decide that it has limitations, which it does. So I will now describe to you the limitations that are in place in the model.

- A spy can work on only one assignment at a time. This means that we cannot schedule a spy to be fighting two or more bad guys (probably a good thing!). Likewise, a bad guy cannot be executing more than one plan at one time.

- A person can have many addresses, but an address can belong to only one person. This means that communal sharing of housing is not recognized. To implement this we need to introduce either another entity (the correct way) or allowing repeating rows of information in the address table (naughty, naughty, naughty).

- We can—and this is relatively serious, if we do not develop our business rules correctly—end up with the scenario of a person belonging to the spies group as well as the bad-guys group! To prevent this we implement *domain constraints*. These will prevent the incorrect values from being entered into either table.

 Domain constraints enables us to limit the values that a column in a table will accept. We can specify a pool of allowable values for a given column. For example, if a value falls between the range of 1–10, then it can be entered, otherwise it will be rejected. As you may can imagine, this is a very powerful tool of database development.

That about wraps it up for the ERD for our application except, of course, for the actual column names within our tables, but we will create these as we develop the tables.

Bringing Our Data Model and Database Together

We have covered a fair amount so far in this chapter, but we really have our application under way now. We have a database, and we have a data model. All we have to do now is implement the data model into our database.

The implementation of the data model will be relatively straightforward, and we will use both Enterprise Manager and Query Analyzer to help us achieve this.

In the rest of this chapter we will discuss some of the best practices that are actually in use out there in the real world. Although these best practices are recognized by many organizations, there are still many differing practices that individual organizations implement.

The good thing about standards is that they are always being refined and redeveloped. As we go through the process of developing (or implementing) our data model we will discuss one of the most common practices—naming conventions.

Developing the First Database Table for the SQL Spy Net Application

Finally, I will stop talking and let you develop your first table, really truly, I promise!

As we go through the development of our tables, we will revisit our ERD and fill in the blanks.

Normally you wouldn't begin coding until you had the initial design complete (barring minor changes), but I know that you must be really chomping at the bit to get the development underway.

Why do we not start coding before the design is complete? Well this normally ends up requiring us to do a lot of rework. We find that we create tables as we go, don't like the design or flow of the application, and end up having to drop and then re-create the tables. On a tight budget, this can end up chewing much of the budget without any real progress.

So I will break the golden rule and allow you to get on with the application development.

All righty then, let's get things under way.

Expand the SQLSpyNet database in Enterprise Manager and click the Tables folder. You will see a list of the tables currently in the database (only system tables at this stage though).

Right-click the Tables folder to open the pop-up menu that gives you the option to create a new table (see Figure 3.16). Doing this will launch the new table window. This is similar to Microsoft Access's new table editor, another new feature of SQL Server 2000. Within this editor we can create columns, primary keys, and indexes, and even provide descriptions of columns (another new feature).

Figure 3.16

*Create new table option
in the SQLSpyNet
database.*

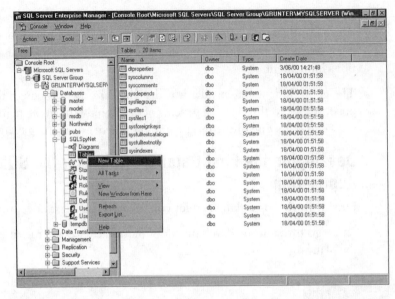

When you implement a data model, you must start at the highest-level entity. This ensures that when we develop the relationships between the tables, the tables will be available. For example, we will start with our Person entity because this entity does not have a foreign key to any other entity. Other possible entities that we could start with are the ActivityType and the AddressType table.

Figure 3.17 shows the table with the columns defined as well as the primary key.

Figure 3.17

*Columns in the Person
table.*

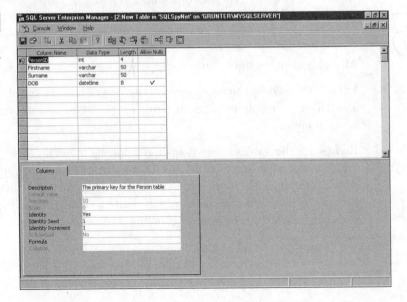

We are going to implement the PersonID as an identity column. An identity column has an automatically incrementing value. For example, the column will start at one, but when the next row is inserted, SQL Server 2000 will increment the row to two (if the identity increment is defined as one, the default). Every consecutive insert will increment the value in the column. Deleting a value will not decrease the column value.

EXCURSION

What Can We Call Our Columns?

Before you actually decide on a name for your column, you should take into consideration some facts.

SQL Server 2000 restricts the characters that you can use when creating or defining a column in table. The first character in the name must include the character sets a–z, A–Z, or _, @, or #. Any characters following on from this must be in the first rule's definition but can also include numbers and the $ sign. The column name must be a minimum of one character long or a maximum length of 128 characters long. Although spaces are allowed in column names, it is not recommended because you must use square brackets ([]) to implement the column names.

The following options will allow us to define the structure of our Person table. We will create the columns and specify the primary key. Besides the limitations I mention in the Excursion sidebar, there are also other limitations that are enforced for your column definitions. SQL Server 2000 has a list of *reserved words* that should not be used as columns names; this list is included in the online help for SQL Server 2000.

 A *reserved word* is a special term that SQL Server 2000 uses to describe something that has special meaning. For example, you cannot create an object in SQL Server 2000 by naming it with the reserved word CREATE. This is exactly the same as in programming languages such as Visual Basic or C++.

 Note You can implement column names that are defined from reserved words if you enclose them in square brackets; for example, [SELECT] is a perfectly legal column name. However, it pays to avoid this type of naming convention because some ODBC drivers do not interpret the square brackets as they should.

- First, ensure the PersonID column Allow Nulls option is *not* checked. To specify an identity column, the column must not allow NULLs. See the Excursion on NULLs for more on my reasoning for this option.

EXCURSION

Preventing NULLs *in Our SQL Spy Net Application*

We briefly discussed NULLs earlier and I gave you an abbreviated description, but just to refresh your memory, a NULL is an unknown value. A NULL is not equal to either a zero or an empty string (""). In fact, a NULL is not even thought of being equivalent to another NULL! When you compare a NULL to another value, a NULL is returned (though this behavior can be changed).

Many differing opinions exist on the roles of NULLs in database design, and I guess I will upset some people by saying this, but as I mentioned earlier I do not like NULLs!

When I design and develop an application, I try to reduce the amount of NULLs in the application as much as is possible. I believe that the extra overhead caused by checking for the existence of NULLs in a client application is tedious. For example, if you try to JOIN two tables together and the columns that you are joining on contain NULLs, you might not receive the results that you would expect. This would require you to change the type of JOIN you execute, causing extra resources to be used on the server.

One way to reduce NULLs in an application is to introduce default values. We will look at other ways shortly, but for now let's discuss Defaults.

Default values, which we specify for our table columns, allow a value to be automatically entered when data is inserted into the database. For example, if we have an Order Date column of data type `datetime`, we can specify that the column automatically gets today's date when a new row is inserted into the table.

We define a default with the keyword `DEFAULT` when we create our tables through code, but when designing a table in Enterprise Manager we enter a value in the Default Value option in the table designer. This ensures that a value is entered into a column even if the user does not enter one.

One other simple way to prevent NULLs is to explicitly specify that we do not want NULLs in our columns by defining them as `NOT NULL`. If data is inserted into a row and a NULL value is attempted to be inserted into a column that specifies `NOT NULL`, the insert will fail.

As we develop our application tables, we will explicitly state each column to either allow NULL values or enforce that NULLs are not allowed. This will help us ensure data integrity and prevent us from having data that is not valuable.

We can attempt to reduce NULLs as much as physically possible, but sometimes it is impossible to avoid them. This is especially true for a column that is not updated until a later stage, or if a value at time of entry is unknown.

So the last word on NULLs is, as much as I try to avoid them, they are actually an integral part of a RDBMS, and all you can do is try to reduce them as much as possible.

SQL Server 2000 has by default NOT NULL specified on a column when created. This is where the Relational Database Management System (RDBMS) differs from the ANSI SQL-92 standard, which states that if NOT NULL isn't specified, NULL is the default. This can be changed so that SQL Server 2000 conforms to the standard, but it is better for us to explicitly state our intentions by specifying either NULL or NOT NULL on every column. That way, if we script our tables to implement into another RDBMS (urgghhh!), we will ensure that our intentions are retained.

- Second, click the Columns property tab at the bottom of the screen (see Figure 3.17). Set the Identity option to yes. This will automatically populate the Identity Seed (beginning number) and the Identity Increment (value to increment by) with one. This will be fine for our requirements.

- To define the primary key for the table, click the PersonID column. This will put an arrow next to the column name. You can then either click the key on the toolbar, or right-click and select Set Primary Key.

This might not mean too much to you at the moment, but SQL Server 2000 creates a unique index on the column you define as a primary key automatically. We will discuss indexes in depth a little later in Chapter 11.

- Next enter all the columns names and data types as shown in Figure 3.17.

- Finally, click the save icon (the floppy disk icon) and enter the table name, which is Person. We have used the entity name here without defining it as a table like some organizations do. For example, I have seen many examples of companies using tblPerson, tPerson, or even PersonTable. There is little need for this. We know it is a table because it resides in the Tables folder. As we discussed earlier, keep it short and sweet.

- You can now close the New Table window. The table you just created will be in the Tables folder (if you don't see it, right-click on the folder and select Refresh). You will see that under the type column the Person table is set to User. This shows that a database user has created the table (in this case sa) rather than it being a system-generated table.

> **Note** The User tables are sometimes known as base tables because this is where the user data is held. Be careful using the term base tables because some developers refer to top-level (highest-level) entities as base tables, which, as you can imagine, could create some confusion.

EXCURSION

A Rose by Any Other Name Still Smells as Sweet

Many companies that I have worked for, and indeed many others around the globe, adopt some type of naming standard for all their database objects, including columns in a table. This is what is called in the industry as *good practice* and allows developers to easily recognize the context of the object.

Many developers/companies will also use *Person_ID* or *PersonID* as the name of the primary key column for the Person table. Whenever you see this throughout the database— that is, in the Spy table—you know that it refers to the Person table. This is a very good naming convention to adopt, but be careful. Ensure that anything that has the suffix *ID* is actually a primary key or foreign key column.

Keep your names simple and meaningful, drop unnecessary datatype definitions from the names, and try to avoid using reserved words.

These naming conventions not only apply to column definitions but also to all database objects.

That was the first database table. Simple, wasn't it? We will now create three more database tables through the user interface and the final four tables through Transact-SQL code, using the CREATE TABLE statement.

You can now create the AddressType table using the same method you used for the Person table. Figure 3.18 displays the columns and the data types as well as the primary key for the table.

The AddressType table is known as a lookup table. The few columns characterize this, as does its placement within our ERD. Lookup tables are usually placed on the peripheral of the ERD, as the AddressType table has been.

This table will be used to record the different types of addresses (postal, physical, and so on) that a person can have. The benefit of modeling in this way means if we want to add more address types (for example, a business address type) at a future date, we can do so without altering the data model.

Another benefit of using lookup tables is that they help us ensure the integrity of our data. If we have a lookup table, we know that every time we use a row with an ID of 5, for example, the row will contain a value of Home Address.

Figure 3.18

Columns in the AddressType table.

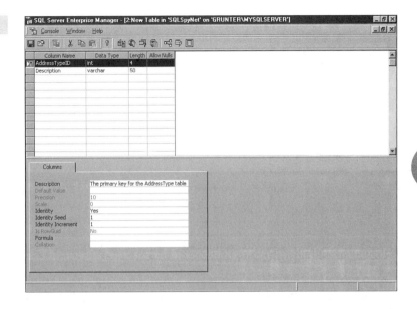

Lookup tables help to prevent people entering information that can be misconstrued due to spelling mistakes.

EXCURSION

Exploring Data Integrity

Data integrity allows the data in our database to remain correct and consistent. If the data in the database does become inconsistent, data integrity is absent.

SQL Server 2000 supports and allows you to implement four main categories of data integrity in our application.

- Entity integrity is the lowest level of integrity and is enforced by the primary key and related indexes. For example, if a person has a Social Security number of 123497859, no other person can have the same Social Security Number.

- Domain integrity enables you to limit the values that a column can accept. For example, you can specify that an Annual Salary column must have a value greater than $10,000.00.

- Referential integrity specifies that the values entered in a column exist in another related table. This is enforced through a foreign key. For example, if you enter a person and his address details (which are held in another table), referential integrity would ensure that the Address table must have a related person in the Person table.

- User-defined integrity enables the developer to define specific business rules that do not fall into one of the other integrity types.

All these categories enable you to develop your own integrity rules.

continues

There is one other way that we ensure the consistency of the data in our application—through data types. Data types in SQL Server 2000 are similar to data types provided by many programming languages. We have strings (such as `char` and `varchar`), integers, money, dates, and many more, including a new type just released in SQL Server 2000 called `SQL_variant`. If you have done any Microsoft Visual Basic programming, this is similar to the variant type in Visual Basic, allowing many data different data type values to be stored in a column.

With data types we can specify that a column in a table will only accept values that are consistent with that type. For example, a Date of Birth column would be defined as a date-time type. This would prevent users from entering invalid values such as a string like `'unknown'` in the column.

We will be implementing most of these categories of data integrity, so you will learn how to create each of these types as we go.

The third table that we will create is another lookup table. The Country table has the same characteristics as the AddressType table, allowing us to add new countries at a later date without having to change the data model. Follow the preceding methods to create this table. See Figure 3.19 for column, data types, and primary key definitions.

Figure 3.19

Columns in the Country table.

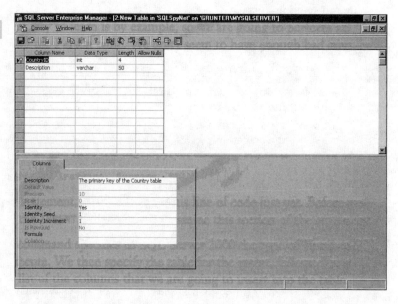

The fourth and final table that we will create through the user interface is the Address table. This is the table that captures the addresses that a person might have.

Once again you will use the same method to develop this table as the previous three. Figure 3.20 shows the columns and the data types, as well as the primary keys for the table.

Figure 3.20

Columns in the Address table.

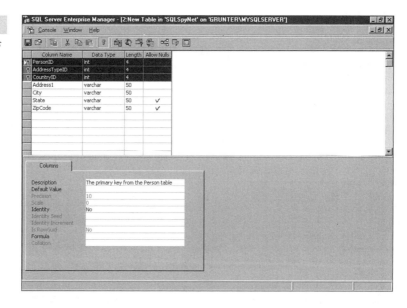

3

EXCURSION

Keys, Keys, and More Keys

Notice that the Address table is a little different in how it defines its primary key. The table has what is known as a *composite* primary key. The combination of the foreign keys from the other tables makes the primary key for the associative Address table. Why? It is guaranteed then that a person can have only one address type for one country, ensuring integrity of the data.

A *composite primary key* is a primary key for a table that is made up of more than one field. For example, in our Person, Country, and AddressType, the associative or junction table that combines these tables needs a foreign key to all three tables. Neither CountryID, AddressTypeID, nor PersonID alone can uniquely identify a row because a person can appear in the table more than once, and likewise with an address type and country. The only way to uniquely identify a row in the table is by combining the three foreign keys into the primary key for the Address table. This guarantees uniqueness for any given row.

Although this is a perfectly valid way to define the primary key for this table (and is the recommended method of relational theory), this table could also have another style of primary key. We could define an AddressID column and set it as an identity value. This could act as the primary key for the associative Address table. Many developers use this method for associative tables, and I might step on some toes here, but it does not ensure data integrity. This method would allow us to insert multiple records of the same address type for the same country and the same person. We could create a unique index on this table to prevent this, but there would be little point when the correct primary key definition would do it for us.

For the sake of data integrity and sticking to the rules of relational theory, we will develop the table to have a composite primary key. Although data updates are a little trickier, I believe that the benefits far outweigh the negatives. We will take a look at how to implement the structure in another way shortly.

Tip If you hold down the Ctrl key you will be able to select more than one column at time.

Because the Address table has the primary key columns from the Person, AddressType, and Country tables, we call these *foreign keys*. This is the first step in creating a relationship between the tables. As we have entered the foreign key columns, we now need to explicitly define the relationships that these tables have.

EXCURSION

3NF, 3NF, Wherefore Art Thou 3NF?

If you look at the Address table that we have just defined, you can see that the relation (table) is not actually in third normal form (3NF). A *transitive dependency* is in the table. See if you can spot it! I will give you the answer at the end of the chapter.

 A *transitive dependency* is if the non-key attributes are not mutually independent. For example, if a dependency exists in our table, such as a ZIP code that is dependent on a city, that is a transitive dependency.

Diagramming Our Database to Build Relationships Between the Tables

Click the Diagrams folder, right-click, and select New Database Diagram. This will launch the Database Diagram Wizard (if it doesn't, don't worry because we are going to do this task without the wizard). Click Cancel. This will give you a blank canvas waiting for you to perform a task. Right-click the blank canvas, and select the Add Table option, as shown in Figure 3.21.

Figure 3.21

Adding a table to the database diagram.

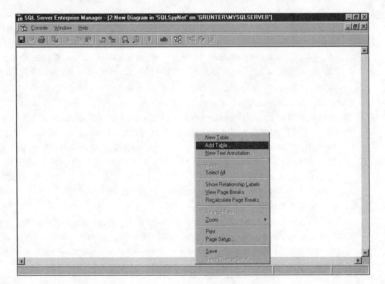

Note   The database diagram tool is a very cool tool! You can perform a multitude of tasks, including drawing diagrams, defining relationships between tables, modifying columns, and creating new tables. It is very simple to use, and most developers prefer to do everything here because it is all in one place.

This will launch the Add Table dialog window, which contains a list of tables in the database, including the system tables. This is shown in Figure 3.22.

Figure 3.22

Selecting tables to add to the database diagram canvas.

Add the tables that we have just created (Address, AddressType, Country, and Person) to the diagram by selecting the table name and then clicking the Add button.

Tip   If you hold down the Ctrl key you will be able to select more than one table at time.

When our four tables have been added to the diagram, close the Add Tables dialog window.

You can move the new tables around on the database diagram canvas by dragging them. This enables you to arrange them so you can see them all together.

Creating Relationships

To create the relationships between the tables, we will start with the Person and Address tables. Click the key next to the PersonID column in the Person table and drag it to the key next to the PersonID in the Address table. This will launch the Create Relationship dialog window, as shown in Figure 3.23.

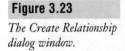

Figure 3.23

The Create Relationship dialog window.

This window is very powerful and introduces one of the many new features to SQL Server 2000.

Let's start at the top. Remember that everything in a SQL Server 2000 database must be uniquely identifiable, including relationship names. As you can see, SQL Server 2000 automatically fills this name in for you. You do have the option to change the relationship name, but this naming convention is fine for our needs.

The default name (FK_Address_Person) describes the relationship well. FK stands for foreign key (the type of relationship we are implementing), the Address is the Address table (the *many* ∞ side of the relationship), and consequently the Person is the Person table (the *one* [key] side of the relationship).

Next we can define the columns on which the relationships depend.

As you can see in the primary key side we have PersonID (the primary key of the Person table). In the foreign key side we have the PersonID (the foreign key in the Address table). If you had many more columns you could specify them in this box. As long as the two PersonID columns are shown, as they are in Figure 3.23, this will be fine.

Next in the dialog box is the Check Existing Data on Creation option. This will ensure that the data in the foreign key table will allow you to create a relationship between the tables. Because we have only just created these tables, we have no data in the tables; this option does not affect our tables. Still leave this option checked.

The Enforce Relationship for Replication option specifies that whenever the table is replicated (copied) to another database the referential integrity (foreign key constraint) will remain in place. Although this does not concern us at this time, our application can grow to a stage where this sort of integrity is required, so leave this option selected.

The Enforce Relationship for INSERTs and UPDATEs option is the whole reason why we are implementing a relationship. This ensures that when data is inserted or updated to the Address table a person actually does exist. Leave this option in place.

Finally, we have one of the new features that SQL Server 2000 implements. This is a feature that Microsoft Access developers have had for a long time, and SQL Server developers have had to admit that at least on one score Access had something that SQL Server didn't. Well no more!

- The Cascade Update Related Fields option updates the foreign key value in the Address table whenever the primary key value in the Person table is updated. For example, if we had a person with an ID of 5 and they had a record in the Address table, if for some reason the primary key value of 5 was changed to 7, SQL Server would automatically update all records in the Address table. Pretty cool, huh?

- The Cascade Delete Related Records option automatically deletes all records in the foreign key table when the primary key table record is deleted. For example, if we have a person with addresses in the Address table and they no longer need to be recorded in the Person table, deleting the Person record would remove all the address records. In relational theory, and before this option was implemented in SQL Server, you had to delete the child records first (foreign key records) before deleting the parent records. If you didn't, you would receive an error preventing you from proceeding with the delete.

Because we do not want to delete records if someone accidentally deletes a person, we will leave the Cascade Delete Related Records option unchecked and do likewise for the Cascade Update Related Fields option. Our Person table has an identity field defined for the primary key, and this cannot be manually changed (well not easily at least), so we will not require this option.

After you have the options set, click OK. SQL Server 2000 will draw a relationship between the tables. The infinity symbol (∞) denotes the many side of the relationship, whereas the key denotes the one side. We have a one-to-many relationship now defined between our Person and Address tables, as shown in Figure 3.24.

The asterisk (*) next to the table names in the diagram shows that the changes have not been made to the database, and will not be made until the diagram has been saved.

Figure 3.24

The relationship between the Person and Address tables.

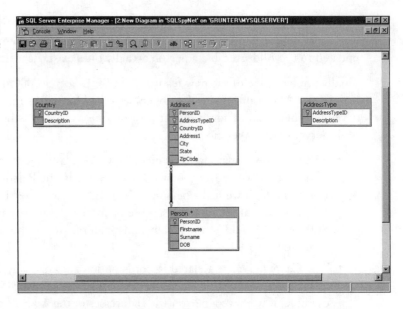

Now I want you to perform the same task for all the tables. Drag the primary key from the AddressType table to the foreign key of the same name in the Address table. Select the same options you did for the first relationship (except, of course, the column names).

Repeat the same task for the Country and Address tables. You should now have a relationship diagram that looks similar to the one in Figure 3.25.

Figure 3.25

The relationship diagram between all our database tables.

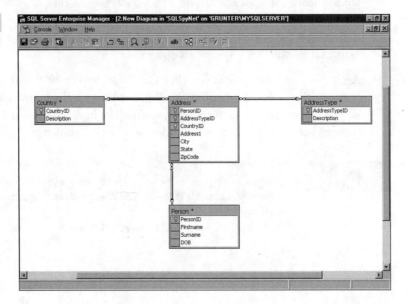

If you now save the diagram by clicking the floppy disk icon, SQL Server 2000 will prompt you for a name for the database diagram. You can enter anything you would like here, but something relevant would be appropriate, for example Current ERD.

After you click OK, SQL Server 2000 will notify you that the tables will be saved to the database, as shown in Figure 3.26. You can save a text file of the tables affected by the changes. This is a very good feature once your application is in a stable state (not undergoing many changes) or when you want to keep track of changes. However, we do not require this, so just click Yes.

Figure 3.26

Save tables to the database.

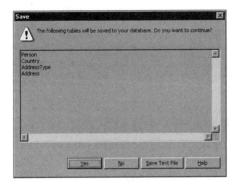

After you click Yes, SQL Server 2000 will perform the necessary database alterations to implement your changes. And that is it! You have now created a relational database. Congratulations! Once again your ability has shined through and you have gained another A+.

Creating Tables the Fun Way—With Code

Boy, you work hard, never giving yourself a break. Because we have implemented half of our database through the user interface, let's create the rest by using Transact-SQL code.

In this section you are introduced to the CREATE TABLE and ALTER TABLE Transact-SQL statements.

The CREATE TABLE syntax is very simple to understand (or at least for our tables it will be!). Once again though, when creating the tables, we should start with the parent table and work our way down to the children tables. This ensures that when we create the relationships the tables exist.

The CREATE TABLE statement for SQL Server 2000 allows us to specify many parameters, including but not limited to the filegroup to which the table belongs, the user who owns the table, the primary and foreign keys, and of course data types and column names.

Most of the parameters of the CREATE TABLE statement you will not need in your day-to-day administration of SQL Server 2000 because they are for more complex data storage issues or for replication and so forth that are not relevant to our application development so will not be covered in this book.

What is the most top-level table left of the four tables in our ERD? The ActivityType table. This table is a lookup table used to define the types of activities that a spy and a bad guy might be involved in. Like the other lookup tables, it allows us to easily add new activity types without having to change the data model.

Note We are going to create our remaining tables with the CREATE TABLE statement. When we create these tables, as we did through the UI, we will only specify the primary key constraints, not the foreign key constraints. We will use an ALTER TABLE statement after the tables have been created to implement the relationships.

Let's create our ActivityType table. Start Query Analyzer and select the SQLSpyNet database from the drop-down list in the Menu bar.

Warning Make sure you have the SQLSpyNet database selected. If you don't, SQL Server 2000 will create the table in whichever database you have selected.

Our ActivityType table will have two columns, ActivityTypeID and Description. Enter the code in Listing 3.3 into the database window.

Listing 3.3—Creating the ActivityType Table Through Transact-SQL Code

```
1: CREATE TABLE ActivityType
2:         (
3:         ActivityTypeID INT IDENTITY(1,1) NOT NULL
4:             CONSTRAINT PK_ActivityTypeID
5:             PRIMARY KEY CLUSTERED,
6:         Description VARCHAR(50) NOT NULL
7:         )
```

After you run this code the ActivityType table will be created in the SQLSpyNet database. Query Analyzer will return a message similar to the one shown in Figure 3.27.

```
The command(s) completed successfully.
```

Figure 3.27

The CREATE TABLE statement executing successfully.

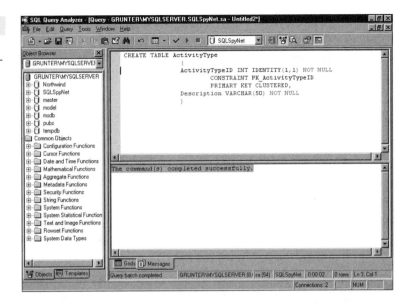

 Note   If you get a message different from this, check the syntax of the statement that you entered and try again.

You can now go back to Enterprise Manager (or the Object Browser in Query Analyzer) and refresh the Tables folder. You will see the ActivityType table in the folder list.

 Note   Although our new table exists in the database, it does not exist in our diagram (Current ERD) that we have just drawn. For this table to exist in the diagram, we would need to add the table to the diagram, as we did with the other tables.

Analysis

So what does the Transact-SQL code mean?

- Line 1 specifies to Query Analyzer that we want to create a table and that its name is ActivityType.
- The opening parenthesis on line 2 specifies that the column names will be defined inside the parentheses.

- Line 3 defines our first column for the table. Its name is ActivityTypeID and it is of data type INT. It is also an identity column. The NOT NULL statement at the end specifies that the column cannot contain a NULL value because it is illegal for identity column and primary key columns to allow NULLs.

- Line 4 supplies a name for the primary key constraint that we are deploying for the table. This can be left blank and allow the system to generate a name for us (similar to the foreign key constraint names we discussed earlier), but here we have specified that the name will be PK_ActivityTypeID (PK = primary key, and the column name).

- Line 5 specifies that the primary key for the table is the column defined in line 2. How? Notice the comma (,)? This marks the end of a column definition. Because the comma follows the PRIMARY KEY CLUSTERED statement and is not separated from line 3 with a comma, the ActivityTypeID column becomes the primary key. The CLUSTERED keyword specifies that the physical storage of the data on disk will be in order of the primary key specified; that is, 1, 2, 3, 4, and so on. This is analogous to the Dewey decimal system at a library, where all books are sorted and stored based on a key value. If the CLUSTERED keyword is not used, SQL Server 2000 will create a clustered index for the primary key, providing that no other clustered indexes exist on the table. But more on this in Chapter 11.

- Line 6 is the second column in our table with a name of Description. It is of a data type VARCHAR that has a maximum size of 50 characters. The Description column cannot contain a NULL value.

- The closing parenthesis on line 7 closes the parenthesis opened on line 2.

With that basic code defined we will now create the remaining three tables. We will start with the Spy table. Enter the code in Listing 3.4 for the Spy table.

Listing 3.4—The Create Spy Table Transact-SQL

```
1: CREATE TABLE Spy
2:      (
3:      SpyID INT IDENTITY(1,1) NOT NULL
4:          CONSTRAINT PK_SpyID
5:          PRIMARY KEY CLUSTERED,
6:      PersonID INT NOT NULL,
7:      SpyNumber VARCHAR(10) NULL,
8:      Alias VARCHAR(25) NULL,
9:      DateCommencedWork DATETIME NOT NULL
10:          DEFAULT (GETDATE()),
11:     AnnualSalary MONEY NOT NULL
12:          CONSTRAINT Check_AnnualSalary
13:          CHECK (AnnualSalary >= 10000),
14:     IsActive BIT NOT NULL
15:          DEFAULT 1
16:      )
```

Analysis

This table definition is similar to the preceding table, but we introduce a couple of new parameters here.

The DEFAULT statement specifies that if a value is not supplied, SQL Server 2000 will automatically insert a value. So on line 10, the default value for the DateCommencedWork column will be today's date.

The GETDATE() function is a special SQL Server 2000 function that returns the server's current date and time. We will take a look at functions again in Chapter 6.

A DEFAULT value also exists for the IsActive column. This automatically is set to 1 if the user does not supply a value.

> **Note**
>
> A BIT data type is normally used for a true/false (Boolean) value. A BIT can only have either a 0 or 1 entered, meaning true (1) or false (0). The name of the column IsActive is the naming convention I use most often when referring to a Boolean value.

Line 13 introduces another type of data integrity. The CHECK constraint specifies that the value entered in the AnnualSalary column can be equal to but not less than $10,000.00 (a pretty small sum for an international spy!).

This is one of the benefits of the flexibility of SQL Server 2000. We can easily build in business rules—the salary rule, for example—and modify these at a later time if needed.

We will now create our BadGuy table. Enter the code in Listing 3.5 into Query Analyzer and let's begin.

Listing 3.5—The Create BadGuy Table Transact-SQL

```
 1: CREATE TABLE BadGuy
 2:      (
 3:      BadGuyID INT IDENTITY(1,1) NOT NULL
 4:          CONSTRAINT PK_BadGuyID
 5:          PRIMARY KEY CLUSTERED,
 6:      PersonID INT NOT NULL,
 7:      KnownAs VARCHAR(25) NULL,
 8:      IsActive BIT NOT NULL
 9:          DEFAULT 1
10:      )
```

This table is a bit simpler than the Spy table, and we have covered all the major points thus far. So let's create the fourth and final table, the Activity table.

Enter the code in Listing 3.6 into Query Analyzer.

Listing 3.6—The Create Activity Table Transact-SQL

```
 1: CREATE TABLE Activity
 2:        (
 3:        ActivityID INT IDENTITY(1,1) NOT NULL
 4:            CONSTRAINT PK_ActivityID
 5:            PRIMARY KEY CLUSTERED,
 6:        SpyID INT NOT NULL,
 7:        BadGuyID INT NOT NULL,
 8:        ActivityTypeID INT NOT NULL,
 9:        IsPlanFoiled BIT NOT NULL
10:            DEFAULT 0,
11:        DatePlanAttempted DATETIME NOT NULL
12:            DEFAULT (GETDATE()),
13:        DatePlanFoiled DATETIME NULL
14:        )
```

Note

You might have noticed that this table is a little different from the other associative entity (Address table) that we created earlier. This table has its own primary key, the ActivityID. If you remember, for the sake of data integrity we did not implement a primary key like this. Now we are actually going to. Why? This will allow you to use both types of primary keys and decide which one suits you best. We have to do a little more work on this table to ensure that our data integrity is maintained. We will need to create a unique index (like a primary key) to achieve this.

As I specified, we need to do a little more work on this table before it is complete. Enter the code in Listing 3.7 into Query Analyzer and run it

Listing 3.7—The Create Unique Index Transact-SQL for the Activity Table

```
 1: CREATE UNIQUE NONCLUSTERED INDEX IDX_Spy_BadGuy_ActType
 2:     ON Activity (SpyID, BadGuyID, ActivityTypeID)
```

Analysis

Okay, so what does the code mean?

- Line 1 defines that we want to create a unique index named IDX_Spy_BadGuy_ActType (index on the Spy, BadGuy, and ActivityType columns). This index must be nonclustered because when we created the primary key for the table earlier we specified that as being clustered. You are only allowed one clustered index per table because the clustered index states the way the data is stored on disk. If we had two clustered indexes, which one would we sort by?

- Line 2 defines the table on which we want to create the index. In this case it is the Activity table. The bracketed column names are the list of column names that we want to define to be unique in the table. Why don't we include the primary key for the table? If we had the primary key in the list we would always have a unique value because the primary key is an identifier column. Every new row inserted has a new value. We might as well not have a unique index.

We also must create unique indexes on the PersonID in both the Spy and the BadGuy tables because the only way to define a one-to-one relationship is to have a unique index on the foreign key column in the table that has the foreign key. Why would we need to do this? A single spy can only come from one person, and a person cannot be more than one spy, so this is a one-to-one relationship (two no's, remember?). The same is true for the BadGuy table.

Enter the code in Listing 3.8, and the Spy table will be almost complete.

Listing 3.8—The Create Unique Index Transact-SQL for the Spy Table

```
1: CREATE UNIQUE NONCLUSTERED INDEX IDX_Spy_Person
2:    ON Spy (PersonID)
```

And enter the same again for the BadGuy table (see Listing 3.9).

Listing 3.9—The Create Unique Index Transact-SQL for the BadGuy Table

```
1: CREATE UNIQUE NONCLUSTERED INDEX IDX_BadGuy_Person
2:    ON BadGuy (PersonID)
```

After you have run this code you will have created all the tables for the database, as well as created *some* of the relationships and the indexes. You should now have eight user (or base) tables. You can check this in either Enterprise Manager or Query Analyzer through the Object Browser.

We still need to define the relationships between the tables, as we did for the Person and Address tables, before we are finished.

Let's define the relationships and get on with it! I am sure that if you looked at the ERD, you could probably define the relationships between the tables in the database-diagram tool. But that would be too easy. Instead, I am going to let you enter the ALTER TABLE syntax, which will allow us to create the relationships through Transact-SQL code.

The first relationship we will define is between the Spy and the Person tables.

If you enter the code in Listing 3.10 into Query Analyzer and run it, we will define our first relationship.

Listing 3.10—Altering the Spy Table So We Can Specify the Relationship to the Person Table

```
1: ALTER TABLE Spy
2:     ADD CONSTRAINT FK_Spy_Person
3:         FOREIGN KEY (PersonID)
4:         REFERENCES Person(PersonID)
```

Analysis

What does the code mean?

- Line 1 specifies to SQL Server 2000 that we are going to change (alter) the definition of the Spy table.

- Line 2 explicitly states that we are going to add a new constraint to the Spy table name FK_Spy_Person (foreign key is between the Spy and Person tables).

- Line 3 states the type of constraint we are defining. In this case it is a referential integrity (foreign key) constraint. The PersonID is the column in the Spy database that is the foreign key to another table.

- Line 4 states that the foreign key we have just created will reference the PersonID column within the Person table.

And that's it. We have now created a relationship between the Person and Spy tables. This is what the database-diagram tool does on your behalf. Now you know why it is so very cool!

We will prove that this relationship has been created in a moment, but first let's enter the other relationship definitions.

The next one to enter is the BadGuy relationship. This is very similar to Spy relationship (virtually a cut and paste job!). See Listing 3.11.

Listing 3.11—Altering the BadGuy Table So We Can Specify the Relationship to the Person Table

```
1: ALTER TABLE BadGuy
2:     ADD CONSTRAINT FK_BadGuy_Person
3:         FOREIGN KEY (PersonID)
4:         REFERENCES Person(PersonID)
```

Next we will add the foreign key constraints to the Activity table.

Remember this table is linked to three other tables (Spy, BadGuy, and ActivityType), so we will have three foreign key constraints.

Enter the code in Listing 3.12 and run it.

Listing 3.12—Altering the Activity Table So We Can Specify the Relationship to the Spy, BadGuy, and ActivityType Tables

```
1: ALTER TABLE Activity
2:     ADD CONSTRAINT FK_ActivitySpy
3:         FOREIGN KEY (SpyID)
4:         REFERENCES Spy(SpyID),
5:         CONSTRAINT FK_Activity_BadGuy
6:             FOREIGN KEY (BadGuyID)
7:             REFERENCES BadGuy(BadGuyID),
8:         CONSTRAINT FK_Activity_ActivityType
9:             FOREIGN KEY (ActivityTypeID)
10:             REFERENCES ActivityType(ActivityTypeID)
```

The only key difference between this code and the preceding code is the multiple foreign key constraints. The keyword ADD is used only once, and commas separate the constraints.

We have now completed the data model successfully. Once again you have excelled and brought upon yourself a standard that others will find difficult to achieve. Congratulations! Another A+, you really are a star student!

Just to prove that the relationships did actually work and I am not congratulating you for no good reason, go back into the database diagram tool in Enterprise Manager.

Open the ERD you created earlier (mine was called Current ERD) by double-clicking the ERD icon.

Now add the new tables to the diagram by right-clicking and selecting the Add Table option. Once again arrange the tables so that you can see all eight tables at once.

The relationships are all in place and defined for you. The diagram you will see should look like Figure 3.28.

Notice the relationships between the Spy and Person tables and also between the BadGuy and the Person tables.

The key at either end signifies a one-to-one relationship. Without the unique index on the PersonID column, these relationships would have been incorrect.

Also you might notice how the ERD in SQL Server 2000 represents our ERD that we created earlier. This means that we have achieved our task of implementing our data model. So once again give yourselves a pat on the back!

Figure 3.28

The completed ERD for the SQL Spy Net application.

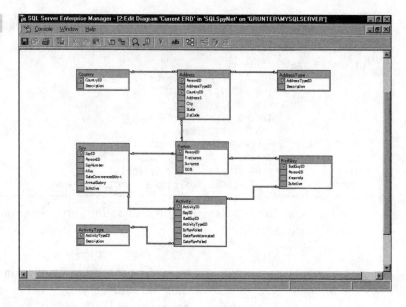

Filling in the Blanks

We have created our database and our base tables. We have implemented referential integrity (relationships), but we haven't entered any data.

This is where you can be as creative as you like! I will show you how to enter the data in the tables and give you a list of values to insert into each table. But you can add and or remove from the lists until your heart is content. Just remember though, this is not *all* of the data we will insert; there will be more as we progress, but this is a starting point.

Like creation of tables, we start at the highest-level tables or parent tables. Why? With referential integrity we must have a record that exists in the parent table before we can insert a record into the child table. You can't have a child without a parent!

Let's insert some countries into the Country table. Select the Country table from the Tables folder in the SQLSpyNet database. Make sure you are using Enterprise Manager.

Right-click the table and select Open Table, and then the Return All Rows option. From now on we will refer to this action as open the *tablename* table in data view. For example: Open the Country table in data view.

When the table is open, click the first row of the table, which should be a blank row. Because the primary key for this table is an identity field (auto-incrementing) we do not need to enter values in the CountryID column. And in fact, SQL Server 2000 will return an error if you try to enter a value in this column. Identity columns make data entry for us very easy!

Select the Description column and type United States in the space. Move to the next row by either clicking with the mouse or pressing the Tab key. You should see the CountryID column automatically assigned a value of 1. See Figure 3.29 for verification.

Figure 3.29

The CountryID identity column automatically incrementing.

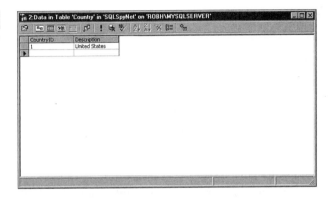

Our identity column works as we expect, so let's enter some more countries into our Country table.

> *Country Name*
>
> United States—Already entered
>
> New Zealand
>
> England
>
> Ireland
>
> Germany
>
> Australia
>
> Russia

You now have a small list of countries. You can expand on this list if you want, but we will probably add more as we develop the application.

Let's do the same for the AddressType table. Once again open the table in data view. Because this table is similar to the Country table (has an identity key), enter the following address types in the Description field:

> *Address Type Description*
>
> Business Postal address
>
> Business Physical address
>
> Home Postal address
>
> Home Physical address

We are now going to repeat the same task for the ActivityType table. Enter the following list into the table:

Activity Type Description
Take over the World!
World domination!
Chaos and mayhem
General disorder
Steal your favorite socks
Wreck havoc!

I guess you can see that all these activities have a common theme, but all bad guys are alike, aren't they?

We have populated our lookup tables with data, but I haven't shown you how referential integrity works yet. To prove to you that the referential integrity constraints that we defined do work, we will attempt to enter an address into the Address table without first defining a person to relate the address to.

We are also going to prove the NOT NULL constraint that we defined on the PersonID column in the Address table.

If you remember back to when we developed the tables, we specified that the PersonID column in the Address table could not contain NULL values. We will test this constraint first, and then prove that the referential integrity constraint is doing what we expect as well.

Open the Address table in data view. Currently we do not have a person in the Person table, so we cannot put a value in the PersonID column; we will leave it empty. When you leave a column empty in SQL Server 2000 it defaults to being NULL.

Click in the PersonID column. Because we do not have a person, press Tab to go to the AddressTypeID. When we try to save this row to the database (by going to the next row in the table), SQL Server 2000 will attempt to put a NULL value in this column.

We entered the address types in the AddressType table previously. The AddressTypeID column will accept values that exist in the AddressTypeID column in the AddressType table.

We are going to supply this address with an address type of Home Physical Address. In my AddressType table this row has an AddressTypeID of 4. Your column might differ from this, depending on the order in which you entered your address types.

Tip   You can find out what ID your column has by opening the AddressType table in data view.

Next enter a value for the Country column. Because we are defining this address for New Zealand, we need the primary key for New Zealand from the Country table. In my Country table this has a value of 2; yours can differ depending on the order in which you entered your countries.

Press Tab to move to the Address1 column. Enter the value of 123 Hickory Street. Press Tab and enter a City of Wellington. Press Tab. Because in New Zealand we do not have the concept of states, we shall leave the State column empty.

Press Tab and move to the ZipCode column. The ZIP code for Wellington, New Zealand is 6001; enter this value in the ZipCode column.

When you leave this row, either by pressing Tab or by clicking the next row, SQL Server 2000 will try to save this row to the database. The integrity rules for the database will be checked, and if the data is valid it will be saved. Try to leave the row now.

If you have followed all the instructions thus far (and I am sure you have, you clever cookie you), and your table definitions are correct, SQL Server 2000 will return an error similar to that shown in Figure 3.30.

Figure 3.30

SQL server error—NOT NULL constraint firing.

This is the first error we were expecting. This shows that our NOT NULL constraint that we defined on the PersonID column is firing correctly. Aren't we clever then?

If you click OK, we will now check the referential integrity constraint that we defined between the Address and Person tables.

Click in the PersonID column and enter the value 100. Because we have not entered any people yet, it doesn't really matter what value we enter here, unlike the Country column. Now try to move to the next row in the table.

Once again, SQL Server 2000 will try to save this row to the database, and because this value for the PersonID column violates referential integrity (because there is no parent record in the Person table with the value of 100) the insert will fail. You will see an error message similar to that shown in Figure 3.31.

Figure 3.31

SQL server error—foreign key constraint firing.

The error notifies you that the value you are trying to insert conflicts with the foreign key constraint (in this case FK_Address_Person) that is defined on the tables. The statement has been terminated message reflects that this change will not be saved to the database.

What do we do to fix this? We define names of some people to enter in the database so we can create addresses for them.

Open the Person table in data view. Once again our PersonID column is an identity field, so you cannot enter a value in this field. Enter the following list of people into the Person table.

Firstname:	Surname:	DOB:
James	Bondy	15 Jun 1963
Austin	Prowess	03 May 1942
Dr.	Eville	09 Sep 1941
Reilly	Ace of What?	10 Aug 1954
Barry	Bon Von Hausen	12 Jun 1972
Greg	Cross	04 Mar 1969
Claus	Von Schmit	31 Apr 1955

Notice how I have set the dates for the DOB column to medium date format? In New Zealand we enter our dates day/month/year (a throwback from our English heritage). Many times I have come across a server using U.S. date format month/day/year (in New Zealand), which has caused nothing but grief. To help prevent any misunderstandings I prefer to use medium date format. When you leave the field, SQL Server will convert the date to short format, but we at least we know what we intended!

Once again this is not a complete list; we will add to it as we progress through our application development. Don't let this stop you from thinking of other people that you would like to add to this list.

Okay, we actually have some basic data in our base tables. We can now populate our Spy, BadGuy, Address, and Activities tables, but we are not going to because in the next chapter we are going to insert data into the remaining tables using Transact-SQL.

And once again you will see the flexibility of SQL Server 2000.

As you can see, it is quite tedious to enter data directly into the tables as we have. It is also quite difficult to ensure that the data we insert is correct, that is, it links to the correct values for the primary keys.

With Transact-SQL we can write some funky Transact-SQL statements that allow us to perform updates with relative ease. I am sure that you are up for the challenge! So let us finish here with a summary of what we have done so far.

Oops, I almost forgot. What is the transitive dependency in the Address table? This would be the City column, and perhaps State, ZipCode, and so on. These are all independent items that could exist as separate lookup tables. We could have a City table that was dependent on the Country, and just link the CityID into the Address table.

Why haven't we done this? Sometimes we need to understand the impact of having a highly normalized structure. To retrieve someone's address we must combine three or four tables, and this can have a large impact on performance. So we denormalize the structure a little to prevent the overhead of joining the tables every time we need an address. Well this, and when I originally performed the analysis for the book, I forgot to implement this design. Tut, tut.

Summary

Well boys and girls, ladies and gentleman, there we have it. Our SQLSpyNet database is built, our base tables are developed, and we have implemented the relationships between the tables.

This chapter really has covered a lot of information, and I wouldn't be surprised if you didn't remember it all.

We really touched only briefly on normalization, and I strongly recommend that you pursue this topic to understand the concepts in more depth. It will save you a world of hurt in the future if you have a better understanding of the topic.

Although we have a basic structure for our SQLSpyNet application, there is room for improvement. A database is not static; it changes as it is developed and as requirements and business rules become clearer. This will happen to our application as well. I do not profess to be perfect, and a good design is one that we can adapt as our needs change.

Having said this though, always try to have a good foundation to work from. If the foundations are well laid, the building will stand strong in all sorts of conditions.

Next Steps

In the next chapter we will look at Transact-SQL, specifically the DML statements, so that we can manipulate and alter the data in our database. We will cover the SELECT, INSERT, UPDATE, and DELETE statements, as well as some pretty cool control-of-flow (COF) language statements.

In this chapter

- *What Is This* SELECT *Statement Then?*
- *Let's Get Some Data in with the* INSERT *Statement*
- *Keeping Everything Up-to-Date*
- *When a Good Spy Dies...* DELETE *'em*
- *What Else Can We Do with Transact-SQL Besides DMLs and DDLs?*

Chapter 4

Manipulating Data with Transact-SQL

We are now at a stage where we can start looking at some further Transact-SQL statements.

We have briefly touched on the subject of Data Definition Language (DDL) and yes, there is more to come. But before we go any further we need to cover Data Manipulation Language (DML). Why? Well most DDL statements are based on some DML or another. There are exceptions, of course. The most notable exception is the CREATE TABLE statement that we have just covered. Most of the other DDL statements retrieve, manipulate, or update data.

Although we will cover the basic DML statements, more examples in increasing complexity are waiting for you. You just need to pursue them. In this chapter, however, we will cover basic DML statements that will assist us in managing the data in our database. With these basic statements we will be able to view, add, edit, and even remove the spies in our database.

The DML statements taught in this chapter all comply with the ANSI-SQL 92 standard, so you can apply the knowledge gained to any ANSI-SQL 92–compliant RDBMS.

What Is This SELECT Statement Then?

Where do we begin? With the SELECT statement! You have already written a SELECT statement--remember when we dropped the SQL Spy Net database? The SELECT statement is by far the most common DML statement that you will write. So learn this statement my student, and learn it well.

The SELECT statement is an easy way to retrieve data from a database. This can be from a single table, a group of related tables, tables that exist in another database, or even tables that exist on another server! Some conditions are imposed on this, such as that you have the appropriate permissions.

Its relative English-like structure makes it quite simple for most developers to pick up quickly. However, do not be fooled in thinking that it is a very simplistic statement.

You can make the SELECT statement as complex or as simple as you like. It enables you to nest other SELECT statements within it (nested queries) or it can even be contained within DDL statements. Talk about versatile! We will cover these extras in the next chapter, but first let's look at the basic structure of the SELECT statement.

In this chapter we will look at the four basic DML statements: SELECT, INSERT, UPDATE, and DELETE. With these four statements we can access and manage all the data within our application. If one of the spies that we have in our system reaches retirement age, we can find his record and then update his active status to inactive.

The SELECT statement as defined in relational theory is a *projection*. We can project data from one table into a list of results. This data can even be summations or aggregations of data.

The SELECT statement is composed of four main parts:

- The SELECT statement itself, which enables you to choose the columns from the table that you want to see.

- The FROM clause, which allows you to specify the table or tables from which you want to retrieve your results.

- The WHERE clause, which allows you to impose restrictions on the data that you want to view.

- The ORDER BY clause, which enables you to specify the columns by which you want to order the results.

The following is the basic syntax of the SELECT statement:

```
1: SELECT Columname1, Columname2, Columname3
2: FROM Tablename
3: WHERE Columname1 = somecriteria
4: ORDER BY Columnname1
```

As we progress through this section we will look at each section of the statement individually and then combine it so we can pull the person's name from the Person table. You should have Query Analyzer ready and the SQLSpyNet database the active database.

> To make SQLSpyNet the active database you can select it from the drop-down list in the menu bar or you can execute the following Transact-SQL statement:
>
> ```
> 1: USE SQLSpyNet
> 2: GO
> ```

The First Building Block for SELECT

The SELECT statement, as mentioned earlier, has four main parts. The first is the list of columns you want to define for your query. These will be the columns that come back in your query results.

Because we will build our statement based on the Person table, we select each Person table column. You do not have to specify either all the columns or the order in which they are defined within the table. This makes it quite simple to customize a query to suit our business needs. We just choose whichever columns fit our criteria and in whatever order we want.

Let's look at the beginning of the SELECT statement.

It is defined with the initial keyword of SELECT. This is followed by a comma-separated (,) list of column names that we want to retrieve.

For example, we might want to retrieve the names of all people in our Person table who have a date of birth that falls within the next month, so that we can send them birthday greetings. What information would we need to achieve this? We more than likely need just their names and dates of birth. So, instead of bringing back all the information in the Person table, we limit the list to the columns we are interested in.

Enter the following code directly in the Query Analyzer window, and we'll add to it as we go along:

```
1: SELECT PersonID, DOB, Firstname, Surname
```

> Some developers use an asterisk (*) to indicate that they want to retrieve all the columns in a table. You should try to avoid doing this because usually it is not necessary. There is an underlying reason why we do not use the asterisk in our SELECT statements. Everything within a SQL Server 2000 database is contained within hidden system tables, including table names (held in the sysobjects table) and column names (held in the syscolumns table). When you specify the asterisk, SQL Server 2000 must look internally in the system tables to find all the column names for the specified table. As you can imagine, this can take some time in a large database! Although writing out the column names for queries is tedious, you will notice the performance benefits as our database grows. Besides which, the new Object Browser in Query Analyzer helps to reduce the tedious task of writing out all the column names.

Notice that the last item on the list, Surname, is not followed by a comma (,). This signifies that the item is the last in the list. That's it for the first part of the SELECT statement. What's next? Oh, that's right, the second part. DOH!

Where Does the Data Come FROM?

The second piece to the SELECT statement puzzle is the FROM clause. This enables us to specify the table or tables over which we want to perform the query.

For the sake of simplicity, we will only perform the query over a single table. It is possible for us to pull data from the Address, Person, AddressType, and Country tables to get all the details about a person (that is, name and address). However, all the information we require at this point is contained in the Person table. Additionally, this would spoil the fun for Chapter 5, "Viewing Data and Automating Updates with DDL," where we build a VIEW to achieve this. Type the following code into the Query Analyzer window after the previous line:

```
1: SELECT PersonID, DOB, Firstname, Surname
2: FROM Person
```

That was really hard, wasn't it? As you can see in the FROM clause, all that is required, in this example at least, is the table name that you want to reference.

EXCURSION

Writing Readable Code

We do not really need to enter the FROM clause on a new line, but for the sake of ease of reading code, it is good practice to separate the logical sections of code. In a simple example it is not hard to read, but if we had a 15-line statement it would be very difficult to read in one line!

> You should also try to indent your code. This makes it not only easy to read, but can also help you derive an answer to a problem because you can logically separate the code into small, manageable chunks.
>
> Although it is not mandatory (because Transact-SQL is not case-sensitive), I like to see the keywords for Transact-SQL in uppercase (as you might have noticed by now). This enables you to easily see the Transact-SQL, and once again makes it easy to follow.

The cool thing is that you can actually run this code now. The rest of the SELECT statement is optional. Let's run the code now. Click the little green triangle.

Tip   If you prefer keystrokes to mouse clicks, use Alt+X or Ctrl+E. You can use either one to execute any Transact-SQL code in the Query Analyzer window.

4

If you typed the column names correctly, you will see all the people you have entered so far in the Person table, as shown in Figure 4.1.

Figure 4.1

The SELECT statement on the Person table and the results.

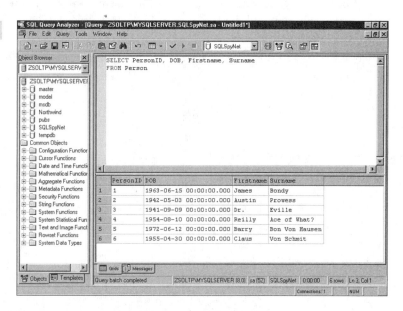

If you don't see any results displayed in the Query Analyzer window, for example, a message stating 0 row(s) affected or an error message, if you received no rows, check that you have entered the people in the Person table that were entered earlier. If you receive an error message, such as Invalid column name 'Somename', check that you have spelled the names of the columns or the table name correctly.

Limiting Data with WHERE

This is all well and fine if we want to see all the data in a given table or tables, but what if we only want to see the data for a specific person? This is where we introduce the WHERE clause.

Within the WHERE clause we can use logical operators, such as =, <, >, LIKE, and so forth, to perform comparisons on our data.

So how does our WHERE clause work? It follows the format WHERE *column-name logical-operator some-value*. If you type the following code into the Query Analyzer window below the previous code, you can find out who the person is with an ID of 3:

```
1: SELECT PersonID, DOB, Firstname, Surname
2: FROM Person
3: WHERE PersonID = 3
```

Once again, this code does not have to be on a separate line, but for the sake of good coding practice...

Like our previous example, this code can be run. So execute the code now. This time your results will look similar to that shown in Figure 4.2.

Figure 4.2

A SELECT statement with the WHERE clause applied.

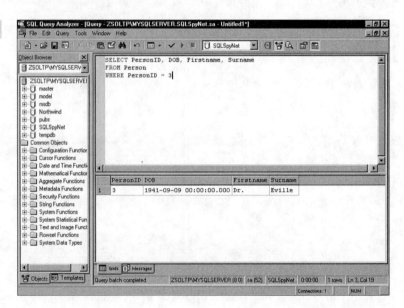

Notice that we have only one row now. This demonstrates to you the effectiveness of the WHERE clause. We can now retrieve either all the data or only one row. What if we wanted to retrieve more than one row?

Let's alter the WHERE clause you have just entered, so that we can find all the people whose last names start with "B." Delete the previous WHERE clause and enter the following line:

```
1: SELECT PersonID, DOB, Firstname, Surname
2: FROM Person
3: WHERE Surname LIKE 'B%'
```

Now execute the statement and view the results. Notice the number of results returned? This has allowed us to widen our search criteria to encompass more rows than our first search, but not as much as our original statement. Your results will look similar to Figure 4.3.

Figure 4.3

A SELECT statement with the wider WHERE clause applied.

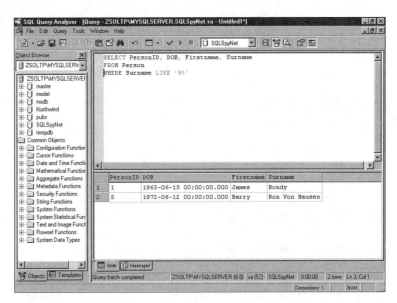

4

> **Note**
>
> Just a little note on the WHERE clause we just specified. The percent % sign indicates that we would like to perform a *pattern match search*. You will see that the % after a character will return *Black* as well as *Brown*. To return all names with a B anywhere within the name, place a % on either side of the character, for example %B%.

Finally, you can specify more than one WHERE criterion for a given statement. To do this, specify the first criterion that the data must meet, and then the second by using either the AND keyword or the OR keyword.

The B in the previous WHERE clause is case sensitive because of the language collation setting that we set for the database. When we created the database we used the Server default, which with my installation is case sensitive. However, this can be different depending on the installation options you choose.

You can check the settings for your database within Enterprise Manager. Click the SQLSpyNet database in the Databases folder. With the SQLSpyNet database selected, right-click and select Properties. On the General tab in the Properties window, you will see the Collation name option. This will have the name of the setting you selected when you created the database. (If it is blank it is the default of the server.)

Notice that it is read-only. This is because if the Collation settings change, everything on disk would have to be re-sorted and re-indexed. Unfortunately, to change the Collation name settings we must drop and re-create the database.

EXCURSION

Narrowing Data with Criteria

The AND and the OR keywords enable us to specify multiple criteria on which to restrict our data. The AND keyword means this criterion *and* this criterion. This is more restrictive than the OR keyword, which specifies this criterion *or* this criterion.

Usually, you will use the AND keyword to narrow the results that you want to retrieve.

The AND keyword has precedence over the OR keyword. For example, in the following list the AND is evaluated first:

```
AND Surname LIKE '%B%'
AND DOB < '15 Jul 1980'
OR Firstname LIKE '%j%'
```

The clause will be evaluated as Surname criteria AND the DOB criteria, and then the OR criteria is applied.

This statement will give you all the people who have a B in their surname and dates of birth that are less than 15th July 1980 or whose First name contains a j.

If you remember back to your first years in high school (I believe this is a freshman in the U.S. It is a third-former in New Zealand), you might remember the old adage BEDMAS: Brackets, Exponents, Division, Multiplication, Addition, and Subtraction. This is the order of precedence for the operators in math. It is the same in Transact-SQL. Every operator has an order, and some are evaluated before others, as we have just seen in the AND and the OR examples. I told you that you would need your mathematics skills!

Put Those Spies in Order!

Let's now take a look at the fourth and final part of the SELECT statement, the ORDER BY clause. This clause enables us to specify the order of the results based on a particular column or columns. Take note of the way the results are ordered in the previous example. We will now place an ORDER BY clause on the SELECT statement to change the way the results are displayed. Type line 4 into the Query Analyzer window under the WHERE criteria to complete the job, as shown in Listing 4.1.

Listing 4.1—Putting Personal Data in Order by First Name

```
1: SELECT PersonID, DOB, Firstname, Surname
2: FROM Person
3: WHERE Surname LIKE '%B'
4: ORDER BY Firstname
```

Now run the query. The results have sorted in ascending order by the Firstname column. Cool, eh?

Like the SELECT statement, we can specify a comma-separated list of column names in the ORDER BY clause. We can also specify the order of the results. We use ASC for ascending (the default if none is specified, as in our previous example), and DESC for descending. We will now alter the ORDER BY clause to demonstrate this.

Change the ORDER BY clause, as shown in Listing 4.2.

Listing 4.2—Sorting Data in Alphabetical Order

```
1: SELECT PersonID, DOB, Firstname, Surname
2: FROM Person
3: WHERE Surname LIKE '%B'
4: ORDER BY Firstname DESC, DOB
```

SQL Server 2000 will now order the results in descending order, first by first name and then within each row the DOB column in ascending order. If we had two Harrys but they had different dates of birth, the oldest Harry would appear first.

That's it! You now have an understanding of the basic SELECT statement. We will expand on this as we develop our application further, including nested subqueries, inner, left, and right joins and so forth.

As you can probably guess, the SELECT statement is a very powerful operational statement. We can test the existence of data, return a result set tailored for our users, and also generate reporting information for senior management.

Let's Get Some Data in with the INSERT Statement

Cool, we know how to retrieve data from the database, but how do we put it in? To do this we use the INSERT statement, so let's take a look at this statement.

As you have probably gathered, this statement enables us to add new values to our database tables. We can insert whole rows at a time and, with the use of the SELECT statement, we can even insert whole tables of data at once! There are, however, a few limits on this, such as security privileges and data integrity.

The INSERT statement is a little different from the SELECT statement, though it does follow a similar format.

The statement is composed of two main parts.

- The initial INSERT INTO statement, which allows us to specify the table and the columns that will be affected by the INSERT.

- The VALUES statement, which allows us to specify the values that will be inserted into the table. There must be a one-to-one mapping between the number of values specified and the number of columns supplied; that is, we must have the same number of each.

Once again the best way to learn is by example, so we are going to perform an INSERT statement on the Person table. We don't seem to have enough bad guys, or spies for that matter, in our database so we are going to use the INSERT statement to add a few more.

Defining the Table and Columns We Want to Insert Into

To begin, type the following code into the Query Analyzer window. Once again though, make sure that you have the SQLSpyNet database selected.

```
1: INSERT INTO Person (Firstname, Surname, DOB)
```

Unlike the SELECT statement, you cannot run this line of code just yet. Before we continue building the INSERT statement, let's examine this section of the statement.

The INSERT INTO command specifies to SQL Server 2000 the type of Transact-SQL that we want to execute. We then specify the table for the insert, followed by a comma-separated list of the columns that we are going to insert into the table.

When inserting a value into every column of a table, you can exclude the column names from the INSERT statement. You must, though, provide a value for every column in the table.

Notice how the Primary Key column of the Person table (PersonID) is excluded from the list? When we created the Person table we specified the PersonID column as an identity column. In general, you cannot insert a value into an identity field, thus we exclude it from our list of columns.

Luckily though, SQL Server 2000 takes care of this for us, so we exclude this column from the list.

> **Note**   You can override the identity column behavior of SQL Server 2000, but we will not be performing this functionality just yet!

Let's Put In Some New Data!

The next part to the INSERT statement is the actual values that we want to insert into the table. Type the following code into the Query Analyzer window:

```
1: INSERT INTO Person (Firstname, Surname, DOB)
2: VALUES ('Margaretha', 'Zelle', '7 Aug 1876')
```

Notice that everything has a single quote (') on either side of it. All data types except the numeric data types (integers, money, floats, and so forth) require this. The easy way to remember this is if it is a string or has anything other than numbers in it (including spaces), then whamo, around go the quotation marks. Some exceptions do exist to this rule of thumb. For example, when using the keyword NULL instead of a value, you do not place quotation marks around the word.

Even dates require single quotes as well. Why? Well if you think about it, most dates actually contain a forward slash (/) or a space to separate the values, so even though they might start with a number they can contain string values.

You can now execute the statement. You should have a notification from SQL Server 2000 specifying that one row has been affected, as shown in Figure 4.4.

Let's do one more INSERT statement on the Person table. Type the following into the Query Analyzer window:

```
1: INSERT INTO Person (Firstname, Surname)
2: VALUES ('Emmat', 'Peels')
```

Notice that we have not specified a value for the DOB column. When SQL Server 2000 inserts this row it will set the DOB column to NULL.

Figure 4.4

An INSERT statement with the notification from SQL Server 2000.

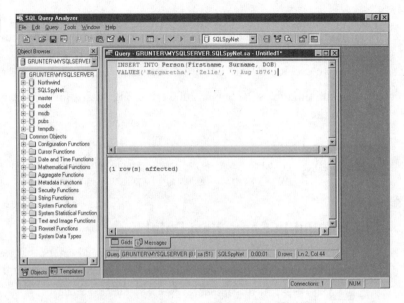

So we have inserted the rows into the table; what now? We must ensure that our inserts worked, and the SELECT statement will verify this for us. Type the following into the Query Analyzer window:

 1: SELECT * FROM Person ORDER BY PersonID

This will retrieve all the rows from the Person table and order them by the PersonID column.

 I have used the asterisk (*) in the preceding example. Naughty, naughty boy! You should avoid this when actually programming for your application. It should even be avoided when checking values as we have here, because it has performance implications for SQL Server 2000.

I have used it in this example to demonstrate the different methods for performing a SELECT. But note that, although I do use it here, I recommend that you avoid using it, if possible.

You will now see all the data in the Person table, including the original data as well as the two new rows that we have just inserted. Because these were the last rows entered they will be near the bottom of the results.

One last thing: Just as in Enterprise Manager, when a row is inserted into a table, SQL Server 2000 checks the constraints that are defined on the table. So if you try to execute the following Transact-SQL code, it will fail (not be inserted), as shown in Figure 4.5.

RunIt
```
1: INSERT INTO Person (Firstname, Surname, DOB)
2: VALUES (NULL, 'Someone', '23 Dec 1977')
```

Figure 4.5

An INSERT statement
failing because of the
NOT NULL constraint on
the Firstname column in
the Person table.

SQL Server 2000 will return an error describing why the statement failed.

As you can see, the INSERT statement gives you the flexibility to insert values at will. But most users would not be able to implement this statement, so what do we do? Well, you will just have to wait and see.

Seriously though, as we develop the application further, you will see how we can hide these seemingly complex statements from the users of the system and offer them an easier way to update the data in the database. We will achieve this in the next chapter when we create a stored procedure to perform data inserts.

Keeping Everything Up-to-Date

This now brings us to the UPDATE statement. As you can probably guess, this statement enables us to alter the values in one or many columns and rows in our tables. Once again, this statement follows a similar format of the preceding statements. It, like the others, is fairly simple to learn and implement. Also, like the preceding statements it has different levels of complexity, so we can write very simple to very complex statements.

One very cool thing about the UPDATE statement is that it enables you to not only update a column in a row or rows, but also update multiple columns at the same time!

The UPDATE statement is for just that: updating values. It does not insert new rows or remove rows.

After your data is in your database, this is probably the next most used (and abused) Transact-SQL statement you will execute, after the SELECT statement, of course.

The UPDATE statement has three parts: the table on which you want to perform the UPDATE, a comma-separated list of column names and values, and (also optionally) any WHERE criteria.

We will build an example from scratch (once again).

Which Table, Please?

One of the names that we have in our Person table has a spelling mistake. We are going to issue an UPDATE statement to fix this issue. Just before we perform the UPDATE, though, we will SELECT the data from the table first to prove that our INSERT has worked.

Within Query Analyzer, type the following line of code:

```
1: SELECT PersonID, Firstname, Surname, DOB
2: FROM Person
3: WHERE PersonID = 8
```

Run a SELECT statement before and after all data updates that you perform to ensure the data alteration takes place.

One of the easiest ways of doing this is to have another query window open with the SELECT statement in it, which you just rerun after you perform the update.

Next we will issue the UPDATE statement. Create a new query window by selecting File, New from the menu bar.

You can also perform this action by using the hotkeys Ctrl+N.

Now type the following line of code within Query Analyzer:

```
1: UPDATE Person
```

This is the first part of the statement, and as you guessed informs SQL Server 2000 that we want to perform an UPDATE. The table on which we want to perform the action follows this. Like the INSERT statement, you cannot run this statement just yet, so be patient.

Correcting Data to Fix Data Problems

Next you specify the column or columns that you want to update. Type the following Transact-SQL code into Query Analyzer:

```
1: UPDATE Person
2: SET Firstname = 'Emma',
3: Surname =  'Peel'
```

This tells SQL Server 2000 that we want to set the value of the column Firstname to Emma and the Surname column to Peel. If we were only updating one column we would exclude the comma (,) and anything after it.

Warning

> Although this code will compile and run now, don't run it! Running this code now will update *all* the rows in the Person table to have the Surname and Firstname we specified.
>
> This feature is by design, and all Relational Database Management Systems perform this action. Why? There might be a time when every column in a table must be set to a certain value. An example would be if all employees in an organization get a 15% pay increase.

WHERE to Put the New Value

How do we update only the row we are interested in? By using the WHERE criteria exactly as we did in the SELECT statement.

To ensure that we update only a single row, we use the primary key of that row. Why? The primary key guarantees uniqueness. We know that only one row will have the primary key value that we specify. So if we add the following line to the Query Analyzer window, we will be able to complete our UPDATE statement, as shown in Listing 4.3.

Listing 4.3—Using the Primary Key to Ensure a Correct Update

```
1: UPDATE Person
2: SET Firstname = 'Emma',
3:    Surname = 'Peel'
4: WHERE PersonID = 8
```

You can now execute the UPDATE statement. SQL Server 2000 will return a message, similar to Figure 4.6, notifying you that one row has been affected.

 Note   If you need further clarification on the WHERE criteria, see the SELECT statement earlier in the chapter.

Figure 4.6

The UPDATE statement succeeding on the Person table.

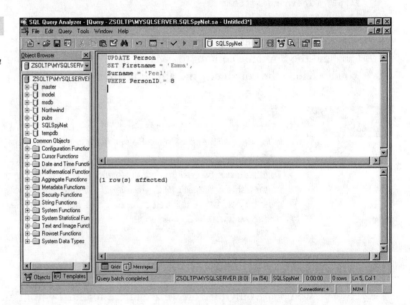

Now perform the SELECT statement again. You will see that the changes we have just specified have been made to the row. And on this note, we are finished with the basic UPDATE statement.

What good is this to the SQL Spy Net application? After the data has been entered, this will be one of the most common statements that you and your staff will perform regularly.

You can imagine that after an assignment is complete, you will need to update the Activities table to reflect that the assignment was either a success or failure. Also, after we gather more details on our adversaries, we will use the UPDATE statement to keep their details up-to-date. We can use the UPDATE statement inside the other DDL statements that we will perform shortly.

When a Good Spy Dies...DELETE 'em

So is that it for the DML statements? Well, no. We can now retrieve, insert, and update data. But how do we get rid of it? In comes the DELETE statement. This is a very powerful statement that enables you to remove all traces of a record, providing certain conditions are met. Similar to the SELECT statement, the DELETE statement follows an analogous structure. With the DELETE statement we can remove all, some, or one record from our database depending on the specification of the DELETE statement that is written.

Accidentally deleting all the rows out of a table is very easy, so be careful!

I hear you: You think I'm molly-coddling you because we've got what, a whole 10 or so entries to safeguard with our lives. I will tell you how to write a DELETE statement; just don't get your knickers in a twist (a little Kiwi saying for you). The point is that someday you'll be managing a much larger pool of spies and you won't want to have to recover from a disastrous situation that could have been avoided. So, remember to delete carefully unless the bad guys are pounding down the door, and then you can delete until your heart is content!

Once again let's build an example, but first let's check the data with a SELECT in a new query window, so that we can prove that our DELETE works.

```
1: SELECT PersonID, Firstname, Surname, DOB
2: FROM Person
```

With that done, let's build the DELETE. Type the following command in Query Analyzer:

```
1: DELETE FROM Person
```

Like the UPDATE statement, this code will compile and run. DO NOT run it though! Why? You will lose all the data you have so far in the Person table. To restrict the rows that we remove, we will place some WHERE criteria on the Transact-SQL code.

Notice that no columns are defined in the statement as they are in every other DML statement. This is because you are deleting the whole row, not an individual column.

> **Tip**
>
> To remove an individual value from a column, use the UPDATE statement to set the value equal to NULL.

Type the following Transact-SQL code after the first:

```
1: DELETE FROM Person
2: WHERE PersonID = 6
```

You can now run the code. Notice that we have used the primary key of the table to ensure that we remove only the single row that we want to get rid of.

After the code has completed, SQL Server 2000 will return a message that the operation has been completed, as shown in Figure 4.7.

Figure 4.7

The DELETE statement succeeding on the Person table.

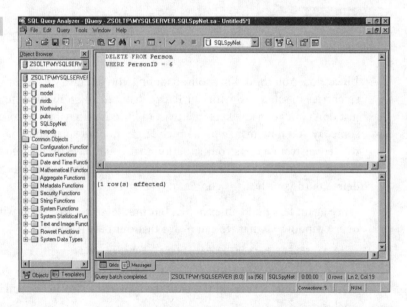

Now rerun the SELECT statement that we ran earlier. This will now have one row less than the previous one.

Our Person row that had a PersonID value of 6 is now gone. Magic! No, not really.

Well my students, you now have passed basic DML 101. It wasn't that hard, was it? You might have noticed that all the DML statements follow a similar structure, and after you learn what each is for; you will have very little trouble in managing the data in your database.

Do not worry; you will get plenty more hands-on experience with DMLs as your career and this book progress. But for now this will suffice; so let's look at the next topic in the chapter.

What Else Can We Do with Transact-SQL Besides DMLs and DDLs?

Remember earlier when I said that Transact-SQL is a set language and not a programming language? Well, that is not quite true nowadays. Should I explain? Yeah, why break the habit of a lifetime?

The original ANSI SQL-92 standard has been extended in most versions of SQL Server (and most other RDBMSs) to give the flexibility of programming-like statements.

As you can imagine, a database in this day and age would not cope with only being able to perform basic tasks such as DDLs and DMLs. We need a little more flexibility than that, so Microsoft has introduced Control-Of-Flow (COF) statements. These statements perform actions similar to their programming language equivalents. You can declare variables, use IF and WHILE statements, and PRINT messages to users, as well as perform a host of other functions.

Okay, other than to extend the functionality of the DMLs and DDLs, what use are they? COF language statements enable us to have greater flexibility in performing data management. For example, when performing an update we can check the existence of a value. We might need to loop through a statement to assess the impact a change can have on other tables. Although these examples are not explicit, they will give you an idea of the benefit of using COF language statements.

But where do we start? Because the COF language statements encompass many of the techniques of programming, some basic programming skills will be mighty handy. However, if you do not possess these skills then I will try to explain the use and application of four basic COF statements:

- Variable declaration
- Assigning a value to a variable
- The IF statement
- The WHILE statement

COF also has CASE, GOTO, and WAITFOR, but we will not cover these statements.

Declaring Variables

One of the first places to start learning about programming languages is usually variable declaration and use. So we will follow this formula and look at how to declare a variable and assign it a value.

When you declare a variable in SQL Server 2000 it is similar to how you would achieve it in a programming language, except one thing. The at symbol (@) is used to prefix a variable's name.

The variable is then assigned a data type and if necessary a relevant size. You can make multiple variable declarations on one line, or you can use multiple lines. Look at the following examples.

```
1: DECLARE @MyChar CHAR(9), @MyINT INTEGER, @MyDate DATETIME
```

Conversely, if you declare the variables on separate lines then you do not need the commas, but you need to use the keyword DECLARE on each line.

```
1: DECLARE @MyChar CHAR(9)
2: DECLARE @MyINT INTEGER
3: DECLARE @MyDate DATETIME
```

Assigning Values to Our Variables with the SET Statement

Cool, you have your variables declared but how do you *initialize* them?

Initialize is a common term in most programming languages and refers to assigning a variable its first value.

Microsoft recommends when assigning values to variables that you use the SET statement rather than the SELECT statement. We will cover both of these to show the difference, but the SET statement is optimized for assigning values. To assign a value to the @MyChar variable, enter the following in the Query Analyzer window:

```
1: DECLARE @MyChar CHAR(9)
2: SET @MyChar = 'SQLServer'
```

Conversely, you can use

```
1: DECLARE @MyChar CHAR(9)
2: SELECT @MyChar = 'SQLServer'
```

These two COF statements are equivalent, and as you can see, the difference in coding is negligible, but we will use the recommendations from Microsoft—who knows the product better than the manufacturers?

That's great! But why would we want to declare a variable and assign a value to it? The most obvious answer is to check for the existence of a value to see whether a condition is true. So how do you achieve this? Well I have shown you how to assign a stagnant value to the variable, but what about when you want to use a value out of a table? Say, for example, that you want to assign the value of the Firstname column from the Person table to a variable to see whether it meets certain criteria, for example that the name does not have a space in it. You can do this with the following code:

```
1: DECLARE @MyChar CHAR(9)
2: SET @MyChar = (SELECT Firstname FROM Person WHERE PersonID = 1)
3: SELECT @MyChar
```

SQL Server 2000 will return the first name for the person in the Person table with an ID of 1. Line 3 in this statement block gets SQL Server 2000 to print the value contained in the variable. If you omit this line, the variable will still be assigned a value, but you will not be able to see the value.

As you can now see, it is fairly simple to combine the DML and COF statements, and we will discover many more examples of this.

We now have a value in the variable, what next? Normally when we assign values to variables we do so for a reason.

The IF Test—Is What We Have in Our Variable What We Expect?

After the variable has a value, you might need to check that the value of the variable is what we expect it to be. How do you do this? With the IF statement.

The IF statement is a very common statement in all programming languages. It enables you to check whether a condition is true and if so, to perform some action or do something else. With the IF statement, you can check for the existence of a value or see whether it is equal to, less than, or greater than another value. The statement is formed of two parts—the IF itself and the ELSE statement.

The ELSE statement is executed only if the IF statement is not true. Let's work our way through an example. In this example, we will assign a value to our variable (@MyDate) and check to see whether it meets a certain condition. Upon deciding if the value meets our condition, we will write out a message to the results window. Type the code from Listing 4.4 into the Query Analyzer window.

Listing 4.4—Testing a Condition (the Date) and Printing the Result

```
1: DECLARE @MyDate DATETIME
2: SET @MyDate = GETDATE()
3: IF @MyDate = GETDATE()
4:    PRINT 'It is today'
5: ELSE
6:    PRINT 'It is not today'
```

You will receive a message from SQL Server 2000 saying "It is today", as shown in Figure 4.8.

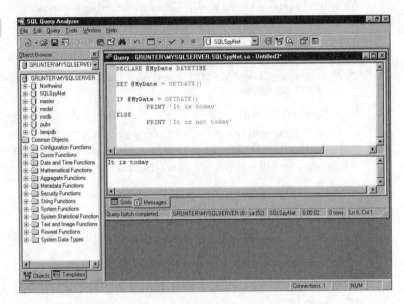

 Note   The GETDATE() function is a built-in system function of SQL Server 2000 that returns the current date for the server. This is similar in concept to the Now() function in VB.

Change the date that is assigned to the variable @MyDate and rerun the statement, as shown in Listing 4.5.

Listing 4.5—Making the Variable Fail the IF Condition to Print the ELSE Message

```
1: DECLARE @MyDate DATETIME
2: SET @MyDate = '01 JAN 2000'
3: IF @MyDate = GETDATE()
4:    PRINT 'It is today'
5: ELSE
6:    PRINT 'It is not today'
```

You will now see that SQL Server 2000 will return a message stating that "It is not today", as shown in Figure 4.9.

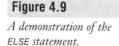

Figure 4.9

A demonstration of the ELSE statement.

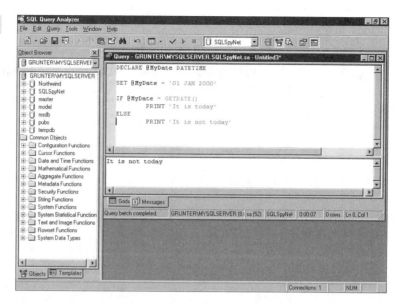

This is a simple but practical example of the IF...ELSE statement. If you think about this laterally you can find many other uses for the IF statement. Suppose you want to check whether a Person exists in the BadGuy table, before you update the Spy table. You can easily achieve this by using an IF statement.

Using WHILE Loops

We have now covered three out of four of the COF statements that we are going to discuss. Without further ado, let's look at the WHILE statement.

The WHILE statement, like most Transact-SQL statements, is composed of several parts. Not all of these parts are mandatory when developing a WHILE statement. The initial WHILE statement follows similar lines as a programming WHILE loop. The loop is executed while a specified condition is true. As soon as that condition becomes false, the loop terminates.

The WHILE loop in Listing 4.6 loops through the code, printing out the value of the counter.

Listing 4.6—Using a WHILE Loop as a Counter

```
1: DECLARE @MyCounter INT
2: SET @MyCounter = 1
3: WHILE @MyCounter < 10
4:     BEGIN
5:         PRINT 'The Counter is now at '
5a:            + CONVERT(CHAR(2), @MyCounter)
6:         SET @MyCounter = @MyCounter + 1
7:     END
```

You will see that SQL Server 2000 will execute the loop until the condition becomes false, as shown in Figure 4.10.

Figure 4.10

A demonstration of the WHILE statement.

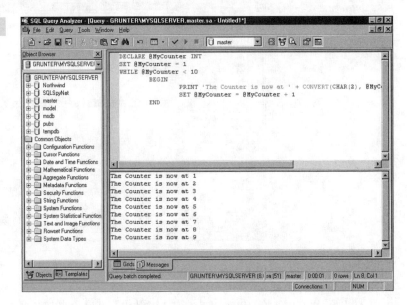

The condition becomes false because we increment the value of @MyCounter each time the loop is executed.

Make sure one of the first things you check before running a WHILE loop is that the condition will eventually become false, or else you can get stuck in what is known as an *infinite loop*.

An infinite loop is when a loop will never terminate; it just keeps on firing and firing and firing. To stop this in Query Analyzer, click the red square on the toolbar.

Analysis

You might notice a couple of things about the loop that we have just built. First, the BEGIN...END pair block on lines 4 and 7 is another COF statement that acts just it does in other programming languages, for example, in Pascal. It allows us to denote that a group of Transact-SQL statements will be executed within the block. The END keyword signifies that there will be no more statements in this block.

The WHILE loop requires a BEGIN...END pair block, and you can contain one or many Transact-SQL statements within the block.

Next to note is the CONVERT function on line 5a. This function allows us to change the data type that @MyCounter has from an INT to a CHAR of size 2. Why? The PRINT COF statement requires that everything is a string. You cannot print data types that are not string values.

The plus symbol (+) is also on the same line. This allows us to have a message and appended to that message the variable @MyCounter. This is how we get SQL Server 2000 to display the incrementing values in the messages that we receive.

I gather you have worked out how to increment the values by looking at line 6. The one thing to note is that we assign @MyCounter the value that it currently has plus one. So if @MyCounter equals 7, it is assigned 7 plus 1. Simple, isn't it?

As I mentioned earlier, the WHILE loop has several parts to it, and we can even combine COF statements (as we have already done). But we haven't discussed one key feature of the WHILE loop yet: the BREAK statement. This allows us to exit a loop gracefully if a given condition is true, or not true, depending on how we define it. Take a look at the example in Listing 4.7, which extends Listing 4.6.

Listing 4.7—Adding a BREAK Statement to a WHILE Loop

```
1:  DECLARE @MyCounter INT
2:  SET @MyCounter = 1
3:  WHILE @MyCounter < 10
4:      BEGIN
5:          PRINT 'The Counter is now at '
5a:          + CONVERT(CHAR(2), @MyCounter)
6:          SET @MyCounter = @MyCounter + 1
7:          IF @MyCounter = 7
8:              BEGIN
9:                  PRINT 'Exiting the loop now'
10:                 BREAK
11:             END
12:     END
```

You will see that SQL Server 2000 will execute the loop until the condition we applied in line 7 becomes true, as shown in Figure 4.11.

Our WHILE condition is still true—@MyCounter is less than 10, but with a nested IF and BREAK statement we can exit the loop early.

Note   Notice how the IF statement has a BEGIN...END pair block? This allows us to capture the Transact-SQL statements in line 9 and 10 together. Without these, the loop would exit as soon as the BREAK on line 10 was reached. Try it and see.

Figure 4.11

A demonstration of the WHILE statement with a BREAK statement.

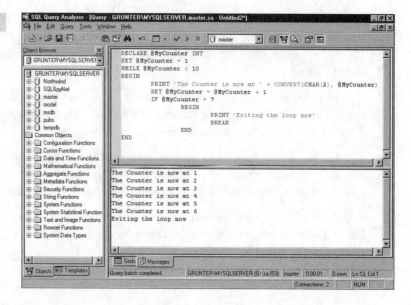

That's lovely, but why would we want to exit our WHILE loop if we already have a condition applied on the loop? Well, it not only allows us to check whether some value is true or not true, but also whether an invalid value has been supplied. We can then exit the loop without incurring the cost of continual execution, or worse still, an error occurring or invalid data being applied to a table.

And so, ladies and gentleman, this brings us to the end of basic COF language statements. Although these examples were not in-depth, they give you a good starting block to launch from, and we will use more COF statements as we progress.

Summary

In this chapter we have looked at the basic DML and COF statements. These have allowed us to

- Run a SELECT statement on our data to retrieve one or more rows from a table.
- INSERT new rows of data into our tables.
- UPDATE data in one or more rows in our tables.
- DELETE data from one or more rows in our tables.
- Cover the declaration and assigning of values to variables.
- Build IF statements, demonstrating the capability to check the existence of a value and perform an action based on the result of the check.

- Build WHILE statements, demonstrating the capability to loop and fire a set of Transact-SQL statements until a condition is reached.

- Look at how to combine our COF statements to provide more flexibility when developing an application.

Next Steps

This concludes our chapter on DML and COF statements. What do I have in store for you next? We are going to build some more DDL statements, such as views, stored procedures, and triggers. You have already encountered some basic DDL statements, tables, indexes, and constraints, and we are going to further this knowledge by combining the basic DML and COF knowledge we have just gained and building very flexible and easy-to-use DDLs. Are you excited yet? You should be!

4

Chapter 5

Pushing the Boundaries of Our DDL Knowledge to View and Update Data

We've been through a fair amount of Transact-SQL, but I guess that's because we are developing a SQL Server 2000 database! And we are not going to stop here. This chapter will extend the DDL knowledge gained in Chapter 3, "Making Virtual Spies—Creating Spy Net in SQL Server 2000," by combining DDL and DML statements to broaden the functionality and richness of our application. With this functionality we will be able to ensure data integrity, provide users with an easy way to retrieve complex data, and discuss some more intricate database objects.

But before we can continue we need to insert some more data.

Adding Information About Our Spies

This time the information will be for the Address table. I will provide you with the initial INSERT statement and a list of values. I'm sure that you will be able to perform the updates by yourself, you clever little thing you!

So fire up the Query Analyzer, select the SQLSpyNet database, and type the Transact-SQL code in Listing 5.1 into the window.

Listing 5.1—Inserting Values into the Address Table

```
1: INSERT INTO Address (
1a:        PersonID,
1b:        AddressTypeID,
1c:        CountryID,
1d:        Address1,
1e:        City,
1f:        ZipCode)
2: VALUES (
2a:     1,
2b:     2,
2c:     2,
2d:     'Level 3, New Kelvin Chambers',
2e:     'Wellington',
2f:     '6001')
```

Analysis

When you enter the preceding listing of code, SQL Server 2000 will return a message stating one row affected. We have just inserted our first person's address. Now guess what? I have a whole list of addresses for you to insert, which will really begin to populate the data in our database.

The list of values that you need to insert into the Address table follows. You do not have to have the exact values that I have here, but ensure that you get the foreign keys correct for the referenced tables.

It is important to get the foreign keys correct because SQL Server 2000 will fail the inserts if you try to reference a person whose ID is not in the Person table. For example, trying to enter a PersonID of 3000 will cause the insert statement to fail.

Isn't referential integrity great?

As you now know, when you want to enter a string into a field in a table, you specify the beginning and the end of the string with a single quote ('). But what do you do when you need to have a single quote *within* your string? For example, Rob's Address.

To do this you must use two single quotes ('') where the single quote would be in your string. So the previous example would look like Rob''s Address.

PersonID	AddressTypeID	CountryID	Address1	City	State	ZipCode
2	3	1	45 Somewhere Street	Los Angeles	California	
2	1	1	PO Box 123	New York		
5	1	3	PO Box 72154	London		
5	2	3	Buckingham Palace	London		
5	3	3	45 Big Ben Road	London		

Now that we have some Address data, we will look at creating a view that returns the Address data as well as some person details for our users.

Finding a Good View

A view is a way of allowing us to define how data can be presented to an end user. This definition helps us build the Transact-SQL that is required to display complex information to a user without the user having to know how to build the statement.

A view acts and behaves like a table in many ways, and you will hear definitions from people that a view is a virtual table. Why is it referred to as a virtual table? A view does not actually hold any data. It just contains a reference to the table or tables that do actually hold the data. So when we update data in a view, we are actually updating the base tables that the view references.

And because of the table-like behavior of a view, we can perform table-like functions on a view. For example, we can use SELECT, INSERT, UPDATE, and DELETE statements to affect data as we would through a table, though some restrictions are on this.

We are now going to build a view that allows us to see the addresses for all our people who have an address. This will bring back not only the addresses, but also the person's name, country name, and address type.

We use views to make it simple for our users to get data back from our database. Views offer us several benefits, including

- Predefined structures of data for our users
- The ability to restrict who can use the views
- Because they are prewritten, we can easily use them for reporting

What is the view going to do for our application? The view we are going to write will make it easy for us to retrieve either a person's address or all the addresses for the people in our Person table.

As you might have noticed from the data that we have placed in the Address table, an address is not listed for every person defined, so we will not bring back anybody who doesn't have an address defined.

Let's get on with it, then... .

Getting Your First Look at a View

Three ways we can build a view in SQL Server 2000 are through a predefined wizard, through Enterprise Manager, and through Query Analyzer.

The wizard is a simple, step-by-step approach. If you would like to give this a go, feel free. Enterprise Manager is also normally simpler for new users, but you have enough knowledge now to do it through Query Analyzer. Have Query Analyzer ready with the SQLSpyNet database selected.

In addition, if you can build a view through Query Analyzer, you will be able to build a view in another RDBMS. So not only is your knowledge transportable, but so is the code!

We will use the code in Listing 5.2 to create our view. You can type this directly into Query Analyzer.

Listing 5.2—Creating Our PersonAddress View to Retrieve Data Without Continually Joining All the Required Tables

```
RunIt →
1: CREATE VIEW PersonAddress AS
2: SELECT
2a:      P.Firstname,
2b:      P.Surname,
2c:      A.Address1,
2d:      A.City,
2e:      A.State,
2f:      C.Description AS Country,
2g:      A.ZipCode,
2h:      AType.Description AS AddressType
3: FROM Person P
4: INNER JOIN Address A
4a:      ON P.PersonID = A.PersonID
5: INNER JOIN AddressType AType
5a:      ON A.AddressTypeID = AType.AddressTypeID
6: INNER JOIN Country C
6a:      ON A.CountryID = C.CountryID
```

Analysis

As you might have guessed, the CREATE VIEW statement tells SQL Server 2000 that we want to create a view named PersonAddress.

The AS keyword is not the end of the statement; it is just the beginning. This clarifies that a Transact-SQL statement will follow so that the view knows what action to perform.

The basic SELECT statement is the same as we learned in Chapter 4, "Manipulating Data with Transact-SQL," but we have a couple of minor differences.

Lines 2a–2h are the list of columns that we want to retrieve. But notice the prefixing—P., A., and so forth. This is what is known as *aliasing*.

Aliasing is a common term in most programming languages. It refers to assigning a friendly (or shortened) name to an object. This enables us to change the name of the object for a short time. We can alias many things in SQL Server 2000 when referring to the objects in code, and in our view definition we have aliased table names (for example, Address is 'A') as well as column names (for example, C.Description is 'Country').

Aliasing these columns enables us to specify the tables from which the columns are derived. But we don't have any tables named A, or do we?

Lines 2a and 2h perform an alias on the column names. This allows us to specify the name that we want the columns to have in the view. So our Country Description column will now be referred to as Country, and the AddressType Description column will be referred to as AddressType.

Why did we do this? A view, like a table, must have distinct column names. Because the Country table and the AddressType table both have Description columns, they would not be unique with their current names. We alias them and give them names that are relevant to what they are for to make them unique. You will see this often when creating DDLs.

Line 3 specifies the table from which we want to perform the SELECT. Notice that after the table name we have defined the table to be aliased as P. We did not really need to alias the table, but for the sake of simplicity it is far nicer to use aliasing. So all of the P. prefixes specify that the columns come from the Person table.

One type of aliasing that we are using is shortened table names. This is a very handy trick when we are accessing multiple tables, and bringing back columns that might exist in more than one table, for example the PersonID column, which is in the Person, Address, Spy, and BadGuy tables.

If we didn't use aliasing we would have to specify each table name in full, for example, Address.PersonID rather than A.PersonID.

This is a perfectly valid technique in most RDBMSs, so this skill is cross transferable.

Lines 4–6a allow us to select data from other tables by using the INNER JOIN statement. This specifies to SQL Server 2000 that we want to join to the table specified after the INNER JOIN syntax. So in lines 3–4a, we specify that we want to join the Person table to the aliased Address table. With the INNER JOIN statement we need to specify how we are going to join the two tables. We achieve this by using the primary key (P.PersonID) from the Person table and joining that to the foreign key (A.PersonID) in the Address table. And that's it! This is how we join tables together.

Lines 5 and 6 also use the INNER JOIN statement, but they join to the Address table rather than to the Person table because this is where the foreign key is for those tables.

Lines 5 and 5a join the Address table to the AddressType table. Using the primary key AddressTypeID in the AddressType table and linking this to the foreign key AddressTypeID in the Address table accomplishes this. We do a similar process for the Country table using the primary key and foreign keys of both tables to join them.

Are you beginning to see how important primary and foreign keys are to a relational database? With all these JOINs it's a good idea to clarify how SQL Server handles them, which I'll show you in the following section.

Like the SELECT statement, we can place WHERE criteria on the view, but at this point we do not need to.

After you run the code, SQL Server 2000 will create the view for you. You can look in the Views folder in Enterprise Manager (you might need to refresh the folder) or the Views folder in the Object Browser within Query Analyzer (this might also be need to be refreshed) .

Looking at JOINS

SQL Server 2000 enables you to perform four basic joins.

- INNER JOIN brings together two tables and displays only the data that is an exact match in both tables. This is the most restrictive of all the joins. Generally it is used the most often.

- LEFT OUTER JOIN joins the data from the table specified in the FROM clause to the table specified in the join statement. This is just as the INNER JOIN statement does, but the difference is that all the rows in the table specified in the FROM clause are returned a NULL for those rows that do not exist in the join table, as well as the data that does exist. So if we specified a LEFT OUTER JOIN on the Address table, we would get all the people from our Person table, addresses for those who have one, and NULLs for those who don't. This would be the next most common join used.

- RIGHT OUTER JOIN is similar to the LEFT OUTER JOIN table except that all the data from the join table is the one returned, and the rows from the FROM table are the ones that will contain NULL values.

- FULL OUTER JOIN is the retrieval of all rows from both the FROM table as well as the join table. This will contain many NULLs but will have the most rows. This is used the least often.

We will now explore the join syntax a little more.

Because joins can be quite a complex topic to understand, let's take a quick look at the different effects they would have on some basic data.

Suppose we have two tables. We will use our Person table and our Address table. In our Person table we have

PersonID	FirstName	Surname	DOB	PhoneNo
1	Greg	Cross	NULL	Not Available
2	Sahara	Desert	NULL	Not Available

In our Address table we have

PersonID	AddressTypeID	CountryID	Address1	City	State	ZipCode
1	1	1	PO Box 123	New York	NULL	NULL
1	1	3	PO Box 72154	London	NULL	NULL

INNER JOIN

So we have two addresses for Greg but no addresses for Sahara. If we perform an INNER JOIN, such as

```
SELECT P.FirstName, P.Surname, A.Address1
FROM Person P
INNER JOIN Address A ON A.PersonID = P.PersonID
```

We would get the following results:

FirstName	Surname	Address1
Greg	Cross	PO Box 123
Greg	Cross	PO Box 72154

As you can see, we only get the rows back that have data that matches in both tables; that is, the PersonID that exists in both tables.

LEFT OUTER JOIN

Now let's change the join syntax to a LEFT OUTER join.

```
SELECT P.FirstName, P.Surname, A.Address1
FROM Person P
LEFT OUTER JOIN Address A ON A.PersonID = P.PersonID
```

We would get the following results:

FirstName	Surname	Address1
Greg	Cross	PO Box 123
Greg	Cross	PO Box 72154
Sahara	Desert	NULL

We now get back Sahara as well, but because she does not have an address in the Address table, a NULL is placed in the Address1 column.

RIGHT OUTER

The RIGHT OUTER join works in a similar way to the LEFT OUTER join syntax, except the data in the table specified in the FROM clause will contain NULL. So if data existed only in the Address table and not in the Person table, the Firstname and Surname columns would contain NULLs, while the Address1 column would have the value of the address.

Because we have referential integrity defined between our Address and Person tables, if we changed the SELECT statement to a RIGHT OUTER JOIN, we would get back the same results as we have in our first scenario (INNER JOIN). Why? Because it is impossible for us to have an Address without a Person (the foreign key specifies so), there cannot possibly be a NULL in the PersonID column of the Address table, so the only rows that can be returned are the ones that contain a match.

Unfortunately (maybe fortunately, if you think about it), I cannot demonstrate a RIGHT OUTER JOIN, but you would use one when you wanted to get all the rows from the Address table regardless of whether they had a matching row in the Person table.

FULL OUTER

The next (and final) join statement we will look at is the FULL OUTER join. What do you think will happen this time?

```
SELECT P.FirstName, P.Surname, A.Address1
FROM Person P
FULL OUTER JOIN Address A ON A.PersonID = P.PersonID
```

We would get the following results:

FirstName	Surname	Address1
Greg	Cross	PO Box 123
Greg	Cross	PO Box 72154
Sahara	Desert	NULL

The results are the same as the LEFT OUTER JOIN statement. Why? For the same reason that the RIGHT OUTER JOIN statement wouldn't give us any extra functionality, the FULL OUTER JOIN acts in a similar way.

Normally a FULL OUTER JOIN on two tables that had some data that did match and some data that didn't match in both tables would return the *Cartesian product* of the two tables.

The *Cartesian product* is the result of the two complete sets being combined. So if Set A contained 1, 2, and 3 and Set B contained 4, 5, and 6, the Cartesian product of the two sets would be 1, 2, 3, 4, 5, and 6.

Comparing Views to Tables

As I said earlier, a view is similar to a table in many ways. We can perform SELECTs, join views to other tables, use them in stored procedures, and apply WHERE criteria to limit the data returned by a view.

To prove this, type the Transact-SQL code in Listing 5.3 into the Query Analyzer window.

Listing 5.3—Using Our New View as a Table

```
1: SELECT * FROM PersonAddress
```

This will return all the results as though you built the SELECT statement that the view contains and executed it. Pretty cool, eh?

Unfortunately, with the view we have just developed we cannot perform any other DML statements because the view references more than one table. If this view were built over a single table, we could run a DML statement over the view as though it were a table. (See the next section, "Restrictions on Views.")

As you probably have guessed, the view that we have just created enables users to see all the addresses a person has, without knowing how to write the complex Transact-SQL.

But this is not the only use that views have. We can write a view to hide sensitive information from all users. For example, our Spy table has an annual salary column. We do not want all users to know how much a spy earns, so what do we do? We write a view that will retrieve the data that the users require, and exclude the annual salary column from the view. Other methods for achieving this are available, and we will explore them in a little while.

Also within views we can reference other views. Views can be built on top of other views. This allows us to build extremely complex Transact-SQL statements that the users are protected from. Pretty cool, huh?

Restrictions on Views

Views are, as you probably guessed, not perfect. They do have some limitations.

- You cannot specify an ORDER BY clause in the SELECT statement contained within the view.
- You cannot pass parameters to the view to dynamically limit the results from the view. For example, we cannot build our view to contain a WHERE criteria that continually changes.
- You can perform updates on a view only if it references more than a single table.

Although these limitations are minor, they can cause you some headaches when developing an application. So is there anything we can do about these limitations? Well, yes. You can use a stored procedure. We will discuss these now.

Streamlining Updates with Stored Procedures

A stored procedure is a set of compiled Transact-SQL statements that are contained within a single object. A stored procedure, like a view, does not contain any data, but only references to the base tables that actually hold the data.

The cool thing about stored procedures is that they are not limited by the same restrictions that a view is.

You can place ORDER BY clauses on the SELECT statements that the stored procedure contains. You can pass in variables to dynamically change the WHERE criteria that you place on the result set.

This means that you can create questions within the code (variables) that you later fill in when you execute the stored procedure. This way you can run the stored procedure with many different answers to do the same task over and over in different situations, which gives you greater flexibility in application development.

However, you still can only update one base table at a time. Because you can have a group of Transact-SQL statements in one object, you can update each table with only one stored procedure!

What other cool things can we do with a stored procedure?

- To protect valuable data we only give users permissions to execute the stored procedure rather than permission to access the base tables.

- Not only can we pass in variables to change the Transact-SQL statements, but also we can retrieve values from the stored procedure. For example, we can update data and retrieve a success or fail flag with which to notify users (among other things). We look at error handling in Chapter 8, "Ensuring Data Consistency with Transactions, Locks, and Error Trapping."

- Stored procedures can contain COF language statements and can include variable declaration and assignment, IF, CASE, and GOTOs.

- Because they can contain many different Transact-SQL statements, we can have SELECT, INSERT, UPDATE, and DELETE statements all contained within one stored procedure.

- Because the Transact-SQL is precompiled, SQL Server 2000 will optimize the stored procedures to run faster and more efficiently.

These are not all the benefits of using a stored procedure, but as you can see, some very good reasons to use stored procedures are evident. We can effectively manage our SQLSpyNet database by using stored procedures.

EXCURSION

Round 1: Stored Procedures Versus Views

I have even built a database without any views at all and achieved all the required functionality just by using stored procedures.

Why would I do this? Well, personally (and this is quite an opinionated view), I find that in SQL Server 2000 and previous versions, views are redundant. They provide limited extra functionality that cannot be derived from a stored procedure.

However, do not count views down and out just yet. With SQL Server 2000 we can index a view, allowing us to have more efficient views that run faster.

So it is anybody's guess which one is going to win this tug-of-war, but I still favor stored procedures over views.

I have probably gotten myself into a *lot* of trouble with many people, so I had better explain myself.

In SQL Server 2000 (and even earlier versions), stored procedures return data. So we can place a SELECT statement within the declaration of the stored procedure. Most other RDBMSs *do not* support returning data from a stored procedure.

This is one example of how most other RDBMSs have strong prerequisites for using views. Also, most of them do not support updating base tables through views. Boy, isn't SQL Server more advanced? Not that I am biased!

I believe there is no real requirement for a view within a database. But you still need to know how to create a view so that you have a complete skill set for managing your data. Many application designers believe wholeheartedly in views, and you might have to debug their applications one day, so it is best to be prepared.

However, just because I feel this way does not mean that you must. Many developers use a combination of views and stored procedures to achieve their client's requirements, and they do so very effectively. Just bear in mind that other ways are possible to achieve the results that you strive for.

Enough of that. What's the stored procedure that we will build going to do? Well, we are actually going to build two stored procedures. These will enable us to pass the stored procedures the values (answers) that we want to insert into the base tables, and this will be done for us.

Which tables will this affect? So far we have data in our Person table, but we do not have any Spies or BadGuys defined in their tables. We will build a stored procedure that will insert data into the Person table, as well as the Spy table, populating two tables at once! We will also build another stored procedure that will update both the Person and the BadGuy tables.

Let's get on with it, then!

Creating the Stored Procedure Code

The first stored procedure we will create will update the Person and Spy tables. These stored procedures will be relatively simple and extend on the DML statements that we learned earlier.

 Note   Remember that stored procedures such as views, tables, and indexes are all objects within our database. So we create the object first, and then we execute (use a Transact-SQL DML statement) that object with the specified values.

Once again have Query Analyzer running with the SQLSpyNet database selected, and type the code in Listing 5.4 the window.

Listing 5.4—Setting Up the Initial Part of Our Stored Procedure

```
1: CREATE PROCEDURE PersonSpyInsert
2:     @Firstname VARCHAR(50),
3:     @Surname VARCHAR (50),
4:     @DOB DATETIME = NULL,
5:     @SpyNumber VARCHAR(10) = NULL,
6:     @Alias VARCHAR(25) = NULL,
7:     @DateCommencedWork DATETIME,
8:     @AnnualSalary MONEY,
9:     @IsActive BIT = 1
10: AS
```

Analysis

Line 1 specifies to SQL Server 2000 that we want to create a stored procedure named `PersonSpyInsert`. The naming convention I use most often for stored procedures is the objects that it will affect and the action that a stored procedure will perform.

The next part of the stored procedure enables us to specify the variables (called *parameters*) that we will pass to the stored procedure.

Lines 2–9 declare and define the data types and any default values that we want the variables to contain. This is similar to when we declared and initialized a variable in Chapter 4, except that we do not need to use the keyword `DECLARE`.

Notice on Line 4 that the variable `@DOB` has a default value of `NULL`. This means that if a value for the variable is not provided when the stored procedure is called, the variable will have the value of `NULL`. This is similar for Line 9. Line 10 is the same as it is in the `CREATE VIEW` statement. The `AS` keyword lets SQL Server 2000 know that there will be further statements to follow.

So what's next? Well we've set up the initial part of the stored procedure, and now we need to build the Transact-SQL statements required to perform the updates. So enter the code in Listing 5.5 in the Query Analyzer window.

Listing 5.5—Creating Our PersonSpyInsert Stored Procedure to Create People and Spies

```
1: CREATE PROCEDURE PersonSpyInsert
2:     @Firstname VARCHAR(50),
3:     @Surname VARCHAR (50),
4:     @DOB DATETIME = NULL,
5:     @SpyNumber VARCHAR(10) = NULL,
6:     @Alias VARCHAR(25) = NULL,
7:     @DateCommencedWork DATETIME,
8:     @AnnualSalary MONEY,
9:     @IsActive BIT = 1
```

Listing 5.5—Creating Our PersonSpyInsert Stored Procedure to Create People and Spies

```
10: AS
11: DECLARE @PersonID INT
12: INSERT INTO Person (Firstname, Surname, DOB)
13: VALUES (@Firstname, @Surname, @DOB)
14: SET @PersonID = IDENT_CURRENT('Person')
15: INSERT INTO Spy (PersonID, SpyNumber, Alias,
15a: DateCommencedWork, AnnualSalary, IsActive)
16: VALUES (@PersonID, @SpyNumber, @Alias,
16a: @DateCommencedWork, @AnnualSalary, @IsActive)
```

Analysis

Because you are so clever, you probably will understand the INSERT statement; if not, refer to Chapter 4, "Manipulating Data with Transact-SQL." The only thing that is a little different about this statement is the use of the variable in the VALUES clause. This enables us to change the values inserted into the table without having to rewrite the Transact-SQL statement. Because we have also defined the data types for the variables, we do not need to worry about using single quotes around the string variables.

So far we have the ability to insert data into the Person table, but how are we going to update the Spy table?

After we have inserted the Person details into the Person table, we need to get back the PersonID from the Person table so that we can then perform the insert on the Spy table.

Notice that Line 11 declares and sets up a variable named @PersonID. Line 14 actually returns the value from the PersonID column, which contains the last inserted row and assigns the value to our @PersonID. Because the PersonID in the Person table is defined as being of type Identity, we need some way of retrieving this value.

SQL Server 2000 provides several methods, but we are using the IDENT_CURRENT function (see Chapter 6, "Getting Clearer Results with Functions," for more on functions). This takes the table name as an argument and returns the last inserted value from the table.

We need the last inserted value so we can create the foreign key in the Spy table. If we know the value of the primary key in the Person table, we can then link the PersonID (foreign key) in the Spy table to the person. This allows us to perform our joins (which we looked at earlier) to link the Spy to an actual person.

We then assign this to a local variable that we pass to the next INSERT statement. We are going to discuss some of SQL Server's built-in functions in the next chapter, but for now let's carry on.

Lines 15–16a perform the INSERT on the Spy table. Run the code now. SQL Server 2000 will return a message stating that the command has been completed, similar to that shown in Figure 5.1.

Figure 5.1

SQL Server 2000 stating that the stored procedure has been created.

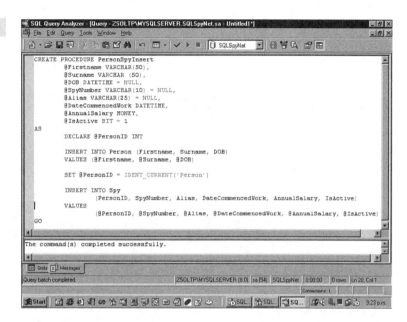

Checking the Table for Places to Fill

We must execute our stored procedure to ensure that it performs as we expect. But before we do, we need to check the data in both the Person and Spy tables to ensure that our inserts do as we expect. So enter the Transact-SQL in Listing 5.6.

Listing 5.6—Checking the Data in Our Person and Spy Tables to Ensure Our Stored Procedure Performs as Expected

```
1: SELECT P.PersonID, S.SpyID, P.Firstname FROM Person P
2: LEFT OUTER JOIN Spy S ON S.PersonID = P.PersonID
```

The results will look similar to Figure 5.2. Notice the large number of NULLs in the SpyID column? This means that no spies are in the Spy table.

We need to use a LEFT OUTER JOIN to ensure that we get all the data from the Person table, especially while we do not have any data in the Spy table. If we used an INNER JOIN, no results would be returned because SQL Server 2000 wouldn't find any rows on which it could perform an exact match.

Figure 5.2

SQL Server 2000 showing the results from the Transact-SQL statement.

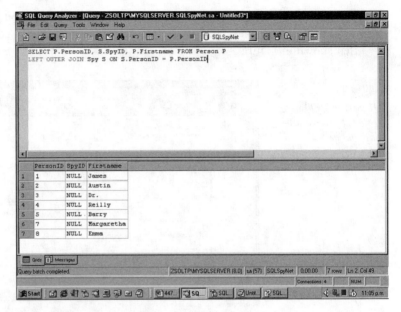

Letting the Stored Procedure Do the Work

We now need to execute our stored procedure. Type Listing 5.7 into the Query Analyzer window.

Listing 5.7—Performing Our First Person/Spy Insert

```
1: EXEC PersonSpyInsert 'Dangerous',
1a: 'Mouse',NULL,NULL,NULL,'15 Jul 2000',75000.00
```

Analysis

Notice that we only pass the parameters that do not have default values assigned. Although we have a large list of parameters for the stored procedure, we do not need to use all of them, though we can if we want to.

If you run the SELECT statement from Listing 5.6 again, you will now see that we have a new value in the Firstname column of "Dangerous" with a SpyID, similar to that shown in Figure 5.3.

Isn't that cool? The inserts have now been performed on two tables, and it only required one line of code. Even though it doesn't look like two tables have been affected, they most certainly have. If you performed individual SELECT statements on the tables, you would see that both tables had new rows inserted.

Figure 5.3

SQL Server 2000 showing the second set of results from the Transact-SQL statement after the stored procedure has been fired.

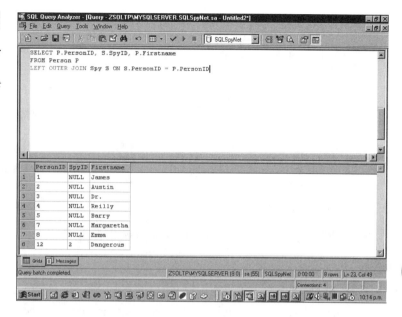

Creating the Stored Procedure to Insert into Both the Person and BadGuy Tables

I will now give you a similar statement for the PersonBadGuyInsert stored procedure. Once again, enter the Transact-SQL code into Query Analyzer (see Listing 5.8).

Listing 5.8—Creating Our PersonBadGuyInsert Stored Procedure to Insert into Both the Person and BadGuy Tables

```
 1: CREATE PROCEDURE PersonBadGuyInsert
 2:    @Firstname VARCHAR(50),
 3:    @Surname VARCHAR (50),
 4:    @DOB DATETIME = NULL,
 5:    @KnownAs VARCHAR(25) = NULL,
 6:    @IsActive BIT = 1
 7: AS
 8:    DECLARE @PersonID INT
 9:    INSERT INTO Person (Firstname, Surname, DOB)
10:     VALUES (@Firstname, @Surname, @DOB)
11:     SET @PersonID = IDENT_CURRENT('Person')
12:     INSERT INTO BadGuy (PersonID, KnownAs, IsActive)
13:     VALUES (@PersonID, @KnownAs, @IsActive)
```

Analysis

This code, as I mentioned, is similar to the PersonSpyInsert stored procedure, and I am sure that you will be able to recognize and follow the structure of the stored procedure easily.

But what is different about this stored procedure from the first one in the previous section? Well, this time we are updating the BadGuy and Person tables. You might have also noticed that the list of parameters that our new stored procedure receives is shorter than for our SpyPersonInsert stored procedure.

After you enter the code and run it, you should see the same `command(s) completed successfully` message (refer to Figure 5.1 for a similar example).

Checking For and Filling In NULLS

The code to get the stored procedure to execute appears in Listing 5.9, but first fire the SELECT statement that I have provided you to ensure that your changes take place!

Listing 5.9—Checking the Data in Our Person and BadGuy Tables

```
1: SELECT P.PersonID, B.BadGuyID, P.Firstname
1a: FROM Person P
2: LEFT OUTER JOIN BadGuy B ON B.PersonID = P.PersonID
```

The results will look similar to Figure 5.4. Once again we have a large number of NULLs (like the statement we ran for the Person and Spy tables in Listing 5.6) in the joined table column. This means that no BadGuyIDs are in the BadGuy table, yet.

Figure 5.4

SQL Server 2000 showing the results from the Transact-SQL statement before the stored procedure is executed.

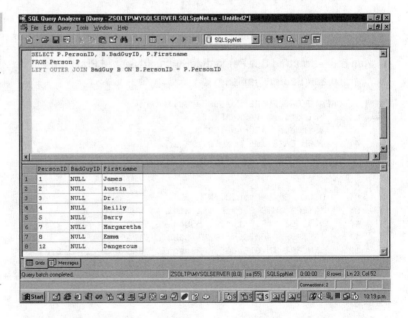

Now we are going to run our stored procedure so that we can get rid of some of those pesky nulls! To execute the stored procedure, use the code in Listing 5.10.

Listing 5.10—Executing Our PersonBadGuyInsert Stored Procedure in the Person and BadGuy Tables

```
1: EXEC PersonBadGuyInsert 'Greg',
1a:'Cross', NULL, 'Gregster', 1
```

Run the SELECT statement that we entered in Listing 5.9 again; the results will be similar to Figure 5.5. And violá you have a new row in both the Person and BadGuy tables. Simple eh?

Figure 5.5

SQL Server 2000 showing the results from the second Transact-SQL statement after the stored procedure has been executed.

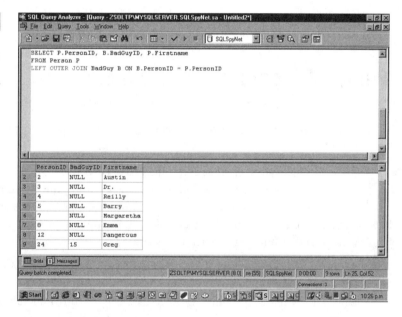

And ladies and gentleman, there it is, your first stored procedures developed and working as you expected. Aren't you doing well?

Guidelines for Using Stored Procedures

Although it is entirely possible to build a database that only uses stored procedures, we would not be able to take full advantage of all the functionality of SQL Server 2000 if we restricted ourselves to only stored procedures.

Stored procedures are very versatile and effective, but the one task that they cannot do is respond to events. So when a row is inserted into a table, you can't get a stored procedure to fire. We have database objects called *triggers* to take care of this, which we will discuss shortly.

Because we require more stored procedures to be developed for our application, I will provide you with the code. However, I will only explain new ideas that come up in the Transact-SQL that we have for the stored procedure. There is little point in re-inventing the wheel.

As you might have guessed by now, we would use a stored procedure whenever we need to do a data update or retrieval operation. With some of the emerging technologies from Microsoft, such as ADO (ActiveX Data Objects), we can call stored procedures from client applications. So it is easy and efficient for us to retrieve data and pass to ADO rather than build Transact-SQL statements and pass individually. We will take a look at this later when we build a user interface for our application.

This brings us to the end of stored procedures. But what's next? Surely this can't be it? Well, never fear, it's not. We will now look at triggers.

Pulling Triggers to Catch Events

So what are these trigger things?…sounds like something spies would use.

Triggers are similar to stored procedures in many ways, except that they are fired by *events*.

Events occur when certain actions take place. (If you have done any Windows programming or used various scripting languages before, the concept of events is probably familiar to you.) For example, when a window opens, it has an onOpen event. The same is true for buttons. They generally have an onClick event. This is a bit of a generalization but pretty much holds true.

An event in SQL Server 2000 is when an action occurs, as in Windows, but the events are usually related to tables. For example, when a row of data is inserted into a table, this is an event. When a row of data is deleted from a table, this also is an event.

How do triggers fit in then? When data is inserted into a table we can fire a trigger to ensure that the data is valid or that a value exists in another table, and so forth. When data is deleted from a table, we can write a trigger that deletes all the children records before the parent record is deleted.

With the new features built in to SQL Server 2000, a trigger that is required to delete a child record when a parent record is deleted no longer is required.

When we created the relationships between our tables in the database-diagramming tool we had the option of allowing SQL Server 2000 to manage the relationship and remove child records when a parent record is deleted. However we haven't taken advantage of this feature.

One of the great features of SQL Server 2000 (that most other RDBMSs don't support) is the ability to have multiple triggers perform the same event on a table.

Traditionally you have only been able to define a single trigger for a single event on a table. This has, in the past, meant that the triggers needed to be very complex to get them to perform the tasks that you needed. With this functionality though, they can be simpler and less complex. SQL Server 2000 also introduces new types of triggers, which I cover in Chapter 15.

Creating a Trigger to Catch Double Spies

I guess you are really biting at the bit now to create a trigger, so let's do it!

The triggers we will create will be associated with the BadGuy and the Spy tables. Currently we have a bit of an issue. Although our data model allows us to define people as being of a specific type (Spy or BadGuy), there is actually a flaw. With the current data model, a person can be both a Spy and a BadGuy. This can happen in the real world, but we will not allow it to happen in our application. We really do not want any double agents working for us now, do we?

To prevent this, we will create a trigger on the BadGuy table (and the Spy table) that checks that the person does not already exist in the Spy table (and vice versa). If they do, the trigger will return an error stating that the action cannot be performed. To be extra careful we will also have to ensure that the trigger does not only cover INSERTs but also UPDATEs.

Note

When we create a trigger on a table we specify with what event the trigger is going to be associated. For example, will it fire on an INSERT, UPDATE, or DELETE?

The triggers we are now going to build are known as AFTER triggers. This means that they fire *after* the change has been made to the table. If we reject the data change we simply roll back the changes (see Chapter 8 on Transactions).

A new feature of SQL Server 2000 is the ability to have triggers that fire before the data is modified, and I mention more about them in Chapter 15. This means that we capture the modification and if we are happy, we then modify the data ourselves.

We will now create the triggers. Enter the code in Listing 5.11 into Query Analyzer with the SQLSpyNet database selected.

Listing 5.11—Create Trigger Syntax for Our First SQL Server 2000 Trigger

```
 1: CREATE TRIGGER CheckBadguyNotInSpy
 2: ON BadGuy
 3: FOR INSERT, UPDATE
 4: AS
 5:    BEGIN TRANSACTION
 6:    DECLARE @SpyID INT
 7:    DECLARE @PersonID INT
 8:    SELECT @PersonID = i.PersonID
 9:    FROM inserted i
10:    SELECT @SpyID = SpyID
11:    FROM Spy S
12:    WHERE S.PersonID = @PersonID
13:    IF (@SpyID IS NOT NULL) AND (@SpyID > 0)
14:       BEGIN
15:          RAISERROR ('The Person you are trying to
15a: Insert/Update already exists in the Spy table.',
15b: 16, 1)
16:          ROLLBACK TRANSACTION
17:       END
18:    ELSE
19:       BEGIN
20:          COMMIT TRANSACTION
21:       END
```

Analysis

By now you will have the general idea of how to create database objects, so I shouldn't need to explain Line 1.

Line 2 is a little different. When we create a trigger we specify that it is for an event. An event occurs on a table, so we must attach our triggers to tables. Line 2 specifies that the trigger we are creating will be on the BadGuy table.

Line 3 specifies to SQL Server 2000 what events we want to use this trigger for. Notice that we are specifying the INSERT and UPDATE events for the BadGuy table. We can specify all events in this list, for example DELETE, INSERT, and UPDATE, or we can specify only one event.

Line 4 is the same as it is for a view and a stored procedure.

Line 5 is a special statement that we will cover a little later, but it allows us to ensure that we can recover from the INSERT if the incorrect value is entered into the table.

 We will cover transactions more in depth in Chapter 8.

Lines 6 and 7 declare some variables that we need to capture the PersonID that has just been inserted, and the SpyID is used to get the value from the SpyID column in the Spy table.

Most of the rest of the trigger uses SELECT clauses to see whether the values already exist. The first special item to notice, however, is Lines 8 and 9.

We set our variable @PersonID equal to the PersonID that has just been inserted. How do we achieve this? Well when SQL Server 2000 performs an INSERT, UPDATE, or DELETE it creates two tables in memory called inserted and deleted.

The deleted table is used when a row is deleted from a base table. The deleted table holds a copy of the row, and so we can query the table (you cannot update these tables) to retrieve information about the deletion.

Likewise, when an insert is performed on a table the inserted table contains a copy of the rows of data that have just been inserted into the base table. So in our trigger we exploit this fact by selecting the PersonID from the special inserted table.

Note

> The inserted and deleted tables, when used for INSERT and DELETE statements, are used individually. But when an UPDATE statement is performed, both tables are used. How? An UPDATE actually deletes the row, and then performs an INSERT, so both tables are used in the background. When performing an UPDATE, you need to take advantage of both tables.
>
> The important thing to note though is that these tables are not permanent tables. They only exist in memory for a short time (usually for as long as the Transact-SQL batch takes to complete), so you cannot access them always. Also, their names are always in lowercase.

Line 13 uses a COF statement to check whether the variable has a value. If it doesn't, then Lines 18 on are executed. Line 20 actually allows the insert or update to be made. Nice, eh?

Lines 15–16 allow us to return a message to the user. We use a built-in SQL Server 2000 function called RAISERROR. We will discuss this statement in Chapter 7 as well. Finally, Line 16 stops the insert/update from being performed. The values are discarded at this point.

And there we are. We now have our first trigger. This trigger will help to ensure that our data's integrity is maintained, so our application will continue to be valuable.

Testing the Trigger

We are now going to test our trigger to make sure it does actually work. First, we'll run some different pieces of code to add spies and bad guys into each table. Then, we'll see whether the trigger checks the integrity of that data when we try to add a double agent.

Enter Listing 5.12 into the Query Analyzer window.

Listing 5.12—Getting Some Data into Our BadGuy Table to Verify That Our Trigger Is Executing

```
1: INSERT INTO BadGuy (PersonID, KnownAs, IsActive)
2: VALUES (3, NULL, 1)
```

This statement will insert data into the BadGuy table—the desired result in case you were wondering.

Now enter Listing 5.13 to update the Spy table.

Listing 5.13—Getting Some Data into Our Spy Table to Verify That Our Trigger Is Executing

```
1: INSERT INTO Spy (PersonID, AnnualSalary, IsActive)
2: VALUES (1, 80000.00, 1)
```

Once again the Spy table will be updated, the desired result. We will now test our trigger with the code in Listing 5.14 (because we have some data).

Listing 5.14—Trying to Insert a Person Who Already Exists in the Spy Table

```
1: INSERT INTO BadGuy (PersonID, KnownAs, IsActive)
2: VALUES (1, NULL, 1)
```

This time when you run the statement, SQL Server 2000 will return the error message that we defined in the trigger, as shown in Figure 5.6.

Now we test the trigger when we perform an UPDATE. Enter Listing 5.15 into the query window.

Listing 5.15—Trying to Update a Person in the BadGuy Table to Someone Who Already Exists in the Person Table

```
1: UPDATE BadGuy SET PersonID = 1
2: WHERE BadGuyID = 11
```

We are trying to update the BadGuy table to a Person that exists in the Spy table. This will fail, and SQL Server 2000 will return the error message that we defined in our trigger.

Figure 5.6

SQL Server 2000 showing the error message that we wrote in the trigger.

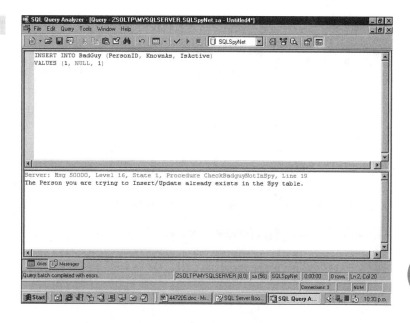

And that's it! You have now successfully created and tested your first trigger. So what now? We build a very similar trigger for the Spy table.

Setting a Trigger on the Spy Table

This trigger will be almost the same, except the table we check against is the BadGuy table rather than the Spy table.

Type the code in Listing 5.16, and then run the sample code that I have provided to ensure that the statements work.

Listing 5.16—Creating a Trigger on Our Spy Table to Prevent Hiring Double Agents

```
1: CREATE TRIGGER CheckSpyNotInBadguy
2: ON Spy
3: FOR INSERT, UPDATE
4: AS
5:    BEGIN TRANSACTION
6:    DECLARE @BadGuyID INT
7:    DECLARE @PersonID INT
8:    SELECT @PersonID = i.PersonID
9:    FROM inserted i
10:    SELECT @BadGuyID = BadGuyID
11:    FROM BadGuy B
12:    WHERE B.PersonID = @PersonID
13:    IF (@BadGuyID IS NOT NULL) AND (@BadGuyID > 0)
14:        BEGIN
15:            RAISERROR ('The Person you are trying to
```

Listing 5.16—Creating a Trigger on Our Spy Table to Prevent Hiring Double Agents

```
15a:      Insert/Update already exists in the BadGuy
15b: table.', 16, 1)
16:          ROLLBACK TRANSACTION
17:       END
18:    ELSE
19:       BEGIN
20:          COMMIT TRANSACTION
21:       END
```

After you have run the code, you must run the statements in Listing 5.17 to check that the trigger fires the way that it should. Because we have some data in both tables, we will just use the data from those tables to perform the checks.

Listing 5.17—Inserting a Double Agent into the Spy Table

```
1: INSERT INTO Spy (PersonID, AnnualSalary, IsActive)
2: VALUES (3, 97500.00, 1)
```

This will return the error message that we defined in the trigger, as shown in Figure 5.7.

Figure 5.7

SQL Server 2000 showing the error message that we wrote for the trigger.

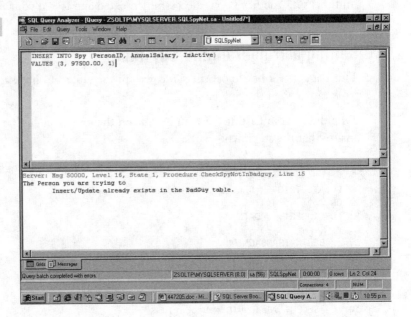

Now we need to test the trigger with an UPDATE statement. Use the code in Listing 5.18 to check this.

Listing 5.18—Updating a Person in the Spy Table to See Whether They Can Be a Double Agent

```
1: UPDATE Spy SET PersonID = 3
2: WHERE SpyID = 2
```

Simple, wasn't it? The triggers now fire the way we expect them to. We can now rest assured that the data will remain accurate and help prevent people from being entered into both tables.

Dropping Objects All Over the Place

What do I do if I don't want one of my DDLs anymore? You might have noticed that all the DDL statements that we have discussed thus far use the syntax CREATE *ObjectType ObjectName*. The same is true if we want to get rid of one of the objects that we no longer require, except we replace CREATE with the keyword DROP (we talked about this in Chapter 3).

So let's see an example! Suppose we did not want the view that we created in the beginning of our chapter.

> **Warning**
>
> Do not run this code unless you really want to get rid of the view that we created. And I suggest that you don't!

We would enter the code as it is shown in Listing 5.19.

Listing 5.19—Getting Rid of Unwanted Database Objects Using the DROP Statement

```
1: DROP VIEW PersonAddress
```

This will destroy the view from our database. The same can be said for any other database object. Just use the keyword DROP, the object type, and the name. Simple.

All the database objects support the capability to alter the statement as well. However, I recommend that instead of altering a database object, you DROP it and re-create it from scratch (excuse the pun).

The ALTER statement is syntactically similar to the DROP statement. How does it work? Like the UPDATE to base user tables, when SQL Server 2000 alters an object it actually drops and then re-creates the object.

Although it is slightly more work for us to drop and then re-create, it ensures that the object we have is exactly as we want it to be.

5

I will get off my soapbox now, and we'll look at the next DDL object for our database.

Going Round and Round Using Cursors

The final thing that we will discuss in this chapter is cursors. We will only discuss these at a high level because they are not needed very often, and at this stage we do not need to use one.

Although cursors are not used very often, you still need to understand what they are and how they work. They are more flexible, in some ways, than other methods for accessing and updating data, but they can be slower sometimes.

What is a cursor? When we use a stored procedure, view, or any of the other data access methods, we perform actions on whole sets of data. This suits our need 90% of the time. A cursor comes in for the other 10%.

A cursor enables us to loop through a table (or view, and so forth) and access each row within that table individually. This means that we can perform an action on this, or move to the next row if it does not meet our needs.

If you have programmed in Microsoft Access (or some other programming languages) you will be used to the concept of a recordset. A recordset and cursor are analogous, and really are the same thing, though their names are different.

When we open cursors, we base them on a SELECT statement. This statement can be over a view or even a single table. But even better than this, we can nest cursors within cursors. Like a stored procedure, a cursor can contain DML, COF, and even DDL statements.

As you can imagine, cursors give us a lot of flexibility, but they do have a very large overhead. When we bring back a large result set, such as a 100,000-row table, we do a single hit on the database, but with a cursor we hit the database for each record in the table. Normally though we would not open a cursor on 100,000 rows.

Well, cursors sound great, but do they have any practical use? In a short answer, yep. I once wrote a system that needed to archive data for a client. This was based on some very complex business rules and involved three tables. Although this does not sound like a lot, the structure caused some headaches.

In the end I developed a cursor that was opened on the parent table and looped through every child record in the subsequent tables. This would be similar to opening a cursor on the Person (parent) table and looping through every record in the Address (child) table. The cursor provided the functionality that I could not achieve with standard methods.

That wraps up this section on Cursors. While we do not have a use for Cursors at this stage, I am sure that you will find a need as your career develops, in fact I can almost guarantee it!

Summary

We have covered some key DDL statements in this chapter. These DDLs are everyday statements that as a developer or DBA you will use again and again. And remember: Practice makes perfect, so don't be afraid to jump right in and have a go.

We have not covered all the DDL statements that SQL Server 2000 has to offer, but this will get you started and is all that is usually required to get your database development started!

Next Steps

In the next chapter we will look at SQL Server 2000's built-in functions (some of these we have seen in this chapter) and discuss user-defined functions and build a sample function. I am sure you are really excited! Right?

Chapter 6

Getting Clearer Results with Functions

One way we can work with data in most applications is to use some sort of function. You might remember that in Chapter 3, "The Language of SQL Server 2000," we used the GETDATE() function to learn the system date to use in our application. Functions are great because we can use the same function that performs an action we want over and over again. We can even use the same functions in different applications. And one nice thing is that SQL Server 2000 has created many handy functions already. Of course, all of this means writing less code in the long run—so when you create a good function, you'll want to keep it.

In this chapter, we'll use some functions that SQL Server 2000 provides, and we'll make some of our own to manipulate the money, dates, names, and so on, in Spy Net.

Before we get to the actual code, it's important to understand how functions work and the types of functions that are available. Also, you can learn here how easily we can put functions together to perform even more complex actions and use data input.

Understanding the Role of Functions

A function is a compiled set of Transact-SQL that takes either none, one, or a set of values as parameters and returns a value, set of values, or performs some action. Functions allow us to easily perform routines again and again without having to rewrite the code for the function's purpose over and over.

These compiled statements that we are referring to, built-in functions, are standard functions that ship with SQL Server 2000. However, you can also create your own functions, called user-defined functions, to suit your own needs or to incorporate built-in functions into a larger set of statements.

A function (both built-in and user-defined), like a stored procedure, is an object that exists within our SQL Server 2000 database. Thus it has two parts, the compiled code that creates the object and the code that executes the object.

When we execute a function, we can give it different values each time, so that we can, generally speaking, get different results each time.

User-defined and built-in functions differ, though, in one important way. The built-in functions that come with SQL Server 2000 cannot be modified, so you cannot alter the compiled code to change the tasks that the function performs. However, built-in functions can be referenced directly through Transact-SQL.

Functions are built on a combination of DDL, DML, and COF language statements. This makes them as flexible as both stored procedures and triggers.

You might think of functions in SQL Server 2000 as being analogous to functions in the major programming languages. For example, VB has the Now() function, which returns the current system date. In SQL Server 2000 we have the GETDATE() function, which, as Now() does in VB, returns the current system date.

Functions can manipulate, modify, and perform calculations on parameters provided either by your code or user input. But wait, there's more! Functions can also query the operating system to return valuable information about the system on which SQL Server 2000 runs; for example, the GETDATE() function that we used in Chapter 3.

Functions can also be nested inside other functions, allowing us to manipulate the value returned by one function within another function. We can include them in SELECT statements and even include them in our triggers, stored procedures, and views, as well as our DDL statements. We can use COF statements to determine which function to fire when.

Functions can also be part of your DDL syntax. For example, we can specify a default value on a column in a table to be one of GETDATE(). When a row is inserted into the table, the default value of the current system date is entered into the column.

Sorting Types of Functions Based on Return Value

Functions perform many different actions, and so many different types of functions exist. But functions can be either *deterministic* or *non-deterministic*.

 Deterministic functions always will return the same result every time they are executed, with the same parameters. For example, if you add the same three numbers, you'll get the same result.

 Non-deterministic functions can return a different value every time they are executed, even with the same set of parameters provided. For example, if you check the records in the same table every time you run a function on it, the table might have the same rows one time but show changes the next.

All functions within SQL Server 2000 are either deterministic or non-deterministic. But although they might not return the same values every time, they do perform a wide range of operations.

Using Built-In Functions

As I mentioned in the previous section, SQL Server 2000 and previous versions of SQL Server have built-in functions that allow us to manipulate, calculate, and extract values from a given value. These functions are extremely valuable and provide a varied way of adding extra capabilities to our database application as well as allowing us, as DBAs, to perform administrative tasks easily.

A whole range of built-in functions enables you to query the operating system, including GETDATE(), which we'll use as a part of our own user-defined function.

What are we going to do now? We are going to use some of these built-in functions in our application, as of course you knew we would.

Using CONVERT to "Make Money"

The CONVERT function is a built-in SQL Server 2000 function that takes a data type and if successful returns that data type as another data type. For example, we pass the CONVERT function a data type of INT and use the function to change it into a VARCHAR.

This enables us to change the behavior of data types when we append them together. For example, when we try to build a string and append a numeric value to the string, SQL Server 2000 will attempt to convert the string into a numeric. Because a string cannot be converted into a numeric value, an error is returned. With the CONVERT function though, we can build strings as we intend them to be.

Sounds good, but how do we use this function? Well, you are actually an old hand already. In Chapter 4, when we discussed the WHILE loop, we actually used the CONVERT function to change our variable @MyCounter into a CHAR of size 2.

In this example we will use the CONVERT function to add a dollar sign to the beginning of our AnnualSalary column in the Spy table. First let's try it without the CONVERT function, as shown in Listing 6.1.

Listing 6.1—Trying to Change the Salary Without the CONVERT Function

```
1: SELECT
2:    SpyID,
3:    PersonID,
4:    Alias,
5:    DateCommencedWork,
6:    '$' + AnnualSalary AS Salary
7: FROM Spy
```

This will cause SQL Server 2000 to raise an error, as shown in Figure 6.1.

Figure 6.1

SQL Server 2000 raising an error when an implicit CONVERT function is performed.

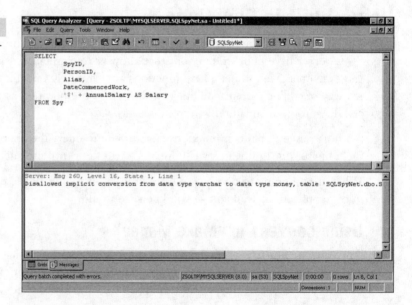

SQL Server 2000 will try to convert the '$' into the same data type as what the column is defined as. This is known as an *implicit conversion*. This occurs when SQL Server 2000 performs the conversion on your behalf. The CONVERT function does not need to be specified.

An *implicit conversion* is when a conversion is performed on your behalf. You do not need to worry about performing the conversion. Nice, huh?

Certain data types, when appended together, perform implicit conversions, such as
DATETIME and MONEY data types. These will append together without you having to
explicitly specify the CONVERT function. However, when appending strings to numerics, we must explicitly convert one of the data types into another data type. Enter the
code in Listing 6.2 into the Query Analyzer window.

Listing 6.2—Explicitly Converting Our Numeric Value into a String

```
1: SELECT
2:    SpyID,
3:    PersonID,
4:    Alias,
5:    DateCommencedWork,
6:    '$' + CONVERT(VARCHAR(10), AnnualSalary) AS Salary
7: FROM Spy
```

This will cause SQL Server 2000 to convert the AnnualSalary into a VARCHAR of size
10 and return the results similar to that shown in Figure 6.2.

Figure 6.2

SQL Server 2000 performing an explicit conversion function.

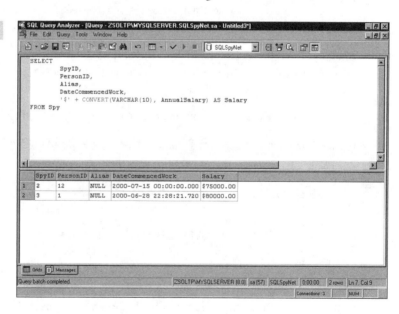

Analysis

Notice now we have a dollar sign in front of the AnnualSalary column. The CONVERT
function is cool, isn't it?

Let's have a quick look at how it is constructed. First we specify the function name,
CONVERT, followed by an opening bracket. Next comes the data type that we want to
convert into. So in this example we want to change our column into a VARCHAR(10).

Following this is the value that we actually want to change. This can be a column, as shown in the example, or a specified value, for example, CONVERT(VARCHAR(2), 22). The value 22 is not derived from anything, but just placed in the function.

This would then change the datatype of the value 22 from a numeric value to a VAR-CHAR value, for example, 22 becomes '22'.

Finally, we finish the function with a closing bracket.

And that, ladies and gentleman, is the basic outline of the CONVERT function. Oh, I guess one other thing to mention here is the CAST function. This has similar functionality to the CONVERT function and allows you change from one data type to another, but the CONVERT function has one more parameter at its disposal over the CAST function: the style parameter.

 Note   The CAST function provides functionality similar to that provided by the CONVERT function but does not take as many parameters.

The style parameter is appended to the end of the function and allows us to specify the style we will use when we change DATETIME, SMALLDATETIME, or most numeric data types into string-based data types (VARCHAR, CHAR, NVARCHAR, and so forth).

In our previous example we can alter Line 6 to what's in Listing 6.3.

Listing 6.3—Changing Our CONVERT Function to Apply a Style to the Returned Field

```
1: SELECT
2:     SpyID,
3:     PersonID,
4:     Alias,
5:     DateCommencedWork,
6:     '$' + CONVERT(VARCHAR(10), AnnualSalary, 1) AS
6a: Salary
7: FROM Spy
```

The results are similar to that shown in our previous example, except we now have commas (,) in our Salary column. This is shown in Figure 6.3.

The style parameter allows us to specify the way we would like our data displayed. It's very powerful, isn't it?

Because of this added functionality I prefer to use the CONVERT function when altering the datatypes of values, but you can use either the CONVERT or the CAST function.

One of the next most common functions is the COUNT function, so let's take a look at that.

Figure 6.3

SQL Server 2000 performing an explicit conversion function with a style defined.

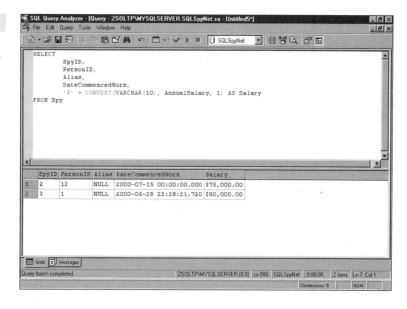

```
SELECT
        SpyID,
        PersonID,
        Alias,
        DateCommencedWork,
        '$' + CONVERT(VARCHAR(10), AnnualSalary, 1) AS Salary
FROM Spy
```

	SpyID	PersonID	Alias	DateCommencedWork	Salary
1	2	12	NULL	2000-07-15 00:00:00.000	$75,000.00
2	3	1	NULL	2000-06-28 22:26:21.720	$80,000.00

COUNT-ing Spies

The COUNT function, as its name suggests, is for performing a count. It will return the total number of items in a group. The return type from the function is an INT (a whole number).

The COUNT function is an *aggregate function* because it summarizes the data for you. The function is also deterministic; it will return the same result every time it is fired, as long as it is given the same parameters.

Aggregate functions focus on numeric data or measurements. These functions take a group of values as input and return a single value. See the section, "Building Your Function Library," later in this chapter, for more information.

The COUNT function is used most commonly to retrieve the total number of items in a table. For example, if you would like to know how many spies are in the spy table, you can perform a COUNT to retrieve the answer.

The COUNT function can be embedded in Transact-SQL statements and used by both DDL and DML statements. So you can use it in stored procedures, triggers, and views, as well as SELECT, INSERT, and UPDATE statements.

Before we use the COUNT function you should know the following:

- If you perform a COUNT on NULL values *only* you will be returned a value of zero.
- You can use the COUNT function on all values in a table by specifying the keyword ALL. With the ALL keyword specified, all values in the column that you are counting over will be counted. This is the default behavior of the function.

- You can also use the keyword DISTINCT in the function. This will then only perform a count on the unique values within the group.
- Finally, you can also use the asterisk (*) to perform a COUNT over all the *columns* and *rows* in a table.

Let's work our way through an example of the COUNT function so that we can see how many people we have in our Person table.

First, we will create a SELECT statement that uses the COUNT function to return the total number of people in our Person table, as shown in Listing 6.4.

Listing 6.4—Counting All the People We Have

```
1: SELECT COUNT(*) AS TotalPeople FROM Person
```

SQL Server 2000 will return the total count of rows within the Person table. As with all SELECT statements, we can apply criteria that will limit the rows returned. We can also join this table to other tables.

That's all well and fine, but what else can we do? As mentioned earlier we can apply the DISTINCT clause to the COUNT function to ensure that we only count unique values. So which table can we have non-unique values in? Why, the Address table, of course. With the Transact-SQL in Listing 6.5, SQL Server 2000 will return the total number of PersonIDs in the Address table.

Listing 6.5—Counting All the People with Addresses

```
1: SELECT COUNT(PersonID) FROM Address
```

In Listing 6.6, however, SQL Server 2000 will return the number of unique PersonIDs in the Address table.

Listing 6.6—Counting the Unique People with Addresses

```
1: SELECT COUNT(DISTINCT PersonID) FROM Address
```

And that is basically it! I am sure that you had no trouble in mastering the COUNT function. Let's take a look at two more before we build our own function, just so that you can be a master of your domain before you get your hands really dirty. Excited yet?

Using the SUM Function to Tally Paychecks

The SUM function, like the COUNT function, is an aggregate, deterministic function. It allows you to total a given set of numeric columns or values. Like the COUNT function it will return a numeric value in the most precise numeric type it can. This can be an INT, FLOAT, MONEY, and so forth.

Of what use is this function? If you have used Excel before, you already have an idea of the power of the function; if not, you soon will!

We will use this function in an example to calculate the total amount of annual salaries paid to spies. Enter the code in Listing 6.7 into the Query Analyzer window.

Listing 6.7—Whoa! We Pay Our Spies How Much?

```
1: SELECT SUM(AnnualSalary) FROM Spy
```

SQL Server 2000 will add all the values in the annual salary column together and return the answer. And just like the COUNT function, we can specify a DISTINCT statement within the function to only add together the unique values from the table. The SUM function becomes even more powerful though when we combine it with another aggregate function. The AVG function returns the average value from a set of numeric values.

Let's combine these together to develop an effective report to show just how much we are paying our spies (see Listing 6.8).

Listing 6.8—We Pay Our Spies Too Much, and On Average They Earn...

```
1: SELECT
2:     SUM(AnnualSalary) AS TotalSalaries,
3:     AVG(AnnualSalary) AS AverageSalary
4: FROM Spy
```

SQL Server will now return not only the total salaries paid to all spies, but also the average annual salary of all the spies. Your results will be similar to those shown in Figure 6.4.

Figure 6.4

SQL Server 2000 returning the sum of all salaries as well as the average salary.

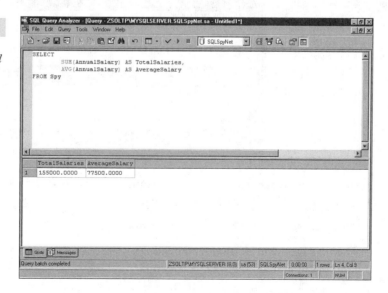

We can now easily see the excessive salaries that our spies earn.

We have briefly looked at two (actually three) aggregate functions. Now we look at one more final built-in function before we create our own.

Putting STUFF into Strings

Let's look at the STUFF function, a scalar function that allows you to manipulate strings in a very flexible way. The STUFF function allows you to remove a user-defined set length of characters and insert another set of characters from a user-defined starting point.

 Scalar functions use a single value and always return a single value. Most configuration functions (that is, checking on your server settings) are scalar. For more types of scalar functions, check out the section "Building Your Function Library," later in this chapter.

The STUFF function is not used as often as the previous aggregate functions, but it is still very powerful and allows you to easily change the way a string looks.

Enter the code in Listing 6.9 into the Query Analyzer window.

Listing 6.9— Stuffing a String into Our People

```
1: SELECT STUFF(Firstname, 1, 0, 'A Person named ')
2: FROM Person
```

SQL Server 2000 will now stuff the string `'A Person named '` at the beginning of the Firstname column. The results will look similar to those shown in Figure 6.5.

Figure 6.5

SQL Server 2000 stuffing the string into the Firstname column.

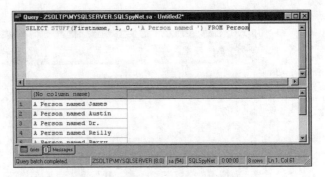

How does it work? The format of the function is defined to be the parameters that the function takes, as shown by this syntax:

```
STUFF(StringToStuff, Start, Length, ValueToStuff)
```

The first argument of the function allows us to define the string that we are going to stuff, in our case the Firstname column.

The second argument of the function enables us to specify the starting position within the string to stuff the new values into. In our previous example we used 1. This specifies that we want to start at the very beginning of our string.

The third argument enables us to state how many characters we want to remove from our initial string. We have specified that we want to remove 0, so no characters are removed from our string. If we had specified any value greater than zero, we would have overwritten that number of characters in our string.

The fourth and final argument enables us to specify the string that we want to use to stuff into the initial string.

 Note   The STUFF function that we just ran does not perform a permanent change to our data. To force a permanent change, we would need to use an UPDATE statement with the STUFF function.

Because the changes do not affect your data, try playing around with the start and length values to see the effect that these have on the string.

We have now looked at some aggregate and scalar functions. Let's look at how to create our own functions. Now doesn't that sound cool?

Creating Your Own Functions to Manipulate Data

Although SQL Server 2000 has a wide and varied range of built-in functions, at times the generalized functions that it has do not suit the specific needs of our applications.

So what do we do? We create our own functions. This means that we can create very rich applications that can perform data manipulation at the database level. If our client's business rules change, we can easily alter the functions that we have created.

So am I telling you that we can build our own functions? Yes, we sure can! SQL Server 2000 has the capability for us to develop small snippets of code that can be called from Transact-SQL and will return a value based on the parameters that we pass them.

Note

As with most of the objects within our database, this actually requires a two-step process. First we create the function with DDL Transact-SQL, and then we execute the function with DML Transact-SQL.

Most user-defined functions are scalar; they return a single value based on none, one, or many parameters. We can also grant certain people access to the use of our functions. Very sensitive information is still protected. We will discuss security in Chapter 7, "Securing Data Entry with Custom Rules and Defaults."

We can also use SQL Server 2000's built-in functions within our user-defined functions. We can incorporate some of SQL Server 2000's functionality and customize it with our own specific needs.

Tweaking Dates from Around the Globe

One function that we need to tweak is the ability to format dates for display. As I mentioned in an earlier chapter, New Zealand (NZ) and the United States (U.S.) have different date formats. In NZ the format is day/month/year. In the U.S. it is month/day/year. This can be very troublesome when updating a server that is configured to U.S. format when in NZ! For example in the U.S., 06/07/00 is the 7th June 2000, but in NZ it is the 6th July 2000! So what to do, what to do?

We will build a function that takes a date parameter and formats the date in a way that ensures we are 100% sure of the date we are being returned. Enter the code in Listing 6.10 into Query Analyzer.

Listing 6.10—Creating a Function for Us to Render Dates in a Precise Format

```
 1: CREATE FUNCTION DateFormatter
 1a: (@Date DATETIME, @DateSeperator CHAR(1))
 2: RETURNS VARCHAR(20)
 3: AS
 4: BEGIN
 5:   DECLARE @ReturnDate VARCHAR(20)
 6:   SET @ReturnDate = CONVERT(VARCHAR(2), DAY(@Date)) +
 6a:     @DateSeperator +
 7:    DATENAME(MONTH, @Date) + @DateSeperator +
 8:    CONVERT(VARCHAR(4), YEAR(@Date))
 9:   RETURN(@ReturnDate)
10: END
```

And there we have it! Our very first date-formatting function. SQL 2Server 2000 will compile and execute the DDL statement and return a success message.

Analysis

Let's analyze the Transact-SQL code that we have just entered:

- Line 1 tells SQL Server 2000 what type of DDL we are going to create.
- Line 1a enables us to specify the list of parameters and their data types that our function will take. So our first parameter will be a date, our second parameter a single character.
- Line 2 enables us to specify the type of data that the function will return to the calling procedure. Why have we used a VARCHAR instead of a DATETIME? We do not want our formatting to be removed by the conversion back into a DATETIME data type. If that happened our function would be rather pointless!
- The rest of the lines I am sure you can work out, but you should note the built-in SQL Server 2000 functions that we are using, specifically DATENAME and CONVERT.
- The only line left that is notable is Line 9. This specifies that we will return the variable @ReturnDate (remember this will be a VARCHAR) to the calling procedure.

And that's about as difficult as this function gets. Remember your functions should not be complex. If they are too complex you might need to break them down into separate functions. Why do I suggest that we keep them simple? When you come back to maintain your application in six months, you will appreciate the simplicity. Additionally, small groups of code will run faster and be easier to compile than large complex blocks of code.

Executing a User-Defined Function

We have built this new-fangled function, but how do we use it? The use of our function is almost the same as using one of SQL Server 2000's built-in functions, except we need to specify the function owner. You will notice that when we call the function we use the prefix dbo. We will discuss the dbo prefix when we discuss security.

Have a look at the following code. Notice the two parameters that we are passing to the DateFormatter function. One is the built-in SQL Server 2000 function GETDATE() and the other is the separator that we want to use when displaying our date.

```
1: SELECT dbo.DateFormatter(GETDATE(), '/') AS DateNow
```

The next line of code, shown in Listing 6.11, uses the function in a SELECT statement that brings back a person's date of birth and reformats it, as shown in Figure 6.6.

Listing 6.11—Executing the Function to Reformat the Dates

```
1: SELECT dbo.DateFormatter(DOB, '-') AS FormattedDOB
2: FROM Person
```

Figure 6.6

Using a function to for-mat the dates of birth.

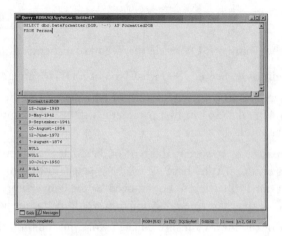

With the way we designed our function, we can actually pass the second parameter as a space. Go ahead and try it!

Building Your Function Library

As you work with SQL Server, you'll begin to build a library of functions. The functions we've used in this chapter should be your first few "volumes." From this point, you can build more functions based on the concepts we've explored here. However, you should keep a few key things in mind about the types of functions and how they work so when you have a particular problem to solve, you'll have a better idea of which "section" of your library of functions can fix the crisis with the fewest alterations.

The following are three main categories of functions, which you've used already in this chapter:

- Scalar functions—These use a single value and always return a single value.
- Rowset functions—These return an object that can be used in place of a table. For example, the OPENROWSET function enables us to reference a SELECT statement rather than a table in Transact-SQL.
- Aggregate functions—These are used for measurement and numeric manipulation. For example, these functions will COUNT, SUM, and provide MAX values. These functions take a group of values as parameters and return a single value.

Scalar Functions

The Scalar functions that are available in SQL Server 2000 come in a broad range of categories:

- Configuration functions— These functions return information about the configuration settings that are currently set.

- Date and Time functions —These functions take dates and times as input values (as a parameter passed in), and they return a number (integer, numeric, and so forth), string, or a date-time value.

- Cursor functions— These functions return information about cursors that are defined within the instance of SQL Server 2000.

- Metadata functions—These functions are very versatile and return information about the database and the objects that it contains.

- Mathematical functions—These take numeric values as inputs, perform some sort of calculation on those values, and return a numeric value or values.

- String functions—These functions take strings as input parameters and return either a string or number (integer, numeric, and so on).

- Security functions— These functions enable you to gain information about the users and the roles that are defined in your database.

- Text and Image functions —These functions take text or an image as an input parameter and return information about the parameter's value.

- System functions—These functions enable you to query and return information about database objects and settings in SQL Server 2000.

- System Statistical functions —These functions return statistical information about the current system settings.

Aggregate and Rowset Functions

So what about aggregate and rowset functions? Do they have similar categories available? Simply put, No! However, all rowset functions are non-deterministic. The results they return vary, even when they are given the same input parameters. Why? A rowset function enables us to bring back rows of data. These rows can be modified by another user, so we cannot guarantee that they will be the same every time we run a query.

Aggregate functions, on the other hand, are deterministic. They return the same values given the same set of input parameters, and so they should. Imagine if, when you performed the COUNT function on a table of data, you got a different result each time—disastrous!

 Tip All aggregate functions, except the COUNT function, ignore NULL values.

You can see a full list of SQL Server 2000's built-in functions in Books On-Line.

Summary

Now you should have a set of functions that you can use to manipulate certain aspects of the Spy Net application and reuse as you create other applications. You also have some idea of the other functions that SQL Server 2000 has already created for you to explore. Keep these and other functions you create (after you've tested them thoroughly), and you can easily insert them whenever you need to perform the same kinds of actions on your data.

And, because you can use functions to test data and make it conform to a set of business rules or standards, as we've shown here, you can help further ensure the integrity of your data.

Next Steps

In the next chapter we will look at transactions and locking. These are key database concepts that apply to all RDBMSs and are very relevant for multiuser environments. So let's keep truckin' on!

Securing Data Entry with Custom Rules and Defaults

Introduction

Data integrity can be one of the hardest parts of application development. I'm sure we would all like to think that our users would be knowledgeable enough to know when information is wrong. But alas, that is not the case. Most users, especially those who are new to a system, will enter invalid data into a field totally by accident.

It is up to us as application designers to be able to handle these little problems as best we can. We do this by setting data integrity constraints.

So far we have seen how to implement data integrity with triggers, stored procedures, and views, but SQL Server 2000 offers us even greater flexibility than this. We can write our own custom data integrity measures using rules, defaults, and custom data types.

In this chapter we will step into the world of rules, defaults, and custom data types to learn how to really protect our data.

We will see why we should use these types of data protection and how to implement them into our application development.

Ruling Your Data World

When we created our tables, what seems like an eternity ago, we specified certain constraints on our tables to ensure the integrity of our data. We implemented domain, entity, and referential integrity. We also implemented the fourth type of integrity, at least in one scenario, *user-defined integrity*.

 User-defined integrity is the ability for us to define our own restrictions on values that can be entered into columns within a table.

How? We build triggers to ensure that a spy could not exist in a table if a bad guy with the same PersonID existed in the BadGuy table.

Why would we need any other types of integrity? Triggers are wonderful if we have quite complex logic, or an event to associate them with. But if we want to have simple logic, or just prevent a user from entering the wrong value immediately, we can create a rule to do this.

A rule is similar to a function in some ways. It is a small, compiled piece of code. It is usually simple in nature and easy to modify.

 A rule does not return a value. However, you can create a rule to use the RAISERROR function to return a custom error message to the user. This allows us to return a useful message back to the user, for example "You must be 60 years old or greater to retire," when the rule is broken. We can attach a rule to the column of a table, although we can attach only one rule to any column in the table.

Checking for Underaged Spies

For example, we do not want to have any people in our Person table under 16 (the legal age for employment in New Zealand). This is a constraint, or business rule, that we can place on the Person table.

This is a perfect candidate for a rule. Why? The requirement is simple enough, so it does not require the complexity of a trigger. Second, the business rule can change over time with new legislation, so that the minimum age is 15. All we need to do then is alter the rule to reflect the new business rule requirement.

 Although we can create and attach a rule to a column in our table, it will not check any existing data. So if you have a person younger than 16 years in the table *before* the rule is attached, this will not be picked up when the rule is attached to the table.

Let's do it, then. You will notice that the syntax for the rule is very simple (see Listing 7.1); it only consists of three lines of code.

Listing 7.1—Creating a Rule to Validate the Age of our Spies and BadGuys

```
1: CREATE RULE AgeValidation_Rule
2: AS
3: @DOB < DATEADD(YEAR, -16, GETDATE())
```

Analysis

You might have noticed that we have used two of SQL Server 2000's built-in functions (DATEADD() and GETDATE()) within our rule. This is perfectly legal, and in fact only enriches the functionality provided to us by the CREATE RULE syntax.

The only line for us to really look at is Line 3 (where it all happens). The variable @DOB is a local variable that holds the value that the column contains. We can call this anything we like, but it *must* be prefixed with the at (@) symbol.

Next, we ensure that our value in our variable is *not* less than 16 years; that is, our statement returns false. If this condition is false, the INSERT/UPDATE is allowed; if not, it fails.

Binding and Testing the Rule

Unfortunately, though, we can't test this yet. Bummer, huh? Why? Because we have not *bound* this rule to a column, which we shall do right now!

Binding a rule, in computer terms, means to associate one thing to another. For example, a bound rule is one that is associated, or linked, to a column. This term is used in many different computer circles and is very common in Microsoft Access development.

To bind our rule to a column, we use one of SQL Server 2000's built-in stored procedures, or alternatively you can use Enterprise Manager.

The sp_bindrule stored procedure is a prebuilt, or built-in, stored procedure that ships with SQL Server 2000. It enables us to programmatically bind a rule that we have just created to a column in a table. It has the following syntactical structure:

```
1: sp_bindrule 'rule', 'object_name', 'futureonly_flag'
```

As you can see, the stored procedure takes three arguments:

- *rule*—The name of the rule that you want to bind. In our case this is AgeValidation_Rule.
- *object_name*—The name of the object to which you want to bind the rule. When referring to a table, we use the *tablename.fieldname* syntax, so for our example we use Person.DOB.

- *futureonly_flag*—An optional parameter, with a default value of NULL (if not supplied). This flag is used for user-defined data types and enables us to specify that the rule will only be bound to future use of the data type, and no existing tables that use the data type will be affected.

Let's bind our rule to our column so we can check that it does limit the values in the column. In Query Analyzer, execute the Transact-SQL code in Listing 7.2.

Listing 7.2—Binding Our Rule to the Person Table's DOB Column

```
1: EXEC sp_bindrule 'AgeValidation_Rule', 'Person.DOB'
```

SQL Server 2000 will return a message similar to that shown in Figure 7.1.

Figure 7.1

SQL Server 2000 binding our first rule to our Person table.

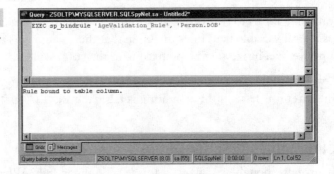

Now if you try to enter a new person in the Person table with an age less than 16 years, SQL Server 2000 will return an error, as shown in Figure 7.2. Try to enter the code in Listing 7.3 into the Person table.

Listing 7.3—Testing Our Rule to Ensure That It Is Working as We Expect

```
1: INSERT INTO Person (Firstname, Surname, DOB)
2: VALUES ('A Firstname', 'A Surname', '01 Jan 1990')
```

Now wasn't that simple?

Notice the error message that SQL Server 2000 has returned to the user. Not very friendly, is it? Well in Chapter 8, "Ensuring Data Consistency with Transactions, Locks, and Error Trapping," we will look at how to capture the errors that SQL Server 2000 returns and return a more meaningful message to our user.

Figure 7.2

SQL Server 2000 rejecting the INSERT INTO statement because of the rule we defined on the Person table.

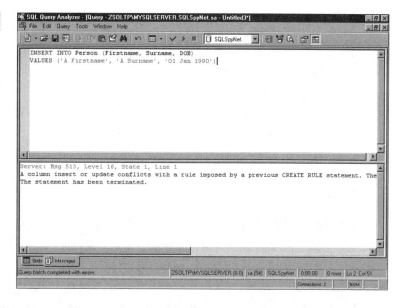

Note

To test this properly you should now try different combinations to ensure that it works as expected. For example, try inserting a new row with a DOB greater than 16 years. Also you could try to add a row with no DOB value supplied.

If you do not supply a value to the column, that is, insert a NULL into the column, the rule will not be activated. Why? Remember in Chapter 1 when we first talked about NULLs? Because a NULL cannot be less than, equal to, or greater than anything else, we cannot compare it to the formula we have.

Cool, we have now learned how to impose more business rules on our application to help ensure that the integrity of data remains intact. Isn't that great?

Next we are going to look at user-defined default values. Talk about exciting!

Setting Default Values

One more way of helping to ensure data integrity is by using default values. When we created some of our tables, we specified default values on a few of the columns of the tables. For example, in the Activity table we specified a default value of GETDATE() on the DatePlanAttempted column.

How do default values help to ensure data integrity? If a user does not know a value, instead of allowing a NULL (which is bad, remember) we put a placeholder value there. So when the user does have the information available he can update the column to reflect the information he has now obtained.

In addition to helping avoid NULL values, a user-defined default is enormously valuable when we want to use the same default in multiple columns. For example, suppose we had a phone number in the Spy, Badguy, and Address tables. When we created these tables we could have specified a default value at that time, but that means that we must write the same logic again and again when we create each table.

A user-defined default, on the other hand, allows us to build the default once, and then just reference it in the tables that require use of the same default.

One of the other benefits of a user-defined default is the ability to change the default and have it reflected throughout the tables, just by changing a single occurrence of the default definition.

Filling in the Missing Data for Our Users

Because you are so anxious, we will use CREATE DEFAULT statements for the SpyNumber and Alias columns in the Spy table, as well as for the KnownAs column in the BadGuy table.

Because these columns allow NULLs, when users enter data they don't actually have to supply values to the columns. We could end up with many NULLs in our table! Bad, bad, bad! So we will create custom defaults to automatically fill in the values in the columns if the user does not supply a value for the column. The default value that we will enter into the columns will be unknown.

Enter the code in Listing 7.4 into the Query Analyzer window.

Listing 7.4—Creating a Default Value for Data That Our Users Do Not Enter

```
1: CREATE DEFAULT Spy_BadGuy_Default AS 'unknown'
```

Once again, like the rule, we can't test this until we bind it to a column or columns. So we need to use the built-in SQL Server 2000 stored procedure sp_bindefault. This stored procedure has a similar syntactical structure to the sp_bindrule stored procedure and looks something like this:

```
1: sp_bindefault 'default', 'object_name', 'futureonly_flag'
```

The only difference between this stored procedure and the sp_bindrule stored procedure that we looked at earlier is the first argument. The *default* argument takes the name of the DEFAULT that you want to bind. In our case it will be Spy_BadGuy_Default.

Execute the code in Listing 7.5 in the Query Analyzer.

Listing 7.5—Binding a Default Value to Our Columns in Our Tables

```
1: EXEC sp_bindefault 'Spy_BadGuy_Default',
1a: 'Spy.SpyNumber'
2: GO
3: EXEC sp_bindefault 'Spy_BadGuy_Default', 'Spy.Alias'
4: GO
5: EXEC sp_bindefault 'Spy_BadGuy_Default',
5a: 'BadGuy.KnownAs'
6: GO
```

Analysis

Notice that we must perform this task three times to bind the DEFAULT to all the columns. We also have specified the GO keyword between the statements to show that they are run as separate batches. SQL Server 2000 will return messages similar to that shown in Figure 7.3.

Figure 7.3

SQL Server 2000 binding our DEFAULTs to the three columns.

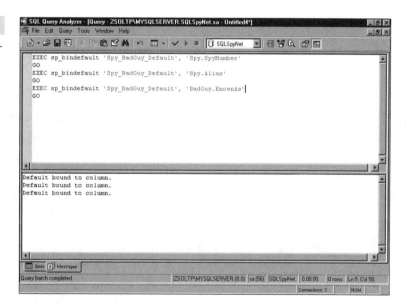

Testing the Default

Once again we need to test that this works. We will enter a row into both the Spy and BadGuy tables without specifying the SpyNumber, Alias, or KnownAs values. These should then be populated with our value unknown.

Enter the code in Listing 7.6 into the Query Analyzer window.

Listing 7.6—Testing That Our Default Value Works on Our Three Columns

```
1: INSERT INTO Spy (
1a: PersonID, DateCommencedWork, AnnualSalary, IsActive)
2: VALUES (2, '23 May 1969', 152000.00, 1)
3: SELECT * FROM Spy WHERE PersonID = 2
```

You should now see similar results to that shown in Figure 7.4.

Figure 7.4

SQL Server 2000 inserting our user-defined defaults into the two Spy columns.

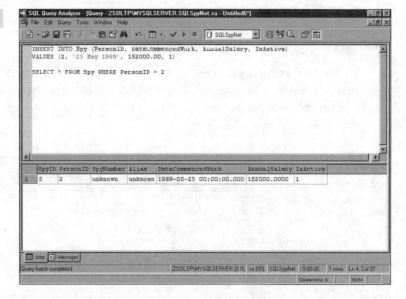

Notice now that our newly inserted data has a default value of unknown in the two columns (on our Spy table) that we bound the default to.

 Note

Once again, to test this effectively you will need to create a series of scenarios. For example, try inserting a new row with an Alias supplied but no SpyNumber and vice versa. Then try it again with both supplied.

Now you need to perform a similar test on the BadGuy table. I am going to leave this up to you, cherub! I am sure you are clever enough to figure out how to achieve this one on your own.

> Because you are a little new to Transact-SQL, I will help you out to find all the Spy records that contain the "unknown" values. You can then update those values by using the UPDATE statement that you learned in Chapter 4.
>
> Here is the code for the Spy table:
>
> ```
> 1: SELECT * FROM Spy
> 2: WHERE SpyNumber = 'unknown'
> 3: OR Alias = 'unknown'
> ```
>
> This will give you all the Spy records that contain our default value in the column. Now you can update the columns with real data.

Adding Custom Data Types to Keep Data Uniform

User-defined data types are based on SQL Server 2000's built-in data types. They allow us greater flexibility when creating tables because we can specify that the new tables will use our user-defined data type, thus ensuring data consistency.

For example, suppose we had a Phone Number column in the Spy, BadGuy, and Address tables. Normally when we create our tables, we would define these columns as being of type VARCHAR(14) and allow NULLs. With a user-defined data type we base our user-defined type on SQL Server 2000's VARCHAR type and allow NULLs also.

But what happens if we have two developers, and the first developer believes that our Phone Number column should be VARCHAR(10) rather than VARCHAR(14)? This creates inconsistencies in our data model.

When we want several columns in our database to all have the same type, size, and NULL-ability defined, we create user-defined data types.

We can then implement our user-defined type in all the relevant tables, and voilà— we have a consistent type throughout the system. Cool, huh?

If we change the data type, it is reflected in all the tables that implement our user-defined data type, making central management of the application very simple.

But not only can we have a consistent data type throughout our data model, we can bind a default to our user-defined data types!

When a value is entered (or not, as the case may be) into the column that contains our data type, the default value will be inserted into the column, as we saw earlier with defaults. We can go one step further than that again. We can even bind a rule to our data type, so that the data integrity we developed earlier is carried across the board as well!

Isn't that great? We can pull all our concepts together to really ensure that our data is as clean as possible. Let's get our hands dirty and create our very own data type!

Validating Phone Numbers

Although we can create a user-defined data type fairly easily, we also must perform several other steps so we can use the new data type properly.

So what are we going to do? We will create a data type called `Person_PhoneNo`. This will be based on the native `VARCHAR(14)` data type of SQL Server 2000. We will then create a default value for the `Person_PhoneNo` data type. When the data type is used throughout our application, the default value will follow.

From this, we will create a rule that does not allow any less than 10 characters to be entered. We will then bind this rule to the data type as well. Finally, we will issue an `ALTER TABLE` statement to change the Person table to have a new column called `PhoneNo` that will be based on our new data type.

 Note

You might have noticed that this is slightly different from the approach we took earlier, where we bound our rules and defaults to columns in a table. The approach we are taking now is the better of the two. If we have our own user-defined types with the rules and so forth bound to them, we have all the business logic encapsulated away from the tables and consistently applied throughout the use of the data type.

To create the user-defined data type, we need to use the built-in SQL Server 2000 stored procedure called `sp_addtype`, which has the following syntactical structure:

```
1: sp_addtype
1a: 'type', 'system_data_type',
1b: 'null_type', 'owner_name'
```

Analysis

Line 1 is pretty self-explanatory. This is the name of the stored procedure we want to execute.

Line 1a allows us to define the name of our data type and the name of the system data type on which it is defined. So for our example this will be `Person_PhoneNo` and `VARCHAR(14)`.

The first parameter of Line 1b allows us to specify whether this column will be `NULL`. If this parameter is not supplied it is set to the default of the database. The second parameter allows us to specify who owns the data type. The default is the current user.

This process has a few more parts to it than usual, so let's sort it out in steps, like so:

1. Enter the code in Listing 7.7.

Listing 7.7—Creating Our User-Defined Type

```
1:sp_addtype 'Person_PhoneNo', 'VARCHAR(14)', 'NOT NULL'
```

You should now see similar results to that shown in Figure 7.5.

Figure 7.5

SQL Server 2000 creating our user-defined data type.

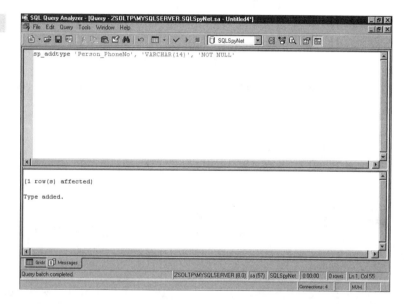

2. Now we need to create the default and bind it to the data type. Enter the code in Listing 7.8 into Query Analyzer.

Listing 7.8—Creating the Default for Our New Data Type

```
1: CREATE DEFAULT PhoneNo_Default AS 'Not Available'
```

3. Then bind the default to the data type with the code in Listing 7.9.

Listing 7.9—Binding the Default to Our New Data Type

```
1: EXEC sp_bindefault 'PhoneNo_Default',
1a: 'Person_PhoneNo'
```

Notice the only difference between this Transact-SQL and the earlier one is the final argument. Here we use the data type name, and earlier we used the column name.

4. Next we need to create the rule and bind it to the data type. Enter the code in Listing 7.10 into Query Analyzer.

Listing 7.10—Create the Rule First, So We Can Then Bind It To the New Data Type

```
1: CREATE RULE PhoneNoLength_Rule
2: AS
3: LEN(@PhoneNo) > 9
```

5. Next we need to bind this rule to the data type, so we use the sp_bindrule stored procedure again.

```
1: EXEC sp_bindrule 'PhoneNoLength_Rule',
1a:'Person_PhoneNo'
```

Once again the only difference is that we specify the data type as the last parameter rather than as a column name.

Let's stop here for a minute. We need to check that this has all gone according to plan before altering our table. Open Enterprise Manager and go to our SQLSpyNet database.

Navigate your way through the folders until you find "User Defined Data Types." Here you will find the data type that we have just created.

> **Tip**
>
> If you do not see the data type in the folder, right-click the folder and select refresh. If you still do not see it, you might need to check the database on which you created the data type!

Double-click the Person_PhoneNo data type. This will present you with a window similar to that shown in Figure 7.6.

Figure 7.6

SQL Server 2000 displaying our user-defined data type.

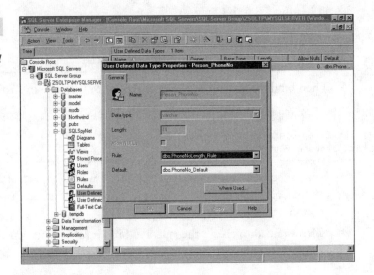

Notice that in the Rule drop-down box we have our new rule shown. This is also the same for the Default drop-down box.

> **Tip**
>
> If you do not see either the rule or the default in the drop-down box, close the window. Next refresh the Defaults and the Rules folders within our SQLSpyNet database. Then go back and open the data type properties window again, and voilà.

Cool, our data type is correctly defined. From the SQL Server 2000's base type of VARCHAR(14), we have a default and a rule bound to the data type. I guess the burning question of the day is, "How do I use it?"

Using the Data Type

Finally we are ready to implement our new data type within our Person table. Enter the code in Listing 7.11 into Query Analyzer.

Listing 7.11—Altering the Table So We Can Implement Our New Data Type

```
1: ALTER TABLE Person
2: ADD PhoneNo Person_PhoneNo
```

SQL Server 2000 will return a success message indicating that action was successful.

Analysis

Simple, wasn't it? Let's have a brief look at the structure of the ALTER TABLE Transact-SQL statement.

- Line 1 specifies that we want to change the structure of our table, and the name of the table that we want to change.

- Line 2 is the change that we want to implement. We tell SQL Server 2000 that we want to add a new column. This is followed by the column name and the column's data type. So in this case our column name is PhoneNo and its data type, you guessed it, is Person_PhoneNo.

> **Note**
>
> We have not specified a DEFAULT or a CONSTRAINT on the column. Why? Because we defined these in our data type, silly!

To check whether our change has actually taken place, in Enterprise Manager go to the SQLSpyNet database and navigate your way to the Tables folder. Then double-click the Person table. You will see a screen similar to that shown in Figure 7.7.

Note

You might have noticed that the column specifies that it will allow NULLs, even though we specified that our data type was not nullable. When you add a column to a table in SQL Server 2000 after a table is created, you cannot add a NOT NULL column. Why? Because you have no data, of course! So even though we explicitly stated that our data type does not allow NULLs, our column, by default, does.

Figure 7.7

SQL Server 2000 displaying our Person table with the new column and our data type displayed.

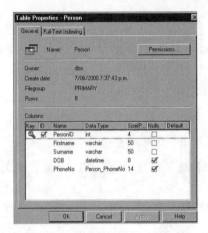

This shows our Person table with the new PhoneNo column added.

What do we need to do now? Test our changes, of course! As per usual I will give you a couple of test examples, but you will need to thoroughly test the changes.

Enter the Transact-SQL code in Listing 7.12 into the Query Analyzer.

Listing 7.12—Testing Our New PhoneNo Column and Data Type

```
1: INSERT INTO Person (Firstname, Surname, DOB)
2: VALUES ('Bert', 'Renault', '10 Jul 1950')
3: SELECT * FROM Person WHERE Firstname = 'Bert'
```

You will see that because we did not supply a value for the PhoneNo column, the DEFAULT value we created is inserted into the column, as shown in Figure 7.8.

Figure 7.8

SQL Server 2000 displaying our DEFAULT constraint firing.

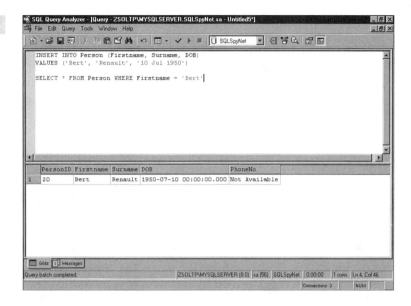

Our `PhoneNoLength_Rule` rule specified that our column must contain a minimum length of 10 characters, so we need to perform testing on this.

Enter the Transact-SQL code in Listing 7.13 into Query Analyzer.

Listing 7.13—Testing That Our `PhoneNoLength_Rule` Rule Works

```
1: INSERT INTO Person (Firstname, Surname, DOB, PhoneNo)
2: VALUES ('The', 'Jokerette', '17 Nov 1962', '123')
```

SQL Server 2000 will fail the INSERT statement because the PhoneNo field violates the rule we bound to the data type.

Here I will allow you to perform additional testing on your own. You should ensure that the field now allows you to insert a value greater than 9 characters, and you should also ensure that if you pass the special NULL value to the field, that the INSERT would also fail. Finally you should check that the rule fires on UPDATE statements as well as INSERT statements.

And here we leave the section on user-defined data types, rules, and defaults. As you can see, their flexibility and ease of implementation is fantastic.

Summary

This chapter has provided us with the finishing touches on ensuring data integrity in our application. You now have skills in implementing data consistency through the four basic methods of integrity: Entity, Referential, Domain, and User-defined. Our application is really beginning to become quite robust now!

It pays to remember that although we have implemented some very good methods for helping to ensure that our application has accurate data entered, we cannot totally prevent our users from entering invalid data. If we tried to stop them doing that, they wouldn't be allowed to enter anything at all.

Data integrity is very important, but so is user training to help ensure data consistency.

Next Steps

From here we will tack a little and take a look at error handling, transactions, and locking. These are key database concepts that apply to all RDBMSs and are very relevant for multiuser environments. So let's get going!

Chapter 8

Ensuring Data Consistency with Transactions, Locks, and Error Trapping

In this chapter, we take a look at how to keep your data safe. Not safe from theft, but safe from the misuse that your users will subject it to!

Whenever you write an application, you make certain assumptions. Although the old adage says "When you assume you make an ASS out of yoU and ME," you have little choice. You need to assume that your users are going to break your application. Whether intentionally or not, someone will enter something that doesn't gel.

To prevent this from happening, you need to look at how you can use transactions, locking, and error trapping to reduce the number of errors that are found and make your application more robust.

You are aiming for 100% bug-free code! And though I have said before that this is not an easy task, if you don't shoot for the stars, how will you ever reach the sky?

To begin with, we are going to take a look at transactions and the pivotal role they play in keeping our data consistent. And like many things, locking goes hand in hand with transactions. We'll look at what a lock is and some of the factors we must take into account when thinking about locking. Finally, we look at error trapping and what do when it all turns to custard!

Keeping Data Consistent with Transaction Wrappers

Thus far, we have seen how to modify the data in our SQLSpyNet database. The statements required to achieve this can be simple or can be complex, but what do we do if, after we've made a change, we suddenly realize the change should not have been made?

Well, we could easily reenter the data, but what about when we have updated the rows in several tables? This could prove to be very difficult to restore the data back to its original state if necessary. So, what do we do? This is where transactions come in.

Transactions enable you to group Transact-SQL statements and execute them sequentially. This, in turn, enables you to create batches of statements that fire one after another. But what is so special about that? You can already group Transact-SQL statements together in stored procedures, triggers, and functions. BEGIN...END pair blocks already give us the functionality to achieve this.

You learn fast, my student! Yes this is true, but transactions offer even more flexibility than this. With transactions, you can perform several database updates at one time, and then either accept or reject the changes that have been made. This is somewhat similar to using the Track Changes option in Microsoft Word. You can either accept or reject the changes that have been made to your document.

Okay, that sounds good, but how does it relate to our application? Well, transactions enable us, and our users, to perform updates. In addition, if an error occurs during the course of the update, we can reject the change and inform the user. This added functionality helps prevent our application from having invalid data, and gives us the option to handle errors nicely, such as preventing our client applications from abruptly halting with errors.

We take a look at error handling in "Handling Errors So Our Application Doesn't Break," later in this chapter.

To help in your understanding of what a transaction is, I will tell you a little story. So sit back and relax.

Let's take a little trip back in time, to a time before you became the program director of SQL Spy Net Limited, in fact so far back it was when you first started as a communications assistant.

While sitting at your desk, you receive an urgent communication with the Presidential seal of approval. Working at a frantic pace, you begin entering the code designed to launch an attack against one of Spy Net's archenemies, Dr. Eville, who has taken over a small island in the Pacific and is using it as a base to launch her assault on the world.

Satisfied that you have done your job well, and not to mention in record time, you sit back and enjoy a nice cup of coffee. Then, you notice on the monitor one of the large missile pods rotating, but the angle looks wrong for it to be aimed at a small Pacific island—in fact, the angle looks totally wrong! You watch in horror as missile after missile is launched upon the world. It looks as though the code you entered has started a full-scale war! Surely, that can't be correct. Why would the President declare war against the rest of the world?

You check the code you have entered against the memo, and to your horror, you discover that you have made a terrible mistake. The code you entered was It grows no moss, so the Black Rock does not move forward, when it should have been The Black Rock does not move forward, so it grows no moss.

Meanwhile, buildings are collapsing, cars are being overturned, and people are being torn apart by explosions that rock the cities of the world—all because of a simple mistake of transposing the code.

But what can you do? Then, it comes to you; you jump up on your chair and shout as loud as you can, "ROLLBACK!"

Watching on the monitor, you see everything happening in reverse—buildings standing upright again, cars being turned back the right way, people being reassembled, even the missiles flying backward and back to their bases. In fact, everything is taken back to the way it was just before you entered the code.

And there you have it; you have just rolled back your first transaction. Okay, sure our story is a little outrageous, but it gives you the general idea of what a transaction is and how a ROLLBACK works.

Let's take a look at what we have achieved with our transaction to prevent the end of the world.

Our transaction began with the code you entered to initiate the launch of the missiles. The entering of the code began an *implicit* transaction. We will take a look at the different types of transactions (implicit, explicit, and auto-commit) in "Choosing a Transaction Type," later in this chapter.

We then specifically stated what we wanted to happen, in this case discard the changes, so we could start again.

A friend of mine suggested that database transactions are like the movie "Groundhog Day." In this movie, the actor (Bill Murray) begins the same day again and again. However, within each day he can do different things to come to different endings. But when he wakes up he knows that everything will be back to the way it was before. This is similar to opening a transaction and performing many different tasks, and then discarding the changes.

We have managed to group a series of events into our transaction—missile pods repositioning, missiles firing, buildings collapsing, and so on—and our transaction follows the basic rules that all transactions must follow.

Making Transactions Pass the ACID Test

Transactions have to follow some rules (who doesn't?). Transactions must be ACID, which stands for *atomicity*, *consistency*, *isolation*, and *durability*.

 Atomicity means that transactions must be all or nothing. Either all their changes are made or none are.

 Consistency implies that when the transaction has finished, the data must be left in a state in which there are no outstanding data changes. Therefore, all the rules of the relational database (such as foreign keys) must be adhered to.

 Isolation. Transactions can be nested inside each other, but they must be isolated from each other. So, if one transaction modifies data, the next transaction must be able to see that data only in the state before the first transaction modified it, or after the first transaction has finished with it. The second transaction cannot see data in a half-finished state.

 Durability. After a transaction has finished, the data modifications must be permanent. The changes persist even in the event of system failure!

Therefore, when designing your transactions, you must think about these rules and ensure that your Transact-SQL code conforms to them. SQL Server 2000 does perform some of this for you, but it should always be in the forefront of transaction design.

So, there we have it! A transaction really is only a wrapper for the Transact-SQL statements we execute. And with this wrapper, we can either let our statements perform the actions for which they were written or reject these changes and restore everything back to the state it was in when the transaction began.

Choosing a Transaction Type

You might be thinking, "How do I start a transaction, and do I really care?" Well, you should! Even though within our application development we will explicitly (defined very shortly) state our transactions, SQL Server 2000 enables you to configure your transaction in other ways.

You can choose from three main ways of defining transactions in SQL Server 2000:

- Implicit transactions—You must manually enable this option for it to be active. You can enable it to be turned on when a user connects to the database, or you can turn the option on with the SET IMPLICIT_TRANSACTIONS ON command. This will begin a transaction for you; then, you must either accept (COMMIT) or reject (ROLLBACK) the changes.

> **Note**
>
> Implicit transactions can provide you with great flexibility when a client application connects to your instance of SQL Server 2000.
>
> You can start a transaction when the connection is established and then as the user performs data manipulation operations (UPDATE, INSERT, or DELETE) you can either accept or reject the changes as you please.

- Auto-commit transactions—This is the default transaction management setting within SQL Server 2000. It will either COMMIT or ROLLBACK the Transact-SQL statement that is executed for you. It tries to finish the transaction after the Transact-SQL statement has executed. This behavior is similar to Microsoft Access. Even if you use implicit or explicit transactions, as soon as they are no longer current, SQL Server 2000 resorts back to this setting.
- Explicit transactions—This is where you explicitly define the start and end of a transaction. After you have finished, similar to the other transactions, you can either COMMIT or ROLLBACK the changes.

We will explicitly state the beginning and end of our transactions from now on. This gives us greater flexibility and control over how and when our transactions are used. However, after our transaction is finished, SQL Server 2000 reverts back to auto-commit transactions.

So, we've talked about what a transaction is and its various settings, but how do you define one? Well, because we are going to use only explicit transactions, this is what we will look at defining.

The explicit Transact-SQL transaction statement really has only two parts to it. Talk about simple! The parts are as follows:

- `BEGIN TRANSACTION` or `BEGIN TRAN`—Initiates the start of the transaction. This is the first part.

  And either

- `COMMIT TRAN` or `COMMIT TRANSACTION`—Applies the changes that have been made within the transaction. This is the second part.

  or

- `ROLLBACK TRAN` or `ROLLBACK TRANSACTION`—Discards the changes that have been made and restores the data back to its original state when the transaction was started. This is also the second part. It means either a `COMMIT` or `ROLLBACK` must be issued.

Within the `BEGIN TRANSACTION...COMMIT/ROLLBACK TRANSACTION` statement, we can have a single Transact-SQL statement or a multitude of Transact-SQL statements. However, this does have some pitfalls, which we will discuss shortly.

EXCURSION

Employing a Two-Phase Commit

Although transactions on the same database are normally easy to manage, transactions that span multiple databases can be a little more difficult to manage.

When everything goes wrong, we roll our transaction back. This is all well and good on one database, but what happens when we are trying to perform an action that spans multiple databases? Take for example the old analogy of transferring money from one country to another.

You go into the bank and transfer $1,000 from your account to an overseas account. Clearly, the two banks do not use the same database, but they still need to manage the process effectively.

When the money leaves your account, you do not want the transaction to be marked as successful until the money is safely tucked away in the overseas account. Otherwise, you might have had the money deducted from your account but never deposited!

Two-phase commit (2PC) enables us to begin transactions on two separate databases and manage those transactions effectively.

Now that you have a rough idea of what two-phase commit is, let's look at how it works.

When the money leaves your account, a transaction is begun, and another transaction is begun when the money reaches the overseas account. But this in itself is not enough to manage the whole process. So, in comes a *resource manager*. This is responsible for ensuring that all involved resources are aware of what is going on.

The resource manager in SQL Server 2000 is known as the *Microsoft Distributed Transaction Coordinator (MS DTC)*. MS DTC requests that each involved resource prepare to commit the changes it has made. This is known as *preparing* the transaction.

As long as all the resources can commit—in other words, no errors exist—all transactions are allowed to complete with no further action by the MS DTC. However if one of the resources can't commit, MS DTC sends a broadcast to all resources notifying them that they need to roll back the transaction. This ensures that all our transactions remain atomic.

This is somewhat similar to a manager who uses negative reinforcement to manage his employees. As long as everything is running smoothly, you never hear from him. But when things go wrong, boy, does he start yelling!

You can now rest assured that your money has been safely withdrawn and deposited in the overseas account without either you or the bank being out of pocket.

Creating a Transaction for Spy Net

I bet all this talk of transactions has you just itching to try one out, right? I knew you'd be excited.

In this example, we look at the basic declaration of a transaction and how it works. We will update the AddressType table with a deliberate mistake. We are going to enter Physical Horse Address instead of Physical House Address. We then will discard our changes by rolling back our transaction.

The example is not really for widespread use throughout our application. That will come when we discover how to handle errors, but for now, it will demonstrate an easy way to see how a transaction is performed. So, let's get on with it!

Start Query Analyzer, once again, and enter the code in Listing 8.1 into the database window.

8

Listing 8.1—Trying Out a Basic Transaction on Our AddressType Table

```
1: SELECT AddressTypeID, Description FROM AddressType
1a: WHERE AddressTypeID = 4
2: BEGIN TRANSACTION
3: UPDATE AddressType SET Description = ' Physical Horse Address'
3a: WHERE AddressTypeID = 4
4: SELECT AddressTypeID, Description FROM AddressType
4a: WHERE AddressTypeID = 4
5: ROLLBACK TRANSACTION
6: SELECT AddressTypeID, Description FROM AddressType
6a: WHERE AddressTypeID = 4
```

Analysis

So what are we doing here?

- Line 1 proves the state of our data before any other actions were performed.
- Line 2 begins the transaction on our Transact-SQL statements.
- Line 3 performs an update on the data in our table.
- Line 4 proves that the change has been made. We can see, in Figure 8.1, that our field has been updated to the value of `Physical Horse Address`.
- Line 5 causes our changes to be discarded. The ROLLBACK statement discards the changes that have been made in the current transaction. It also closes and finishes the transaction.
- Line 6 proves that our code has been reverted back to what it was before the changes took place.

In Figure 8.1, you can see the changes made and then discarded with the previous code.

Figure 8.1

Demonstrating the BEGIN *and* ROLLBACK TRANSACTION *statements.*

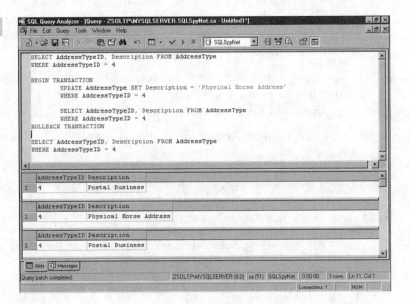

So, there we have it—a basic transaction that shows how data can be manipulated and then returned to how it was, ensuring that the rules (ACID) of transactions are met.

> Using a transaction with a ROLLBACK statement can be very useful when you are testing Transact-SQL statements and do not want to corrupt your data. For example, suppose you want to update all the Spy salaries in the Spy table because you have very generously given everyone a pay raise of 10%!
>
> Before you actually want the update to be saved to the database, you want to check that the total of the spies' pay raises will not blow out the budget for the year.
>
> With a transaction, you can apply the changes, check the totals against your budget report, and discard the changes if they can't be met. I reckon you should tell the spies that they can't have their pay raises after all!
>
> With a little thought, you will find many more examples of being able to use transactions for testing.

There are some things we can do to make our transactions more effective. Let's take a look at some of the best practices we should use when creating our transactions.

Getting the Most from Your Transactions

Keep this list in mind when you create transactions for your applications:

- Transactions should be kept as short as possible—Why? For SQL Server 2000 to ensure that our transactions are ACID, it uses numerous resources, so long-running transactions are expensive. Although this might not be much of an issue in a system that has a few users, such as ours, in a system that supports many users the performance of the system will be severely degraded if the transactions are too long.

- Define effective locking strategies to prevent users from reading data that has been modified, but not had the transaction committed—I tell you more about locking in the next section of the chapter.

- Avoid allowing users to input information during a transaction—Human response times are inherently slower than those of a PC, and as mentioned before, transactions are very expensive on resources. So get all the user input before a transaction is begun.

- Avoid opening a transaction while browsing through data—This helps reduce locking issues. In addition, transactions, after all, are really the most valuable for updating data, not retrieving it.

- Reduce the amount of data you access in your transactions—If you need to perform an update on only a single row, ensure that you hold a lock on only that row, not on the whole table. This helps reduce possible locking problems for other users.

Although we can set several other options when designing our transactions, this will put you on the right path until we look at locking options.

8

Maintaining Data Integrity with Locks

Locking, like transactions, is a key database concept in all RDBMSs. Even though we probably won't need to explicitly manage locks for our application now, we want any application we create to scale or grow without having to start over. Therefore, understanding locks now can help us prepare for the days when Spy Net goes to the enterprise level.

One of the great analogies for explaining locks is another banking one. Suppose you are married, and you have $400 in your joint checking account, with no overdraft facility. You go into the bank and attempt to withdraw $300. While you are in the bank, your wife goes into another branch and attempts to withdraw $200. The teller at your bank processes the request, sees $400 in the account, and issues the money. However, before she is finished, the teller at your wife's branch processes the $200 request and also issues the money. When the transactions are committed, the account is suddenly overdrawn by $100.

What should happen here? When the first teller begins the withdrawal, a lock should be placed on the record. This prevents the second teller from even beginning her request until the first teller has finished. We will discuss more about locking shortly, but just bear in mind that we should be careful when designing our transactions.

Locking enables us to prevent users from reading data that is being modified; we can also prevent two users from updating the same data at the same time. This ensures that our data remains in a consistent state. Although we cannot totally stop users from inputting incorrect data, we can at least manage that data after it is in our application.

How SQL Server 2000 Automates Locking

SQL Server 2000 manages most connections for you without any real intervention required from the DBA or developer—talk about easy! In Enterprise Manager, we can actually view the locks that a user has on a resource.

So, let's take a quick look at where to find the locks manager in SQL Server 2000:

1. Open Enterprise Manager and navigate your way to the Management folder.

2. Within the Management folder is the Current Activity folder. Here, you can view what users are doing, which locks are held, and which processes are running.

3. So, to see whether any locks exist on a database, open the Locks/Object folder. In Figure 8.2, you can see that a lock is held on the SQLSpyNet database.

4. Double-click the SQLSpyNet icon in the Locks folder to see which user is holding the lock.

When you look at locks held on database objects, users in the system are represented by the ProcessID (or SPID). This is a dynamically assigned value by SQL Server 2000 that can represent the current user's process.

See, even SQL Server 2000 uses primary keys internally!

How do we go from Username to SPID? Every task that is being run on the server is held in an internal table called *sysprocesses*. This table contains the SPID, and the LoginName (among many other things). This can tell us which user is running what process on the server.

Figure 8.2

SQL Server 2000 showing that a lock is held against the SQLSpyNet database.

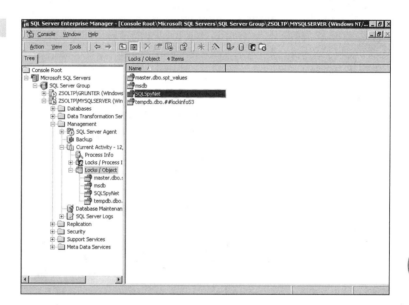

SQL Server 2000's built-in locking management normally takes care of most of the locks required on a resource. SQL Server 2000 decides whether it needs to take a granular lock or a more fine-grained lock, based on the query and the underlying schema.

Although this is the default behavior of SQL Server 2000, we can take control and force locking to happen the way we want it to happen.

EXCURSION

Forcing SQL Server 2000 to Lock the Door (Oops, Table) When We Want To

 To do this, we need to use the locking hints in our Transact-SQL statements. *Locking hints* allow us to specify the type of lock that SQL Server 2000 uses. This forces the query optimizer to use the lock that we specify for the SELECT statement that we are executing. Several other hints types are available, including table, view, and join hints.

For example, in the following code line we use an exclusive lock on the Person table, forcing SQL Server to use an Exclusive lock when retrieving rows:

```
1: SELECT Firstname FROM Person WITH (TABLOCKX)
```

This forces SQL Server 2000 to use a lock it would not normally use when performing a SELECT.

By the way, it is not recommended that you use an exclusive lock for selecting data!

A lock on information is basically a hold over a piece of information for a given period of time. An example from our application might be if you need James Bondie's file from the filing cabinet. While you have that file in your possession, you can read and update the file, but no one else can. You have exclusive control over the file. However, after it is placed back in the filing cabinet, your lock on the file is released and anybody else can read or modify the file.

Locking works in a similar way in SQL Server 2000. After a user has a piece of information, no one else can do anything with that piece of information until she has finished, though we do have control over this behavior.

Several degrees of locking exist, from very low-level row/column locking to high-level table locking. The various levels of locking affect the performance of our application.

> **Note** Because transactions are resource intensive, locking can be, too. Poor locking design can effectively stop an application! Accidentally locking a resource and not freeing that resource up after you're finished with it can cause other users to be locked out, preventing them from continuing with their daily tasks.

Developing a Locking Strategy

If you want your application to scale, you'll need an effective locking strategy in place. Then, you can confidently allow more users to access your application without impeding performance too heavily. So, it pays to think ahead a little, especially when designing for a large-scale application.

Dealing with Data Concurrency Problems

When you have more than one user accessing data at once, you have the potential for *data concurrency* problems. These are grouped into four main categories:

- Lost update problem—Two people make changes to a spy's details in the Spy table. The change made by the first person is lost.

- Dirty read (uncommitted dependency problem)—One person makes a change to a spy's data. Then, a second person reads an uncommitted change, and the first person realizes an error has occurred and rolls back the changes. The second person does not realize that the changes have been rolled back and bases their decision on the uncommitted changes.

- Non-repeatable read (inconsistent analysis problem)—The first person reads a spy's information twice, but between readings, a second person updates the spy's information, which causes it to completely change.

- Phantom (phantom read problem)—One person reads and updates the spy's data. Then, a second person takes the spy's data and integrates changes into the application, but on doing so, she finds that unexpected changes have been made by a third person.

So, how do we prevent each of these issues? The very best way is to implement locking that does not allow another user to either read or update the information until it has been completely finished with by the first user.

Sounds obvious you say? Ahh, but it is not always possible to prevent other users from having a resource. After all, they still need to continue with their jobs as well.

Matching the Lock to the Problem

What do we do then? This is where we specify the type of locking we will use. For example

- Lost update problem—Do not allow another user to make changes until the first user has committed his changes. This does not prevent her from reading the data, but she cannot perform updates.

- Dirty read— In this scenario, we need to ensure that no users read the data while the updates are being performed. To do this, we use an exclusive lock (the file scenario discussed earlier is an exclusive lock) on the resources we need.

- Non-repeatable read—Similar to the dirty read issue, we must ensure that no one can read the changes until they have been committed.

- Phantom read— In this scenario, we must prevent users from accessing the data until the first and third users have totally finished with the data.

You can see we face several issues with a multiuser environment, but we also have a lot of flexibility with the way we can structure and implement the locking of our records. So, what are these?

8

Selecting Levels of Locking

When we refer to the levels of locking, we are actually using what is known as the *granularity* of locking.

Granularity refers to how fine you want a lock to be. For example, do you want to lock the whole table (a coarse-grain lock), or do you want to lock only a specific row (a fine-grain lock)?

You face certain issues with the depth of your locks. With a very fine-grain lock, you acquire a lot of resources to manage the lock but ensure data consistency. With a coarse-grain lock, you use fewer resources but increase the risk of data inconsistency, and might even prevent other users from performing their tasks. Usually, SQL Server 2000 takes care of locking for you, though.

SQL Server 2000 uses dynamic locking to decide the most cost-effective locks for transactions. Depending on the query and the underlying schema, SQL Server 2000 chooses the level of locking it requires to perform the requested task.

But what about when you want to specifically set the level of locking? Normally, you don't need to do this for an application that has only a few users, but sometimes you might find that locks are not being released on resources as quickly as you might like. If that happens, you can specify the granularity lock for what you require.

You can place locks on the following resources (from fine-grain to coarse-grain):

- Row identifier—This enables you to lock an individual row in a table. It's the finest-grain lock you can acquire.

- Key—With this, you can obtain a row lock within an index.

- Page—This enables you to obtain a lock on the underlying data page of the table or index. This is finer than a table lock because a table can contain (and most often does) more than one page.

- Extent—This enables you to obtain a lock on a group of eight side-by-side data pages.

- Table—With this, you can obtain a lock on the table, including all data and the indexes for the table.

- Database—A lock can be obtained on the whole database! This, as you can imagine, is the coarsest-grain lock available!

Within each of these resources, you can set the *mode* of locking you want to perform on the resource. SQL Server 2000 has six basic locking modes:

- Shared lock—This is the most general lock and allows all users to read data. However, no updates to the data can be performed until the lock is released. The lock is released when the data has been read.

- Update lock—This lock mode helps prevent deadlocking (see "Avoiding Deadlocks" in the excursion a little later on) from occurring. Only one transaction at a time can hold an update lock on a resource. If the transaction tries to modify the resource (using DELETE and so on), the lock is switched to an exclusive lock; otherwise, it is switched to a shared lock.

- Exclusive lock—This prevents all other users from updating or even reading data from the resource. It is one of the coarsest-grain locks SQL Server 2000 offers.

- Intent lock—This lock actually locks the resource below with either a shared lock or an exclusive lock. So, when you place an intent exclusive lock on a table, this actually places an exclusive lock on the pages the table contains and prevents any other transactions from acquiring a lock on that resource. Why use this? Internally, it is more efficient for SQL Server 2000 because it needs to check locks at only the table level to see whether any other transactions can gain locks on the table, rather than having to check every row or page.

- Schema lock—Two types of schema locks exist: shared and exclusive. Beginning to see a pattern yet? An exclusive schema lock is used when adding a new column to a table, for example. A schema shared lock, on the other hand, is used when compiling a query. This allows other transactions to run but prevents changes to the database schema from being performed.

- Bulk update lock—This is used when you bulk copy data into a table. This lock prevents other transactions (non-bulk copying) from altering or reading the data from the table.

As you can see, you have a large amount of flexibility over the way SQL Server 2000 handles your transactions and locking, but there is one more thing that can bite you! It's called a deadlock, and you must make sure you try to prevent this. So read on....

8

EXCURSION

Avoiding Deadlocks

This is probably one of the worst fears that DBAs have. It's a special situation that not only occurs in SQL Server 2000 but also can occur within many other Windows applications.

So, what is this oh-so-scary deadlock? A *deadlock* (or *deadly embrace*) occurs when one user has a resource locked and requires a lock on a second resource. Unfortunately, the second resource he requires is actually locked by another user who, like the first user, requires a lock on the first resource.

The first user cannot obtain a lock on the second resource and will not let go of the first until he gets it, and the second user has the second resource locked and will not let go until she gets the lock on the first resource. Not a nice situation!

One way to think about a deadlock is to imagine a couple of kids fighting over toys: One has a truck and the other a grader, and neither will give up until he gets the other toy as well as his own. You begin to get the idea of how problematic a deadlock can be on a database.

Luckily for us, SQL Server 2000's internal management uses an algorithm to spot deadlocks. If it finds a deadlock, SQL Server 2000 finishes one user's transaction (usually by a rollback) so the other user's transaction can complete.

However, although SQL Server 2000 manages most deadlocks for you, you still need to be careful when designing the locking of your rows for users.

Locking Considerations

Similar to transactions, you need to be a little careful when designing your locking strategies. Just using one type of lock (fine-grain) for all your transactions might be fine for a couple of users, but when you scale up your application, you might find that your server's performance becomes less than optimal. So, keep in mind the following concepts when designing your locks:

- Follow the transaction guidelines!
- Stress-test the application! This is the process of performing the same actions with the number of users you expect your application can have.
- Allow your users to terminate long running queries. For example, if a search brings back 2 million records, this can take a while. Therefore, you should allow the user to cancel the query.
- Prevent user input during queries to reduce the time they take to run. While a query is running, it is holding a lock of some sort on a resource.

Although you can alter the locking of your queries and objects, for now let SQL Server 2000 manage the locking of your application. In the future, this might need to be revisited, but let's cross one bridge at a time.

Handling Errors So Our Application Doesn't Break

Sometimes things break. No matter how careful you are as a programmer, you cannot guarantee that someone is going to use your application in the way you intended it to be used.

This can cause some unexpected actions to occur. In the worst-case scenario, the error goes undetected and the update/delete/insert performs successfully, resulting in invalid data in the database. Or, the application might crash and leave it in a state that has the user screaming and abusing you. Believe me; let's not go there!

So what do you do? Well, SQL Server 2000 has some very good error-handling capabilities you can use to

- Determine whether an error has occurred
- Decide on a course of action
- Either recover from or blow away the changes
- Inform the user that something bad has happened

With SQL Server 2000, you can even define your own custom error messages to let the user know what is going on. But first, let's start with how to catch an error.

What Is an Error Composed of in SQL Server 2000?

In the next section, we take a look at implementing error handling in stored procedures, but first let's take a look at what happens if you try to enter a bad guy without there being a corresponding Person record in the Person table.

As you know by now, you cannot have a child record without having a parent record. If we enter the code in Listing 8.2, SQL Server 2000 will fail the insert because the Person record does not exist.

Listing 8.2—Trying to Insert a Bad Guy into the BadGuy Table Without a Corresponding Person Record

```
1: INSERT INTO BadGuy (PersonID, KnownAs, IsActive)
2: VALUES (10000, 'A real bad dude', 1)
```

SQL Server 2000 fails this insert because a Person does not exist for the record, but just take a look at the error message it returns (see Figure 8.3)!

Figure 8.3

SQL Server 2000 failing our insert and displaying a system error message.

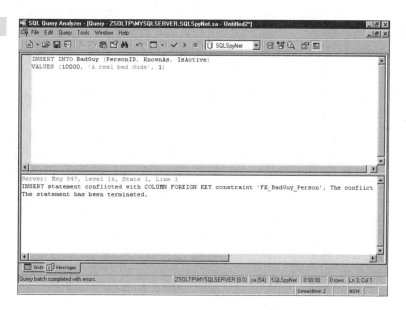

Most users would not understand the error being returned. It would only confuse and frustrate them. Therefore, you need to implement error handling to prevent this from happening.

SQL Server 2000, like Visual Basic and other programming languages, has a very rich error object. It has several attributes you can use and manipulate to provide the best options for your users:

- Error number—This is the number of the error and what populates the value of the @@ERROR function (see "Catching an Error," later in this chapter). These numbers are all unique for each error.

- Error description or error message string—This is the informative message that comes back with each message. SQL Server 2000 can substitute certain values in the string to make the messages more informative—for instance, Update on *tablename* failed. Every time this message is called, the *tablename* attribute is swapped for the actual name of the table. Each description is unique for each error.

- Severity—This indicates how severe the error is. Low numbers (2 or below) are low-level informative errors or warnings, whereas higher numbers are errors that will prevent the task from occurring.

- State code—This is used when a given error is called from many places within the source code of SQL Server 2000. A unique state code is assigned to the error message every time the error is called and allows a Microsoft SQL Server Engineer to help diagnose the problem.

- Procedure name—This is populated if the error occurs within a stored procedure.

- Line number—This indicates the line number on which the error occurred for a stored procedure.

SQL Server 2000 stores all its error messages within the Master database, in a special system table called *sysmessages*.

All the interfaces (ODBC, ADO, and so on) that talk to SQL Server 2000 have the capability to report on the basic error attributes (number and description), but they vary when it comes to reporting on the more detailed error attributes.

That is how an error is defined in SQL Server 2000, but how do you catch one?

Catching an Error

SQL Server 2000 enables us to check whether an error has occurred with the `@@ERROR` function. This function returns an integer. If the value returned is a zero (`0`) then all is well. But if the value is something other than zero, you know an error has occurred and you need to decide what you to do.

 Warning

> You must be careful when checking the value of `@@ERROR`. Every time a new Transact-SQL statement is fired, the value of `@@ERROR` is cleared. So, you need to either check the value immediately or assign the value to a local variable for use later.

So, how do you use the `@@ERROR` statement? You use the `IF` statement you learned about in Chapter 4, "Manipulating Data with Transact-SQL." The following is an example:

```
1: IF @@ERROR <> 0
2:     BEGIN
3:     --Perform some action
4: END
```

In this example, we initially check to see whether the value of `@@ERROR` is not equal to zero. If this is true, we perform whatever action we deem appropriate.

Imagine we are updating the data in a table. If we wrap the update in a transaction and find there is an error, we can roll back the transaction and notify the user that an error has occurred. This goes a long way in helping us build a robust and stable application.

We can also check for the existence of a specific error. Imagine you are updating the Spy table but no `PersonID` exists for the spy you are trying to insert, as in our previous example. You can use the `@@ERROR` function to check for the specific error number 547, which is a foreign key constraint error. From this, we can return a custom message to our user, saying that she must first enter the details into the Person table before the Spy table.

Making Errors Work for You

You've caught the error, but what do you do now? Panic! No seriously; when you have caught the error, you can perform several actions:

- Fail the task(s)—When your task(s) raises an error you can trap, the first priority should be to undo any changes that have occurred within our Transact-SQL statements so far. This ensures that your data remains consistent. Remember the rules!

8

- Exit immediately or try to continue execution—When you trap an error, you can either exit the Transact-SQL statement immediately or continue with execution. If the error is only a low-level warning or does not affect performance, it might be okay to continue; otherwise, you should get out of there.

- Give the user a message that explains the error—Although returning the SQL Server 2000 internal error message might mean something to a developer or DBA, it normally is of little use to the user, so you should display an informative error message for the user's benefit.

So, let's take a look at modifying the stored procedures we wrote in Chapter 5, "Viewing Data and Automating Updates with DDL," to implement some error handling.

Changing Our Stored Procedure to Implement Error Trapping

We wrote two stored procedures in Chapter 5 that use the INSERT statement to make entry of a Person and either her Spy or BadGuy details easier.

As our stored procedures currently are, we can actually end up inserting partial data rather than ensuring total execution happens. So, if we fire the stored procedure and the first INSERT is successful, we have a Person record as expected. However, if the second statement fails we end up with an orphaned Person record because no corresponding Spy or BadGuy record will exist. Worse still, if the user fires the stored procedure again, we end up with the same Person details and still no Spy or BadGuy record!

 I will step through the changes required to the stored procedures, but I will show you only how to implement those changes in the PersonBadGuyInsert stored procedure and leave the alteration to the PersonSpyInsert stored procedure up to you.

To begin, fire up Query Analyzer and select the SQLSpyNet database. Enter the code in Listing 8.3 into the window.

Listing 8.3—Altering Our PersonBadGuyInsert Stored Procedure So We Can Implement Error Handling

```
1: ALTER PROCEDURE PersonBadGuyInsert
2:    @Firstname VARCHAR(50),
3:    @Surname VARCHAR (50),
4:    @DOB DATETIME = NULL,
5:    @KnownAs VARCHAR(25) = NULL,
6:    @IsActive BIT = 1
7: AS
8:    DECLARE @LocalError INT
```

```
 9:    BEGIN TRANSACTION
10:      INSERT INTO Person (Firstname, Surname, DOB)
11:      VALUES (@Firstname, @Surname, @DOB)
12:     SET @LocalError = @@ERROR
13:     DECLARE @PersonID INT
14:     SET @PersonID = IDENT_CURRENT('Person')
15:     INSERT INTO BadGuy (PersonID, KnownAs, IsActive)
16:     VALUES (@PersonID, @KnownAs, @IsActive)
17:     SET @LocalError = @LocalError + @@ERROR
18:     IF @LocalError = 0
19:         BEGIN
20:             COMMIT TRANSACTION
21:             PRINT 'You have successfully added a new Person
                ➥and their Bad guy details'
22:         END
23:     ELSE
24:         BEGIN
25:             IF @LocalError = 547
26:                 BEGIN
27:                     ROLLBACK TRANSACTION
28:                     PRINT 'Oops. You must add a Person before
                        ➥you add a Bad guy!'
29:                 END
30:             ELSE
31:                 BEGIN
32:                     ROLLBACK TRANSACTION
33:                     PRINT 'Oops an error occurred please try again!'
34:                 END
35:         END
```

Analysis

The lines to notice are

- Line 8, where we declare a local variable to hold the @@ERROR value after each of our statements is executed.

- Line 9, which begins a transaction so we can roll back and keep our data consistent if an error occurs.

- Line 12, where we actually assign the value of the @@ERROR function to our variable. If an error has occurred then our @LocalError variable holds the error number; otherwise, it is assigned a zero.

- Line 17, which is slightly different from line 12. Here, we actually assign our @LocalError variable the value it currently contains, *plus* the value of the @@ERROR value. This persists the value throughout the scope of the procedure.

- Lines 18–35 are our error trapping procedures. If our variable has a value of zero then everything is fine and we commit our transaction. Otherwise, we return a custom message to the user depending on the value in our variable. Cool, huh?

Note If you want to return the SQL Server 2000 description of the error, you can access the error messages through the sysmessages table in the Master database. With this, you can retrieve the description of the error from the table with a simple SELECT statement using the @@ERROR as the WHERE criteria.

For example

```
1: SELECT * FROM master.dbo.sysmessages WHERE error = @@ERROR
```

You might have noticed a couple of things with the error trapping we have implemented here.

First, if the first Transact-SQL statement generates an error, we potentially can have a value of 547 (or some other value) in our @LocalError variable. However, if the next statement fails and gives us the same error number, our @LocalError variable could contain a value of 1094!

When we try to check against the sysmessages table, we either get an error message that does not relate to the error or get back no message whatsoever.

Second, this error trapping is based on continuous execution. If the first statement fails, we do not exit straight away but try to fire the second statement instead. We can alter this at a later stage if we believe the transaction holds the resources up for too long, but for now, this will do.

Go ahead and add your error trapping to the second stored procedure; just remember to change the message you return back to your user.

Summary

So, what have we done in this chapter? This chapter has enabled us to explore the ways in which we can ensure our data remains in a consistent state by

- Wrapping our changes in transactions
- Implementing locking to prevent inconsistencies in data updates
- Implementing some basic error trapping in our two stored procedures to enable us to undo any changes without impacting on our users

Next Steps

In the next chapter, we look at security in our application. This includes creating a new user and examining the roles SQL Server 2000 provides. We will assign our new user permissions based on what we believe they should be able to do.

8

Chapter 9

Implementing Security in Spy Net

Our application is really rockin' now! We actually have an application that enables us to begin sending our spies on assignments. But because we are running an application that has the potential to cost people their lives, we really should start to think about security within our application. After all, we do not want anybody getting in there and causing malicious damage now, do we?

Fortunately, SQL Server 2000 has a very good security model that allows us to specify our security all the way from restricting database/server access right down to restricting access to a column in a table. Talk about thorough!

Why would we want to have so much control over our application? That question really depends on the type of access we want our users to have. Confident users who really understand the application can require (and be able to handle) more access to get their jobs done than a user who doesn't really understand the application.

Not only do we need to understand and design our application well, but we also need to fully understand and appreciate our user's needs. This enables us to ensure that our system will meet their requirements.

Our users will need to access the data within our tables, but they shouldn't be allowed to alter the structure of either our database or the objects that the database contains. We should also try to stop users from unnecessarily accessing other databases on our server, such as master, tempdb, and model.

In the next few sections we will look at a typical user, some security and auditing approaches, and how to give rights and roles to our users. So let's get going then!

Sharing Spy Net with Other Users

By default there is only one user in our database when it is first created. This is the default user sa. As you have discovered, there is no restriction on the sa account.

 Note

You may have more than one user within your instance of SQL Server 2000 depending on the type of operating system you have. For example, if you are running a Windows 2000 or NT machine, you will have the default BUILTIN\Administrator group account on your server.

Our sa account is configured as the dbo, or *database owner*.

 Database owner means that this user has the ability to attach, configure, create, and drop databases as he or she wants. In other words, the dbo is an owner so he has full control of the database. Although this is great for us, we do not want to give all our users the ability to drop our database! After all, I do not want to have to build everything from scratch again.

How do we protect users from themselves? For each user that we want to have in our database we create an account and assign them different permissions, which means just what you'd think: access granted or denied. These permissions can be server-, database-, or object-related within our instance of SQL Server 2000. If you have had much to do with NT before, you will be well equipped to deal with the concept of security in SQL Server 2000. If not, don't panic! You will get there and I am sure you will excel as usual.

Before we create our first user, we need to discuss the concept of logins.

 A *login* is an account that is used to establish a connection to the instance of SQL Server 2000 that contains our SQLSpyNet database. Because we have been using the special sa account (installed by default) we have not had to create a login account before.

When our users try to establish a connection to SQL Server 2000 they need to have a login so that SQL Server 2000 can authenticate their details. One of the properties of a login is the databases that the user can access. SQL Server 2000 uses the details users provide to allow them access.

SQL Server 2000 supports two types of authentication: Windows Authentication Mode and Mixed Mode (Windows Authentication and SQL Server Authentication). Because we are operating on a Windows 98 system, which is not network connected, we cannot take advantage of Windows Authentication. We will look at these terms and what they mean later in the chapter in the "Creating Logins to Spy Net" section. However, as mentioned, Windows Authentication is not supported in Windows 98, so we need to use SQL Server Authentication.

Creating Logins to Spy Net

SQL Server Authentication allows us to create users and logins of our own, perfect when you are not running on a Windows 2000 or NT machine. We can reset passwords and manage the users independently of the operating system. Most developers prefer this type of security because it is very simple to create a new user and grant them access, but Microsoft recommends using NT authentication when you have that option. Let's have a go now and create a login (SQL Server Authentication) for our SQL Server.

1. Open Enterprise Manager and navigate to the Security folder. Within this folder are four options (Logins, Server Roles, Linked Servers, and Remote Servers).

2. We'll use the Logins option. Right-click the Logins option and select New Login. This will give you a dialog box similar to that shown in Figure 9.1.

Figure 9.1

The dialog box for creating a new login for SQL Server 2000.

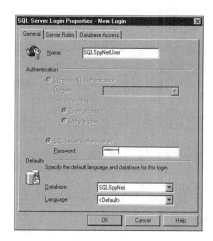

9

Because we've installed SQL Server 2000 on Windows 98, the Windows NT Authentication option is grayed out with the SQL Server Authentication option selected. But let's take a look at the types of SQL Server 2000 logins that we can have.

If you click the Logins option under the Security folder, you will see all the current logins defined in your server. For most of us only one login is defined so far. However, if you are running NT 4.0 or Windows 2000 you will see a second login defined for the database. This is the special BUILTIN\Administrator account. This account is used to allow local administrators on the machine to connect as SQL Server 2000 dbos by using Windows NT Authentication.

- Windows NT Authentication—This enables users to connect to SQL Server 2000 without having to supply their login credentials manually. The login is authenticated using the user's NT user account. It must contain the domain information as well as the username, for example DISNEYLAND\Mickey. Unfortunately, this is not available on a Windows 98 PC that is not connected to an NT network. When a user connects with NT security, he does not have to provide his password. This saves users the trouble of entering their login information every time they connect to SQL Server 2000. With Windows Authentication we get a few more features than we do with SQL Server Authentication, such as password expiration, encrypted passwords, and lockout capabilities.

- SQL Security Authentication—This is the login type that we need to create. This is an internal login that SQL Server 2000 uses to establish security information. The sa account we are using is based on SQL Security Authentication. When users connect to the server they must supply their username *and* their password.

Remember that when you first installed SQL Server 2000 you had the option of setting the authentication mode, either Windows Authentication or Mixed Mode. If you only wanted your users to connect by using their NT user accounts, you would have selected the Windows Authentication mode option. But because we are not on an NT domain we cannot take advantage of this.

3. Click the General tab to give our login some details, like a name. You can enter something like SQLSpyNetUser. This defines that we are creating a user for the SQL Spy Net application. You can name the login anything that you want, but it is always a good idea to name it something relevant.

4. The next item on the screen is setting the password for the user. As the sa you can assign and change the login's password at any time. The user can also change their password to something relevant to them. So we will initially set the password to something the user will remember, for example, Password.

Tip You can assign a login a blank password, but this is not recommended because it will allow anyone to log in using the sa account. Also, you cannot force users to change their passwords when logging in, unlike in Windows NT where an administrator can force a password change when the user first logs in.

5. Next we can specify the default database that the user has. When the user logs in to Query Analyzer (for example) the default chosen database is the one specified in the list. Choose the SQLSpyNet database from the list.

6. Next we set the default language for the login. This setting affects how the server displays certain information for the login. For example, if you choose British English then dates would be in the format dd/mm/yy.

7. Click the Database tab and you'll see a screen as shown in Figure 9.2.

Note If you click OK on the General tab without going through the other tabs, SQL Server 2000 will ask you to first confirm the password for the user. It then will return a warning saying that the login you just created does not have access to the default database.

8. Select the SQLSpyNet database from the list, and you will then be able to assign a role to the user. For now, let the role default to public.

   We'll go through the permissions associated with the public role in the next section.

9. Click OK. SQL Server 2000 will now create the login for us. You will be able to see the login in Enterprise Manager window.

10. To check (which is very good practice) that our login (and user) have been created successfully, go to the Users folder within the SQLSpyNet database, as shown in Figure 9.3.

Figure 9.2

The dialog box for granting access to the databases within our instance of SQL Server 2000.

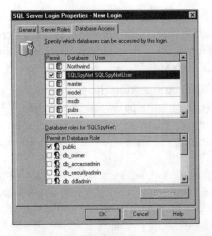

Figure 9.3

Enterprise Manager displaying our newly created login for the SQLSpyNet database.

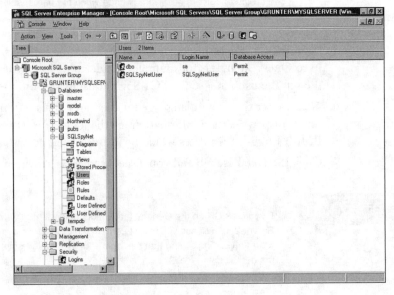

And there we have it! You have now successfully created your very first login for our application. Very cool!

Logging In as SQLSpyNetUser to Test Permissions

When we created this user we gave them a default role of public. This means that the user will have all the permissions and access that the public role has. And by default, in SQL Server 2000, this is very limited!

Currently one of the only things that this user can accomplish is to establish a connection to SQL Server 2000, and the only database they will be able to connect to is SQLSpyNet.

So let's give it a try then! Start Query Analyzer from the Start menu. SQL Server 2000 will prompt you for your login information, as shown in Figure 9.4. Enter the SQLSpyNetUser and the password for the account in the dialog window, and then click OK.

Figure 9.4

Query Analyzer prompting for the login information.

This will log you in to the application as SQLSpyNetUser. We will now try to look at some of the data in one of our tables. Enter the code in Listing 9.1 into the Query Analyzer window.

Listing 9.1—Checking the Permissions of Our SQLSpyNetUser

```
1: SELECT PersonID, Firstname, Surname FROM Person
```

SQL Server 2000 will return an error stating that the user does not have permission to even see the data in the table! This also means that they cannot UPDATE, INSERT, or DELETE data from any of the tables.

We now need to assess the permissions that our user will require.

Assigning Roles for Our Users

Before we give our users any access to our application, we need to consider the roles that we want our users to have.

EXCURSION

One Year "Roles" into the Next

So what is a role? Supposedly, roles came about in SQL Server 2000 when the Windows team suggested that they would change the name of the NT *groups* to *roles*. The SQL Server team thought they would be proactive and changed the name to agree with the changes that the Windows team was going to implement, but alas Windows 2000 was released with groups instead of roles. Aww well guys, there is always next year!

A role is similar in concept to the idea of a group in NT. We can assign permissions to either a role or an individual user. If we assign permissions to a role, then every user that we add to that role will *inherit* the permissions from the role.

 Inherit is the capability of an object (in this case a user) to derive all the attributes from another object (in this case a role).

By default, SQL Server 2000 has 10 basic database roles defined. These roles all allow for different levels of access to the database.

There is one very special role, however: the Public role. Every single user who is defined within the database belongs to the Public role. The Public role has almost no permissions except the very basic ones that allow a user to make a connection to the database and so forth. This role has some basic rules around it.

- It is contained within every database.
- It cannot be dropped.
- Every user belongs to the Public role, including the sa account.
- Because every user belongs to the role by default, you cannot add or remove users from the role.

 The permissions that the Public role has, as mentioned, are very limited. You can alter this, but buyers beware. Because every user belongs to the role, you might accidentally assign too much control to someone who does not know how to use it.

So what sort of permissions does each role have?

- db_owner—This is the most God-like role that a user can have. This role allows a user *complete* control over the database. The sa user is a member of the dbo_owner role, hence the reason the sa account can do anything it wants to the database.
- db_securityadmin— This role allows a user to manage all the roles and members of those roles. This role can also manage assigning permissions to the roles. If we had a user that we trusted to manage the security of our database but didn't need full control, we would assign them this role.
- db_accessadmin—This role is used to give a user the rights to add or remove users within the database. As with our db_securityadmin role, we would normally grant the user this role as well to ensure that they can give users the necessary access they need.

- `db_ddladmin`—This role allows a user to manipulate all the objects within the database. For example, a user can create, modify, or drop the database's objects. This role has permission to run all SQL Server 2000 DDLs.

- `db_backupoperator`— This role allows the users assigned to the role to perform database backups.

- `db_datawriter`—This role allows a user to modify the data in all the user tables defined within the database.

- `db_datareader`—This role allows a user to view the data from all the user tables defined within the database.

- `db_denydatawriter`—This role prevents a user from modifying any of the data in the user tables within the database.

- `db_denydatareader`—This role prevents a user from viewing any of the data in the user tables within the database.

A user can belong to none, one, or many of these roles. If a user belongs to more than one role, the user will have the collective of all the permissions of the roles with respect to the rules of precedence.

For example if our user, `SQLSpyNetUser`, belonged to the `db_datawriter` and the `db_backupoperator` roles, they would be able to not only modify data within a table, but also perform database backups.

However, if our `SQLSpyNetUser` user belonged to the `db_denydatawriter` and the `db_datawriter` roles then our user wouldn't be able to update data within our tables. What? Why? Because denying access to a database is more restrictive than granting access, and denying access has a higher precedence than granting access.

So be careful when assigning roles to your users. You might accidentally restrict users from a table or other database object that they really need access to.

Assigning Roles to the SQL Server Instance

Not only can we assign roles for our users within our SQLSpyNet database, but we can also assign users roles for the whole SQL Server 2000 instance. This allows us greater flexibility in deployment, especially in a large site. This means that we can allow only certain people the rights to, for example, back up our database. With this we can then ensure that no one tries to perform a backup without fully understanding what he or she is doing!

So what are the server roles that SQL Server 2000 has available?

You can view the server roles for your instance of SQL Server 2000 under Security, Server Roles. All the current server roles installed for your instance of SQL Server 2000 will be within the Server Roles folder.

- sysadmin—This role has *full* control over the whole instance of SQL Server 2000. This is the role to which the sa account belongs.
- securityadmin—This role can create and manage logins for the server.
- serveradmin—This role can set the configuration options of the instance of SQL Server 2000. This role also has the ability to shut down the server.
- setupadmin—This role has the ability to manage startup procedures and linked servers.
- processadmin—This role has the ability to manage the processes that SQL Server 2000 has running. This means that this role can issue the KILL command, which finishes a user's session. If the user has any open transactions, their transaction is rolled back before the session is terminated.
- diskadmin—This role can manage the files on disk, for example filegroups (see "Creating the SQL Spy Net Application Database" in Chapter 3) and so on.
- dbcreator—This role can create, alter, and drop databases.

Most of these roles allow members of the role to add other users to the role. For example, if our SQLSpyNetUser belonged to the dbcreator role, he could then add any other users to the role.

But be careful because not all roles allow the addition of new members to the role. For example, the db_datawriter role does not allow users to add new members to the role.

Okay, I know there are some actions that these roles perform that we haven't discussed yet, but hey, we will get there!

What happens when these roles do not really suit our business rules? Let's take a look at some options now.

Creating a Role Model

If I have 10 new users but am not really sure that I want to grant them as much access (or as little) as the built-in server/database roles provide, what can I do?

SQL Server 2000 allows us to create our own roles. If all of our users are to have similar access, the best idea is to create a role, add each user to the role, and then grant and deny the permissions on each object that they will be allowed to perform.

That sounds really cool! The perfect solution for my problem!

However, we currently have only one user. Is it really worth creating a whole role for just one user?

Well luckily for us, SQL Server 2000 allows us to grant/deny permissions on every object within the database to a single user/users. So, for example we might allow our SQLSpyNetUser to alter addresses in the Address table (SELECT, INSERT, UPDATE, and DELETE), but prevent them from altering any of the Spies details.

 Note   This sort of flexibility is available to us within SQL Server 2000 (and in fact all previous versions), but SQL Server 2000 also allows us to prevent our SQLSpyNetUser from viewing the AnnualSalary column in the Spy table! We have that fine of granularity control over the permissions that our users have.

Within the next couple of chapters, however, we are going to create a second user for our SQLSpyNet database. This user will be for our Web front-end that we are going to build.

For us to leverage the best from our application we are now going to create a role for our database and then assign our user accounts to the role. Our role will be assigned basic permissions that allow our users assigned to the role to perform some tasks against our database.

First let's create the database role.

1. In Enterprise Manager, go to the SQLSpyNet database and then navigate your way to the Roles folder.

2. When you are there, right-click and select New Database Role. This will give you a screen similar to that shown in Figure 9.5.

3. Like most database objects, we need to give our role a name with which SQL Server 2000 can use to identify the object. Let's give our new role a name of SQLSpyNetRole. Once again you can name this anything you like, but it is better to use a descriptive name.

4. Select Standard Role for the database role type, but notice that SQL Server offers these two roles:

Figure 9.5

Creating a new role for our SQLSpyNet database.

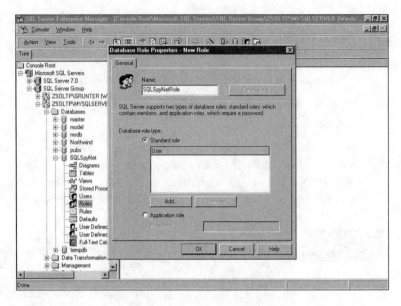

- Standard role—This type of role is generally similar to the groups in Windows NT. This role can contain users, and permissions can be applied. When a user connects (and they are a member of the role) they inherit the permissions of that role (as well as any other permissions the user might have) .

- Application role—These are special roles within SQL Server 2000 because they do not contain any members (or users). In some ways you can think of these special roles as user accounts. Application roles act like users because they require a password to be activated. However, when the role is activated (by supplying a password and using the `sp_setapprole` stored procedure), the connection loses all the permissions that the users, roles, and NT Groups have while the connection is active. It becomes the responsibility of the application to take over the task of user authentication, but because SQL Server 2000 must authenticate the application when it establishes a connection, the application must supply a password.

5. The next thing that we need to do is add our SQLSpyNetUser to the role, so click the Add button and you will see a screen similar to that shown in Figure 9.6.

Figure 9.6

Assigning our SQLSpyNetUser to the SQLSpyNetRole within Enterprise Manager.

6. This screen contains a list of our current users in the database, but because we have only one, this is all that is shown! If you have more than one user, simply click the users you want to add.

And there we have it! Our user is now a member of the SQLSpyNetRole and will inherit all the rights that the role has (which are none at the moment!).

Tip   Do not close the Database Role Properties window just yet! You can launch the Permissions window from this one, and we are going to assign the permissions very soon!

Now let's have a go at granting our `SQLSpyNetRole` some basic permissions within the database. There are two ways to accomplish this task—either through code or through using the graphical tools in Enterprise Manager. This time however we are going to use the graphical tools in Enterprise Manager. I just heard you say, "Whew!"

Deciding Permissions for Specific Tasks

Before we begin granting/denying permissions to our role, shouldn't we have a clear idea of what they (the users who are members of the role) need to do? Yep. You are so right! Our users are general users of the system. They are entitled to view and edit some data, but not all of it.

So what *can* they do?

- Insert, update, and delete addresses
- Insert, update, and delete countries

9

- Insert, update, and delete address types
- Insert and update within the Person table
- Insert and update within the PersonAddress view
- Run our date formatter function

So what *can't* they do?

- View or alter the data in either the Spy or BadGuy tables
- View or alter the data in the ActivityType table
- View or alter the data in the Activity table
- Execute the PersonBadGuyInsert/PersonSpyInsert stored procedures
- View or alter the data in the Activity table
- Alter the data structures in any way
- Create any other database objects
- Perform any sort of administration task

Is there anything else? Well there very well might be. As our application develops further, we can assess the restrictions we have placed on this role, and best of all, we can easily adjust the permissions the role has. But at this point in time I think we have pretty well covered it!

So how do we grant or deny our role (and our users within the role) access?

Granting Specific Permissions

Let's grant our role the access we have just defined.

 Note   If we do not specifically assign rights to any of the other objects within the database to our role (and/or users), they will not be able to use those objects.

1. If you haven't closed the Database Role Properties window, click the Permissions button. If you have to open the window again, double-click the SQLSpyNetRole role in the Roles folder in the database, and then click the Permissions button. This will give you a window similar to that shown in Figure 9.7.

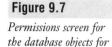

Figure 9.7

Permissions screen for the database objects for our SQLSpyNetRole.

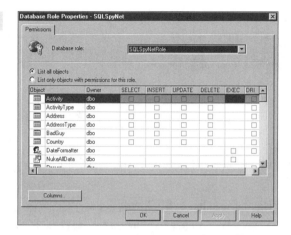

This screen provides a list of database objects and all the permissions that we can assign to our SQLSpyNetRole. As you can see, so far our users have no rights to do anything within our database, except of course connect to it.

> **Tip**
>
> To see what permissions a role (or user) has in the database, select the List Only Objects with Permissions for This Role option.

2. To give our SQLSpyNetRole role the rights that we have decided they can have, click each option, such as SELECT, INSERT, UPDATE, and DELETE from the Address table, as shown in Figure 9.8.

Figure 9.8

Assigning permissions to our SQLSpyNetRole on each database object.

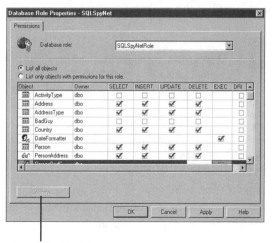

Click a table to enable;
Click here for column permissions

It should be pretty obvious to you by now that SELECT, INSERT, UPDATE, and DELETE are for the permissions options. However, EXEC and DRI might be two terms you are unfamiliar with.

EXEC refers to the ability to execute a stored procedure.

DRI refers to Declarative Referential Integrity, which allows a user to alter the structure of the relationships between the objects in the database.

3. Use the data in Table 9.1 for the permission options you should set for our role.

Table 9.1—The Permissions Granted to SQLSpyNetRole

Object	SELECT	INSERT	UPDATE	DELETE	EXEC	DRI
Address	X	X	X	X		
AddressType	X	X	X	X		
Country	X	X	X	X		
DateFormatter					X	
Person	X	X	X	X		
PersonAddress	X	X	X	X		

4. Click Apply, and our role will now have rights to those objects that we have just assigned.

Notice the Columns button at the lower right of the screen. This allows us to grant SELECT and UPDATE permissions on a specific column within the database, giving us very fine control over what our users can do.

If the Columns button is disabled, click a table in the list, for example the Address table, and the button will then become enabled. Click the button and you will see the columns for the table listed.

Well that's cool! But what other rights can we grant or deny to our users and roles?

Checking Database Permissions

If you stretch your mind back to when we created the SQLSpyNet database in Chapter 3, we looked at several options, and one of these was the Permissions tab. At the time we didn't set any permissions for our users because we didn't have any users!

Now, whenever you have a database with one or more users, you might want to know the various permissions on that database. For example, you might want to know which users are capable of writing to the database or which ones can back up the database.

To find the *database* permissions, follow these steps:

1. Click the SQLSpyNet database within Enterprise Manager.

2. Right-click and select Properties.

3. Click the Permissions tab. This will give you a screen similar to that shown in Figure 9.9.

Figure 9.9

Checking the permissions that SQLSpyNet database offers various users.

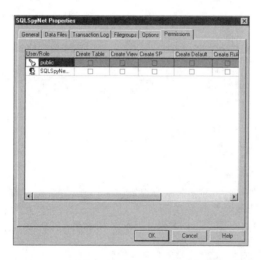

You can see that our SQLSpyNetUser is now in the list. We can assign our user the ability to create database objects such as views, tables, and so on.

We can also give users who are members of certain roles permissions to perform administrative tasks. For our user, do not assign any administrative permissions because we're following the list we created in the "Deciding Permissions for Specific Tasks" section.

At some stage in the future, administrative tasks such as backup and restore can be assigned to a more experienced user when we have expanded our user base. After all, you do not want to be the only one doing the administrative tasks, do you?

Exercising Our Rights

Our user has some rights now. How do we prove it? One of the easiest ways of proving the permissions that our user has is to log in to Query Analyzer as the user. In this way we can impersonate the user and test how the permissions have been assigned.

Fire up Query Analyzer now, and let's get testing! When you have logged in to Query Analyzer as SQLSpyNetUser, we will perform some basic tests to make sure that we can't access anything we shouldn't, and that we can access everything that we should! (If you can't remember the correct procedure, refer to the section "Logging in as SQLSpyNetUser to Test Permissions" when we logged in earlier in the chapter.)

Enter the query in Listing 9.2 into the Query Analyzer window.

Listing 9.2—Checking the Permissions of Our SQLSpyNetUser on the Person Table Now That the User Belongs to the SQLSpyNetRole

 1: SELECT PersonID, Firstname, Surname FROM Person

This should return all the records in the Person table as shown in Figure 9.10.

Figure 9.10

Demonstrating that the SQLSpyNetUser user has correct table permissions.

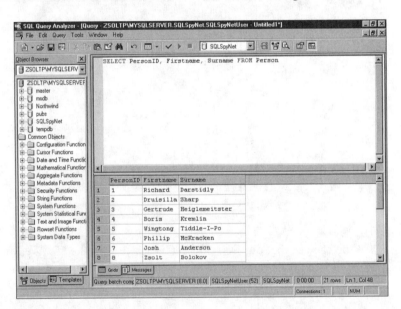

We will now try to perform a similar task on the Spy table. This is a table to which we did not grant permissions to our role. Enter the code in Listing 9.3 into the Query Analyzer window.

Listing 9.3—Checking the Permissions of Our SQLSpyNetUser on the Spy Table Now That the User Belongs to the SQLSpyNetRole

 1: SELECT SpyID, PersonID, SpyNumber, Alias FROM Spy

This will return an error stating that our user does not have permission to perform a SELECT on the table, as shown in Figure 9.11.

Figure 9.11

SQL Server 2000 denying access to our SQLSpyNetUser from viewing the records in the Spy table.

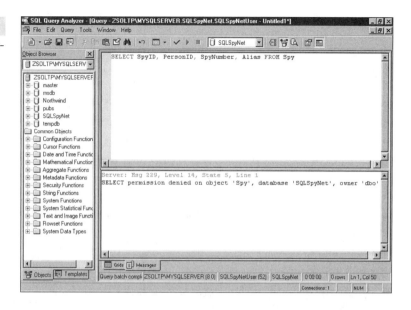

 Note

If you see all the data in the Spy table returned, first check who you are logged in as within Query Analyzer. You can see who you are logged in as by executing this piece of code:

```
SELECT SYSTEM_USER
```

If this is fine, check the permissions by following the earlier steps.

There we have it! We have done a quick check to see that the permissions are assigned correctly. You should go ahead now and check the rest of the objects within the database by performing similar tasks.

Although we can grant and deny access to our users and roles, is there a way to actually watch what they are up to? In a short answer, yes! Let's take a look at auditing.

Auditing: Yes, Big Brother Really Is Watching!

SQL Server 2000 as a total database management system allows us to perform auditing on our instance of SQL Server 2000. This means that we can track activity on the server such as failed login attempts, granted/denied permissions to a user, and backups and restores. Even the process of starting and stopping auditing can be an event record in the audit log!

Why would we want to perform auditing on our instance of SQL Server 2000? Quite simply, to track potential problems, whether these are of a secure nature or just what our users are doing on our system, so we can help with errors.

With a combination of the auditing features of SQL Server 2000 and SQL Profiler we can track a user's activity from the time they log in to the time their connection is terminated.

SQL Server Version 7.0 had auditing capabilities, but they have been updated in SQL Server 2000. If auditing is turned on, the server will behave a little differently from how it would in other circumstances. When auditing is turned on, SQL Server 2000 creates an audit log, which has a default size of 200MBs. It creates this file at startup time, so the server might start up a little slower than normal.

If the file cannot be created because of disk space limitations, SQL Server 2000 will shut down the SQL Service! This is how integral auditing is within SQL Server 2000. Likewise, if for some other reason auditing fails within SQL Server 2000, the SQL Service will be shut down and users will not be able to connect to the server.

Why is there such a tight security model? SQL Server 2000 comes with two auditing models. The first model, Basic Auditing, allows us to capture basic user events; we will discuss this a little more shortly. The second security model, C2 Auditing, is a little more intense, and quite rightly so. Before we get into C2 Auditing let's take a look at Basic Auditing.

Basic Auditing in SQL Server 2000

SQL Server 2000 allows us to capture many events that the users can perform within our database and even within our instance of SQL Server 2000. How do we achieve this? We can use two applications to begin auditing with—SQL Profiler (which we introduced in Chapter 2, "Exploring the Tools of SQL Server 2000") and the built-in auditing tools in Enterprise Manager.

SQL Profiler is a very versatile tool that allows us to capture many events that our users perform on our database. We can tailor the events we capture to a specific user, database object, or database. This allows us to basically track anything that we want! We can also set configuration options within the instance of SQL Server 2000 that you might want to capture auditing information in. We can capture successful logons by our users, unsuccessful logons, or both.

But why would we want to capture all events that a user performs on our database; isn't that a little overboard?

Our data is sensitive! This is especially so in our case. With an ODBC connection it is relatively easy to create a connection to a database. After the connection is made, the user/hacker can try to gain access to the privileged information contained in our tables.

Now what would happen if Dr. Eville managed to get hold of that information? She could effectively shut down our operations and thus leave the world unprotected, and her onslaught to take over the world would go unhindered!

If we have an effective security strategy, we can limit the objects that a user can access, as we have done with the SQLSpyNetUser, but with auditing we can also monitor what our users are up to.

Okay, so what if the basic auditing is not enough for us to see what is going on? What do we do then? Luckily for us, SQL Server 2000 provides the sort of auditing that is required for very sensitive organizations like ours. Let's take a look at the next step in auditing.

Looking at C2 Auditing

C2 Auditing is based on the C2-Level Security issued by the United States Department of Defense. As you can imagine this is pretty heavy stuff! Not only are user connections captured but also *any* security-related actions, such as grant/deny logins, creating new user accounts/roles, and so forth are captured.

Windows 2000 supports C2-Level Security, and more information can be found on the Radium Web site

```
http://www.radium.ncsc.mil/tpep/epl/entries/TTAP-CSC-EPL-00-001.html
```

C2 Auditing is the ability to capture all the events that could compromise security within a computer system. C2-Level Security is a government standard that defines the level of security of your system. This includes such items as the following:

- Restricting or granting access to a database or server to either an individual or a group of users. SQL Server 2000 achieves this through logins and roles.
- You must be able to uniquely identify a user on the system. SQL Server 2000 will not allow you to create two logins with the same name, so at any point you can identify the user within the system.
- Administrators must be the only ones who can grant/deny access to the resources on the instance of SQL Server 2000.

This is not a total list. As you can imagine, the Department of Defense does not take this lightly!

We are not ready to implement auditing at this point in time because our application is not ready for release yet, but as soon as it is, we might need to implement auditing.

In Chapter 14, "Troubleshooting and Debugging in SQL Server 2000," we will take a look at SQL Profiler and how to set up tracing for our application. This will give you a basic start in getting to know SQL Profiler (and some hints on how to get auditing up and running) so that you have the platform on which to build your knowledge!

Considerations for Developing a Security Strategy

Can we really enforce this without a large overhead of maintenance? Here are some things to keep in mind for permissions:

- To help reduce the maintenance that we face in the future, you are better off using roles. After a role is established (remember you can create hundreds of these if you need to), you then only need to add/remove members from the role, thus reducing the overhead of looking after many users.

- SQL Server 2000's security is such an important part of the system that *every* database object is checked prior to execution to see whether the user has permission to use the object. This is even true for the sa account! This approach helps to ensure that the security model is enforced correctly.

- We can grant and deny our users access to objects within the database, but if they have rights to create a view or stored procedure can they create one over a table that they do not have access to? Yes, the user can *create* the object, assuming they have the correct permissions to create database objects. However, when they try to *execute* the stored procedure or view, they will receive an error stating that they do not have permission to access the tables or object that the stored procedure uses.

  Once again we can rest assured that our security model remains in place, even if we have clever users. Why does this happen? Because the database checks permissions on every object that the user accesses, it finds that the tables contained within the stored procedure do not have permission. Pretty cool, huh?

What else do I need to know about auditing? Heaps! The concepts of auditing are simple enough, but there are ramifications of auditing our users' activities, so keep these points in mind:

- First of all, when SQL Server 2000 starts it will try to create an audit log. This file is 200MBs in size—no smaller, no larger. It won't take long before your disk is full, and then SQL Server 2000 will refuse to start because auditing will fail.

  You must ensure that you have a very good plan to archive the audit logs. There is no sense in having them just to fill up disk.

- Second, auditing will have a performance hit. If every event that our users are performing is being captured, the database has to write this to disk, thus slowing performance. This can be really noticeable in a system that supports hundreds of concurrent users. Although basic auditing will have a performance hit, C2 auditing will have a larger performance hit, mainly because of all the security activity being logged as well.

- Finally, why are we logging these events? It would seem a little ridiculous to capture all these events in an audit log if we were never going to use the information.

  If we are auditing our application extensively and have a large user base, this would tend to create many entries in our audit logs. This could then become a full-time job for someone. Sitting in a back room scanning through the logs—boy what a job! Where do I sign up?

Summary

Well, ladies and gentleman, this brings us to the end of yet another chapter. And one step closer to the goal of completing our project, yippee!

We have looked at the types of authentication that SQL Server 2000 provides as well as the different levels of security that we can provide to our users. From there we moved into looking at auditing in our application and what types of capabilities SQL Server 2000 provides us in this area.

Finally, we briefly discussed some of the considerations to keep in mind when designing security for our application. Although security might be one of the last things you implement in your future applications, remember that it *is* important within any application. But it takes a little time to define the security model well. Spend the time and it will make life a lot easier in the future!

9

Next Steps

In the next chapter we are going to take a look at how to ensure our data is available to our users when they need it. We are going to look at some of the more common DBA tasks such as backing up our data and restoring it after a failure. So let's get going!

Chapter 10

Ensuring Data Availability

Once again it is time to change hats! We have been involved in many roles in developing our application. Initially we started out as analysts, and then we moved into a development role. Next we moved to being security specialists, and now we move into the true of world of being a DBA!

I bet you never knew that your pool of skills was so diversified! Wait until you apply for your first database development job. You will be able to fill in many different areas of knowledge.

Let's get back on track. As a DBA we have many tasks to perform to ensure that we meet the objectives stated earlier in the book. So far this book has been project-oriented, but this chapter deals with a DBA subject where we must talk strategy *before* we apply the knowledge to our application.

How do we ensure that our database is available? We cannot guarantee that our database will always be there when need it, but we can ensure that when something does go wrong, we have the ability to bring it back up very quickly.

As DBAs, we have a responsibility to our developers, managers, and clients, ourselves in this case, to ensure that we can safeguard against all types of failures.

How do we achieve this? By creating a good disaster recovery plan and by using the backup and restore operations that SQL Server 2000 has available we can save our database in a consistent state, and then if it all turns to custard, we can restore the database back to the consistent state it was in. The basic elements of a good data availability strategy include

- Planning ahead
- Understanding transaction logs and how to use them to restore data

- Performing database backups
- Restoring data

As a part of the learning process, we'll go through some of the basic ideas behind creating a plan and then show you how to create backups and restore the database.

At the end of this chapter, I give you another checklist to prompt you in designing your own backup plan.

Creating a Database Backup Strategy

Database backups are an integral part of a DBA's job. Without an effective backup strategy, we might find that we are in a situation where we have a corrupt database but no backups current enough to restore from. Part of the strategy is understanding the models available to you, knowing when to run a backup, and knowing where to store your precious files.

With an effective backup strategy we can recover from many failures that occur, including

- Invalid user data, such as running the end of month rollover before the end of the month
- Hard drive failure
- Failure of the server

Although these are not everyday situations, they do happen in the real world, so you must be prepared for the worst.

Backups also provide us with one other feature, free of charge (even better, huh?). With a backup we can create a copy of our database (or any other SQL Server 2000 database), including *all* database objects as well as data, simply and easily. This means that we can migrate our database to a totally different server without building anything at all from scratch.

Warning   With this feature of SQL Server 2000 it is also easy for someone to take a copy of sensitive data and create their own database from it. This is why we restricted the roles of the user in Chapter 9, "Implementing Security in Spy Net." We don't want just anybody getting our data now, do we?

How to Prevent Losing Everything

With an effective backup strategy, as mentioned, we can restore "when good databases go bad!"

How do I know that I have an effective strategy? Don't I really find out when I need to? To a certain degree this is true. You will never really find out how good your strategy is until the time comes, but there is a lot you can do to help ensure that it runs smoothly.

- Back up regularly (this will depend entirely on use).
- Protect your backups by using passwords, holding them in a fireproof safe, and so on.
- Have *full* database backups held off site.
- Perform consistency checks regularly.
- Manage your backups effectively.
- Plan for the worst!

This is by no means a definitive list. Having a truly effective backup strategy requires consultation among many groups. In fact, everybody who has a dependency of some sort (such as all stake holders) on the data needs to have their input. We can then assess their needs and build them into our strategy. Luckily for us, we only have ourselves to worry about!

Using Transaction Logs in Backup and Recovery

A transaction log is internally used by SQL Server to keep track of updates, inserts, and deletes that occur within your (or other) databases. SQL Server has one transaction log per database by default (but there can be more if you require).

A transaction log is an extremely important concept to SQL Server 2000. Because it keeps a record of the *changes* to the data within a database, you can use them (along with a full backup) to restore a database back to consistent state.

| Tip | Because transaction logs grow with time, you must maintain them. Chapter 14, "Troubleshooting and Debugging in SQL Server 2000," gives you some tips for keeping the logs in check to avoid letting them take up all your available disk space. |

EXCURSION

Logs, Logs, and More Logs

By now you may be wondering about all the different types of logs that SQL Server 2000 has.

We looked at audit logs in the second half of Chapter 9. This type of log is used to capture what users are doing within your instance of SQL Server 2000 and normally are related to security monitoring. For example, when a user (an administrator) adds another user to a database role, reconfigures the server, or stops and starts the SQL Service, these actions are written into the audit log.

In Chapter 11 we will take a look at the activity log. This log is similar to Windows NT/2000's internal logs. The activity log keeps track of the actions that occur within your instance of SQL Server. For example, when the SQL Service starts it is recorded in the log; similarly, when an error occurs, it is also recorded in the activity log.

In this chapter, however, we are looking at transaction logs. These logs keep track of all the data changes that have occurred within your database. For example, when Sally updates Richard Darstidly's address, the **UPDATE** statement is recorded within the transaction log.

The benefit of recording the logs means that we can back up the transaction logs, and when the database fails (as it will at some point in its life), we can restore the entire database, and then apply the transaction logs, one at a time, and in order to ensure that our data is as up-to-date as possible.

Choosing the Appropriate Recovery Model

By now it should be obvious why we perform backups, but what types of backups do we perform? SQL Server 2000 supports three recovery models.

Note

When I use the term *log* I am actually referring to the Transaction log, which holds all the transactions and the modifications those transactions make within our database.

- Full—This is by far the most complete of the three recovery models. If a hard drive fails, it allows you to recover to when the failure occurred or to any given point in time. To allow this to happen, all operations are logged. Because everything is logged, bulk operations will cause the log to grow extensively.

  Point-in-time recovery enables us to recover our database to any given point. This is a very powerful feature when we have a production database that must have data availability 24/7. It enables us to ensure that we lose as few database changes as physically possible.

Point-in-failure recovery enables us to recover to the point where the failure occurred, as long as the transaction log is present and undamaged.

- Bulk-logged—This is a complete database backup, but the transactions in the log for bulk operations are minimal so the logs are not filled as quickly as they are for a Full backup. However, if your hard drive fails, you can recover with the Bulk-logged model, but it does not give you point-in-time recovery.

- Simple—This is the easiest of all the backup options. It takes the least space on disk (log size is smaller) and is the least resource intensive, but it exposes you to higher data loss capabilities. This model does not allow us to recover to a point in time or even to the point of failure. This is the current model of SQLSpyNet.

All these models have pros and cons. Which is best? That depends on your individual requirements. A database that has many transactions and needs to be fully recoverable at the drop of a hat would benefit from the Full model. A database that has had many large bulk inserts, such as SELECT INTO, and does not need to recover individual user transactions, would benefit most likely from the Bulk-logged model.

The Simple model is really for non-critical systems, such as applications in the middle of development. Because you cannot recover from the point of failure, you will need to restore the database from the most recent backup and have the users re-enter their transactions. This is the type of model we are using while we are currently developing SQLSpyNet. When we go live it would be better to switch to the Full model, or at the very least the Bulk-Logged model.

Don't worry, I will tell you how to switch models shortly.

Checking the Recovery Level of Spy Net

The recovery level of the database is set when the database is created and is based on the model that is set in the model database, just as many other configuration options are. We covered the model database when we first created our database; see Chapter 3, "Making Virtual Spies—Creating Spy Net in SQL Server 2000," for more information.

You can find what recovery model our database is using by executing DATABASEPROPERTYEX, shown in Listing 10.1. This is a new built-in function to SQL Server 2000 that returns all sorts of useful information about your database. You can find out more about this function in Books Online.

10

Listing 10.1—Looking Up a Recovery Model

```
1: SELECT DATABASEPROPERTYEX('SQLSpyNet', 'RECOVERY')
```

Switching Recovery Models

You can switch from one recovery model to another, but there are some things you should do before and after doing this, such as the following:

- Full to Bulk-logged—Requires no change in your backup procedures.
- Full to Simple—You should back up the log immediately before changing. This ensures that you can recover to that point. When switched over, discontinue backing up the log.
- Bulk-logged to Full—If point-in-time recovery is required, you should execute a log backup immediately.
- Bulk-logged to Simple—You should take the same actions as Full to Simple.
- Simple to Full—You should execute a database backup immediately after switching; from then on continue backing up your database and log regularly.
- Simple to Bulk-logged—Take the same actions as Simple to Full.

Most of the time though, after your database recovery model is set, you will not need to change it often. An exception would be with a Full model if you find that the logs are becoming too large in size, or the performance of your database is being affected by logging all the transactions.

To change the recovery model we use, you must issue an ALTER DATABASE statement, similar to that shown in Listing 10.2.

Listing 10.2—Changing a Recovery Model

```
1: ALTER DATABASE SQLSPyNet SET RECOVERY FULL
```

This will set the recovery model for our SQLSpyNet database to Full.

Finding the (Right) Time

Well this is all cool, but when should I look at backing up my database? This is really the million-dollar question, more from the point of view of your users rather than impact it will cause on the system.

SQL Server 2000 allows backups to be executed while users are connected to the system. This means that there is no downtime while the database is being backed up; however, you should bear in mind some considerations when performing these online backups.

- ALTER DATABASE statements that use the ADD FILE or REMOVE FILE options specified will cause the backup to stop running.
- INSERT, UPDATE, and DELETE statements can be performed while a backup is in progress.

- Shrink database or shrink file will cause the backup to fail. We will take a look at these terms again in Chapter 14.

Backups can take a long time (depending on the size of the database), so schedule backups for the quietest times. In a system that runs 24 hours a day 7 days a week (24/7), you will need to assess the times that the system is the least busy (normally around 2 a.m. or 3 a.m.), and perform the backups then.

What? You expect me to be at work at 2 a.m. to back up a database? You've got to be kidding! Well my student, them's the breaks of being a SQL Server 2000 DBA.

Where Do I Back Up To?

We can back up our database to a couple of places, and SQL Server 2000 will perform most of these for us.

- To disk—This allows us to back up our database as a single file (normally a `.bak` extension) and place it somewhere on our hard drive. We need to specify the full Universal Naming Convention (UNC) pathname, for example, `C:\Program Files\Microsoft SQL Server\MSSQL$MYSQLSERVER\BACKUP\ SQLSpyNet.bak`.

- To tape—This allows us to back up our database to a tape drive. With a tape drive we must also specify the full path of the tape drive, for example, `\\.\TAPE1`.

Because we can make a backup of our database directly to disk, we can specify a mapped server drive, so that our backup is held off our server. If we are backing up to tape, a copy of the tape should be stored off site as well or in a fireproof safe. Once again, it is better to be safe than sorry.

What Do I Back Up?

This is where some of the more versatile features of backups come into play. Although we can specify the type of recovery model we want to use, we can also specify which portions of the database we want to back up.

10

We might need to assess the recovery model we are using before we decide which type of backup we are going to perform.

We can specify for our database backups the following options:

- Database—complete—This is a direct copy of the database as it stands, including all the database objects (tables, views, stored procedures, and so on) as well as the data. With this backup we can restore the database onto another server.

- Database—differential—This backup only copies the changes that have occurred since the last complete database backup was performed. So if you have added a new table, it will append the new table to the backup; likewise, with data changes it will append the data changes to the backup.

- Transaction log—This makes a copy of the transaction log (all the user's transactions, including INSERTs, UPDATEs, and DELETEs). This enables us to restore a database to a given point in time. Because we have all the users' transactions and what-not, we can recover the work they have entered.

- File and filegroup—This allows us to back up a portion of the database at a time. This really should be used only for very large databases that take an extremely long time to back up with any other means. You must also be backing up the log to be able to recover.

We have the basic theories covered well enough for us to get into it! Like most things in SQL Server 2000, two methods for backing up a database are available. We can perform a backup through Enterprise Manager and use the GUI tools, or we can enter the code directly into Query Analyzer. You guessed it; the second way is my preferred way!

However, let's take a quick look at both ways so you will be a totally prepared DBA.

 Note

The most common area for the GUI (in my experience) to fail is when performing a database backup. Normally we would not repeat ourselves, but I think it is essential that you know how to perform the operation in both methods, so if the interface does fail, you can still backup your database.

Backing Up Spy Net Using Enterprise Manager

Now we have our mission-critical database that we want to protect. We know that we want to perform backups that allow us to restore easily, and our user transactions are small enough for us to log every event (full recovery model). Because this is our first backup, we want to perform a complete (full) backup.

1. Start Enterprise Manager and navigate to the SQLSpyNet database. Right-click the database and select All Tasks, and then Backup Database, as shown in Figure 10.1.

Figure 10.1

Where to find the backup database option for our SQLSpyNet database in SQL Server 2000.

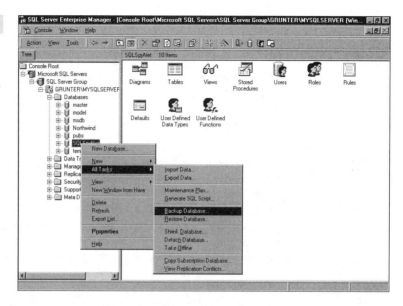

When the option has been selected, a new screen will appear similar to that shown in Figure 10.2.

Figure 10.2

The backup database screen for our SQLSpyNet database.

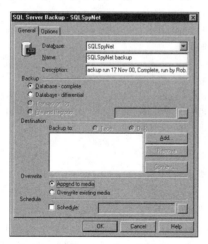

2. Within this screen we can set several options for our database backup. The first is the database that we want to back up. This should be set to SQLSpyNet.

3. Then we can specify a logical name for our database backup. This is something that is meaningful to us, so we can easily identify backups that we have performed. This is a mandatory field. Something like SQLSpyNet backup should do it.

4. Next we can enter a description to fully describe our database backup. This can be something like `SQLSpyNet Database Backup run 17 Nov 00, Complete, run by Rob`. This field is optional.

5. Next we choose what type of backup we want to perform. As already stated, we are going to perform a Database—Complete backup. Ensure this option is selected.

> You might notice that the transaction log and filegroup options are not available. The log option is not available because when we created our database we set the Truncate Log on Checkpoint option on. This option removes old records from the log, thus preventing us from backing it up.
>
> So if our database fails we will only be able to restore from the last complete database backup we took, rather than to any given point in time. This option is not a viable idea in a production system because if the database fails, you will have to restore it, and then get the users to enter all their work again. And believe me, they won't be happy.
>
> We use this option because we are only developing our database, so the current data we have is not going to be a great loss if it disappears—we can re-enter it easily enough.
>
> To alter this configuration you can use one of two methods (but you knew that, right!).
>
> First issue the following Transact-SQL statement to change the truncate log on checkpoint setting:
>
> ```
> sp_dboption 'SQLSpyNet', 'trunc. log on chkpt', 'true'
> ```
>
> Alternatively, you can change the option through the Properties window for the database through Enterprise Manager. We learned how to do this in Chapter 3, when we configured our model database.

6. In the Destination section we specify where we want the backup to be saved to. Click the Add button. This will launch a new dialog window that allows you to type the UNC file path manually, as shown in Figure 10.3.

7. Enter a file path with the name of the file also specified, for example `C:\Program Files\Microsoft SQL Server\MSSQL$MYSQLSERVER\BACKUP\ SQLSpyNetEM.bak`.

Alternatively you can click the ellipsis (...) button. This will launch a window that will allow you to navigate your way through your file system. After you find the location in which you want to save the file, type the name of the database backup file, as shown in Figure 10.4.

Figure 10.3

Specifying the file path for our database backup on the SQLSpyNet database.

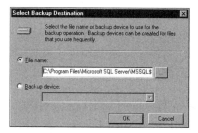

Figure 10.4

Storing our database backup for the SQLSpyNet database in an alternative location.

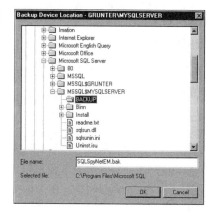

8. Click the OK buttons until you return to the first screen. You will now see that there is an entry in the Backup To list box.

What do the other buttons next to the list box do?

- The Remove button allows you to remove a database backup from the list of backups available.

- The Contents button shows you the number of current backups. For example, if you back up a database today, and then again tomorrow, and then again after that, in the contents screen you will have three entries with the date and time of the backups, size, and so forth.

- The Overwrite option allows you to overwrite the previous backups. If you specify Overwrite you cannot roll back to a previous version. For example, if you perform a backup today, and another tomorrow specifying the overwrite option as Overwrite Existing Media, this means that the backup set from today will no longer be available. Leave this option set to the default of Append to Media.

- The Schedule option is the next option. I know I made you panic about having to come into the office at 3 a.m. just to do a database backup, but our friends at Microsoft wouldn't be that mean to us.

10

The Schedule option allows us to specify a schedule for performing the backup. This is a little like setting a reminder in Outlook. We can specify that the task is a recurring task that occurs every so often. For now just leave this option blank.

9. We have one more thing to look at. You might have noticed that one more tab is available at the top of the screen. The Options tab allows us to specify some further backup options that might be relevant.

    - The Verify Backup Upon Completion option opens a message box informing you that the backup has completed successfully when the media integrity has been checked. You can select this option for this backup.

    - The Check Media Set Name and Backup Set Expiration option allows us to validate the details for the media so you do not overwrite an existing backup that you want to keep. For more information on media sets, check out Books Online.

    We can actually define a name for our media on which we are performing the backups. Every time SQL Server 2000 performs a backup on the media we can get it to validate the details for tracking and inventory purposes. Leave this option blank.

10. Click OK now; SQL Server 2000 will perform a database backup. You will see a screen similar to that shown in Figure 10.5.

Figure 10.5

SQL Server 2000 performing our first database backup for us.

How long the backup will take depends on your machine, the size of the database, the speed of your hard drive, and several other factors, but because our database is relatively small it shouldn't take too long, even on my Pentium 75! When SQL Server 2000 has completed the backup, you will see a message box stating that the backup operation and verification have been completed successfully.

And there we have it ladies and gentleman, our first ever SQL Server 2000 database backup. That wasn't hard, was it?

Note You should now have a quick look in your file system in the path where you specified the backup file to be saved to. You should see the file (with a .bak extension) within the directory.

Backing Up Spy Net Using Transact-SQL in Query Analyzer

You can see how simple Enterprise Manager is to use to create a backup, but the number of steps involved makes performing backups a little slow. We are now going to do exactly the same backup, but this time in Transact-SQL code. So fire up Query Analyzer, and let's get on with it!

The Transact-SQL code needed to perform the backup appears in Listing 10.3.

Listing 10.3—Backing Up Spy Net

```
1: BACKUP DATABASE SQLSpyNet
1a: TO DISK = 'C:\Program Files\Microsoft SQL Server\MSSQL$MYSQLSERVER\
    ➥BACKUP\SQLSpyNetQA.bak'
1b: WITH NOINIT, NOSKIP, STATS = 10
```

This will back up the database and give a running statistic to show how far through the backup procedure you are. This is shown in Figure 10.6.

Figure 10.6

SQL Server 2000 performing our second database backup.

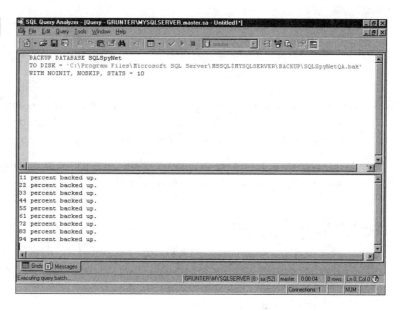

Analysis

Let's take a quick look at the BACKUP DATABASE statement.

- Line 1—This specifies to SQL Server 2000 that we want to perform a database backup on the SQLSpyNet database.
- Line 1a—The TO DISK option allows us to specify that the backup will be placed in a file in the specified location.
- Line 1b—This part of the statement is optional, but let's configure the statement to have the same actions as Enterprise Manager. The WITH statement means that there are some options to follow. NOINIT means that the backup set is appended rather than overwritten. This is the same as our Overwrite option in Enterprise Manager. By not selecting the Overwrite option in Enterprise Manager, we append the backup to the existing backup sets. NOSKIP specifies that the media name and details be verified. This is the same as the Check Media Set Name and Backup Set Expiration option in Enterprise Manager, and checks the expiration date (if any) of the backup sets before being overwritten. Finally, the STATS = 10 option indicates that SQL Server 2000 will give you a running commentary of the progress; for example, 10% backed up, 20% backed up, and so on.

> **Note**   Even though we specified the STATS = 10 option, the percent completed count might not be in 10% steps. Do not worry if the first step is 8%, the next is 19%, and so on.

If you take a look in the file system, you should now see two database backup files. One has EM (Enterprise Manager) and the other has QA (Query Analyzer) in the names, providing of course you followed my naming convention!

And there we have it. Two database backups performed and completed. So it is now up to you to decide which way you like best!

Restoring Spy Net

We have seen how to develop half of our backup plan. Now we need to look at what to do when we need to use the backups that we have created. This is so when everything has turned to custard—and it will, it will—you will be really glad that you had those backups available.

But just because we have a backup of our database and our transaction log, that doesn't guarantee that our database will be in exactly the same state as it was before we had a disk fail (or some other catastrophe).

When we do a complete database backup we take a copy of the state of our database. When we restore the database, we restore it to the same state the backup was in. If any incomplete transactions are in our backup, these transactions are rolled back when we restore. This helps to ensure that our database is in a consistent state. It wouldn't be any good having incomplete database updates floating about now, would it? Remember transactions must be ACID (see Chapter 8).

If a user were partway through some processing (hence the reason for late-night backups, to avoid this) when we took the backup, if chaos happens and we need to restore the database, the user's last lot of work would be lost. So although our back-ups will provide us with a lot of the work, it will not usually be 100%.

How to Get It All Back

So we've completed our database backup, and now a user comes running up to us. "Umm, I've got something to tell you," they begin a little sheepishly, "I've kind of deleted all the spies from the Spy table, kind of accidentally. And before you ask, no, I didn't use a transaction."

After 10 minutes of preaching to them about the importance of using transactions when performing database updates, you go in search of the last backup. Looking on disk you see that there are more than 20 backups. Now which one would you use?

Luckily for us, SQL Server 2000 actually holds all the database backup information in the msdb database. So when we perform a database backup every night, all this information will be stored in the msdb database. SQL Server 2000 will use the information contained in this database to suggest a restore option. This makes our lives a little easier than digging through 20-odd backup files to find the most relevant backup.

With the screens in the restore database utility, we can view the descriptions and names that we applied to backup, so this also aids us in performing a restore.

Looking at Database Restores

So what happens when I do a restore? If the database that you are restoring does not exist, SQL Server 2000 will create the database for you. Cool, huh? For example, if our hard drive fails and we need to rebuild our server, the database, of course, doesn't exist. So we perform a database restore and as part of the restoration, SQL Server 2000 will create the database as part of the operation without you having to worry about data file or log sizes, or even any of the basic configuration options of the database.

10

This does *not* mean that an error occurs if the database exists when you go to perform a restore. SQL Server 2000 will simply overwrite the current database you have and replace *everything* within the database with the backup you are using to restore from.

In earlier versions of SQL Server you had to have the server with the same collation settings (see the installation section in Appendix B, "What Happens If I Selected the Custom Install Option?") as the database had when you performed the backup. Well no more! Support for multiple collation settings is one of the cool new features of SQL Server 2000.

We can even restore databases from a Windows 98 operating system to a Windows NT server, and vice versa. But it doesn't stop there; we can also restore to a Windows 2000 server with no issues. And in fact, when Spy Net does go live, I suggest an upgrade to Windows 2000 server.

One other very nice feature is the implicit upgrade that can be performed when restoring a SQL Server 7.0 database. If you back up your SQL Server version 7.0 database in the method described earlier, you can restore that database into a SQL Server 2000 database without having to do anything extra. Now that makes upgrading very nice indeed.

Although upgrading from version 7.0 to 2000 is a simple process, versions of SQL Server prior to 7.0 have a different internal storage system. This means that to upgrade a 6.5 database to 2000 you will need to use the Upgrade Wizard. More on this can be found in Books Online.

When we looked at backups, we found it was possible to back up only certain parts of our database, logs, and filegroups. So how do we use these if we back them up?

Applying Transaction Logs

Why do we back up the transaction logs? With a full database backup being completed every night, if we back up the logs hourly we will be able to restore the database to the state it was in since the last log backup or the point of failure.

Let's look at it from the point of view of not backing up the log. Suppose we have our database backup performed at 3 a.m. every morning (you must be getting sleepy by now).

Your users come in at 8 a.m. and because of very heavy demand in the underground spy world, they are all working like demons until 2 a.m. The next database backup is due to take place at 3 a.m., but the hard drive fails! This is an absolute catastrophe. Smoke is coming from inside the server, and you are sure you can see little bits of the drive poking out of the casing. Boy, when this went, it went in a big way.

So, being the diligent DBA that you are, you rebuild the server and apply the last backup you have, but this one is almost 24 hours old. All that hard work that your users have done is lost. Some very agitated and tired people are looking at you when you tell them the news!

What happens if you did have the log backups? If you have an overnight complete database backup and back up the log hourly, you can recover to the last hour's backup, or even to the point of failure! This way your users will only lose their last hour's work (at worst). This is better than the last 23 hours, isn't it?

> With our current database settings we cannot perform log backups. This is because we have the Truncate Log on Checkpoint option turned on. This option prevents our log from continual growth but is not really satisfactory in a production environment, as the example we have just discussed shows.
>
> Because we do not need to have high recovery level of the data in our database, we have the Truncate Log on Checkpoint option enabled. This suits our current needs better because the log does not continually grow and fill up valuable disk space.

Before we can restore our database with our backed up transaction logs, there are some rules that we must follow (when aren't there?).

- The complete/differential database must be restored first.
- There must be an unbroken sequence (a continuous chain) of log backups since the last complete/differential database backup.
- The transaction logs must be in the correct sequence from the time the last complete/differential database backup was completed.
- After the database has been restored, no more transaction logs can be applied to the restoration, unless you want to do the whole process again.

So like the database backup, the database restore can be performed in one of two ways, either using the GUI tools in Enterprise Manager or through Transact-SQL in Query Analyzer. So once again let's have a go at restoring our database from the backups we created earlier.

10

Note

We will not perform a transaction log backup or restore. If you want to try this, see Books Online for more information, specifically looking for the BACKUP LOG and the RESTORE LOG Transact-SQL statements.

Restoring Spy Net Using Enterprise Manager

As with the backup process, Enterprise Manager helps you with all the details.

1. Open Enterprise Manager, find the SQLSpyNet database, right-click, select All Tasks, and then Restore Database. This will give you a screen similar to that shown in Figure 10.7.

Figure 10.7

Restore screen within SQL Server 2000 for our SQLSpyNet database.

The General tab provides quite a bit of flexibility in the type of restore that we can perform.

2. First, select the database we want to restore. If it is an existing database select it from the drop-down box. If not, type the name of the new database, and when the restore proceeds, SQL Server 2000 will create it for you. For us though, select the SQLSpyNet database from the list.

3. The Restore section allows us to choose the type of restore we want to perform. The following options are available:

   • Database—Allows us to restore a selected database. The list box will show the most recent backups for our database. This is driven from the msdb database.

   This is the one that we are going to restore from, so select this option.

- Filegroups or Files—Allows us to restore either a file or filegroup, which is a subset of a complete database restore.

- From Device—Allows us to restore from a device. This is the type of restore you select if you want to restore from a file that you have on a tape or located on a drive. This is the option that you will need to select if there is no backup information in the list box below.

 The rest of this section deals with performing a restore from the Database option.

4. Next we can choose the database from which we want to see a list of backups. Make sure the SQLSpyNet database is selected.

5. The First Backup to Restore option is a list of the most recent backups, in descending order; that is, the last backup first. Ensure that you have the most recent backup selected. If you select another backup from the list, it will be added to the list box. This would allow you to restore multiple backups one after another.

6. If you highlight the database restore in the list box, you will see that the Properties button becomes available. This will allow us to edit the properties of the restore, for example, change the file that the database is going to restore.

7. Like the backup screen, we have another tab on the screen, Options. Within this screen are several further options that allow us to alter the way the backup is configured.

 This is only a discussion of the Options tab. Generally the default options of a SQL Server 2000 restore will suit our needs, and in this case they do. So leave the options as they are by default.

10

- Eject Tapes (If Any) After Restoring Each Backup—This will force the tape out of the tape drive after the restore has been completed.

- Prompt Before Restoring Each Backup—SQL Server 2000 will ask you whether you want to continue when performing multiple restores.

- Force Restore Over Existing Database—This will allows us to "blow away" the existing database. This will delete the current database and re-create the database based on the information contained in the backup set.

- Restore Database Files As—If you want to use other database files for the restore, you can enter these here.

- Recovery Completion State—The different option settings can allow us to add additional transaction logs if required. With this option set, we can rebuild a database to its state before it crashed by applying the transaction logs in the correct order.

8. Make sure the backup set we prepared earlier is checked on the General tab. Then click OK. You will see a screen similar to that shown Figure 10.8.

Figure 10.8

SQL Server 2000 restoring our SQLSpyNet database.

And that's it! SQL Server 2000 will now give you a message stating that the database has been restored successfully.

That is how we restore a database through the GUI in Enterprise Manager. Let's now do the same thing through Query Analyzer.

Restoring Spy Net Using Transact-SQL in Query Analyzer

Fire up Query Analyzer, and enter the Transact-SQL statement in Listing 10.4 into the window.

Although it is not usually required, you should perform your backup and restores with the Master database as the selected database in the drop-down in Query Analyzer.

Listing 10.4—Restoring Spy Net with Transact SQL

```
1: RESTORE DATABASE SQLSpyNet
2: FROM DISK = 'C:\Program Files\Microsoft SQL Server\MSSQL$MYSQLSERVER\BACKUP\
   ➥SQLSpyNetQA.bak'
3: WITH STATS = 10
```

Warning   If the RESTORE statement fails, make sure that the SQLSpyNet database is *not* the active database in Enterprise Manager. In other words, if the database is selected, select another, for example Master. This ensures that no connections are held on the database, so the restore can continue.

Analysis

Listing 10.4 accomplishes the backup as follows:

- Line 1—Specifies to SQL Server 2000 that we want to perform a restore on the SQLSpyNet database.
- Line 2—Specifies where to find the backup to restore from. In this instance it is from a disk location.
- Line 3—Specifies that statistics (progress) will be displayed when the restore operation is being performed.

And there we go. We have just restored our database again, this time through Transact-SQL code (yahoo!), but emulating a similar operation to that which we performed in Enterprise Manager.

Finalizing Your Plan

So is there anything else I need to know about the backup and restore options? First of all, when thinking about disaster recovery we need to think of the cost to our business of *not* having our data. This will determine the type of planning and maintenance that you need to have in place. The recovery plan must be well thought out and offer you the most protection as well as the ability to recover quickly.

Some of the things you should consider as you finalize your plan involve security, using extra resources to ensure availability, and creating a checklist. This section offers you a few hints and tips.

Keep Track of Copies

In Chapter 9 we discussed how to grant or restrict permissions to someone who might perform a backup and then restore our database. SQL Server 2000 now allows us additional protection by securing backups with passwords. So even if someone could get a copy of our backup from somewhere, they couldn't restore it.

Microsoft says that this is really only a base level type of security. The password option does not encrypt either the data or the backup set. And someone with a third-party tool could potentially crack the password and get access. But it is a start. It is a

10

little like locking your house. If you lock it, a thief will go elsewhere (most of the time) where the goods are easier to get.

Although you can perform database copies by doing backups and restores, you are better off using the new Copy Database Wizard. When you use the wizard you also copy all of your server logins as well as your user accounts. If there are any scheduled tasks (see Chapter 11, "Administering Spy Net,") for the database, the wizard will copy these as well. We will review the Database Copy Wizard in Chapter 15.

Mark the Transaction Log

The transaction log allows us to use named marks, similar to a bookmark, to specify a given point in the log. With this we can mark the log before a potentially damaging update.

For example, if we have an update that can affect several thousand rows, we mark the log specifying a given point. We can then begin the transaction, and if an error occurs, which causes all the rows in our database to be updated incorrectly, we can simply roll the changes back by restoring the transaction log to the mark that we created within the log.

To mark the transaction log, you can use the BEGIN TRANSACTION WITH MARK TransactionName Transact-SQL statement to insert the point where you want to mark within the transaction log. We looked at transactions in Chapter 8, "Ensuring Data Consistency with Transactions, Locks, and Error Trapping."

To recover to a marked transaction, use the RESTORE LOG Transact-SQL statement and specify the WITH STOPATMARK = TransactionName option.

Create a Warm Server

We also have another new feature called *log shipping*. This allows us to constantly back up our database logs and restore them on another server, allowing us to keep a "warm" server waiting in the wings that is roughly consistent with our current server.

A *warm server* is a server that mimics our current server and is running, waiting for our first server to go down. We can then unplug the first server from the network and plug in the second server, and voilá, we are back in business within minutes.

SQL Server 2000 offers numerous other features and enhancements for backups and restores, but we take a look at these a little later. These are just a few to whet your appetite.

Create a Checklist of Resources and Practices

I've included some of the resources that you should consider as a part of your plan. Although this is only a light list, it will give you an idea of some of the considerations that you need to have when developing a disaster recovery plan. Be sure to create your own list and keep it handy for when you or the person on duty needs it.

__ Designate a recovery champion—This person is responsible for ensuring that the plan is in place and well designed.

__ Back up all databases regularly—This includes not only user databases, but also system databases.

__ Keep track of the builds of servers—This is a list of all the software, service packs, hot fixes, and so on that have been installed on the server or servers.

__ Have run-throughs—Rebuild another server from your disaster recovery plans. This allows you to check how well designed your plans are.

__ Prepare a warm server—If possible, a warm server that can be swapped in for the failed server is a very good approach.

__ Ensure support is available—As well as having a champion for the process, ensure that the support is available when you need it; that is, have both a primary and secondary response contact.

Make and Follow Your Recovery Steps

So what do I do when it all turns to custard? PANIC!! No, that is the wrong approach! Approach the problem slowly and calmly, following your plan to meticulous detail. This is why you spent hours making sure it was correct.

One possible way to recover is to follow these steps:

1. Rebuild your server applying the software, service packs, hot fixes, and so on, from your software list.

2. When SQL Server 2000 has been replaced on the server, restore the system databases first. This will normally require a reboot of the server.

3. Restore the user databases.

4. Establish a connection to the server from the client applications.

5. Perform some brief testing on the application.

6. When you are happy with the previous steps, allow your users back onto the system.

7. Monitor performance and functionality for at least the next 24 hours.

10

And there we have it, a brief rundown on disaster recovery and planning. But one final thought for you—plan for disaster, and do it now! If you put it off, Murphy's Law dictates you will most definitely need a disaster recovery plan when you don't have one.

Summary

In this chapter we have covered *the* most important part of a DBA's role, ensuring that when the worst happens we can get up and running again with minimal effort. Although we have covered the basics of the backup and restore statements, there is much more to both of them than we have time (and word count) for in this chapter. I strongly encourage you to learn about them in more detail before using them in a production environment.

Also, although we have talked about capacity planning, we have not really defined the rules for this. This does depend largely on the needs of your users, managers, and developers. I strongly suggest that you plan your backup and recovery strategies *very* carefully. You must test them, and then test them, and then for good measure test them again!

Unfortunately for us, we will never really know how good our plan is until we really need it. Microsoft has some very good guidelines for developing a backup and recovery plan, and you can find these guidelines in Books Online by searching for Designing a Backup and Restore Strategy.

One other thing that we briefly touched on was managing our backups. Make sure that you know when, whom, and what the backups are for. Very good guidelines for this by Microsoft are also in the previously referenced section.

Next Steps

In the next chapter we will look at scheduling our backups to run during the night, so we don't have to get up at 3 a.m. to perform a database backup! "Whew!" I just heard you say. You don't really think that Microsoft (or myself) would have been that mean to you, do you?

Chapter 11

Administering Spy Net

We now are getting into the nitty-gritty of database administration. In this chapter we will look at the real jobs of the DBA, so you will need to keep the DBA hat on for a little while longer.

So far we have seen how to design a database, implement that design, and perform backup and restores of our database. Now we look at how to keep it all running smoothly, with some of the built-in tools and functionality of SQL Server 2000.

In this chapter, you get a good start on several important database administration tasks. These are tasks that you will use frequently as a DBA. In fact, so often that you'll want to find out much more about these tasks—and believe me, dozens of books have been written on just administration alone.

As I mentioned early in the book (way back in Chapter 2!), SQL Server 2000 provides some very rich tools to perform all sorts of functionality, and the administration part of SQL Server 2000 is no exception! The GUI makes life for administrators much easier, but it does not replace the planning and thought required to successfully administer the server.

As a DBA, it is our responsibility to ensure that not only our databases are available, but also that our server runs efficiently. This means that when the server runs poorly, we are ultimately responsible.

Another part of our role is to ensure that users of the system have access to the server and the database when they require it. With our configuration settings correct we can achieve one of our stated objectives.

Configuring SQL Server 2000

When we install SQL Server 2000 many options are set by default. Most of the time these settings are fine, but if SQL Server 2000 is running inefficiently or slowly, we can adjust the way the server uses its resources.

We have very granular control over the configuration settings of the server. We can even specify how much RAM (memory) SQL Server uses. By right-clicking the server name (GRUNTER\MYSQLSERVER) in Enterprise Manager and selecting the Properties option we can get to the properties for the server, as shown in Figure 11.1.

Figure 11.1

Where to find the server configuration settings for our SQL Server.

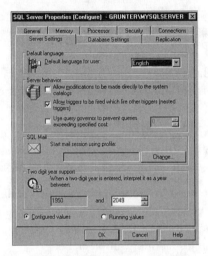

Within the property manager screen are many configuration items. You won't need to alter most of these options, but you know where to find them when you do.

The following are some of the more interesting configuration options to check out:

- In the Server Settings tab we can specify the default language for our server, and hence our users.

- The server behavior option Allow Modifications to Be Made Directly to the System Catalogs allows users to modify the system tables.

Allow this option only if you are certain that you want this to be allowed. If the *system catalogs* get out of sync, our databases can cause some severe issues or be totally useless to us!

System catalogs are made up by the system tables within a database. The system tables contain the definitions of objects within our database; for example, an object's name, columns (if relevant), type (table, view, and so on), and all the other attributes of our database objects. Making direct modification to the system tables is not allowed by default—you must enable this option, but heed the warning.

- The SQL Mail option is a bit more interesting. In here (if you have it set up on your machine) you can specify a valid mail profile name, and your instance of SQL Server 2000 can be configured to send and receive emails. This allows us to configure the server to email someone if something goes wrong. Cool, eh? We will talk about this shortly.

- The Memory tab allows us to specify how much memory SQL Server uses. By default, SQL Server 2000 will use as much memory as is available. After all, it's there, so why not use it? However, if you find that other applications are performing too slowly, you can configure SQL Server 2000 to use only a specified amount.

Limiting the amount of memory SQL Server 2000 uses can alter the performance of the applications, so change the settings carefully. SQL Server will use all available memory—but it is not greedy. If other applications require the memory for their tasks, SQL Server 2000 will release the memory to that application. That's nice, isn't it?

Because SQL Server will use as much memory as is available, if you have multiple instances of SQL Server 2000 on a machine, they will all be allocating and de-allocating memory resources as they need them. Each instance of SQL Server 2000 will treat another instance of SQL Server 2000 as just another application, so be careful in how many instances of SQL Server 2000 you install on your machine.

- The Processor tab is the next tab that might require reconfiguring, depending of course on your operating system. Although we are only talking about a Windows 98 configuration in this book, when you release this system to live, it will more than likely be released on a Windows NT/2000 system. When this happens you can come into this section and set the NT/2000-specific options.

And that about wraps up the Server Configuration option. As I stated earlier, many options allow us to configure our server, but you will need to check these out on

11

your own, and a good place to start is in Chapter 15, "Exploring SQL Server 2000 on Your Own."

So what now? Let's take a look at some of the more general administration tasks that as a DBA you will need to perform.

Performing General Administration Tasks

Besides checking server settings and backing up databases you'll be doing a lot of other tasks as a DBA. If being a DBA were too easy, you wouldn't want the job! How boring would that be?

As already mentioned, you must ensure that the server is running smoothly and that your databases are fast and efficient. The good news is that most of these tasks can be done for us automatically. After we have defined which tasks need to be completed and when, we can build scheduled jobs that will run when we specify them.

Let's take a look at setting up a scheduled job that performs a database backup for us during the night, so that we don't have to get up at 3 a.m. to do the backup. Like I would have made you do that? Maybe your new boss will, but I won't.

Scheduling Jobs

What is a scheduled job? Well this is like a reminder in Microsoft Outlook. We can schedule a task or job to fire at a designated time, for example we can set a database backup for 3 a.m. These jobs are simple to set up, and the configuration options for each job are very versatile.

 **Note**   Like most things in SQL Server 2000, scheduled jobs can be created either through Enterprise Manager or through Transact-SQL. This time we are going to go for the GUI in Enterprise Manager, but if you would like to know how to set them up with Transact-SQL look up sp_add_jobschedule in Books Online.

1. Fire up Enterprise Manager and navigate your way through the folders until you find Management, and then open the SQL Server Agent folder. Inside this folder you will find three options.

    - Alerts—These allow us to configure what actions happen if a specific error occurs.

    - Operators —These are user accounts that allow us to email, Net send (on Windows NT/2000), or even send a page to someone's pager when something goes wrong.

- Jobs—These are tasks that can have one or more steps performed. These steps are Transact-SQL statements that SQL Server can execute. Our jobs can occur one time or can be recurring events.

2. Select the Jobs folder, right-click, and click New Job from the menu shown in Figure 11.2.

Figure 11.2

Selecting the New Job option to create a new job in SQL Server 2000.

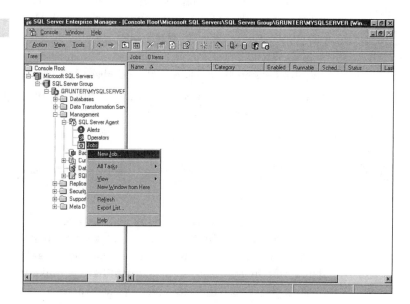

This will bring up a screen similar to that shown in Figure 11.3.

Figure 11.3

Setting the General properties of the new job.

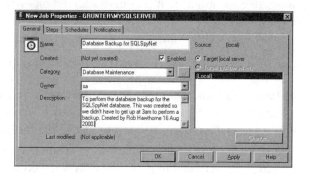

3. Because we're creating a job to perform our SQLSpyNet database backup, give the job a name that describes the task and the database it is for, such as Database Backup for SQLSpyNet. This allows us to specify a descriptive name so that anyone else will be able to recognize what the job is for. The name can't be any longer than 128 characters, which is more than enough for us!

4. Next we need to enable the job. Make sure the Enable option is checked. The Target Local Server option allows us to have this job performed on our current instance of SQL Server 2000. If we had *linked servers* (if we were connected to a network) attached to our server, then we would be able to create our job to run on the other servers, even though it is only enabled on our server.

Linked Servers are data sources that SQL Server 2000 can communicate with (for example, other SQL Servers, Excel, or Access). We can then perform queries on those servers to retrieve and manipulate data.

5. Next we can assign our job to a particular category so we can better organize our jobs. Let's assign our job to the Database Maintenance category.

If we have a multitude of jobs, we can sort the jobs by category, so it is a good idea to assign our jobs to categories.

If you click the ellipsis button ..., you will see all the current jobs in this category.

6. Next we can assign an owner to the job. If the job is owned by another login, we need to ensure that the login has sufficient privilege to run the job. For example, we could assign this job to our SQLSpyNetUser, but they wouldn't be able to run the task because they do not have permission to perform database backups. Make sure the sa account is the owner.

7. Let's add a description to our job. This will allow us to understand the job, why it was created, and by whom. In the future we can review the job and assess whether we still need it. We have a limitation of 512 characters for the description field.

The description I have entered appears in the Description box.

```
"To perform the database backup for the SQLSpyNet database.
➥ This was created so we didn't have to get up at 3am to
➥ perform a backup. Created by Rob Hawthorne 16 Aug 2000."
```

8. Next we need to tell SQL Server 2000 what task to actually perform. Click the Steps tab. This will give you a screen similar to Figure 11.4.

9. Click the New button. This will allow us to create our first (and only) step that we want SQL Server 2000 to perform for us when doing a database backup. This will give you a screen similar to that shown in Figure 11.5.

Figure 11.4

Setting up the steps in our new job to perform our database backups.

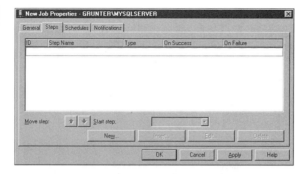

Figure 11.5

Telling SQL Server 2000 the actual commands we want our new job to perform.

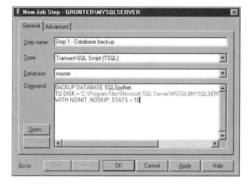

10. First we need to assign a name for our step, something like Step 1 Database Backup. This name cannot exceed 128 characters and must be unique.

11. Next we can choose the type of command that we want SQL Server 2000 to execute for us. Most of the time you will want to use the Transact-SQL option, but you do have the ability to get SQL Server 2000 to run operating system commands, such as batch files (these are files that have operating system commands within them) and so forth, as well as a multitude of other scripts. For our task though, leave the option set to Transact-SQL.

12. Next we can specify the database against which we want to perform the task. Because we are performing a database backup it doesn't matter whether we have the Transact-SQL execute against the master database. Why? Well we specify the name of the database in the backup statement, so SQL Server 2000 knows which database we are backing up. We covered this in Chapter 10, "Ensuring Data Availability," remember?

13. Finally, let's enter the command that we want SQL Server 2000 to perform. Let's put in our backup statement that we wrote in Chapter 10. It's a good thing we learned how to write the statement as well as use the GUI, isn't it? Otherwise you might be having a few late nights!

11

```
1: BACKUP DATABASE SQLSpyNet
1a: TO DISK = 'C:\Program Files\Microsoft SQL Server\
    ➥ MSSQL$MYSQLSERVER\BACKUP\SQLSpyNetJob.bak'
1b: WITH NOINIT, NOSKIP, STATS = 10
```

The only change we have made here is the filename that we create. This time it has a job suffix.

> **Note**
>
> The suffixes on the filenames are not compulsory. It is just something that I believe allows us to easily identify where the backup file came from. It is best to practice and all that, right?

The Open button shown in Figure 11.5 will allow us to select a saved Transact-SQL script to load. So maybe we should have saved our script from earlier, bugger! Another little Kiwi saying for you.

The Parse button will check that your syntax is correct. Click this now because it's better to be safe than sorry.

14. In the Advanced tab we can specify what actions SQL Server 2000 takes when the job either succeeds or fails. The defaults for this screen suit our needs fine, so we will leave them as they are.

   • On success action—Go to the next step.

   • Retry attempts—0.

   • On failure action—Quit the job reporting failure.

   Click OK. You will see our job appear in the Steps list box. If we had several steps in our process, we could reorder them so that some fired before others.

15. Next we need to specify when our task will run. Click the Schedules tab. Then click the New Schedule button. This will give you a screen similar to that shown in Figure 11.6.

Figure 11.6

Scheduling how often SQL Server 2000 will run the new job.

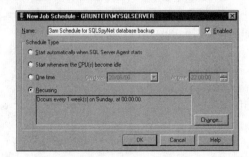

16. Like our step names, our schedule names must be descriptive, no greater than 128 characters, and unique. Enter something similar to "3 a.m. Schedule for SQLSpyNet database backup." Make sure the Enabled option is checked.

17. Next we need to setup a schedule. Let's take a quick look first at the options that we do have.

    • Start automatically when SQL Server Agent starts—This will get the job to start when the SQL Server Agent starts. You can set the SQL Server Agent to start when the operating system starts by using the SQL Service Manager. See Chapter 2, "The Tools of SQL Server 2000 for Managing an Instance," for more details.

    • Start whenever the CPU becomes idle—We can specify the CPU idle time for our instance of SQL Server 2000. When the CPU is idle we can get our job to start.

    • One time—We can set our job to run once only, at a specified time.

    • Recurring—This is the option that we are going to select. It allows us to have our job repeated for a specified set of time or until some indefinite period.

    Select the Recurring option, and click the Change button. You will see a screen similar to that shown in Figure 11.7.

Figure 11.7

Defining when we want our job to run in SQL Server 2000.

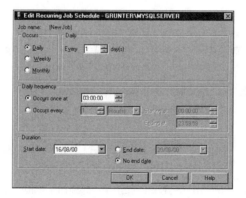

18. The screen is self explanatory, especially if you have set up recurring items in Outlook before. We need to set the following options:

    • Occurs—Daily.

    • Daily—Every 1 day.

    • Daily Frequency—3:00:00 a.m.

    • Duration—Start date, set that to today's date. Do not specify an end date.

11

19. Click OK. This will take us back to the New Job Schedule screen. Once again click OK. You will now see our new schedule in the job screen.

Gee, that was easy, but what do we do if it fails? I'm glad to see you thinking ahead! We can never, ever guarantee that something will work, so it pays to know what to do when it goes wrong. Hence the reason for the Notifications tab. Click this tab. You will see a screen similar to that shown in Figure 11.8.

Figure 11.8

Defining what happens if our job fails or succeeds.

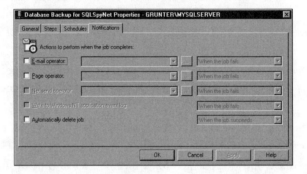

The most common option for this screen is to write to the Windows NT Event log. Unfortunately, because we are using Windows 98 as our operating system, we do not have the ability to write to the NT Event log (because it doesn't exist). So what do we do?

This is where we introduce operators. With an operator, we can specify a specific recipient to SQL Server 2000 to which an email or page (using a third party's paging software) can be sent. But we will take a look at this shortly.

If you now click OK, our new job will be written away, ready to run in the morning at 3 a.m. There are two things you should note about this though:

- Your computer must be on for this task to perform. Although it seems obvious, I have heard of people setting up jobs and having them never run because they shut off the system!

- Check regularly that the task has run. In the Jobs folder you can see a list of jobs and the last time they ran, and whether they succeeded or failed. Next you should check where you specified that the file be saved to for the backup. This will allow you to check that the file has been successfully created.

- Create a secondary database into which you restore the file occasionally just to check that it is actually backing up correctly.

And that, ladies and gentlemen, brings us to the end of yet another section of administration. Let's next take a look at operators.

Calling on SQL Server Operators

An operator allows us to define a person that can be notified when certain events take place. For example, if our backups fail, we would like an email sent to us specifying that the backup failed.

Operators require certain things to be available before we can use them effectively.

- Our instance of SQL Server 2000 must be able to send emails. You set this property under the server configuration options that we looked at earlier, or under the properties for the SQL Server Agent. Right-click on the SQL Server Agent icon, and select Properties. To find out more information about using and setting up mail profiles, see the Microsoft Exchange or Outlook documentation.

- The Net Send capability for an operator can be used only if we are using Windows NT/2000.

- The Pager email name uses an email address to send the pager a notification, so the email profile must also be established. You will need to use a third party's software to convert the email to a page.

 Note | Generally there are not too many differences between running SQL Server 2000 Personal Edition on Windows 98 and running SQL Server on Windows NT/2000. However, within the SQL Server Agent folder the differences become quite apparent. You can leverage several options if you are running an NT/2000 operating system. Keep these options in mind when you upgrade or scale your application to a multiuser environment.

I realize that we are designing for a Windows 98 operating system, so we cannot setup the Net Send option, but operators are very important to allow us to have our system up 24/7, so it is a good idea to have a brief coverage of them!

If you do not have a mail profile setup on your machine, you won't be able to take advantage of the operator function either. But I will still tell you how to set up an operator.

1. Select the Operators folder under the SQL Server Agent folder. After you have found the folder, right-click and choose the New Operator option, as shown in Figure 11.9.

11

Figure 11.9

*Selecting the New
Operator option.*

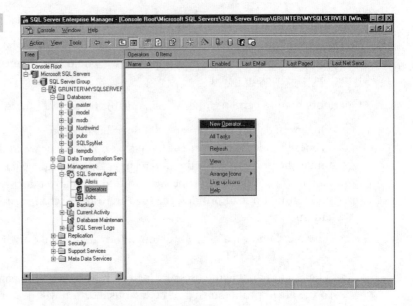

The screen that opens will be similar to that shown in Figure 11.10.

Figure 11.10

*The New Operator
screen.*

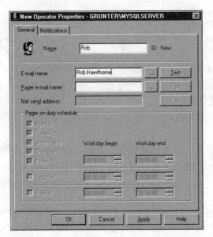

2. Like all we have done so far, we must define a name for our operator. Once again you are restricted to 128 characters, and the name must be unique; that is, no other operators can exist with the same name.

3. Let's give our operator a name that we will easily recognize. For mine I have used my own name.

4. Next we can specify the email name. This is the display name of the user to whom you want to send an email. If the name is not clear, you can enclose the email address in square brackets, for example `[SMTP:someone@somewhere.com]`. The Test button will send an email to the operator.

 Note   If the email test fails, check your mail profile with which you have set up your server. If the name is invalid, the server will not be able to send mail for you.

5. Next is the pager email name. If you have the email address of the operator that you want to page, you can enter their address here. Like the email name, we can test this entry with the Test button. If you assign a pager email name, you can then specify the hours of operation for the operator.

6. After you have assigned an operator an email address, you can click the Notifications tab. Here you can specify what events occur that the operator is sent notification about.

    Two options are on the screen initially, Alerts and Jobs.

    • The Alerts option is for system-generated errors that can occur; for example, the demonstration alert `tempdb` is full. Alerts are the next part in our scenario, but because our database is still very immature we won't leverage their functionality. Administration plans, on the other hand, we will implement, so hang on a minute or two more and we will address administration plans.

    • The Jobs option allows us to view the jobs that will notify the operator. Currently we do not have any notifications assigned to operators because we didn't have the jobs to start with.

7. We now have an operator and a job, and we need to assign that operator to a job to receive the notifications. Close the New Operators screen by clicking OK.

8. Open the job by going to the Jobs folder and double-clicking the Database Backup for SQLSpyNet job. Click the Notifications tab. This will give you a screen similar to Figure 11.11.

9. The Notifications screen allows us to specify an action to be taken if the job either fails or succeeds. Because we really only want to know when our job fails, select the Email Operator option, and select our operator (in my case Rob) from the list. The next option we want to select is a notification when that operator is called, so select the When the Job Fails option. Click OK.

11

Figure 11.11

Assigning our job to an operator for notification purposes.

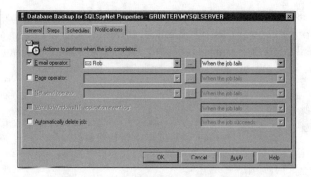

There we have it. Our new operator will now be notified if our when the job fails by way of email. As you can imagine in a real-life production system, these tools are very powerful.

There is one more thing that we can create to give us even more flexibility in the administration of our server and databases: an alert.

Using Alerts

We design an alert when we would like SQL Server 2000 to raise an event when certain conditions become true. For example, if our database suddenly becomes very large because of some heavy transaction processing, we can have SQL Server 2000 send us an email and also call a job that backs up the transaction log. Now that's flexibility!

Because our job is relatively simple and our database is still in development, we will not set up an alert, but you should realize that when our system goes live you will get some great flexibility from using alerts. You can find out more about alerts by checking them out in Books Online. See Chapter 15 for tips on using Books Online.

What Do SQL Server Logs Do?

In Chapter 10, we took a look at a few of the types of SQL Server logs you'll be using for various tasks and how you can use them. In this section, we'll examine one of the greatest aids in performing SQL Server 2000 maintenance—the SQL Server activity logs.

These logs track and monitor what is happening within our instance of SQL Server 2000. Every time SQL Server 2000 is stopped and restarted, the server cycles the activity log. So when our system is rebooted we will get a new log.

The logs can be found under the Management folder of the Server, and then under SQL Server Logs, within Enterprise Manager, as shown in Figure 11.12.

Figure 11.12

Finding the Activity logs in Enterprise Manager.

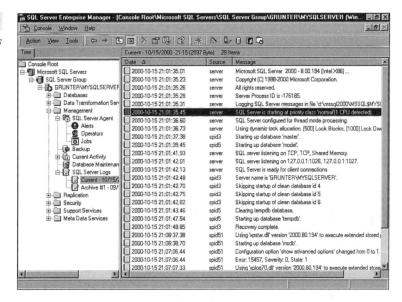

By double-clicking any of the logs, you will see the events that the server has recorded.

For those of you familiar with Windows NT/2000, the logs look very much like they do in Windows NT/2000. You can view more detailed information about the event by double-clicking any of the items in the log, as shown in Figure 11.13.

Figure 11.13

Viewing the entries in our Activity logs.

When you look through the log you will probably see many events for our SQLSpyNet database starting up. This is because of the Auto Close option that we set when we created the database.

As you can see with these logs, this creates a lot of overhead, opening the database every time someone makes a request to the database. But this option is by far the

11

most efficient for our desktop database. When we move to a multi-user system, it would be far better to reconfigure this option.

When SQL Server 2000 encounters an error, it is logged into the log file. Every now and then you will receive an error from SQL Server 2000 that states you should look in the logs for more information. After you retrieve the error message, you can search in Books Online (or one of the other numerous resources we discuss in Chapter 15) to help resolve the problem.

Generally though, you will not really use the logs until SQL Server 2000 encounters an error. So let's get on with the rest of our discussion on maintenance.

Running Consistency Checks

What's next in the administration tasks that we need to perform? We must occasionally check the consistency of our database. These checks that we run will help to ensure our database remains consistent and notify us of any problems early on. The checks perform logical and physical checks on our databases, tables, indexes, and file-groups.

The consistency statements are grouped into four categories:

- Maintenance statements —These statements perform maintenance checks on our database, indexes, and tables.
- Miscellaneous statements— These statements enable you to configure row-level locking or remove the leftovers of a `.dll` from memory.
- Validation statements— These statements validate that the database objects (databases, tables, and the like) are consistent and in good order.
- Status statements— These statements give the status of objects within our databases; for example, how fragmented an index is.

The main consistency statement that we execute is the `DBCC CHECKDB` statement. This is a validation statement, and the one that you will probably run more often than not. This statement returns a report on the current state of our database; that is, the number of pages that our tables are using on disk.

There are a multitude of DBCC statements that we can execute, including index defragmentation checks, database repair, and several others. These all offer different functionality, and you can find more information in Books Online.

Well when all is said and done, SQL Server 2000 will really take care of the database and configuration options. We only need to run DBCC checks occasionally just for our own peace of mind.

You should run the DBCC checks to be sure that everything is as you expect. Microsoft has done a lot of work in this area to make the only real reason to run the checks to be reassured by them, rather than actually having a requirement to run them.

Let's take a look at running the DBCC CHECKDB statement. As you have probably guessed, because these statements are Transact-SQL based we will need to run the statement in Query Analyzer.

Enter the code in Listing 11.1 into the Query Analyzer window.

Listing 11.1—Running a DBCC Check to Ensure That Our Database Is Okay

```
1: DBCC CHECKDB('SQLSpyNet')
```

This will return a large amount of information about our SQLSpyNet database, including how many rows are in each page of each table in our database.

The main thing to check though is to quickly scan through and see if there are any errors. You will see them pretty quickly if there are, but I am pretty sure that everything will be nice and clean for you.

If you do have any errors, check with Books Online for other parameters that you can specify to help repair the problems.

> DBCC CHECKDB is one of the best statements you can run because it checks and repairs the consistency within our database and fixes the widest range of possible errors. It performs the job of both DBCC CHECKALLOC and DBCC CHECKTABLE statements, so there is no need to run these statements as well.
>
> In the past, SQL Server version 6.5 and earlier, a DBCC CHECKDB statement could take hours to execute. Microsoft has worked hard to bring down the time of the statement to execute without compromising the effectiveness of the statement, but the statement can still be very resource intensive. So do not run a DBCC CHECKDB in busy periods, especially on a larger database!

We have now seen how to generate a database backup and how to set it up to run in the quietest hours. We've seen how to check the consistency of our database, but this also has to be run in downtime (preferably), and although I could schedule a job to run this task, I do not get the feedback from the statement. How do we combine these tasks? Well, in steps the Maintenance Plan Wizard!

11

Generating a Maintenance Plan for Database Consistency and Availability

A *maintenance plan* allows us to combine our consistency checks with our database backups into a single unit of work. We can also have our maintenance plan update the statistics of our database.

If the statistics of our database are kept up to date, our database will give us better performance because SQL Server 2000, for example, can decide whether to use an index or perform a table scan to retrieve our results. Although these statistics are kept updated by SQL Server 2000, this is only done periodically. Forcing the statistics to update allows SQL Server 2000 to use the most recent information for parsing our queries.

The Maintenance Wizard can also make our data files smaller by removing any unused data pages. This will save us space overall.

The wizard allows us to configure several other options, but instead of talking about them, let's get into it!

Using the Maintenance Plan Wizard to Create Our Maintenance Plan

To start the Database Maintenance Wizard follow these steps:

1. Right-click the SQLSpyNet database, choose All Tasks, and then Maintenance Plan, as shown in Figure 11.14.

Figure 11.14

Finding the Database Maintenance Wizard within SQL Server 2000.

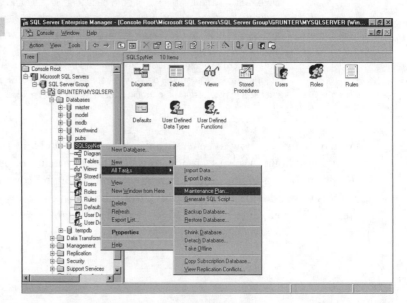

This will launch a wizard like that shown in Figure 11.15.

Figure 11.15

The Database Maintenance Wizard within SQL Server 2000.

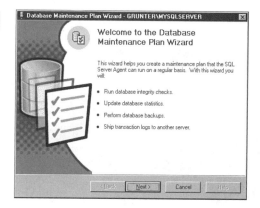

2. The options are limited on this screen, so click Next. This will open a screen where we can choose the databases on which we want to perform the maintenance tasks.

 Note

So far the only maintenance that we have performed has been on the SQLSpyNet database, but we also need to ensure that our system databases run well. If they do not run well, our database won't either. The system databases are the key to the whole operation.

3. In this wizard screen, select not only the SQLSpyNet database, but also the model, master, and msdb databases, as shown in Figure 11.16.

Figure 11.16

Selecting the databases on which we want to perform maintenance tasks.

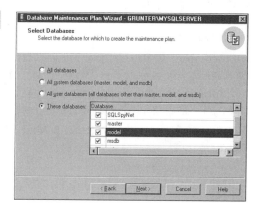

The other databases, Northwind and Pubs, are sample databases that come with SQL Server 2000 (you might not even have these installed). Click Next.

4. This will open a screen similar to that shown in Figure 11.17.

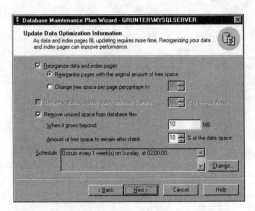

5. Within this screen we can configure how our indexes are shuffled around and maintained. We also can specify what happens to any unused free space on data pages. Let's take a quick look at the options that this screen provides.

- Reorganize Data and Index Pages—When this task runs, SQL Server 2000 drops and re-creates the indexes on our tables, with either a new fill factor or the original fill factor.

    Select Reorganize Pages with the Original Amount of Free Space.

- Update Statistics Used by Query Optimizer Sample—This will sample the data in the pages within the tables of our database. By doing this, the query optimizer can use the information to navigate its way through the data pages to find the required data. The higher the sample, the more accurate the statistics are, so the better our queries will perform, but the sampling will take longer.

- Remove Unused Space from Database Files—This gets rid of any unused space, thus reducing the size of our data files. We can specify the size that our database files become before they are shrunk. Because we are only running our database on a small PC, we should set this size to 10MB.

    Leave the Amount of Free Space to Remain After Shrink option to the default of 10%.

- Schedule—This allows us to set the date and time that the data optimization tasks will occur. The Change button allows us to alter the schedule of the task. The screen for changing the schedule of the task is the same as it is for the schedule screen when creating a job. This time, however, we want the data optimization task to occur weekly, on a Sunday at 2:00 a.m.

6. When you click Next you see the option to perform database consistency checks, as shown in Figure 11.18.

Figure 11.18

This screen allows us to check the integrity of databases and indexes.

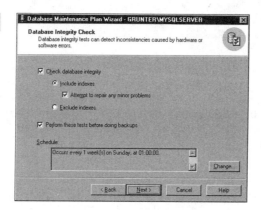

7. When we select the Check Database Integrity option, several other options are available for us to configure our maintenance program.

- Include Indexes—The consistency check will verify that our indexes are okay. Select this option.

- Attempt to Repair Any Minor Problems—SQL Server 2000 will try to repair problems that it finds when the consistency check is run. Microsoft recommends that this option be selected.

- Perform These Tests Before Doing Backups—This will force the checks to be run before a backup is performed. If the checks find any inconsistencies, the backups will not be run. Select this option.

- Schedule—Once again we can set the day and time that we want these tasks to run. Set it for Sunday at 1 a.m.

After you've set the options, click Next. This will take you to the Specify Database Backup Plan screen, as shown in Figure 11.19.

11

Figure 11.19

Setting when the database backup will occur.

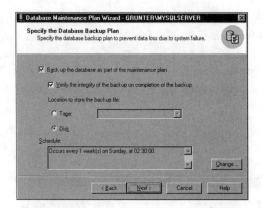

As you might remember, we already have a task to back up our database that occurs every day at 3 a.m. We are now going to create one that occurs on Sunday at 2:30 a.m. A real-life situation can have two backup processes: a differential backup that occurs every day and a complete backup that occurs every week.

8. Select the Back Up the Database as Part of the Maintenance Plan option. This will enable the other options.

   - Verify the Integrity of the Backup on Completion of the Backup—This will force SQL Server 2000 to check whether the backup is complete.

   - Location to Store the Backup File—We can either specify tape or disk. Because I assume you do not have a tape drive, specify the disk option.

   - Schedule—Set this to occur every Sunday at 2:30 a.m.

Warning

We must be a little careful scheduling our tasks. If we have a long running process it can cause another process to be queued, or worse still, not run at all. This is not a problem with database backups, but you should try to have them back up at different times if possible.

Click Next. This will give us the screen shown in Figure 11.20.

Figure 11.20

This screen allows us to specify where the database backup file will be saved.

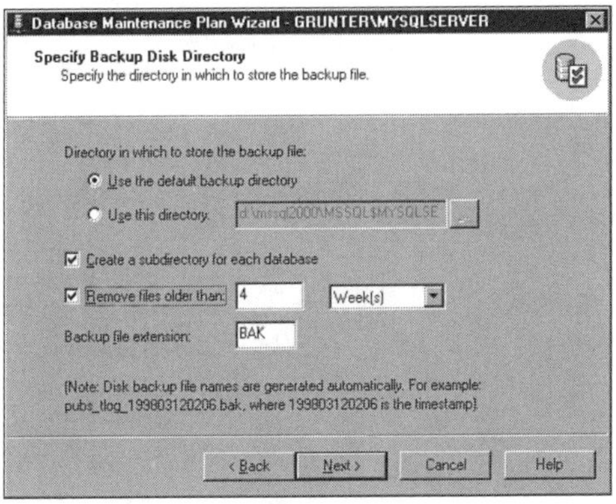

9. The options to specify for this screen are the following:

   - Directory In Which to Store the Backup File—We can either select a specialized directory or use SQL Server 2000's default directory. The default is fine for our needs.

   - Create a Subdirectory for Each Database—Because we are backing up multiple databases, they will be easier to manage in their own directories.

   - Remove Files Older Than—SQL Server 2000 will delete files older than a specified period. If you require a detailed history of your database, do not select this option. For our needs set this option to four weeks.

   - Backup File Extension—You should leave this as the default of BAK. You can specify another file extension, but the default in this case is fine.

Note   You might notice at the bottom of the screen that the wizard informs us that the filename is dynamically created. It includes the timestamp, which is a special data type that, like its name suggests, stamps a date-time value into the field, or in this case filename.

Once again click Next. You will see the Specify the Transaction Log Backup Plan as shown in Figure 11.21.

11

Figure 11.21

This screen allows us to specify the transaction log backup plan.

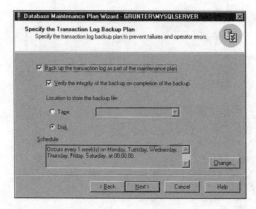

10. We will have transaction log backup performed for us, so specify similar options to the database backup, except the schedule. Have the log backed up every day except Sunday at 12:00 a.m. This is the default. Click Next.

11. This will give us a screen similar to the one we saw in Figure 11.18. Select the same options as we did for the Specify backup disk directory screen, except leave the Backup file extension default to TRN.

12. Click Next. This will open the Reports to Generate screen, as shown in Figure 11.22.

Figure 11.22

This screen reports the steps taken and errors that occur.

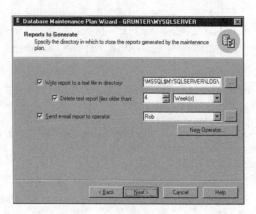

13. With the Reports to Generate screen we can specify that SQL Server 2000 generate a report based on the steps that the maintenance plan has performed, and any errors that have occurred.

The following options become available when we select the Write Report to a Text File In Directory option:

- We can select the directory to which the file is saved.
- Delete Text Report Files Older Than—Set this option to 4 weeks.
- Send Email to Operator—If you managed to successfully set up an operator earlier, you can select that the report is sent to them by way of email.

After you've completed this screen, click Next. This is the penultimate screen of the wizard—only one more after this one.

14. The Maintenance History screen, shown in Figure 11.23, allows us to keep historical information about the steps that the server has taken in completing the plan. This is the report entered into a table.

Figure 11.23

This screen records the steps taken and the errors that occur and logs them into a system table.

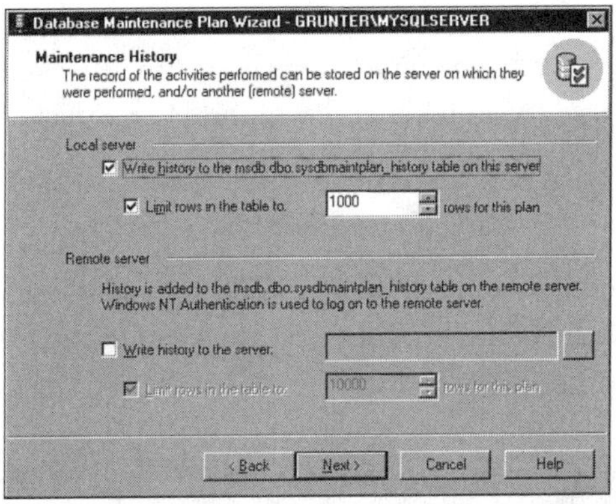

This screen inserts rows into a system database (msdb) and table (sysdbmaint-plan_history). Like the report, it captures the steps taken, the database name, success or failure, and so on. There is one row for each activity executed. If there is more than one database with the same activity performed, then there is a row for each database.

Set the number of rows to never exceeded 1000 rows. This means when the table reaches 1000 rows, the older rows will be deleted from the table.

Now we have set this up to write history to our server, but we can also set this up to write the history away to another server or another instance of SQL Server 2000. Leave this option unselected, and click Next.

And that's it! We now have the final screen, as shown in Figure 11.24, in the wizard, where we can name the maintenance plan.

11

Figure 11.24

Specifying a name for the maintenance plan.

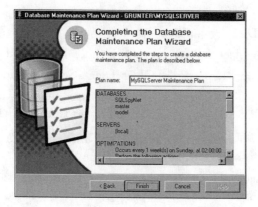

15. In the list box you can see the configuration options that we have selected. This is the last chance you have to get the settings right, before finalizing the plan. When you are happy, give the plan a name that is meaningful, something like MySQLServer Maintenance Plan, and click Finish.

Well done! Another task excellently completed. I am sure you are really excited about the prospect of becoming a real-life SQL Server DBA.

SQL Server 2000 will now write away our database maintenance plan. You can view the plan under the Management folder, and then under the Database Maintenance Plans folder, as shown in Figure 11.25.

Figure 11.25

The database maintenance plan defined within our instance of SQL Server 2000.

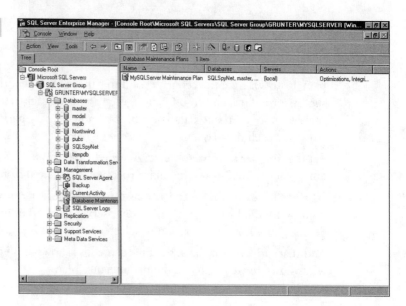

There we go guys, we now have a plan that will keep our databases running nicely, and a bit of a plan in case the worst happens.

This DBA stuff is a walk in the park. What else does a DBA do? So far the tasks we have done are very general DBA style tasks, and we are presuming that everything is running fine. Do not be mistaken; being a good DBA takes a lot of skill. They need to have very effective problem-solving skills, as well as the ability to think things through carefully and plan a course of action.

Identifying Indexes

So far I have talked a lot about indexes throughout our application development, but we haven't seen any real examples of how they are used or implemented within our application.

There is a method to my madness, I assure you! Indexes are an integral part of database development, but most of them are created for us without our even knowing it! For example, when we create a primary key, SQL Server 2000 creates a unique index on the column that has the primary key defined on it automatically.

SQL Server 2000 supports two types of indexes, *clustered* and *non-clustered*.

Clustered forces the ordering of the index to that of the column on which it is defined. For example, if we define a clustered index on a numerical column, the index will be ordered in numerical order, 1, 2, 3, and so on. Because this type of index forces the ordering of the data, you can have only one per table. Any inserts are placed into the index in the order in which they should appear. By default a primary key is a clustered index.

Nonclustered indexes are not ordered on disk, so you can have multiple nonclustered indexes on a table. They contain a small sample of data and a pointer to where the rest of the data resides on disk.

But this doesn't explain what an index is. You will hear most authors and developers say (and I agree with them) that an index for a database table is like an index in a book. You use the index in the book to quickly find relevant information.

SQL Server 2000 uses the same principle. If an index is available, SQL Server 2000 will use the index to retrieve the information. However, if an index is not available, SQL Server 2000 will scan the table and go through *every* row until a match is found. As you can imagine, this can become very time consuming and resource intensive if you have very large tables in your database.

11

How Indexes Work

An index contains a small amount of the data that the column contains and has a reference (or pointer) to where on disk the data exists within the table. For example, if we defined an index on the Person table for the Firstname column, and one of our columns contained Jimmy the Rotten, SQL Server 2000 may very well have the value Jimmy contained in the index (maybe even the whole value!) and a pointer to where the rest of the value is residing on disk, as shown in Figure 11.26.

Figure 11.26

Accessing data from indexed values.

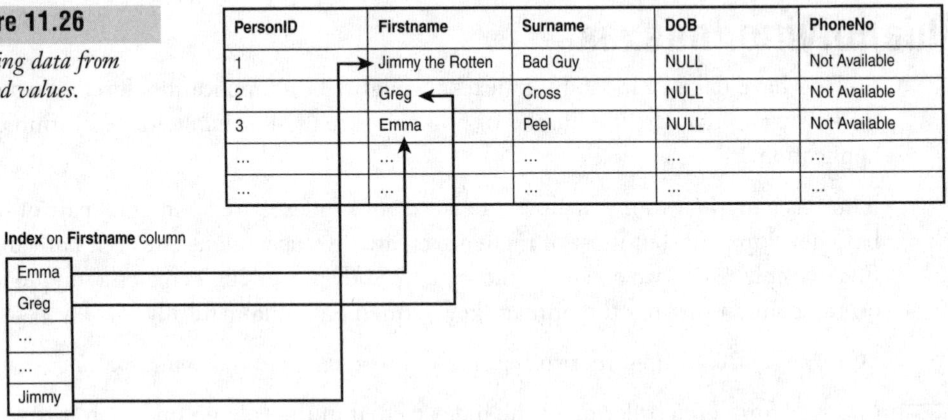

PersonID	Firstname	Surname	DOB	PhoneNo
1	Jimmy the Rotten	Bad Guy	NULL	Not Available
2	Greg	Cross	NULL	Not Available
3	Emma	Peel	NULL	Not Available
...	...	...	...	...
...	...	...	...	...

Index on **Firstname** column

Emma
Greg
...
...
Jimmy

Because an index contains a small amount of the data that is in a table, if SQL Server 2000 can retrieve the information that you need from the index, it won't even hit the table, thus increasing data retrieval performance.

Why wouldn't I define an index on every column? Surely that would allow SQL Server 2000 to find my data very quickly.

Everything has its price! Although indexes can speed up data retrieval, they can cost you in other ways. Tables that have indexes on them require more storage space because the index is an object within the database (aren't most things?) and also a copy of the data is kept for each row.

Indexes also have a performance hit on standard database tasks such as INSERT, UPDATE, or DELETE. Why? SQL Server 2000 must maintain the indexes internally. If you are inserting 10,000 or more rows, the index must be updated to reflect the new data changes.

When to Use an Index

As a DBA we must find a balance between the number of indexes we have and the number of data changes our users are potentially going to perform. Some of this pain has been eased though with SQL Server 2000 because we can define indexes on views. This is just one of the cool new features of SQL Server 2000. Defining an index on a view works in a similar way as it does for tables.

However, SQL Server 2000 goes one step ahead of this. If the view is not directly referenced in a `FROM` clause of a Transact-SQL statement, the query optimizer might find it more efficient to use the index that the view has for retrieving data (as long as the query is relevant, of course!).

 Note   Indexes on views (an indexed view) are not available in the version of SQL Server 2000 that we are using. You must be using Enterprise Edition to take advantage of this cool new feature.

Creating an Index on Our Person Table to Increase Query Performance

We now are going to create an index on our Person table to help increase the performance of any queries run against the table. Well, that's not true really! Because our application is so small at the moment, this exercise will not dramatically increase performance, but it will in the future when we have a lot more data.

Before we continue we are going to execute a query without implementing our index. But this time before we execute the index we are going to use another one of SQL Server 2000's debugging tools, the *execution plan*.

 An *execution plan* is a graphical representation of how SQL Server 2000 actually executes a query. They are brilliant for debugging complex queries because you can easily see areas that performance costs are the highest.

SQL Server 2000 supports two types of execution plans: estimated execution plans and the actual plans *after* the query has executed.

The estimated plans are used to analyze the query you have just entered into the Query Analyzer window, to give you an idea of the performance of the query. This can be especially useful for long-running queries to get an idea of how they will perform.

Execution plans delivered after the query has run display the actual results of the execution plan, providing invaluable information when pinpointing poor performance in queries.

Checking a Pre-Index Query with Execution Plan

To turn on the graphical execution plan in Query Analyzer, follow these steps:

1. Choose Query, Show Execution Plan (as shown in Figure 11.27), or press Ctrl+K.

Figure 11.27

Where to find the execution plan within Query Analyzer.

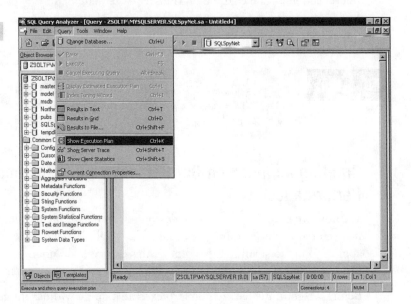

2. After you have selected to view the execution plan, enter the Transact-SQL code in Listing 11.2 so that we can see our execution plan.

Listing 11.2—Executing a SELECT Statement Without Our Index Defined on the Person Table

```
1: SELECT * FROM Person
2: WHERE Firstname LIKE '%a%'
```

The results pane of the Query Analyzer window will contain a tab called Execution Plan. If you select that tab, you will see results similar to those shown in Figure 11.28.

 Tip   If you hold your mouse over the Person.PK_Person image you will see information that shows how SQL Server 2000 performed different operations to bring the results of the query back.

Figure 11.28

Showing the results of the query with the execution plan turned on within Query Analyzer using the clustered index defined on the PersonID column.

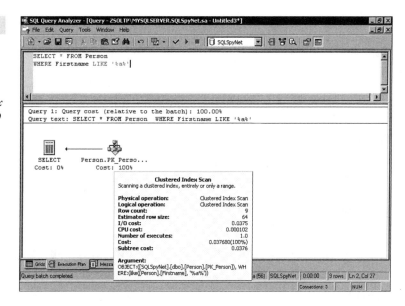

Analysis

Although a lot of information is returned to us (sometimes a little too much!), what we are really looking at (in this instance, at any rate) is the Physical Operation value. This specifies that the query uses the current clustered index defined on the table (that is, the primary key we have defined on the table).

Although this is fine for the few rows we currently have in our table, when we have hundreds of rows, it may not be a good idea to use the primary key for the query because the WHERE criteria is applied to the Firstname column.

Let's create an index on our Firstname column so when we do have hundreds more rows, the Query Optimizer will use the index to retrieve our data.

Indexing the Person Table

The type of index we will create is a nonclustered index. The main reason we cannot create a clustered index on our table is that it already has a clustered index specified on the table. When we created the primary key PersonID, SQL Server 2000 automatically created a clustered index on the PersonID column, and we are not allowed more than one clustered index on a table.

To create our index, enter the Transact-SQL code in Listing 11.3 into Query Analyzer.

11

Listing 11.3—Creating an Index on Our Person Table to Enhance Future Performance

```
1: CREATE NONCLUSTERED INDEX idxPersonFirstname
2: ON Person (Firstname)
```

And there we have it. Our first index! It's simple really, but before we continue, let's just take a quick look at the structure of the statement.

Analysis

Line 1 specifies the type of index we want to create, in this instance a non-clustered index with the name `idxPersonFirstname`.

Line 2 specifies the table (Person) and the column (`Firstname`) that we want the index to be created on.

Checking the Performance Change After Indexing

Let's execute our query again, but this time we will make a little change to the query (see Listing 11.4).

Listing 11.4—Executing a SELECT Statement with Our Index Defined on the Person Table Forcing Us to Use the New `idxPersonFirstname`

```
1: SELECT * FROM Person
2: WITH (INDEX(idxPersonFirstname))
3: WHERE Firstname LIKE '%a%'
```

Analysis

Line 2 alters our query to force SQL Server 2000 to use our new index. We need to do this because the Query Optimizer will not use our index. There simply is not enough data for the Optimizer to justify using the index.

> **Note**
>
> It is not usually classed as good practice to force SQL Server 2000 to use an index to retrieve results. This is the job of the Query Optimizer, which understands the intricacies of the inner workings of SQL Server 2000 far better than we can.
>
> The method I have demonstrated is really just for demonstration purposes only.

Now when you look at the execution plan, as shown in Figure 11.29, you will see that SQL Server 2000 has used our index to perform the query.

Figure 11.29

Showing the query results using the non-clustered index.

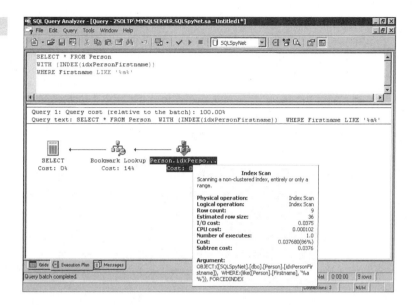

Holding your mouse over the `Person.idxFirstname` icon, you can see that we have forced SQL Server 2000 to perform an index scan to retrieve the data from our table.

We have now created an index and seen how to use one. Now let's take a look at managing our indexes for optimal query performance.

Maintaining Our Indexes to Keep Our Application Performing Efficiently

Although indexes can enhance the performance of our application, like everything else within our database they must be maintained, especially if the database is very transaction intensive and performs hundred of thousands of data modifications per day.

We can add new indexes and alter or delete existing indexes without affecting our database schema, and because indexes can enhance the performance of our application it does not hurt to experiment with the creation or modification of indexes until you get the mix right.

But once we have indexes defined on our tables (or views), we need to make sure that they are kept up to date and current so that they do not become out of date and thus affect query performance.

There are generally two ways to keep our indexes up-to-date.

11

You can delete and then re-create the indexes on your tables. This can be expensive to system performance because, in the case of our Person table, you have more than one index defined on a table. SQL Server 2000 must drop and re-create the nonclustered index twice.

The first time you drop the clustered index, the nonclustered index is dropped and then re-created. The second time you re-create the clustered index on the table, the nonclustered index is once again dropped and then re-created.

You can get around this overhead by specifying to SQL Server 2000 that you want to drop and re-create the index in one step. Using this method lets SQL Server 2000 know that all we are doing is rebuilding an existing index rather than dropping and re-creating an index.

The second method for re-computing the indexes defined on our tables is to use the DBCC DBREINDEX statement. This is one of the easiest ways of re-computing the statistics for your index. We are going to use this way to work through an example (see Listing 11.5).

Listing 11.5—Executing a DBCC Check to Re-Index the Indexes on Our Person Table

 `1: DBCC DBREINDEX(Person)`

With the DBCC DBREINDEX statement, we can re-index either all the indexes defined on a table or just an individual index.

 Note

To re-compute an individual index; just specify the index name after the table name in the DBCC DBREINDEX statement, similar to this:

DBCC DBREINDEX(Person, PK_Person)

This will rebuild the PK_Person index only on the Person table.

SQL Server 2000 has now rebuilt all the indexes defined on the Person table, as shown in Figure 11.30.

This is all fine and good, but the best part is that you do not have to perform this operation very often, if at all!

Like most things, SQL Server 2000 handles the recalculating of the statistics of indexes for us. Isn't that nice? Except, however, if you create an index on which you explicitly specify that you do not want SQL Server 2000 to re-create the statistics, but this is not a recommended practice.

Although this is pretty cool stuff, we are now going to look at some more of the interesting parts of the DBA role. Let's now take a look at performance monitoring.

Figure 11.30

Execution plan turned on within Query Analyzer using the nonclustered index defined on the Firstname column.

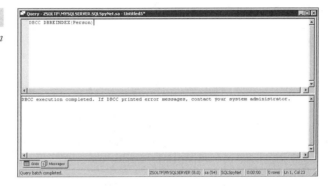

Performance Monitoring

Performance monitoring is one of the most enjoyable parts of being a DBA, at least in my opinion. It allows us to get in and view what is happening on the server, and then we can take corrective measures to fix any issues we face. Although this might sound simple enough, it can be a challenging task, especially in a volatile network or in a system that performs hundreds of thousands of transactions!

How do we monitor the activity of our server? Navigate your way through the folders in Enterprise Manager until you get to the Management folder. Under this folder you will find a Current Activity folder.

This folder allows us to see what each user is doing on each of our databases, and even more than that, on what tables. We can even go the other way and see what tables are having tasks performed on them by which users.

So let's take a look at the Current Activity folder and objects.

Monitoring Current Activity

As I mentioned, the Current Activity folder enables us to see what is happening on our server. Three main objects are under the activity folder:

- Process Information—This displays the current activity on the server.
- Locks/Process ID—View user activity within the server.
- Locks/Object—View database activity within the server.

What does the activity look like when it is running? Let's start a long running process so we can see the activity in the window.

Fire up Query Analyzer, but this time when you log in use the SQLSpyNetUser login. Enter the code in Listing 11.6.

Listing 11.6—Running a Loop to Examine User Information

```
1: DECLARE @Counter INT
2: SET @Counter = 1
3: WHILE @Counter < 1000000
4:     BEGIN
5:         PRINT 'Counter is ' + CONVERT(VARCHAR(10), @Counter)
6:         SET @Counter = @Counter + 1
7:     END
```

This will cause SQL Server 2000 to go around and around in a loop 999,999 times! This batch will take a fair amount of time to run.

If you now look in Management, Current Activity, Locks/Objects, and then SQLSpyNet, you will see a *SPID* for the current user. If you double-click the SPID, you can see the command that the user is running, as shown in Figure 11.31.

Figure 11.31

The process details for the SQLSpyNetUser in the SQLSpyNet database.

SPID is the unique system process ID, which is assigned to each user connection. It is not a permanent number.

One of the most powerful tools that a DBA has is the KILL command. This allows us to terminate a user's SPID. If we use the KILL command it will stop the user's work and roll back the command.

If a user is processing a long-running command, as we did, we may issue the KILL command or hit the Kill Process button. This will terminates the user's work and issue a rollback command so that the user's changes are undone.

If the user has a process that takes 45 minutes to run, and you kill their process at 40 minutes, it could take a further 40 minutes to roll back the changes that the user has tried to commit.

The KILL command can be issued in Transact-SQL, but you need to know the user's SPID.

We've now had a general overview of the activity functionality that SQL Server 2000 provides. Remember, though, this has been a very brief overview. If you want to learn more you should start the Transact-SQL statement that we ran earlier, and take look in the other folders to see what processes are running and the impact it is having on the server.

Summary

We've covered the very basic administration tasks of SQL Server 2000. You are getting the building blocks that you need under your belt to really look at becoming a SQL Server 2000 DBA in the very near future!

Although these steps we have just gone through are not the be-all and end-all of a DBA's role, they do give you some very good insight in what to expect as a DBA. Fun isn't it?

From here you can build on this knowledge and really get your hands dirty by administering the instance of SQL Server 2000 that you have on your machine to suit your own needs. So get into it!

Next Steps

In the next chapter we are going to switch our hats once again and look at developing a front end for our application. After all, we can't expect our users to have the SQL skills that you have obtained! We will build a very basic Web front end leveraging some more of Microsoft's technologies (who else's?) to deliver our content to a browser. So let's go!

11

Designing a Front End to Support Our SQLSpyNet Database

Welcome back to the developers' corner! It's time to start coding again!

We now have a database that suits our needs. The basic design is stable, we have a backup plan that assists in the system being available 24/7, and we have looked at implementing basic multi-user support. But we cannot assume that our users (other than ourselves, of course!) have enough skill to execute accurate and clever Transact-SQL statements to perform their daily tasks.

What do we do to help them? This is where we combine our artistic design skills with our vast knowledge of programming to build a friendly and easy-to-follow front end that enables our users to enter and retrieve data quickly and easily. The front-end design must be intuitive, offer the chance to back out if it all goes wrong, and be secure.

These objectives seem simple enough to achieve, but an inexperienced programmer could take months to come to grips with the intricacies of a programming language, let alone build a fully functional system.

In addition to these considerations, the developer also must decide which technologies will suit his application the best. And if that weren't enough, the developer also must decide what architecture that he will use when deploying the application.

Luckily for you, you've got me! Just follow along and before you know it, you will build a (basic) Web front end from which you can extend the functionality of at your own pace.

First of all though let's take a quick look at the architectures we can use when designing our application.

Understanding Basic Client/Server Architecture to Implement for Our SpyNet Application

Good architectural design is the key to having a successful application. If the design is thought through properly, the system can be expanded and the functionality can be enhanced at a later stage.

Those of you who have programmed before should have a basic understanding of client/server architecture. We briefly looked at this when we installed SQL Server 2000. If you need a refresher course, refer to Appendix B.

There is a little more to client/server architecture than just the roles that each performs. There is also the functionality of the different parts. This is where the concept of thin/fat client comes in.

When we have client/server architecture, we also have the concept of logical layers within the architecture, as shown in Figure 12.1. These layers are encapsulated functional areas that perform certain tasks.

 A *layer* is a distinct functional area within our architecture, but a layer does not exist only by itself. It has a high interaction with other layers thus creating the required functionality for our application.

- Presentation layer—This is the nice GUI that the user is presented with. This layer contains code that formats and displays data in an easy to read way. It also captures user input. The data captured from user input is passed to the business rules layer.

- Business rules layer—The business rules for the application are held here. For example, if a person must be older than 16 years, this layer verifies the data and either succeeds (and passes to the data layer) or fails and returns an error to the presentation layer.

- Data layer—This layer retrieves the validated data from the business rules layer. It then attempts to insert the data into the database, but if a key field is missing, it will return an error to the business rules layer, which, in turn passes it back to the presentation layer.

So, armed with this new-found knowledge, let's take a quick look at fat client architecture.

Figure 12.1

Client/server layers on a continuum between back-end server and user interface.

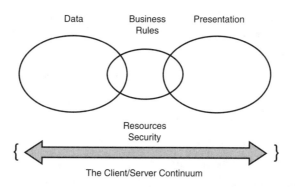

Server

Client

What Is a Fat Client?

Fat client, sometimes referred to as *two-tier client/server*, is where a very rich front end talks to a back-end database. An application such as Microsoft Access can run on our local PC and talk to a server, which contains our SQL Server 2000 database. This rich front end has many of the logical layers in client/server architecture built in, such as presentation, business rules, and even some data layer, as represented in Figure 12.2.

Figure 12.2

A fat client carries more of the load and power at the user end.

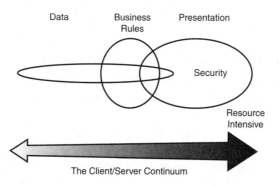

Server

Client

12

Because this type of application has most of the logic contained within the application, it allows us to check data input and return error messages very quickly, thus avoiding a round trip to the server.

But what are the real benefits of this type of architecture? Fat-client architecture will allow us to

- Validate the data very quickly
- Manage security easier
- Normally develop very easily and quickly
- Reduce network traffic
- Take advantage of the operating system components
- Use low-cost servers
- If the server crashes, availability of the local application might still be possible

However, fat-client architecture is not perfect. It does have these drawbacks:

- It must redeploy on every PC if a code change is required
- It's very expensive on client PCs because fat client tends to be resource intensive
- It can be very hard to maintain, especially if the application is deployed on many client PCs
- Its cost of support can increase dramatically

These are not all the pros and cons for fat client architecture, but they do give you a taste for some of the issues we face as developers when choosing the right design.

Let's now take a look at thin-client architecture.

Why Use a Thin Client?

Thin client, sometimes referred to as *multi-tier client server*, allows us to get more of a definitive split between the layers of our application.

 Note Thin client refers to more of the wave of recent Web-based applications that have become more prevalent throughout the world.

With this type of architecture we can place the presentation on the client PC, the business rules on a central server, and the data layer on our SQL Server, as shown in Figure 12.3.

Figure 12.3

Using a central server to shift the resources away from the client end.

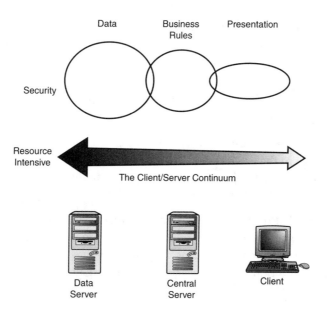

As you can imagine, this makes more sense than fat-client architecture because each layer is logically separated (distinct) from the other. Although each layer is separate, they still rely on each other heavily for the application to work as we expect.

The following are some of the benefits of thin client:

- If a code change is required, you need to change it in only one place
- It's very easy to deploy
- It's easy to maintain because all code is held in a central place
- Because the presentation layer is only run on the client PC, very few resources are needed
- It logically follows the client/server architectural model

There are some drawbacks as well.

- Network traffic is increased because each request requires a trip to the server
- Expensive servers are needed to run and manage the application
- Generally no access to the operating system is available, so we lose this functionality
- Security can be a bit of a nightmare
- The code base can be very large and hard to maintain

This is a brief overview of thin client/server architecture. Remember, I have not given you a definitive list of pros and cons for this model, but it should get you on the road.

12

Which Configuration Is Best?

Really that comes down to your needs when deploying an application. If you have 200 users, all with different specifications for their machines, even some old 486s, you might need to think about thin client architecture. However, if you are deploying to 50 users and the network is quite slow but the local PCs are high specked, then fat client architecture might suit you better.

There are several reasons why you would choose one architecture over another. The knowledge of the programmers is one reason. If your programmers haven't built a Web site before, it will take them a lot longer to develop an application using thin client architecture than fat client.

Just know that there is no real right or wrong answer. Just because in situation A you chose thin client doesn't mean that when you come across a similar situation you will choose the same way! As long as the solution you choose fits the client's needs and you can deliver on time, within budget and with all the functionality required, who could ask for more?

Choosing a Front-End Development Environment for Our Application

You now have an idea of client/server architecture, both fat and thin client. Let's take a look at the development environments we can use to build the front end to Spy Net.

Note In case you haven't realized yet, I am quite a Microsoft bigot. I love the development tools that Microsoft provides and enjoy the ease of development and deployment that the tools offer. However, this is not to say that any other vendor's products are not any good, just that I prefer Microsoft's. So in this section we will take a look at some of the Microsoft products that are offered for building our front end.

We are going to look at three (yep, only three) of the development tools that Microsoft offers to build our front end with: Visual Basic, Microsoft Access, and Active Server Pages (ASP).

Microsoft Visual Basic (VB)

When it comes to client/server architecture, VB 6.0 has it all! VB allows us to build all sorts of applications, and future releases will only offer us more flexibility.

 Note   Microsoft has recently announced that the new version of VB (VB 7.0) will be based on the new .Net platform. This will extend the richness and functionality of VB, and developers will have all the functionality that their Delphi and Java counterparts have had. VB.Net will be truly object-oriented and give us such lovely things as inheritance, polymorphism, and encapsulation. I can hardly wait!

The development environment is easy to work in, there are GUI tools for drawing forms, and the drag-and-drop capabilities make it easy to pick up and use.

The programming language is based on the original BASIC language, but it is far more sophisticated now. No longer do we have GOTO (though it is still supported), but functions, procedures, and so forth make the language far easier to read and simpler to use. Most programmers will pick up the programming language very easily.

With VB 6.0 we can create rich forms with message boxes and navigational controls, so this gives us our fat client architecture. We can create Web classes also, which allow us to deploy to a browser, so we then meet our thin-client requirements.

VB sounds like the perfect development tool. Is there anything you should be aware of? Well really, no.

The only thing that would stop most people from developing in VB is the initial cost of the software. Compared to some of the other environments that Microsoft supplies (for example, Access and FrontPage), it is relatively expensive. However, compared to other development environments, VB is very well priced.

In this chapter we will not be using VB to build our interface, mainly because I can't guarantee that everyone reading the book has VB.

Microsoft Access

Next on the list we have Microsoft Access 2000 from the Office 2000 suite. This is a great beginner's development tool, but senior developers will appreciate the richness of the development environment as well. It uses what is known as VBA (Visual Basic for Applications) as a programming language.

12

Although I talk about Access 2000, SQL Server 2000 can have any version of Access (even version 1!) running over the top of it. However, with Access 2000 you get some extra functionality that you just don't get with older versions. Gives you even more reasons to want to upgrade, doesn't it?

VBA is a trimmed-down version of VB. It looks and acts mostly like the familiar VB language but doesn't have all the rich capabilities of VB. However, this line is becoming more blurred with each new release of VBA.

Microsoft Access is a desktop database. It allows for simple and cost-effective database development. It provides a very rich front end and allows you to store data locally in the tables that it has behind it. But you can do even a little more than that. You can link into SQL Server 2000, capture the information locally, and then update the SQL Server with the changed information.

Desktop Databases are used to store information locally on a PC. They provide the ability to create tables and build referential integrity and queries. Normally a desktop database also will enable you to develop a front end using rich forms and Windows controls. Microsoft provides two desktop databases, Access and Visual FoxPro. These provide similar functionality, but in New Zealand at least, Access is by far the most common.

The one major problem Access has is that it does not scale well. It really is only good for fat client/server architecture. Although Web forms and pages have been built into Access 2000, they are not at a stage yet that you can take full advantage of them.

What's so different about Access 2000 and Personal Edition of SQL Server 2000? Even though Personal Edition of SQL Server 2000 is not as rich as Enterprise Edition, it is still a full RDBMS. On the other hand, Access is a hybrid of VB and SQL Server, with cut-down functionality from both.

In Access you can build the basic structure of your database, but Enterprise-wide deployment is not really an option (unless your Enterprise has only a few users) because Access doesn't scale well.

The rich controls and functionality that Access provides are great, and you have the capability to access standard Windows APIs, but when it comes to redeployment it can be expensive.

When I originally scoped the book, I was going to have you develop the front end in Access, but once again, I can't guarantee that everyone reading the book has copy of Access on his or her PC. So we are going to develop a front end for the Web! Excited? I knew you would be.

Microsoft Active Server Pages (ASP)

Active Server Pages (ASP) are a Microsoft initiative that allows HTML pages to be created dynamically based on information contained within a database.

EXCURSION

Another Piece of the Alphabet Soup

Out in the development world you will hear many three-letter acronyms being banded about, and with so many, there will always be double-ups. ASP is no exception.

Here's the first ASP acronym: Active Server Pages are Web pages that allow dynamic content to be delivered, and they're what we now are going to explore.

Here's the second ASP acronym: Application Service Providers are companies that basically allow you to "rent" software from them. For example, a company might license a version of Microsoft Office and deploy that on their machines, but when the next version of Office comes out, they must purchase licenses all over again. An ASP, though, allows a company to download the latest software by paying a monthly rental charge, sort of like leasing. Neat idea huh? And it provides an invaluable service for small- to medium-sized businesses.

ASP is a technology that allows us to deliver content that previously would have taken hundreds of static HTML pages to write.

ASP pages are run on a Web server by using Internet Information Server (IIS) or Personal Web Server (PWS). When the page is called from a browser, it is sent to the browser as a stream of HTML (text). This means that any browser can interpret the page and display it. And they said that Microsoft had a monopoly! The Web is great, isn't it?

ASP uses VBScript (or JavaScript) to leverage their powerful functionality. VBScript is a cut-down version of VB. It has even fewer features than its VBA counterpart, but this just means programming is a little more fun!

In VBScript there is no concept of a datatype. Everything is treated as a Variant (a special datatype that can contain all datatypes), similar to the Variant datatype in VB. When a variable is assigned a value (for example, a string) for the first time, it means that any other values assigned to the variable are treated as strings. Likewise for integers and so on, so you must be a little careful when assigning values. This will become more obvious to you when you start writing code.

12

ASP sounds really cool. Is there anything to watch out for? Well yes! ASP is a great technology but you need to realize that anything sent to the browser is only HTML. It is very hard to control user input and so on. We can do this through some very clever *client-side scripting*, but not all browsers support scripting.

Scripting is probably the buzzword of the last wave in Web and component development. It covers several areas, including ASP, Windows Scripting Host (WSH), and client-side scripting. Client-side scripting in a browser context refers to the message boxes and basic data validation that is performed on a Web site. Just try surfing out there for a while to see what I mean.

Additionally, the pages are not compiled until they are run, so if an error is in a page, you can't find it until you call the page from your browser.

What about a development environment? Now this is the cool thing about ASP! Those of you out there who are lucky enough to have access to Visual InterDev (VID, part of the Visual Studio suite) will have a rich development environment, but others who do not have access to such a great development tool can actually write ASP in Notepad.

Visual InterDev (VID) rocks! It is absolutely brilliant for developing Web applications in. You can use drag and drop, write code, and even link to a database so that all your data, tables, and structures are integrated in your development environment. VID allows you to write stored procedures, execute them, and view the results, without having to open one of SQL Server 2000's tools! You also have a full and rich development environment with breakpoints, immediate windows, and so on. If you get a chance to use this tool, grab it!

Because ASP is known as a scripting language, and HTML/ASP pages are really only text, you can develop a whole application in Notepad or any other text editor such as WordPad or MS Word. It is not the easiest thing in the world to do, but at least you can carry on developing.

To view your ASP pages in Notepad or any other text editor, you will need to open Notepad first, and then use either File, Open or drag and drop the ASP file into the open Notepad window.

Alternatively, you can associate the ASP file extension to be opened with Notepad. This can be done under Tools, Folder Options in an open folder/explorer window. Consult the Windows help for more information.

We will develop our ASP pages in FrontPage. A light version of this comes with Internet Explorer 5.0, which I know you have or you wouldn't be able to run SQL Server 2000. You need to make sure this is installed. Optionally, you can download FrontPage from the Microsoft Web site.

The only other thing that you must have installed is some type of Internet Web server on your machine. For Windows 95, 98, and NT 4.0 Workstation this is PWS (Personal Web Server). For Windows 2000 (all versions) and NT 4.0 Server this is IIS (Internet Information Server) .

 Note   You will find the PWS Install option on your Windows 98 CD when you run setup, and in Appendix A at the end of the book, you will find the install/configuration guide for setting up your PC as a Web server.

Establishing a Connection to Our SQLSpyNet Database

Before we get into the nitty-gritty of developing our front end, we need to take a quick look at the different ways of establishing a connection to our database.

There are two mainstream ways of establishing database connections.

Using the Tried and True Method of ODBC (MSDASQL)

Open Database Connectivity (ODBC) is a standard way of establishing a database connection. Most client/server applications use this method because the ODBC drivers can be easily configured within the control panel of Windows. Within the client application we specify the data source name (DSN) connection name, and voilà we have a connection!

If a server is moved, you do not need access to the source code to change which server the connection is pointing to. You just open control panel and edit the connection properties right there.

ODBC acts as an interpreter for more than one type of database. ODBC drivers exist for SQL Server, Access (Jet), Oracle, DB2, Excel, text files, and so on. When you make a request to your database through ODBC, the request you are making is interpreted to the native SQL of the database you are querying.

As you can imagine, this can impede the performance of the application. The trade-off for ease of maintenance is performance. It's not a good trade, really. Having said that though, the drivers that are being written for ODBC are getting better and better, so maybe in the future the trade-off won't be quite so noticeable.

> Microsoft recommends that ODBC be used only for backward compatibility, such as establishing a connection to legacy applications. The new method of using OLE DB, which we will check out next, is the recommended way to establish a connection to a database.

Using the New-Fangled OLE DB Provider for SQL Server (SQLOLEDB)

What else can I use instead of ODBC? SQL Server 2000 (and earlier versions) enables you to talk to SQL Server 2000 almost directly through a native provider called SQLOLEDB. Bit of a mouthful, huh? This driver allows you to create a connection to the database by supplying some connection string parameters, a little like ODBC. But the biggest drawback for SQLOLEDB is when the server moves. Because you specify the connection string information in the client application, not just a central DSN, the source code must be available for you to change the application to point to a new server.

Using SQLOLEDB, we get access to some features that are not supported by the ODBC connection. This gives us greater flexibility, and the performance is great! So when it comes to our application, we will use SQLOLEDB.

> Using SQLOLEDB and having to move servers is not really an issue in an ASP Web application. The connection string information is held in one place, and because ASP is really only a text file, the server connection information is very easy to modify.

Building the SpyNet User Interface

In this section we will build a very basic front end that makes a connection to our database, validates a user's login, and retrieves (searches for) data. Although this is just a start, it will provide the building blocks you need to develop it further for your own needs.

This chapter, unlike the others, is more like a recipe: planning the pages, creating a user to access the pages, and so on. Follow the recipe and you will get a cake (well actually a GUI) at the end.

Because we're focusing on SQL Server 2000 instead of the art of building user interfaces, I don't give much explanation of the code or development process. I do show you how to turn a basic query against the database into an interactive Web page. You never know, I might just write another book on front-end development!

Determining the SpyNet Web Pages

Our interface will be relatively simple, all of about 7–10 pages, and three of these pages will be used for establishing and closing a database connection. We'll also use welcome and query pages to let the user enter search criteria. Our Web site will have the following pages:

- Default.htm—This is the first page that is hit when our Web site is called. This page will be briefly seen by our users.

- Login.asp—Used to validate the user's login information. This page will be seen by our users.

- Global.asa—The initial page that holds the database connection information in application-wide variables. It's a system-only file.

- adovbs.inc—The file used to give us constants, provided by Microsoft. We will use a cut-down version because we do not need a full file. This will be an include file and is a system-only file.

   Include files are files that contain general functions that we need to use throughout the site. They are called include files because we include them in the page as you would include header files in C++ or Java, or make references like in VB.

- Connection.asp—The file used to actually make a connection to the database. This will be an include file and is a system-only file.

- ConnectionClose.asp—The file used to close the connection to our database. This will be an include file and is a system-only file.

- Welcome.asp—The first page our users will be sent to after successfully logging in. This page will be seen by our users and will act as their home page.

- Search.asp—This is where our users are able to perform searches against our database. This page will be seen by our users.

This is the basic structure of our Web site. Now we should take a brief look at the software you will need on your machine.

Setting Up Your Machine to Run the SpyNet Application

Before creating the actual Web pages, you first need to prepare your machine to act as a server by installing some software.

As mentioned earlier, you will need to install PWS. You can find this under the add-ons folder on the Windows 98 CD, or you can download it from `http://www.microsoft.com/windows/ie/pws/main.htm`.

> **Note**   To find out how to set up your machine as a Web server, take a look in Appendix A, "Setting Up Your PC as a Web Server."

Of course, you'll want to use the files I've created so you don't have to rewrite all the code. The files for the application are on the book's Web site under Que's site (`www.quepublishing.com`). Download those and tuck them away until you need them.

Next you will need to have ActiveX Data Objects (ADO) installed. Luckily for you this is done when you install SQL Server 2000 as part of the Microsoft Data Access Components (MDAC) upgrade. The MDAC upgrade also installs SQLOLEDB for you.

The last thing that you need to have installed is Microsoft FrontPage. This comes with Internet Explorer 5.0, so if you do not have it installed already, just rerun the Internet Explorer setup and select the component from the list.

> **Note**   You do not have to use Microsoft FrontPage. As mentioned earlier, you can use Notepad, Word, or any other text editor. If you have a copy of Visual InterDev you should use that because VID is designed for the development of both small- and large-scale Web sites.

And that's it! We are now ready to begin creating our first Web site. So let's get going. Just remember, if you do not fully understand something you will need to do more research on your own!

Setting Up Our Web Site to Run Under PWS

Before we create our Web site we need to set a place where our files will be saved.

1. Navigate your way through the file system until you see where PWS has created the standard Web site that comes with the software. This will be something like *x*:\Inetpub\wwwroot\, where *x* is your hard drive.

2. When you have found this folder, create a new folder under this one called SpyNet.

3. Under the SpyNet folder create two new folders, Includes and Images. Your file system will look something like the one shown in Figure 12.4.

Figure 12.4

How your file system should look so we can start building our SpyNet Web site.

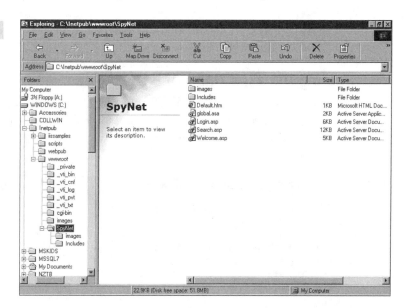

The SpyNet folder will hold all our main files for the Web site. The Includes folder will hold our include pages, and the Images folder will hold all our images. As we develop (or copy) each page, I will let you know where they all go so that the site doesn't break. To begin, put all the images under the Images folder.

That's about all we need to do now. Let's start building!

Creating a New User to Establish a Connection

Because this is a brand-new Web site, we do not have any users who can access our site. Remember when we created the SQLSpyNetUser? If not, you can skip back to Chapter 9 and check it out in "Creating Logins to Spy Net."

Now we need to create a new user who has only limited rights. We don't want anybody hacking the site, now do we?

Warning

Although we have developed a user for our site and restricted access, it is by no means totally secure. You would need to research security on the Web a little more to find the most appropriate method for securing the site.

12

1. Create a user called SpyNetIntranetUser and give them a password that is easy to remember.

2. The new user must have access to our SQLSpyNet database, but make sure the new user is *only* a member of the Public role.

3. When you have created the user, the only permission you are going to give them is SELECT permission on the Person table, for reasons that will soon become clear.

Creating Our First Page, the Global.asa

The first page we are going to create is the Global.asa. In an ASP application this is the first system page that is called, and it holds information that is available to the whole application. So create a file with the name exactly as it is, Global.asa, and enter the code in Listing 12.1 into the file.

Listing 12.1—Creating a Connection with Global.asa

```
1: <SCRIPT LANGUAGE="VBScript" RUNAT="Server">
2: Sub Application_OnStart
3:     Application("Conn_ConnectionString") = "Provider=SQLOLEDB.1;
       ➥Initial Catalog=SQLSpyNet;Data Source=GRUNTER/MYSQLSERVER;"
4:     Application("Conn_ConnectionTimeout") = 15
5:     Application("Conn_CommandTimeout") = 30
6:     Application("Conn_CursorLocation") = 3
7: End Sub
8: </SCRIPT>
```

Analysis

You need to make a couple of changes to get this to run on your system. In Lines 3 and 3a the Application("Conn_ConnectionString") will need to be modified to have your server name entered where I have the server name GRUNTER. This then needs to be followed by your instance name, which is MYSQLSERVER in my example. Your code will need to be in the form *InstanceName\ServerName*.

Tip

You can easily get your server name/instance name from the Service Manager tool. By opening the tool, you will see a list of SQL Servers running on your system (and network if connected). Choose the one you want, copy the name by using Ctrl+C, and paste it into your code. Voilà! All done.

To learn more about Service Manager, refer to Chapter 2, in the section "Checking Out SQL Server 2000's Other Tools."

Notice the Application prefixes (that is, **Application**("Conn_ConnectionString")) on some of the lines; these variables with the prefix hold information that is available to the *whole* application. We will use these variables and pass them to the connection object.

This page goes under our SpyNet folder, which is known as the *root* of the Web project. The Global.asa file must always be placed in the root of any Web project.

Creating the Default.htm Page

Next we need to create the Default.htm page. This is the first page, by default in PWS, which is served up when the user hits the site. The special name of Default.htm is the name that PWS (and IIS) looks for. You can configure this to be something different, but the default is fine for us.

 Note   There is nothing really special about this page; it is just a plain old HTML page. There is no dynamic content, but this page is core to our system development.

Create a new page, and once again call the page exactly the name specified. Then enter Listing 12.2 into the page.

Listing 12.2—Default.htm

```
1: <HTML>
2:    <HEAD>
3:       <TITLE>Spy Net Limited</TITLE>
4:       <META NAME="RedirectPage" HTTP-EQUIV="REFRESH"
          ➥CONTENT="0;URL=Login.asp">
5:    </HEAD>
6:    <BODY></BODY>
7: </HTML>
```

When this page is called it redirects us (see line 4, specifically looking at the CONTENT tag) to the Login.asp page. We actually have enough now to run our Web site. Groovy baby!

If we run our Web site by typing our address http://*servername*/*websitename*; that is, http://grunter/SpyNet, into our browser, the Default.htm will redirect us to our Login.asp page, which doesn't actually exist yet, so we will get the good old 404 (page not found) error!

12

All this code is available for you to download. Because the code is available, you do not have to create all these pages from scratch. However you will need to modify the Global.asa page so that the Web site will run on your system.

For those of you who do like looking through code on paper as well as on screen, I have included all the source code in the next couple of sections, so read till your heart is content.

The Default.htm file is also placed in the root of the Web project. This means that we do not have to configure our Web server (PWS) to find a new file; this one will be found by default.

Building the Include Pages

First let's take a quick look at include files and why we use them. Include files save a lot of repetitive coding. We create our subroutines to perform a given set of functionality and we just call that same subroutine again and again when we need it. Anything to make our lives easier!

There are a couple of ways for us to make a connection to the database, and there are also a couple of ways to retrieve the data. In my opinion none is as good as ADO.

ADO stands for ActiveX Data Objects. ADO allows us to easily connect to a database and retrieve and update data. ADO has a very simple object model, consisting mainly of Connection, Command, and Recordset objects. These combine to provide great data management capabilities.

ADO allows us almost complete flexibility when we are developing a Web site. We can make database connections, have multiple recordsets, and so forth.

All the include files must be placed under the Includes directory. I have made specific references to them in the code, so they should be under the directory or else they can't be found and the code will fail.

Using Connect.asp for an ADO Connection

To establish a connection to SQLSpyNet database with ADO, we need to supply the Connection object (a subcomponent of ADO) with the correct parameters. This includes *servername*, *databasename*, *username*, and *password*. Listing 12.3 shows the code for this page, called simply enough, the Connection.asp page.

Note If you do not know, in VBScript a comment is prefixed with a single quote ('). So look for any of the code that has a single quote as a comment for some clarification.

Listing 12.3—Connecting to the Database Through ADO

```
 1: <%'Declare a variable called Conn
 2: Dim Conn
 3: 'Check to see if our Connection already exists if it does, don't do anything
 4: If Not isObject(Conn) Then
 5:     'If it doesn't set our variable to type ADO Connection Object
 6:     Set Conn = Server.CreateObject("ADODB.Connection")
 7:     With Conn
 8:         'Specify some parameters for our Connection object
 9:         .ConnectionTimeout = Application("Conn_ConnectionTimeout")
10:         .CommandTimeout = Application("Conn_CommandTimeout")
11:         .CursorLocation = Application("Conn_CursorLocation")
12:     End With
13: End If%>
```

Analysis

If you are a little insightful you will see that we specified some of these parameters in our Global.asa. The only ones we didn't specify are the username and password because our users must enter these when they log on. By giving the connection object the connection string information, as we do in Connection.asp, we can get a connection to our database for everything we need to SQLSpyNet database with ADO, .

Cleaning Up the Connection

The next include file we are going to take a look at is the ConnectionClose.asp page, shown in Listing 12.4. All this page does is tidy up after we have finished with the connection object. As any middle-tier developer will tell you, "Always, always clean up the objects when you have finished with them!"

Listing 12.4—ConnectionClose.asp

```
1: <%If isObject(Conn) Then
2:     Conn.Close
3:     Set Conn = Nothing
4: End If%>
```

12

Analysis

When we include the ConnectionClose.asp page in our page, we discard the connection that we have been using by first closing it (line 2), and then destroying the object from memory in line 4 (Set Conn = Nothing).

Using adovbs.inc to Make the VBScript Work Properly

The adovbs.inc file is the third and final include file. Because nothing is *strongly typed* in VBScript and we do not have access to all the libraries that VB has, we need to have our constants (values that do not change) in a single place.

Strongly typed refers to the datatypes that a development language uses. VBScript is not strongly typed because everything is treated as a Variant (a special type that can contain anything) until it is assigned its first value. VB 6.0, on the other hand, is a strongly typed language because when you declare a variable you specify the datatype at creation time.

We use constants because they allow us to use English-like names for specified values instead of the more ambiguous numbers that VBScript recognizes.

In our site we are only using a cut-down version of the adovbs.inc file, which I've put into Listing 12.5. There is a lot of overhead in opening the file every time a page is loaded, so if we keep the page trim, it will load faster.

Listing 12.5—Storing the VBScript Constants in adovbs.inc

```
1: <%
2: '-------------------------------------------------------------------
3: ' (SOME) Microsoft ADO
4: '
5: ' ADO constants include file for VBScript
6: '
7: '-------------------------------------------------------------------
8:'---- CursorTypeEnum Values ----
9: Const adOpenStatic = 3
10:
11: '---- LockTypeEnum Values ----
12: Const adLockReadOnly = 1
13:
14: '---- CursorLocationEnum Values ----
15: Const adUseClient = 3
16:
17: '---- ObjectStateEnum Values ----
18: Const adStateClosed = &H00000000
19: Const adStateOpen = &H00000001
20:
21: '---- ParameterDirectionEnum Values ----
22: Const adParamInput = &H0001
```

```
23: Const adParamOutput = &H0002
24:
25: '---- CommandTypeEnum Values ----
26: Const adCmdStoredProc = &H0004
27:
28: '---- DataTypeEnum Values ----
29: Const adVarChar = 200
30: %>
```

Validating the User's Login

This is one of the cooler pages that I am sure you will enjoy developing. This page actually takes the user's name and password and passes that to the ADO connection object. Listing 12.6 shows the code for the Login.asp page.

Listing 12.6—Using Login.asp to Verify User Access

```
1: <%@Language="VBScript"%>
2: <%'The Option Explicit makes sure that all variables are declared
3: Option Explicit
4:
5: 'Response.Expires ensures that the page is not cached in the browser
6: Response.Expires = -1000
7:
8: 'Response.Buffer means that the page is buffered on the web server.
9: 'The browser will not receive
10: 'the page until the contents have finished rendering on the browser
11: Response.Buffer = True
12:
13: 'This variable is at page level scope, so that we can give
14: 'back custom error messages
15: 'See below
16: Dim sErrorMessage
17:
18: 'Check to see if the user has pushed the button.
19: 'If they have then call the dologin function
20: If Len(Trim(Request.Form("M")))<>0 Then
21:     'If the login information is true then redirect
        ➡the user to the Welcome page
22:     If DoLogin Then
23:         Response.Redirect("Welcome.asp")
24:     End If
25: End If%>
26:
27: <HTML>
28:     <HEAD>
29:         <META NAME="GENERATOR" Content="Microsoft Visual Studio 6.0">
30:         <TITLE>Spy Net Limited</TITLE>
31:     </HEAD>
32:
33:     <SCRIPT LANGUAGE="JavaScript">
```

continues

12

Listing 12.6—continued

```
34:        function CheckLogin(){
35:             /*This script just checks the user has entered a
36:             Username before we submit the page.
37:             It is called from the Login button at the bottom of the page
38:             If they have supplied a user name then we submit the page*/
39:             if (formMain.UserName.value == "")
40:                  {
41:                  alert('Oops, you have forgotten to type your User Name.
                    ➥Please enter to continue.');
44:                  formMain.UserName.focus();
45:                  }
46:             else
47:                  formMain.submit();
48:             }
49:    </SCRIPT>
50:
51:    <BODY LEFTMARGIN="0" TOPMARGIN="0" MARGINWIDTH="0" MARGINHEIGHT="0"
       ➥BGCOLOR="#666666" LANGUAGE="JavaScript"
       ➥ONLOAD="formMain.UserName.focus();">
52:        <TABLE CELLPADDING="0" CELLSPACING="0" BORDER="0"
           ➥WIDTH="100%" BORDERCOLOR="RED">
53:             <TR>
54:                  <TD WIDTH="411"><IMG SRC="images/topstrip.jpg" WIDTH="411"
                    ➥HEIGHT="147" VSPACE="0" HSPACE="0"></TD>
55:                  <TD WIDTH="38"><IMG SRC="images/topstripmid.jpg" WIDTH="38"
                    ➥HEIGHT="147" VSPACE="0" HSPACE="0"></TD>
56:                  <TD WIDTH><IMG SRC="images/topstripright.jpg" WIDTH="100%"
                    ➥HEIGHT="147" VSPACE="0" HSPACE="0"></TD>
57:             </TR>
58:        </TABLE>
59:
60:        <TABLE CELLPADDING="0" CELLSPACING="0" BORDER="0"
           ➥BORDERCOLOR="GREEN">
61:             <TR>
62:                  <TD ROWSPAN="3"> <IMG SRC="images/figure.gif"
                    ➥VSPACE="20" HSPACE="0" WIDTH="172" HEIGHT="285"></TD>
63:                  <%If Len(Trim(sErrorMessage))<>0 Then
64:                       Response.Write("<TD WIDTH=""324"" HEIGHT=""99""
                        ➥VALIGN=""CENTER""><FONT FACE=""arial,
                        ➥verdana, helvetica"" SIZE=""2""
                        ➥COLOR=""#ffffff""> " & sErrorMessage &
                        ➥"</FONT></TD>")
65:                  Else
66:                       Response.Write("<TD HEIGHT=""99""> </TD>")
67:                  End If%>
68:                  <TD ROWSPAN="3"><IMG SRC="images/logo.jpg" WIDTH="295"
                    ➥HEIGHT="290"></TD>
69:             </TR>
70:             <TR>
71:                  <TD valign="top"><IMG SRC="images/title.jpg" WIDTH="324"
                    ➥HEIGHT="63"></TD>
```

```
72:             </TR>
73:             <TR>
74:                 <TD> </TD>
75:             </TR>
76:         </TABLE>
77:
78:         <FORM NAME="formMain" ACTION="Login.asp" METHOD="POST">
79:             <TABLE CELLPADDING="0" CELLSPACING="0" BORDER="0" WIDTH="100%"
                ➥BORDERCOLOR="BLUE">
80:                 <TR>
81:                     <TD ROWSPAN="5" valign="top">
82:                         <IMG SRC="images/bottomstrip.jpg" WIDTH="100%"
                            ➥HEIGHT="162"></TD>
83:                     <TD WIDTH="235">
84:                         <IMG SRC="images/logintopstrip.jpg" WIDTH="235"
                            ➥HEIGHT="17"></TD>
85:                     <TD ROWSPAN="5" valign="top">
86:                         <IMG SRC="images/bottomstrip.jpg"
                            ➥WIDTH="100%" HEIGHT="162"></TD>
87:                 </TR>
88:                 <TR>
89:                     <TD BGCOLOR="#000000" HEIGHT="17">
90:                         <FONT COLOR="#ff8c00" STYLE="FONT-FAMILY: Verdana;
                            ➥FONT-SIZE: x-small;">Username:  
                            ➥       
                            ➥ Password:</FONT>
91:                     </TD>
92:                 </TR>
93:                 <TR>
94:                     <TD BGCOLOR="#000000" HEIGHT="17">
95:                         <INPUT TYPE="TEXT" NAME="UserName" SIZE="15">
                            ➥ <INPUT TYPE="PASSWORD" NAME="UserPwd"
                            ➥SIZE="15">
96:                     </TD>
97:                 </TR>
98:                 <TR>
99:                     <TD BGCOLOR="#000000" HEIGHT="17" ALIGN="RIGHT">
100:                        <IMG LANGUAGE="JavaScript" ONCLICK="CheckLogin();"
                            ➥STYLE="Cursor:Hand" SRC="Images/Login.gif"
                            ➥VALUE="Login" ID="Login"
                            ➥NAME="Login" WIDTH="101" HEIGHT="13"> 
101:                    </TD>
102:                </TR>
103:                <TR>
104:                    <TD>
105:                        <IMG SRC="images/loginbottomstrip.jpg" HEIGHT="83"
                            ➥WIDTH="100%">
106:                    </TD>
107:                </TR>
108:            </TABLE>
109:            <INPUT TYPE="HIDDEN" NAME="M" SIZE="15" VALUE="Login">
110:        </FORM>
```

continues

12

Listing 12.6—continued

```
111:    </BODY>
112: </HTML>
113:
114: <%Function DoLogin
115: 'This statement allows us to trap errors that may occur
116: On Error Resume Next
117:    'bResult is a boolean variable (True or False)
           ➥that we use in the function
118:    Dim bResult
119:    'sConn is a varaible that we use to build the connection
           ➥string information that we need to
120:    'create a connection to the database with
121:    Dim sConn
122:    'These are the include files we need!!%>
123:    <!--#INCLUDE FILE = "Includes/adovbs.inc" -->
124:    <!--#INCLUDE FILE = "Includes/Connection.asp" -->
125:    <%If isObject(Conn) Then
126:        sConn = Application("Conn_ConnectionString") & ";User Id=" &
           ➥Request.Form("UserName") & ";PASSWORD=" &
           ➥Request.Form("UserPwd") & ";"
127:        Conn.Open sConn
128:        If Conn.State = adStateOpen Then
129:            bResult = True
130:        Else
131:            bResult = False
132:        End If
133:    End If
134:
135:    If Err.number<>0 Then
136:        'This is the error code for a login failure
137:        If Err.number = -2147217843 Then
138:            bResult = False
139:            sErrorMessage = "Oops, we cannot log you in.
               ➥Please check the credentials you have supplied."
140:        Else
141:            bResult = False
142:            sErrorMessage = "Oops, something has gone wrong internally.
               ➥Please try again, and if the problem persists contact
               ➥your System Administrator."
143:        End If
144:    End If
145:
146:    'If the attempted results are are successful we will store the
147:    'information in a session variable so other database connection pages
148:    'can use the same information
149:    If bResult Then
150:        Session("UserName") = Request.Form("UserName")
```

```
151:            Session("UserPwd") = Request.Form("UserPwd")
152:        End If
153:        '**********************************************************************
154:        'NOTE:
155:        'IT IS NOT RECOMMENDED TO STORE PASSWORDS IN A SESSION VARIABLE
156:        'While session variables are only for the logged in user, they are not
157:        'encrypted, so suspect to hacking. In a real site you would need to
158:        'find some other architecture
159:        '**********************************************************************
160:
161:        'Finally give back the results of the attempted login
162:        DoLogin = bResult
163: End Function%>
```

Analysis

The most important thing to get from this long listing is how ADO attempts to establish a connection to the database with the user's credentials. If successful, the user is allowed in and redirected to the Welcome.asp page. If unsuccessful, the user receives an error message, informing them that their attempt was unsuccessful.

The two text fields on the screen capture the user information and when submitted back to the server (by the user clicking the login button), we take this information and try to make the connection.

Where does it all happen? If you take a look at the function DoLogin, you will see that this function takes the username and password and passes it to our Connection.asp page. If the connection succeeds the user is in, if it fails, the user must try again.

Login.asp is placed in the root of the Web project.

Greeting Users with the Welcome.asp Page

This is the main screen that our users will see. We have a nice greeting on the page welcoming them to our site. When our site is running, the user will be able to navigate around the site from this page to perform a search, to log out, and maybe in the future to update the data that lives in the database.

Our Welcome.asp page, shown in Listing 12.7, is rich in the fact that it provides valuable information, up front and to the point. However, in a development aspect this page is very simple. It is almost pure HTML, making it very easy to understand.

Listing 12.7—The Welcome.asp Page

```
1: <%@Language="VBScript"%>
2: <%'The Option Explicit makes sure that all varibles are declared
3: Option Explicit
4:
5: 'Response.Expires ensures that the page is not cached in the browser
6: Response.Expires = -1000
7:
8: 'Response.Buffer means that the page is buffered on the web server.
9: 'The browser will not receive
10: 'the page until the contents have finished rendering on the web server
11: Response.Buffer = True
12:
13: 'If the User wishes to log out, we destroy the session variables
14: 'When it gets to the next line, they will be redirected back to Login.asp
15: 'Cool huh?
16: If Len(Trim(Request("Destroy")))<>0 Then
17:     If CInt(Trim(Request("Destroy"))) = 1 Then
18:         Session("UserName") = ""
19:     End If
20: End If
21:
22: 'Check to see if the UserName has been stored in a session variable.
23: 'If not send the user to the Login.asp page.
    ➥This will then force them to login again.
24: 'This helps to prevent someone from just typing the URL
25: 'of the page into the browser window and getting into the site
26: If Len(Trim(Session("UserName")))=0 Then
27:     'Why do we just check UserName? Well the user may have no password!
28:     Response.Redirect("Login.asp")
29: End If%>
30:
31: <HTML>
32:     <HEAD>
33:         <META NAME="GENERATOR" Content="Microsoft Visual Studio 6.0">
34:         <TITLE>Spy Net Limited</TITLE>
35:     </HEAD>
36:
37:     <SCRIPT LANGUAGE="JavaScript">
38:         function VerifyLogout(){
39:             var bConfirm = window.confirm('This will log you out of Spy Net.
                ➥Are you sure you wish to continue?');
40:             if (!bConfirm)
41:                 window.event.returnValue = false
42:         }
43:     </SCRIPT>
44:
45:     <STYLE TYPE="text/css">
46:         A:link    {color: #ffffff;text-decoration:none}
47:         A:visited    {color: #ffffff;text-decoration:none}
48:         A.b       {color: #ffffff; text-decoration:none;}
```

```
49:        A.r          {color: #ffffff; text-decoration:none;}
50:        A.bb    {color: #ffffff; text-decoration:none;}
51:        A.bb:visited     {color: #ffffff; text-decoration:none;}
52:        A:hover    {color:#ff8c00;text-decoration:underline;}
53:        A.bb:hover      {color:#ff8c00;}
54:    </STYLE>
55:
56:    <BODY LEFTMARGIN="0" TOPMARGIN="0" MARGINWIDTH="0" MARGINHEIGHT="0"
       ➥BGCOLOR="#666666">
57:
58:        <TABLE CELLPADDING="0" CELLSPACING="0" BORDER="0" WIDTH="100%">
59:            <TR>
60:                <TD VALIGN="top"><IMG SRC="images/welcometopstrip.jpg"
                   ➥WIDTH="100%" HEIGHT="101" VSPACE="0" HSPACE="0"></TD>
61:                <TD WIDTH="38" VALIGN="top">
62:                    <IMG SRC="images/welcometopstripmid.jpg" WIDTH="38"
                       ➥HEIGHT="101" VSPACE="0" HSPACE="0"></TD>
63:                <TD WIDTH="303" VALIGN="top"><IMG SRC="images/menu.gif"
                   ➥WIDTH="303" HEIGHT="100" useMAP="#menu" BORDER="0" >
64:                    <MAP NAME="menu">
65:                        <AREA SHAPE="rect" COORDS="156,43,210,56"
                           ➥HREF="search.asp" TITLE="Search"
                           ➥ALT="Search">
66:                        <AREA SHAPE="rect" COORDS="97,44,151,55"
                           ➥ONCLICK="VerifyLogout();"
                           ➥HREF="Welcome.asp?Destroy=1"
                           ➥TITLE="Logout" ALT="Logout">
67:                        <AREA SHAPE="rect" COORDS="38,44,92,56"
                           ➥ HREF="welcome.asp" TITLE="Home" ALT="Home">
68:                    </MAP>
69:                </TD>
70:            </TR>
71:        </TABLE>
72:
73:        <TABLE CELLPADDING="0" CELLSPACING="0" BORDER="0" WIDTH="600">
74:            <TR>
75:                <TD ROWSPAN="2" VALIGN="top"> 
76:                    <IMG SRC="images/figure.gif" VSPACE="20" HSPACE="0"
                       ➥WIDTH="172" HEIGHT="285">
77:                </TD>
78:                <TD HEIGHT="99" VALIGN="top" COLSPAN="2">
79:                    <IMG SRC="images/welcome.gif" WIDTH="167"
                       ➥HEIGHT="77">
80:                </TD>
81:            </TR>
82:            <TR>
83:                <TD WIDTH="30"> </TD>
84:                <TD VALIGN="top">
85:                    <FONT FACE="arial, verdana, helvetica" SIZE="2"
                       ➥COLOR="#ffffff">
```

continues

12

Listing 12.7—continued

```
86:                      <P>
87:                          Welcome to Spy Net LTD. This site
                             ➥runs in conjunction with the
                             ➥SQL Server 2000 Database Development
                             ➥from Scratch book by
                             ➥<A HREF="mailto:rob-marg@xtra.co.nz">
                             ➥Rob Hawthorne</A>.<BR><BR>
88:                          The development of this site is part of the
                             ➥book, and is designed to give you an
                             ➥overview of how easy it is to create
                             ➥a SQL Server 2000 database and then
                             ➥implement that on the web!
89:                      </P>
90:                      <P>
91:                          On the top right of the screen, you will see
                             ➥three buttons "Home," "Logout,"
                             ➥and "Search".
92:                          <LI>The "Home" button will always bring
                             ➥you back here.
93:                          <LI>The "Logout" button will log you
                             ➥out of the system, and return you to the login
                             ➥page.
94:                          <LI>The "Search" button will take you to the
                             ➥search screen, so you can perform a
                             ➥search for People in the system.
95:                      </P>
96:                      <P>
97:                          So have a play and familiarize
                             ➥yourself with the site.<BR>
98:                          If you wish to add to it later, that
                             ➥would be great!<BR>
99:                          Some suggested ideas are
100:                         <LI>Have a data entry screen for
                             ➥ Spies and Bad Guys
101:                         <LI>Have a reports screen to see who
                             ➥is on what activity
102:                         <LI>Implement a notification system to a Spy
                             ➥when they are reassigned i.e. an Email
103:                     </P>
104:                     <P>
105:                         PS: If your PC supports it, this site looks
                             ➥great in 16-bit (or higher color)
                             ➥and a 1024x768 (or greater) resolution.
106:                     </P>
107:                     </FONT>
108:                     <FONT FACE="arial, verdana, helvetica"
                         ➥SIZE="2" COLOR="#ff8c00">
109:                     <P>
```

```
110:                                This site's awesome graphics were provided
                                ➥by a very talented Graphic Artist.
                                ➥Thank you Jillian for all your hard work!
111:                        </P>
112:                    </FONT>
113:                </TD>
114:            </TR>
115:            <TR>
116:                <TD> </TD>
117:            </TR>
118:        </TABLE>
119:
120:        <TABLE CELLPADDING="0" CELLSPACING="0" BORDER="0" WIDTH="100%">
121:            <TR>
122:                <TD ROWSPAN="3" VALIGN="top">
123:                    <IMG SRC="images/bottomsTRip.jpg" WIDTH="100%"
                        ➥HEIGHT="162">
124:                </TD>
125:            </TR>
126:        </TABLE>
127:    </BODY>
128: </HTML>
```

Welcome.asp is also placed in the root of the Web project.

Creating the Search.asp Page to Retrieve Data from SpyNet

With this page we have some real Web site functionality. We can dynamically search for information within our database, and in the future we can provide links so we can view and edit the data.

What do we need to do to get the Search.asp page running? First of all we need to think about what we are searching for, for example, is it a person, a spy, or an address?

Luckily for you, I have already decided; isn't analysis fun? For the moment the search will be over the Person table, allowing us to find people by their first name or their surname. But we will go one step ahead of this and allow the user to enter the initial character of a surname (or first name) and return a result. For example, if they entered Ha, they would get Hawthorne as well as Harrison.

Creating a Stored Procedure to Search Against SpyNet

Let's create our stored procedure. It is up to you whether you use Query Analyzer or Enterprise Manager to create the stored procedure. I am sure by now you are becoming proficient with both tools!

Enter the code in Listing 12.8 into the tool of your choice.

12

Listing 12.8—The Stored Procedure to Search the Person Table

```
1: CREATE PROCEDURE PersonSearch
2:     @FirstName VARCHAR(50) = NULL,
3:     @Surname VARCHAR(50) = NULL
4: AS
5:     SELECT
6:         PersonID,
7:         Firstname + ' ' + Surname AS Fullname,
8:         dbo.DateFormatter(DOB, ' ') AS DOB,
9:         PhoneNo
10:    FROM Person
11:    WHERE (@FirstName IS NULL OR Firstname LIKE @FirstName + '%')
12:      AND (@Surname IS NULL OR Surname LIKE @Surname + '%')
13:    ORDER BY Firstname, Surname
14: GO
```

Analysis

The only lines here that are a little different than what we have come across before are Lines 11 and 12. The special clause that we have entered (@FirstName IS NULL) allows us to evaluate whether the parameter has a NULL value. If it is true, then the OR clause is not executed. The same principle applies for @Surname. So you can actually execute this stored procedure without any parameters supplied, and get back all the people in the Person table! However, if you do supply a value for the parameters, the search will be restricted by the values supplied. The '%' on the end of the LIKE statements allow us to append a wildcard to the parameter for searching.

You should go ahead and test the stored procedure (I'm sure you know that though!), with a combination of parameters, shown in Listing 12.9, to make sure it returns the data as you want, for example.

Listing 12.9—Testing the Search

```
1: EXEC PersonSearch @Surname = 'T'
2: GO
3: EXEC PersonSearch
4: GO
```

Analysis

The first search is a limiting search and will return the records that have a surname beginning with T. The second search is a more generalized search that returns absolutely everything in the table because no parameters are supplied to restrict the search.

Granting the New User Permission to Search

Now that our stored procedure is created we must give our new user access to it. Enter the statement in Listing 12.10, or go through Enterprise Manager and assign execute permissions to the new user.

Listing 12.10—Granting Search Permissions to the User

```
1: GRANT EXECUTE ON PersonSearch TO SpyNetIntranetUser
```

Our stored procedure is created; our user has access; now we need to create the screen to actually search for the data.

Creating the Search Screen

The Search.asp page is divided into two main sections. The first is the basic HTML outline that includes the text boxes for the user to enter their search criteria, and the second is the function that actually performs the search. This function makes a connection to the database and executes the search.

Within this function though, we introduce two more ADO objects, which you'll see in Listing 12.11.

- Command object—This allows us to specify that we are going to create a stored procedure and use certain parameters for a search. The command object allows us to build a command that we want to execute against the database.

- Recordset object—This allows us to bring back a group of records. After we have a set of records, we can write these out to the screen.

The ADO objects are very cool! They have many properties that you can manipulate, and in fact whole books have been written on ADO! To help you follow along, I add several comments, including sections marked with single quotes (') and asterisks (*) to show you where the action is.

Listing 12.11—Creating the Code for the Search.asp Page

```
1: <%@Language="VBScript"%>
2: <%'The Option Explicit makes sure that all variables are declared
3: Option Explicit
4:
5: 'Response.Expires ensures that the page is not cached in the Browser
6: Response.Expires = -1000
7:
8: 'Response.Buffer means that the page is buffered on the web server.
   ➥The Browser will not receive
9: 'the page until the contents have finished rendering on the Browser
10: Response.Buffer = True
```

12

continues

Listing 12.11—continued

```
11:
12: 'If the User wishes to log out, we Destroy the session variables
13: 'When it gets to the next line, they will be redirected back to Login.asp
14: 'Cool huh?
15: If Len(Trim(Request("Destroy")))<>0 Then
16:    If CInt(Trim(Request("Destroy"))) = 1 Then
17:        Session("UserName") = ""
18:    End If
19: End If
20:
21: 'Check to see if the UserName has been stored in a session variable. If not
22: 'send the user to the Login.asp page.
    ➥This will then force them to login again.
23:'This helps to prevent someone from just typing the URL of the
    ➥page into the Browser 20: window and getting into the site
24: If Len(Trim(Session("UserName")))=0 Then
25:    'Why do we just check UserName? Well the user may have no password!
26:    Response.Redirect("Login.asp")
27: End If
28:
29: 'A page scoped variable because it will be used in more than one place
30: Dim sErrorMessage%>
31: <HTML>
32:   <HEAD>
33:     <META NAME="GENERATOR" Content="Microsoft Visual Studio 6.0">
34:     <TITLE>Spy Net Limited</TITLE>
35:   </HEAD>
36:
37:   <SCRIPT LANGUAGE="JavaScript">
38:     function VerifyLogout(){
39:         var bConfirm = window.confirm('This will log you out of Spy Net.
           ➥Are you sure you wish to continue?');
40:         if (!bConfirm)
41:             window.event.returnValue = false
42:     }
43:   </SCRIPT>
44:
45:   <BODY LEFTMARGIN="0" TOPMARGIN="0" MARGINWIDTH="0" MARGINHEIGHT="0"
      ➥ONLOAD="formMain.Firstname.focus();" BGCOLOR="#666666">
46:     <FORM NAME="formMain" ACTION="Search.asp" METHOD="POST">
47:         <INPUT TYPE="HIDDEN" NAME="M" VALUE="DoSearch">
48:         <TABLE CELLPADDING="0" CELLSPACING="0" BORDER="0"
           ➥BORDERCOLOR="RED" WIDTH="100%">
49:             <TR>
50:                 <TD VALIGN="top">
51: <IMG SRC="images/welcometopsTRip.jpg" WIDTH="100%" HEIGHT="101" VSPACE="0"
    ➥HSPACE="0"></TD>
52:                 <TD WIDTH="38" VALIGN="top">
53: <IMG SRC="images/welcometopsTRipmid.jpg" WIDTH="38" HEIGHT="101" VSPACE="0"
    ➥HSPACE="0"></TD>
```

```
54:                          <TD WIDTH="303" VALIGN="top"><IMG SRC="images/menu.gif"
                          ➥WIDTH="303" HEIGHT="100" USEMAP="#menu"
                          ➥BORDER="0">
55:                            <MAP NAME="menu">
56:                                <AREA SHAPE="rect" COORDS="156,43,210,56"
                                ➥HREF="search.asp" TITLE="Home"
                                ➥ALT="Home">
57:                                <AREA SHAPE="rect" COORDS="97,44,151,55"
                                ➥ONCLICK="VerifyLogout();"
                                ➥HREF="Search.asp?Destroy=1"
                                ➥TITLE="Logout" ALT="Logout">
58:                                <AREA SHAPE="rect" COORDS="38,44,92,56"
                                ➥HREF="welcome.asp" TITLE="Home"
                                ➥ALT="Home">
59:                            </MAP>
60:                          </TD>
61:                        </TR>
62:                    </TABLE>
63:
64:                    <TABLE CELLPADDING="0" CELLSPACING="0" BORDER="0"
                    ➥WIDTH="600" BORDERCOLOR="GREEN">
65:                        <TR>
66:                          <TD ROWSPAN="2"> <IMG SRC="images/figure.gif"
                          ➥VSPACE="20" HSPACE="0" WIDTH="172"
                          ➥HEIGHT="285"></TD>
67:                          <TD VALIGN="top" COLSPAN="2" HEIGHT="77">
68:                            <IMG SRC="images/search.gif" WIDTH="167"
                            ➥HEIGHT="77"></TD>
69:                        </TR>
70:                        <TR>
71:                          <TD WIDTH="30"> </TD>
72:                          <TD VALIGN="top" HEIGHT="200">
73:                            <FONT COLOR="#ff8c00" STYLE="FONT-FAMILY: Verdana;
                            ➥FONT-SIZE: x-small;">Firstname: 
                            ➥      
                            ➥      
                            ➥      
                            ➥      
                            ➥Surname:</FONT><BR>
74:                            <INPUT TYPE="TEXT" NAME="Firstname" SIZE="28"
                            ➥ALIGN="right"
                            ➥VALUE="<%=Request.Form("FirstName")%>">
                            ➥  <INPUT TYPE="TEXT"
                            ➥NAME="Surname" SIZE="28" ALIGN="right"
                            ➥VALUE="<%=Request.Form("Surname")%>">
75:                            <BR><BR>
76:                            <INPUT TYPE="Image" SRC="Images/go.gif"
                            ➥VALUE="Search" ID="Search" NAME="Search"
                            ➥ALIGN="right" WIDTH="54" HEIGHT="10">
77:                            <BR>
78:                            <%'If our page has been submitted the hidden value M
```

12

continues

Listing 12.11—continued

```
                                ➥(see top of HTML, just under the
                                ➥opening form tag)
  79:                           'will exist, so do our search
  80:                           If Len(Trim(Request.Form("M")))<>0 And
                                ➥UCase(Trim(Request.Form("M")))="DOSEARCH"
                                ➥Then%>
  81:                               <!--#INCLUDE FILE = "Includes/Connection.asp"-->
  81a:                               <!--#INCLUDE FILE = "Includes/adovbs.inc" -->
  82:                               <%'We include the Connection.asp file here so
                                ➥that both of the functions
  83:                               'below can see the Conn object
  84:                               Call DoPersonSearch
  85:                               'Now close the connection object (always
                                ➥cleaning up after ourselves!!)%>
  86:                               <!--#INCLUDE FILE =
                                ➥"Includes/ConnectionClose.asp"-->
  87:                               <%End If%>
  88:                           </TD>
  89:                       </TR>
  90:                   </TABLE>
  91:
  92:                   <TABLE CELLPADDING="0" CELLSPACING="0" BORDER="0"
                       ➥BORDERCOLOR="BLUE" WIDTH="100%">
  93:                       <TR>
  94:                           <TD ROWSPAN="3" VALIGN="top">1
  95:                               <IMG SRC="images/bottomsTRip.jpg" WIDTH="100%"
                                ➥HEIGHT="162"></TD>
  96:                       </TR>
  97:                   </TABLE>
  98:           </FORM>
  99:       </BODY>
 100:</HTML>
 101:
 102: <%'*********************************************************************
 103: 'This is where make the database connection
 104: '*********************************************************************
 105: Function DoLogin
 106: 'This statement allows us to trap errors that may occur
 107: On Error Resume Next
 108:     'bResult is a boolean variable (True or False)
             ➥that we use in the function
 109:     Dim bResult
 110:     'sConn is a varaible that we use to build the connection
             ➥string information that we need to
 111:     'create a connection to the database with
 112:     Dim sConn
 113:
 114:     If isObject(Conn) Then
 115:         sConn = Application("Conn_ConnectionString") & ";User Id=" &
             ➥Session("UserName") & ";PASSWORD=" &
             ➥Session("UserPwd") & ";"
```

```
116:        Conn.Open sConn
117:        If Conn.State = adStateOpen Then
118:            DoLogin = True
119:        Else
120:            DoLogin = False
121:        End If
122:    End If
123:
124:    If Err.number<>0 Then
125:        'This is the error code for a login failure
126:        If Err.number = -2147217843 Then
127:            DoLogin = False
128:            sErrorMessage = "Oops, we cannot log you in.
                ➥Please check the credentials you have supplied."
129:        Else
130:            DoLogin = False
131:            sErrorMessage = "Oops, something has gone wrong internally.
                ➥Please try again, and if the problem persists contact
                ➥your System Administrator."
132:        End If
133:    End If
134: End Function
135:
136: '****************************************************************
137: 'This is where actually perform the search
138: '****************************************************************
139: Sub DoPersonSearch
140: On Error Resume Next
141:     'Used to validate the user's login information, by calling the
            ➥DoLogin function (see below)
142:     Dim bValid
143:     'Used to check if an Error has occurred.
            ➥If it has this Boolean will be set to True (see below)
144:     Dim bError
145:     'Cmd is for the ADO Command Object
146:     Dim Cmd
147:     'rs is for the ADO Recordset Object
148:     Dim rs
149:     'This variable is used to write out the font style,
            ➥as I am too lazy to write it our over and over
150:     Dim sFontStyle
151:     'These two variables are used to hold the page we are on,
            ➥and what the total number of pages are
152:     Dim iPageCurrent, iPageCount
153:
154:     'Set out error variable to False to make sure it
            ➥does not accidentally have a True value!
155:     bError = False
156:
157:     'Our fontstyle variable
```

12

continues

Listing 12.11—continued

```
158:      sFontStyle = "<FONT FACE=""arial, verdana, helvetica"" SIZE=""2""
          ➥COLOR=""#ffffff"">"
159:
160:      'Our bValidUser variable will contain either a true or false
          ➥from the DoLogin function
161:      bValid = DoLogin
162:
163:      'If they are not a valid user, then let's give the user a message
          ➥and get out of here
164:      If Not bValid Then
165:          Response.Write(sFontStyle & sErrorMessage & "</FONT>")
166:          Exit Sub
167:      End If
168:
169:      'If all of the above is fine, let's do the search
170:      Set Cmd = Server.CreateObject("ADODB.Command")
171:      Set rs = Server.CreateObject("ADODB.RecordSet")
172:      rs.CursorLocation = adUseClient
173:
174:      With Cmd
175:          .ActiveConnection = Conn
176:          .CommandType = adCmdStoredProc
177:          .CommandText = "dbo.PersonSearch"
178:          'Execute the sp with the correct values to get the values back
179:          If Len(Trim(Request.Form("FirstName")))<>0 Then
180:              'If they have entered value execute the SP
                  ➥with the value they entered
181:              .Parameters.Append
181a: .CreateParameter("",adVarChar,adParamInput,50,Trim(
      ➥Request.Form("FirstName")))
182:          Else
183:              'If they haven't entered value still execute the
                  ➥SP but pass a Null
184:              .Parameters.Append
                  ➥.CreateParameter("",adVarChar,adParamInput,50,Null)
185:          End If
186:          'Do the same thing for the Surname
187:          If Len(Trim(Request.Form("Surname")))<>0 Then
188:              .Parameters.Append
                  ➥.CreateParameter("",adVarChar,adParamInput,50,Trim(
                  ➥Request.Form("Surname")))
189:          Else
190:              .Parameters.Append
                  ➥.CreateParameter("",adVarChar,adParamInput,50,Null)
191:          End If
192:
193: '***********************************************************************
194:          'WARNING: Because we are not using the parameters.refresh,
                  ➥and explicitly naming our parameters we
195:          'need to make sure they are passed into the SP in
```

```
               ➥EXACTLY the same way as they are declared.
196:        'Why not use the parameters.refresh command then?
               ➥Because that takes a trip to the SQL Server to get
               ➥all the parameter information back to the Command
               ➥object, and the less trips to the server the better
197:  '****************************************************************
198:
199:        'Finally assign our recordset the values that have been
               ➥returned from the Command object
200:        Set rs = .Execute
201:    End With
202:
203:    If Err.number <> 0 Then
204:        'This is the error code for a Execute permission denied on object
205:        If Err.number = -2147217911 Then
206:            sErrorMessage = "Oops, you do not have permission to
               ➥perform this functionality.
               ➥See your System Administrator for assistance."
207:            bError = True
208:        Else
209:            sErrorMessage = "Oops, something has gone wrong internally.
               ➥Please try again, and if the problem
               ➥persists contact your System Administrator."
210:            bError = True
211:        End If
212:    End If
213:
214:    'Only called if an Error occurs due to the user not
               ➥having permission to Execute the SP,
215:    'or some other error occuring
216:    If bError Then
217:        Response.Write(sFontStyle & sErrorMessage & "</FONT>")
218:        'Remember to clean up everything
219:        rs.Close
220:        Set rs = Nothing
221:        Set Cmd = Nothing
222:        'It turned to custard so let's get out of here
223:        Exit Sub
224:    End If
225:
226:    rs.PageSize = 3
227:
228:    'Check rs is not empty
229:    'If it is tell the user, clean up our objects, and get out of the page!
230:    If rs.EOF Then
231:        sErrorMessage = "Your search produced no results.
               ➥Please re-enter some new search criteria, and try again."
232:        Response.Write(sFontStyle & sErrorMessage & "</FONT>")
233:        'Clean up everything
234:        rs.Close
235:        Set rs = Nothing
```

continues

Listing 12.11—continued

```
236:        Set Cmd = Nothing
237:        Exit Sub
238:    End If
239:
240:    iPageCurrent = Request.Form("PageCurrent")
241:    If Len(Trim(Request.Form("Next.x")))<>0 Then
242:        iPageCurrent = iPageCurrent + 1
243:    ElseIf Len(Trim(Request.Form("Previous.x")))<>0 Then
244:        iPageCurrent = iPageCurrent - 1
245:    Else
246:        iPageCurrent = 1
247:    End If
248:
249:    rs.AbsolutePage = iPageCurrent
250:    iPageCount = rs.PageCount
251:
252:    'If we get to here our rs is not empty, so write out the results.
            ➥Simple ehh!
253:    Response.Write("<TABLE BORDER=""0"" BORDERCOLOR=""ORANGE"">")
254:
255:    'Record and page count stuff
256:    Response.Write("<TR>")
257:    'Wrote the font style our for this one because we are
            ➥using a different color
258:    Response.Write("<TD COLSPAN=""10""><FONT FACE=""arial,
            ➥verdana, helvetica"" SIZE=""2"" COLOR=""#ff8c00"">")
259:    Response.Write("Your search returned " & rs.RecordCount & " records
            ➥and you are on page " & iPageCurrent & " of " & iPageCount)
260:    Response.Write("</FONT></TD>")
261:    Response.Write("</TR>")
262:
263:    'Hide the current page, so that we can move back and forth
264:    Response.Write("<INPUT TYPE=""HIDDEN"" NAME=""PageCurrent""
            ➥VALUE=" & """" & iPageCurrent & """" & ">")
265:    Response.Write("<TR>")
266:    Response.Write("<TD COLSPAN=""4"">")
267:    If iPageCurrent > 1 Then
268:        Response.Write("<INPUT TYPE=""Image"" ALT=""Previous Records""
                ➥SRC=""Images/Previous.gif"" VALUE=""Previous""
                ➥NAME=""Previous"" WIDTH=""54"" HEIGHT=""10""> ")
269:    End If
270:
271:    If iPageCurrent < iPageCount Then
272:        Response.Write("<INPUT TYPE=""Image"" ALT=""Next Records""
                ➥SRC=""Images/Next.gif"" VALUE=""Next"" NAME=""Next""
                ➥WIDTH=""54"" HEIGHT=""10"">")
273:    End If
274:
275:    Response.Write("</TD>")
```

```
276:     Response.Write("</TR>")
277:
278:     'Table header stuff
279:     Response.Write("<TR>")
280:     Response.Write("<TD>" & sFontStyle & "<B>Person's
         ➥Name</B></FONT></TD>")
281:     Response.Write("<TD>" & sFontStyle & "<B>Date of Birth<B></FONT></TD>")
282:     Response.Write("<TD>" & sFontStyle & "<B>Phone No.</B></FONT></TD>")
283:     Response.Write("</TR>")
284:
285:     Do While rs.AbsolutePage = iPageCurrent And Not rs.EOF
286:         Response.Write("<TR>")
287:         Response.Write("<TD>" & sFontStyle & rs("FullName") &
             ➥"</FONT></TD>")
288:         Response.Write("<TD>" & sFontStyle & rs("DOB") & "</FONT></TD>")
289:         Response.Write("<TD>" & sFontStyle & rs("PhoneNo") &
             ➥"</FONT></TD>")
290:         Response.Write("</TR>")
291:         rs.MoveNext
292:     Loop
293:     Response.Write("</TABLE>")
294:
295:     'Remember to clean up everything
296:     rs.Close
297:     Set rs = Nothing
298:     Set Cmd = Nothing
299: End Sub%>
```

Analysis

Notice in the code that I have taken advantage of some of the Recordset object properties. These properties allow me to specify that I want only 10 records on the screen to be shown at any one time. Why would I want to do this? If you have many more than 10 records per screen, scrollbars will appear, and who wants scrollbars onscreen?

There we have it, ladies and gentleman, a basic Web site (with some very cool graphics—thanks again Jillian), so we can search our Person table.

I bet you guessed it, but the Search.asp page is also placed in the root of the Web project.

Now you could expand this so that you search over more than one table, or you bring back the person's address at the same time. But before you do I have a couple of best practice examples that I suggest you do when developing for the Web.

12

Watching Speed and Consistency

The biggest issue most times in Web development is speed! Nothing is worse than waiting for a Web page to load. After all, 15 seconds in front of a PC feels more like 15 minutes! To keep Web pages fast, follow these basic rules:

- Keep the pages small. Too many lines of code (more than 400) and you will begin to degrade performance.
- Do not switch between HTML and VBScript too often. The compiler must context-switch as it renders the page on the server, thus slowing performance.
- Use the Command object. Although you can actually build a site not using the Command object, it tends to be slower because ADO must guess what you are sending to the database.
- Finally, design your stored procedures to be as efficient as possible, while still providing the same results.

You can do many more things to enhance a user's Web site experience, but this is just a general guide to get you started.

Well done, a large part of the application is developed. You are not only learning how to be a DBA, but also an ASP programmer!

Surfing the SpyNet Site

Let's see our Web site running! Follow these steps:

1. Open a browser window and type your server name and SpyNet in the browser window, that is, `http://grunter/SpyNet`. You will see a screen similar to that shown in Figure 12.5.

Figure 12.5

The Login.asp page waiting for our users to enter their login information.

2. Enter the username—`SpyNetIntranetUser`—and the password, and click the login button. The next screen you see will look similar to Figure 12.6.

Figure 12.6

Welcome.asp greeting our user after they have logged in.

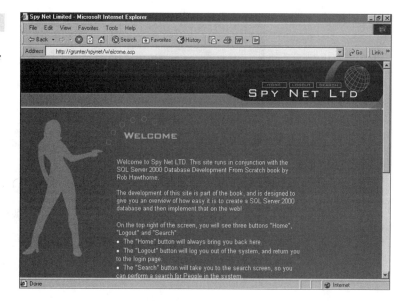

3. At the top right of the screen is the search button (as well as the home and logout buttons). After you click this you can enter your first search. The screen will look similar to Figure 12.7.

Figure 12.7

Search.asp bringing back our search results based on the criteria we entered.

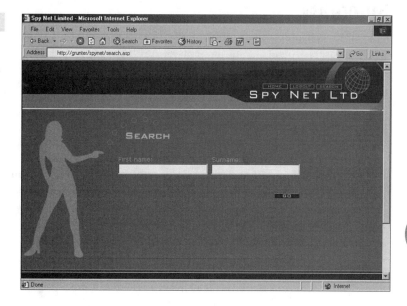

4. Type a letter or string in the field. I have entered Greg as the string, and Figure 12.8 shows a sample result.

Figure 12.8

Pulling up data from SpyNet to match the criteria.

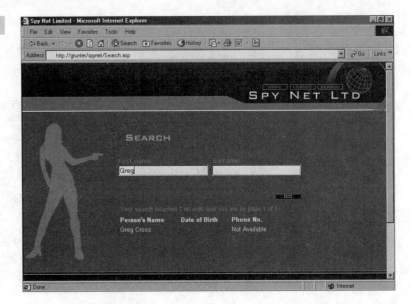

There we have it! It is a simple interface that gives a good foundation on which to build a cool site.

Summary

In this chapter we have looked briefly at programming a basic Web site to cater to our users. To get the full benefits of ASP though, you need to practice, practice, and then do some more practice! Although I have included comments with the code I have written, you need to get stuck in and have a go!

Next Steps

In the next chapter we are going to take a look at the DTS Wizard and the flexibility it offers for importing data into our application. Chapter 13 will involve using the Excel spreadsheets that are available on the Que Publishing Web site, so download these now so we can get on with it!

Chapter 13

Putting All the Pieces Together

So far we have taken our idea from design to implementation and developed a simple front end for our users to retrieve and view data. You have been given a fair amount of information along the way, and your head must be swimming a little bit by now. A bit of an information overload! Well, just sit back and relax, this chapter is going to be nice and easy and relatively stress free.

Although we have not done absolutely everything in SQL Server 2000, you should have a pretty good idea by now of the basic concepts of SQL Server 2000 and how to find your way around the interface. This chapter helps you clean up your spies and bad guys and get some new fresh data ready for presentation.

So far our data has been rather limited. The data has been simple and based on whatever I have thought of as we have gone along. But now we are going to take advantage of the Data Transformation Service within SQL Server 2000 and import data from an Excel 2000 spreadsheet.

 Note The import does not have to be done from an Excel 2000 spreadsheet. SQL Server 2000 will import from almost any version of Excel. But for you take advantage of the prepared data, it is in the Excel 2000 format.

This spreadsheet could be a feed of spies' names that you get from other spy organizations around the world. Or it could be an electronic copy of the information that we have had on paper for years that one of your staff has compiled for you.

Also in this chapter, I talk about some future expansions that our application can undergo. And guess what? You are going to do them. No, I'm just kidding. Any future enhancements that we have are not going to be implemented in the remainder of the book. I wouldn't be so cruel! The next two chapters give you some other avenues for exploration as you hone your DBA skills and look at some features SQL Server 2000 offers.

Putting New Data into SQLSpyNet with the DTS Wizard

The DTS Wizard is a very flexible tool that allows us to import data from almost any data source, including Excel, DB2, Oracle, Access, and even Text files. Why do we need this? Many organizations have data spread throughout the company. Charles will have a spreadsheet of his customers, Mary will have a small Access database that has all her suppliers, and Jenny, the secretary, might have a text file (word document) with the names and phone numbers of all the staff members.

With all of these disparate types of information floating around the office it's pretty obvious that data management can become a real nightmare! Duplication of data is inevitable, and retrieval is almost impossible.

But here comes SQL Server 2000 to the rescue! With the introduction of DTS in SQL Server version 7.0, many organizations have been able to relieve the pain of trying to get all these disparate pieces of information together. The DTS Wizard is a point-n-shoot approach to import (or even export) data into our database. We go through a series of steps, selecting the database into which to enter the data, where the data is to come from, and so forth.

This is all fine for simple data, but what happens when we have more complex data that doesn't have a clear definition between first name and surname? DTS can even take care of this, with your help of course.

Within a DTS package we can define VBScript that can be used to manipulate, format, or rerun a process. This gives us great flexibility when it comes to altering our data either before, during, or after the insert to the database.

There are many aspects to DTS packages, and we will only have a quick look at the basics. I suggest that you play with DTS packages in SQL Server 2000 because they rock! And the flexibility and control you have over the import/export process will surprise you.

Before we actually insert the data into our database, we are going to delete *all* the data out of our database. This will allow us to start from a clean slate. But just before we do this though, let's back up our database.

Note

You should always get into the habit of making a backup or a way to recover the data if you are making large data modifications.

13

Backing Up the Database Before the Transfer

You might be wishing you didn't have to do this, but do you want to know the cool thing? You do not have to write the backup statement again! Because we wrote a backup task earlier (see Chapter 11, the section titled "Scheduling Jobs"), we can actually force it to run immediately. This means we can create a full database backup just by right-clicking on the job (under Management, SQL Server Agent, and then Jobs), and selecting Start Job, as shown in Figure 13.1.

Figure 13.1

Forcing a job to start immediately within Enterprise Manager.

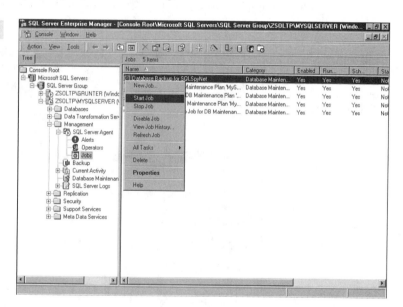

You will see that the status of the job is set to executing. When the job has finished, the status will change to either Succeeded or Failed.

So there we go, a backup done nice and simply, with no extra code!

Creating a Stored Procedure to Clean Out the Data

Now let's go ahead and create a stored procedure to delete our data for us.

 Note

You do not have to delete all the data from your database before using DTS, but we want our database to be clean, so this is the best way to achieve this.

Because we might want to do this task again, we are going to create a stored procedure that actually performs the DELETE for us. But this time for something a little different we are going to create the stored procedure within Enterprise Manager. The other thing that we need to do is lock the stored procedure down so that only the dbo role, or any user mapped to that role, can execute it. After all, we do not want just anybody deleting all the data from our database!

Using Enterprise Manager to Create a Stored Procedure

Here are the steps to create a stored procedure to delete all the data from Spy Net:

1. Start Enterprise Manager and navigate your way through the SQLSpyNet database until you find the Stored Procedures folder.

2. Right-click the Stored Procedures folder and select New Stored Procedure as shown in Figure 13.2.

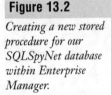

Figure 13.2

Creating a new stored procedure for our SQLSpyNet database within Enterprise Manager.

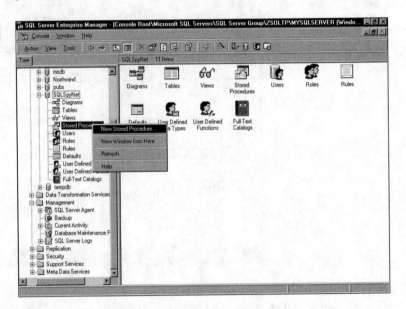

This will open a new screen, which has the basic outline of the stored procedure structure, as shown in Figure 13.3. Simple isn't it?

Figure 13.3

The new stored procedure screen in Enterprise Manager showing the basic structure of the CREATE PROCEDURE statement.

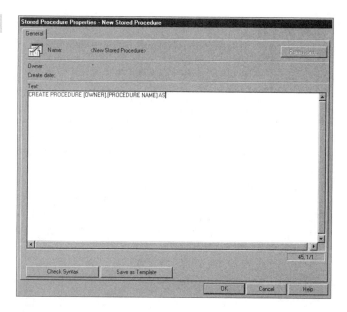

13

EXCURSION

Learning Code the "Hard Way"

I can hear you asking now, "Why did you make us type it out through code then?" I believe that if you know how to write stored procedures from scratch in code, you will never have a problem creating a stored procedure inside Enterprise Manager.

But more than this, if you know how to write code from scratch, you will be able to find errors within code far more effectively than if you use the templates to write the code for you. Besides, you never know when the interface will fail and you will actually have to write code. Remember, practice makes perfect.

3. Now we will give our new stored procedure a name, something meaningful like NukeAllData, because that's what it is going to do.

4. Enter the code in Listing 13.1 into the New Stored Procedure window.

Listing 13.1—Creating a Stored Procedure to Delete the Data

```
1: CREATE PROCEDURE NukeAllData
2:     @Confirm INT = 0
3: AS
4:     IF @Confirm <> 0
5:        BEGIN
6:            BEGIN TRANSACTION
7:            DECLARE @LocalError INT
8:            SET @LocalError = 0
9:            DELETE FROM Activity
```

Listing 13.1—Continued

```
10:          SET @LocalError = @LocalError + @@ERROR
11:          DELETE FROM ActivityType
12:          SET @LocalError = @LocalError + @@ERROR
13:          DELETE FROM BadGuy
14:          SET @LocalError = @LocalError + @@ERROR
15:          DELETE FROM Spy
16:          SET @LocalError = @LocalError + @@ERROR
17:          DELETE FROM Address
18:          SET @LocalError = @LocalError + @@ERROR
19:          DELETE FROM Person
20:          SET @LocalError = @LocalError + @@ERROR
21:          DELETE FROM AddressType
22:          SET @LocalError = @LocalError + @@ERROR
23:          DELETE FROM Country
24:          SET @LocalError = @LocalError + @@ERROR
25:          IF @LocalError <> 0
26:              ROLLBACK TRANSACTION
27:          ELSE
28:              COMMIT TRANSACTION
29:      END
30:  ELSE
31:      PRINT 'You cannot execute this Stored Procedure at this time'
32: GO
```

Analysis

What does this stored procedure do? The stored procedure will delete *all* data from *all* the tables in our database. It wraps this in a transaction, just in case something does go wrong.

> **Warning**   Remember, we can't delete parent records before child records, so we need to delete all the data from the child tables first!

The parameter that we supply to the stored procedure just checks that something other than a zero is supplied. Although this does not stop someone from running the stored procedure, it does help to ensure that we know that they do really want to run the procedure.

Denying Access to the Power of Deletion

The next thing that we have to do is specifically deny access to this stored procedure from the other users and roles in our database. The sa account or anyone belonging to the dbo role will still be able to execute this stored procedure. Enter the code in Listing 13.2 into Query Analyzer.

Listing 13.2—Safeguarding the Stored Procedure

```
1: DENY EXECUTE ON NukeAllData TO SQLSpyNetUser
2: GO
3: DENY EXECUTE ON NukeAllData TO SpyNetIntranetUser
4: GO
5: DENY EXECUTE ON NukeAllData TO SQLSpyNetRole
6: GO
7: DENY EXECUTE ON NukeAllData TO Public
8: GO
```

Analysis

The DENY statement specifically removes a user's (or role's) privilege from executing a stored procedure. You can think about it as a negative GRANT statement. Instead of specifically giving permission to use the stored procedure, we are specifically taking it away.

Running the Stored Procedure

Now we need to run our stored procedure and remove all the data from our database. Enter Listing 13.3 into Query Analyzer.

Listing 13.3—Deleting the Data

```
1: EXEC NukeAllData 1
```

> If you try to execute this stored procedure without the one (1), you should get a message back stating, "You cannot execute this stored procedure at this time." Just to prove it works, go ahead and have a go!
>
> If you need to know what the 1 (one) is for, take a look back at when we created the stored procedure, and all will be revealed.

And there we go, we have backed up our database, we've deleted all the data, and we are now ready to go ahead and import the data into our application.

Using the DTS Wizard to Reload Our SQLSpyNet Database with Data

Let's have a go now at creating our own DTS package to bring in the new data for our spies, bad guys, and so forth.

> **Note**
>
> With the DTS Wizard we actually have to perform the import process thrice, the first time for the primary tables the second time for the secondary tables, and the final time for the Activity table.
>
> You will find three `.xls` files on the book's Web site (`http://www.quepublishing.com`), called SpyDatabasePrimaryTables.xls, SpyDatabaseSecondaryTables.xls, and SpyDatabaseActivityTable.xls.
>
> Why do we run three times? As you know, you cannot have child records in a database without first having the parent records. The first import inserts the parent records, and the second import will proceed because the necessary parent records are available. The third import will succeed because all the necessary records are now available.

To import the primary tables, follow these steps in the wizard. Then, refer to this set of steps later in this section when you import the remaining tables.

1. Once again, navigate through the server until you see the Data Transformation Services folder. Right-click the folder, select All Tasks, and then Import Data, as shown in Figure 13.4.

Figure 13.4

Finding the DTS Package Wizard in SQL Server 2000 inside Enterprise Manager.

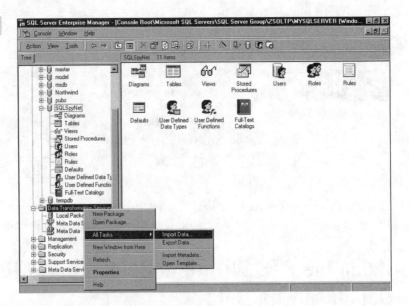

This will launch the DTS Import/Export Wizard, which allows us to begin specifying the different options for our import process. The initial wizard screen looks similar to Figure 13.5.

Note

This is not the only way to launch the DTS Wizard, but I guess you knew that SQL Server 2000 supported other ways, right? The DTS Wizard can be launched through the Start menu from Programs, Microsoft SQL Server, Import and Export Data.

Alternatively you can launch the DTS Wizard from Tools, Data Transformation Services, Import (or Export) data through Enterprise Manager.

Figure 13.5

The DTS Import/Export Wizard ready for us to begin.

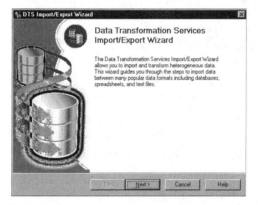

2. Like most of the wizards, the first screen doesn't allow you to do too much, so click Next.

3. The next screen, as shown in Figure 13.6, is a little more interesting and allows us to specify the source from which we want to retrieve our data.

Figure 13.6

DTS Import/Export Wizard ready for us to select the source where we want to select our data.

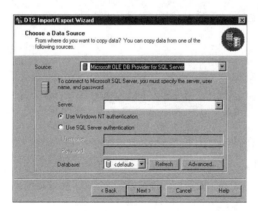

The Source drop-down box allows us to specify the place our data comes from. Select Microsoft Excel 97-2000. This will change the screen so that it has only a filename box available, similar to Figure 13.7.

Figure 13.7

DTS Import/Export Wizard ready for us to select the file path of where our Excel spreadsheet is in the file system.

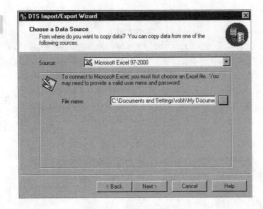

4. After you have entered the file path of where the Excel Spreadsheet is or navigated your way through the file system with the ellipsis (...) button, click Next.

5. The next screen allows us to select the data source that we want the import process to import our data *into*, as shown in Figure 13.8. This can be a SQL Server 2000 database or almost any other data source.

As you can imagine, because you can choose a non-SQL Server database to import from and import into, you can actually perform data transformation to and from Excel spreadsheets, or virtually any other data sources. You do not have to actually import into (or export from) SQL Server 2000. DTS can just act as the middleman in the whole process.

Figure 13.8

Setting the Destination options for the wizard.

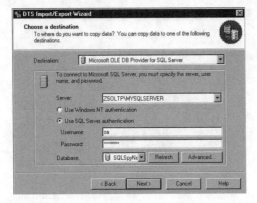

You need to set the following options for the Destination step in the wizard:

- Select Microsoft OLE DB Provider for SQL Server in the Destination drop-down box.
- Select your server from the Server drop-down box.
- Use SQL Server authentication, and enter sa in the Username box and the password for sa in the Password box.
- Select the SQLSpyNet database from the Database drop-down box. If the database drop-down does not contain anything, click the Refresh button.

6. When you've set the configuration options, click the Next button.

 Note

> The Advanced button next to the Refresh button allows us to set more complex options, such as the connection timeout, for the connection that we make to the Destination source database.

7. The next screen, Specify Table Copy or Query, allows us to choose whether we are going to copy whole tables or specify our own query to copy the data. Because we are copying from an Excel spreadsheet, we are going to specify the first option, Copy table(s) and view(s) from the source database, as shown in Figure 13.9.

Figure 13.9

Setting the type of Import we are going to perform.

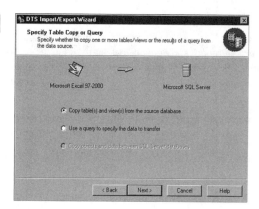

8. After you've selected the option, click Next. This will bring up the screen shown in Figure 13.10.

Figure 13.10

Selecting the source tables to which the data will be copied.

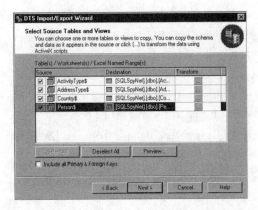

9. This screen allows us to select the tables that we want to copy into, as well as specify the columns that we want to copy into.

   We need these mappings:

   - ActivityType sheet—ActivityType table
   - AddressType sheet—AddressType table
   - Country sheet—Country table
   - Person sheet—Person table

10. Do not check the Include all Primary & Foreign Keys option.

 Note   If the tables did not exist when the data import was being performed, this would create the Primary and Foreign keys for us. If the tables do exist, some options would not be enabled that allow us to alter the constraints on the tables.

11. When you have the mappings right, click the Next button.

12. This screen, as shown in Figure 13.11, allows us to specify whether the task is run immediately or scheduled for later use. We want to run the task immediately.

   The Save DTS package option allows us to specify whether we want to save the package so that we can run it again in the future. If we save the package not only can we run it again later, but we can also modify the package to have custom tasks added.

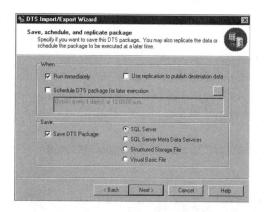

Figure 13.11

Setting whether the task is run immediately or scheduled for later execution.

13

Tip

If the Save DTS Package option is not enabled, click the Schedule DTS Package Option for Later Execution option, and then deselect the option again. This will enable the save package option.

13. Select the Save DTS Package option as a SQL Server package. The different save options offer us

   - SQL Server—The package is stored in the msdb database within the sysdtspackages table.

   - Meta Data Services—This allows us to save the package within the Meta Data Services.

   - Structured Storage File—Allows us to save the package as a COM (Component Object Model) storage file.

   - Visual Basic File—Allows us to save the package as a VB file.

14. When you are happy, click Next.

15. The following screen, as shown in Figure 13.12, allows us to specify a name for the package that we are going to save.

   Like everything else, we need to enter a name and description for the package that is descriptive and identifies what we are doing, like so:

   - Name— SQL Spy Net Excel Primary Table Import.

   - Description—An Excel spreadsheet import that repopulates the database primary tables, run by Rob 21 Aug 00.

   - Owner Password—This option allows us to specify a password for the owner to protect the package. Leave this blank.

- User Password—This option allows us to specify a password for the user. This means the user can run the package but cannot view the package contents. Leave this option blank.

- Server details—Set these to the server that SQLSpyNet database resides in, using the username and password. This is the server that the DTS package will be saved to.

Figure 13.12

Entering the package details when we are saving the package.

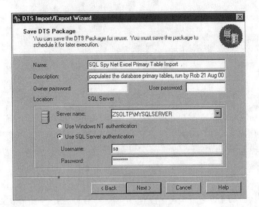

  Note

You can select another server from the drop-down box (if there is one) on which to store the package. A server other than the one you are currently connected to is known as a remote server. You will need to have a valid account and password to gain access to the server to store the DTS package on it. This allows you to create a DTS package on your machine, and then store it on another server for later use or as a backup.

16. After you have set the options, click Next.

17. The final screen, as shown in Figure 13.13, is the last step in the wizard.

18. When you are happy, click Finish. This will execute the DTS package immediately and import our data.

    You will see a screen similar to that shown in Figure 13.14.

Figure 13.13

*The DTS
Import/Export Wizard
summary (final) screen
for the package.*

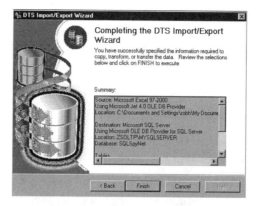

Figure 13.14

*DTS Import/Export
Wizard executing the
package for us.*

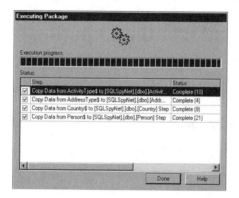

When the wizard has finished importing our primary tables, we need to import the
secondary (or child) tables. Run the wizard again, creating a new DTS package. This
time use the SpyDatabaseSecondaryTables.xls file, and map the following tables to
the worksheets in the .xls file:

- Spy sheet—Spy table
- BadGuy sheet—BadGuy table
- Address sheet—Address table

As before, save the DTS package, using the following options:

- Name—SQL Spy Net Excel Secondary Table Import.
- Description—An Excel spreadsheet import that repopulates the database secondary tables, run by Rob 21 Aug 00.

So, and I know this gets repetitive, run the wizard again, creating a new DTS package. This time use the `SpyDatabaseActivityTable.xls` file, and like the first two times, map the Activity worksheet in the .xls file to the Activity table in the SQLSpyNet database.

Like the first (and second) time, save the DTS package, using the following options:

- Name—SQL Spy Net Excel Activity Table Import.
- Description—An Excel spreadsheet import that repopulates the database Activity table, run by Rob 21 Aug 00.

After the package has finished running, we should perform a quick check on the tables to ensure that our data has come across successfully.

Checking the Results of the Import

How do we know if we have any rows in a table? We use the COUNT function to return a count of the number of rows in a table. If you enter Listing 13.4 into Query Analyzer we can check the data insert for the Spy table.

Listing 13.4—Checking the Data After the Import

```
1: SELECT COUNT(PersonID) FROM Person
```

This will return the current number of rows (well actually PersonIDs) in the Person table.

You should now go ahead and check that the rest of the tables have data in them. By the way, they all should have!

Okay, so now what? Well because we saved our DTS packages, we can take a quick look at what SQL Server 2000 does when it creates a DTS package. Navigate your way to Data Transformation Services, Local Packages, and then you should see our three new packages. If you double-click one of the packages, you will get a graphical representation of what the package looks like, as shown in Figure 13.15.

This package allows us to alter it or run the package again. To view some of the information SQL Server 2000 uses when importing the data, right-click the different icons, including the arrows, and choose Properties from the menu, as shown in Figure 13.16.

Figure 13.15

The DTS package that we saved from the DTS Import/Export Wizard.

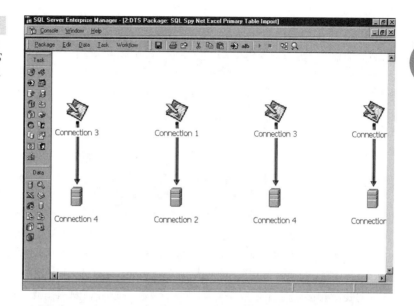

Figure 13.16

Where to find the properties for each component of a DTS package.

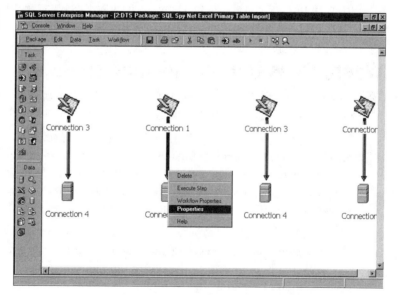

The properties window enables you to manipulate the DTS package in many ways, and an example of the properties window for Connection1 (one of the arrows) appears in Figure 13.17.

Figure 13.17

The properties window for Connection1 of the newly created DTS package.

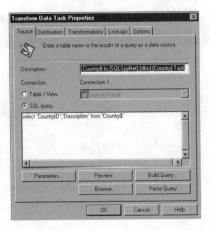

Have a good look around DTS. Because you can easily re-create the wizard that we used earlier, do not be afraid to try some things out in the DTS package designer.

Here is a challenge for you. See whether you can figure out a way to import the data from all three spreadsheets in a single package! It is possible, though it might require some in-depth investigation on your behalf and some clever VBScript.

Where Does Our Application Go Now?

Our application is now in a stable state, the database design hasn't changed from our original concept, but there are many more things that our application could include.

Because our SQLSpyNet application is for recording spies' movements and bad guys' activities, the next logical step would be to add monitoring of spies' equipment while on assignment. Currently our spies go out to fight bad guys, but we have no way of measuring how much equipment they use. Now in James Bond films, Q is always nagging 007 about being careful with equipment. Shouldn't we be doing the same thing?

What change would this require? Because our model is relatively stable we can add new tables without impacting the rest of our database too much. The amount of change required would be to add probably two more tables to the structure. One would be a lookup table that contains a list of equipment. The second table would be a junction table, which breaks up the many-to-many relationship that would exist between our new lookup table and the Activity table.

So Rob, how did you come up with this? When a spy is involved in an activity is when they require resources (equipment). However, a spy can have more than one piece of equipment while on assignment. This creates a many-to-many relationship between Resource and Activity, so a junction (or associative) table is required.

13

If we implement this change, what else can we get our application to do? The next logical step is to use our application as a management-reporting tool. This would allow senior management to create graphs on the performance of our spies over the bad guys.

We can also create reports, either Web-based or using reporting tools such as Crystal reports or Access, to monitor performance, salaries, and the number of staff on the books. These reports are simple to develop and only require you to create some stored procedures (or views) to retrieve the data, and then build a front end.

Other enhancements to the application could include

- Adding a financial component to the application so we can record expenses. This would allow us to find out how much per year it costs us to fight crime.
- Adding another person type to the application. This could be so human resources (HR) could manage the number of staff we have.

As you can see, there are several enhancements that we can perform on our application to make it perform more than just the basic functionality. However, in a real-world scenario the first thing we would need to do is roll out the application to our users so they can assess the application and give us feedback on performance, look and feel, and most importantly, functionality!

So there we have it: an application that has not only provided you with hours of entertainment in developing, but also has the possibility of providing many more hours of delight. So let your imaginations run wild!

Summary

Compared to some of the other chapters we have gotten through so far in the book, this one was really lightweight.

We looked at creating a DTS package to import our spies and bad guy details from Excel spreadsheets. I guess you can easily see how this could be expanded to include data feeds from other sources in the future.

We then looked at where the Spy Net application is currently and where we could potentially take the Spy Net application. Remember that these are just some of my ideas; you might have some more outstanding ideas for the next release of Spy Net, and hey—if you do, let me know. You never know, I might write another book, and your idea could be just what I need.

Next Steps

In the next chapter we are going take a look at debugging. By using the tools within SQL Server 2000, we will discover ways to find and prevent the errors that can arise when developing an application.

So break out your dancing shoes; we are going to get the show on the road.

In this chapter

- *Using SQL Profiler to Find Errors*
- *Using the Client Network Utility to Resolve Connection Problems*
- *Debugging Stored Procedures*
- *What? No More Room?*

Chapter 14

Troubleshooting and Debugging in SQL Server 2000

Although most things run smoothly in SQL Server 2000, sometimes you get an error that you just can't seem to find. And, if your database really starts growing, you're likely to run into trouble if you don't manage your server's resources effectively.

In this chapter I will take you through some of the experiences that I have had and give you some idea of what you can face out there in the real world.

Using SQL Profiler to Find Errors

One of the best tools for helping to solve problems in SQL Server 2000 is SQL Profiler. SQL Profiler as a problem-solving tool can show you exactly what has been sent to the SQL Server by a client application.

Within the last few weeks I have had to upgrade a SQL Server from version 6.5 to version 7.0 (yeah, I know it should have been 2000 but the client couldn't wait). The client had an old Visual Basic interface (written by someone else) and no source code available for the client application. I used SQL Profiler to trace the Transact-SQL statements that were sent to the database from the client application to ensure that the upgrade to SQL Server version 7.0 would go smoothly. The tool was invaluable, and allowed the upgrade to go as easily as possible.

Let's take a look at SQL Profiler and see what it has on offer. In this section we will set up a trace to capture the commands that the client application (Spy Net) sends to our SQL Server 2000 application.

Creating the Trace

We will start the trace and capture *all* (no specific) of the commands that the browser sends to our SQLSpyNet database, including login information and a basic search.

The ability to capture information from the browser as it goes to SQL Server is one of the best forms of debugging that you can do! It is simple yet very effective, so if you are going to do any sort of front-end development, pay close attention.

1. SQL Profiler can be launched from within Enterprise Manager (under Tools, SQL Server Profiler) or from within the SQL Server menu group in your Start menu, by selecting Programs, Microsoft SQL Server, Profiler.

2. When you have SQL Profiler launched, the first thing you need to do is set up a trace definition. You can do this by selecting File, New, Trace, as shown in Figure 14.1 (or use Ctrl+N).

Figure 14.1

Launching the new trace definition screen.

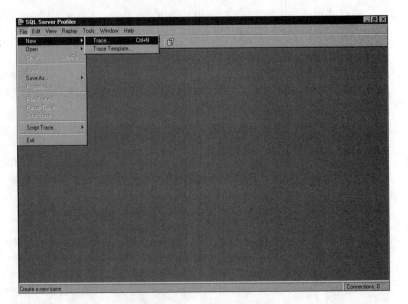

This will prompt you for your login information so that your connection information can be validated against the database on which you want to perform a trace.

3. Fill in the login information and you will see a screen similar to that shown in Figure 14.2.

Figure 14.2

Setting the properties for the new trace definition.

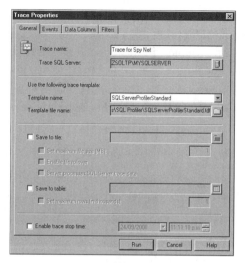

14

4. Next, define the trace. As you can see on this screen, you have several options (and even more on each of the tabs). Fill in the blanks on the General tab as described in the following:

   - Trace Name—Allows you to enter the unique name for your trace to identify the individual traces later on. Enter `Trace for Spy Net`.

   - Trace SQL Server—Specifies the instance of SQL Server on which you want to perform a trace. Make sure the instance (if you have more than one) that contains SQLSpyNet is selected.

   - Template Name—Allows you to choose from a list of predefined templates that ship with SQL Server 2000. These templates are designed to assist you with the different aspects of a DBA role. For example, a SQLProfilerTuning template will assist you in tuning your SQL queries and database performance. Select the SQLProfilerStandard template.

   - Template File Name—This allows you to choose another template (custom written, for example) that you can use instead of the predefined ones that come with SQL Server 2000. These template files have a `.tdf` file extension. You do not need to change this option for our needs.

   - Save to File—This, as you can imagine, allows you to save the trace to a file. So if you wanted to implement auditing in your application (see Chapter 9 for more details), you could capture all events against your server/database and save the trace file to disk. You don't need to do this.

- Save to Table—Alternatively, you can save your trace to a table within your database. This allows you to save the events in either an existing table or in a new table within any databases that you have access to. Like the Save to File option, you do not need to do this.
- Enable Trace Stop Time—This allows you to specify how long you would like to run a trace. Leave this unchecked for now.

This is invaluable if we are auditing our application! We can specify the times that we want to trace for, meaning we can capture the peak time traffic or the after-hours potential hacker traffic!

5. Click the Events tab. As shown in Figure 14.3, this window allows us to specify the event classes that we want to trace against.

Figure 14.3

Setting the events we want to capture for the new trace definition.

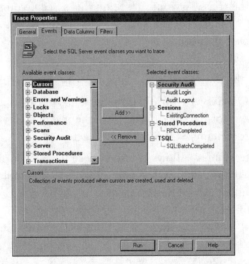

The event classes allow us to capture when an event is prepared, executed, or completed for all the major Transact-SQL categories. We can capture when a stored procedure was started, recompiled, or completed, for example. For our needs though, the defaults of the SQLProfilerStandard template are fine.

14

Note

If you save your trace and review the trace properties at a later date, the only events that you will see are the captured events; the Available Event Classes box will be disabled.

6. Click The Data Columns tab, as shown in Figure 14.4. This dialog allows us to specify the columns of information that we want to see displayed in our trace.

Figure 14.4

Setting the columns we want to see for the new trace definition.

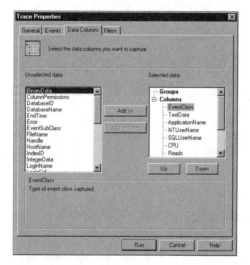

7. Because we are not on an NT-based system, remove the NTUserName column from the Selected Data select box. Click the NTUserName column, and then click the Remove button.

Tip

If you do not see the NTUserName column, look under the Columns group (written in bold).

8. To see the last and one of the most-used tabs in the Profile Trace Properties screen, click the Filters tab.

   The Filters tab allows us to apply filters to our traces so that we can narrow our traces to specific databases, users, or even applications.

9. Because we are only interested in what happens to our SQLSpyNet database (in this instance), find your way to the DatabaseName column, click the plus (+) symbol, and enter SQLSpyNet in the Like box, as shown in Figure 14.5.

Figure 14.5

Setting the filters for the new trace definition.

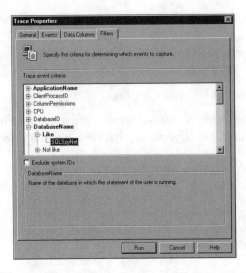

This will restrict the filter to show only those events that occur in the SQLSpyNet database.

10. And that's it! Our trace definition is now ready to go. Click the Run button and the Trace will start.

Sometimes this can take a little while, depending on the speed of your machine and how busy it is processing requests, so be patient.

When the trace starts, it will capture some basic information about the existing connections (if any), so you might notice several entries appear in the window that *seem* as though they are not relevant to our application.

EXCURSION

Am I Already Connected?

What the trace is doing is logging that a connection is already established against the SQL Server. This can show you that users are already connected, so performing a large query could impact them.

If you are seeing that the trace is reporting an existing connection (considering we are in a single-user environment) you probably have Enterprise Manager, Query Analyzer, or Spy Net open, or even a combination of all three.

If you close these applications, stop the trace (by clicking the red square in the toolbar) and clear the trace window by selecting Edit, Clear Trace Window from the menu bar, you will have a fresh trace screen. Now restart the trace (by clicking the green triangle in the toolbar) and voila[ag] no more existing connection information!

Spying on Users

So there we go; our trace is started. How do we check what our users are doing?

 Note Make sure you still have the SQL Profiler window open with the trace running to complete the steps in the following section.

14

1. Open the Spy Net application, and enter your login information, then go to the Search screen.

2. Perform a search. Figure 14.6 shows that I've performed a search for Greg and an entry is logged in the trace window.

Figure 14.6

Spying on our users to see what they are doing.

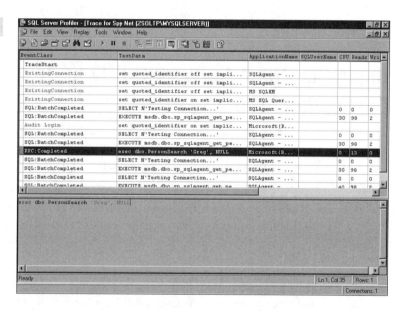

This shows that a user (ourselves) has executed the stored procedure PersonSearch with the parameters `'Greg'` and NULL.

3. We can then copy this command and paste it into a Query Analyzer window to see the results that SQL Server 2000 will return for the query.

Tip

You can copy the command that was sent to the SQL Server by the client application by clicking the command and then highlighting the text in the Results window. Right-click and select Copy or use the shortcut keys Ctrl+C .

See what I mean about help when you are debugging? If you can see the commands sent to the SQL Server from the client application, you can easily see what parameters are missing or check to see whether they are malformed and so forth. As you can imagine, this becomes very powerful when you continually have an error returned from a client application and you just can't figure it out! Capture the command, submit it to the SQL Server through Query Analyzer, and nine times out of ten, your problem will be resolved.

Now that we have learned the basics of SQL Profiler, what other tools can help with troubleshooting ?

Using the Client Network Utility to Resolve Connection Problems

Chapter 2, "Exploring the Tools of SQL Server 2000," briefly looked at the tools of SQL Server 2000. In this chapter we discovered the client network utility. A client network utility tool allows us to change the way that a client machine talks to SQL Server 2000.

On our installation all that is really available to us is TCP/IP, but on a Windows NT/2000 machine, we see several other protocols. The most common, other than TCP/IP, is Named Pipes. See Appendix B, "Installing and Configuring SQL Server 2000," for definitions of these terms.

Occasionally you get an error that does not seem to make sense. Your Web site or client application is running smoothly, and for what seems to be no reason, establishing a connection becomes a problem.

The ODBC driver or another connection mechanism will report an error that a connection cannot be made to the specified SQL Server. This can be because of several things; you will find that switching from TCP/IP to Named Pipes will normally resolve these connection issues for you.

You can specify a Named Pipes connection through either the client network utility or the ODBC driver manager (within Control Panel). So if you do start to get connection problems, try changing the protocol first.

Because this book was written for SQL Server 2000 to run on a Windows 98 machine, the ability to change network protocols is not an option. However, we will take a quick look at how to change these settings for a Windows NT or 2000 machine. Something a little extra for the NT/2000 guys out there!

Do not change these settings unless you are having connection issues! You could potentially change the protocol from TCP/IP to Named Pipes and find that you cannot establish a connection anymore.

You will find the Client Network Utility within the SQL Server menu group in your Start menu by selecting Programs, Microsoft SQL Server, Client Network Utility. This launches a screen similar to that shown in Figure 14.7.

Figure 14.7

The Client Network Utility.

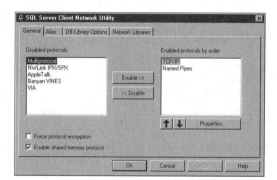

The first tab in the Client Network Utility shows which protocols are enabled for your installation. As you can see on the Windows 2000 machine I am running here, we have two protocols enabled, TCP/IP and Named Pipes. For a Windows 98 machine, we would only have TCP/IP enabled.

Let's take a look at the Alias tab, shown in Figure 14.8.

Figure 14.8

The Client Network Utility Alias tab.

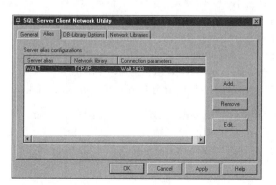

This tab allows us to configure the way we talk to the SQL Server. We can change the protocol we use by selecting an alias from the list, in this case WALT, and clicking the Edit button. This will give us a screen similar to that shown in Figure 14.9.

Figure 14.9

The Edit Network Library Configuration screen.

By changing the Network Libraries option from TCP/IP to Named Pipes we can get our client utilities (Query Analyzer, Enterprise Manager, and so on) to use the Named Pipes protocol to talk to SQL Server 2000.

Once again several other options are available within the Client Network Utilities screen, but they're a bit beyond our needs. Changing this option should take care of any connection issues that you have.

The following are some things to remember about the Client Network Utilities:

- You cannot change the protocols to Named Pipes on a Windows 98 machine.
- You shouldn't change the protocols unless you have an absolute reason to do so.

But there we have it, another nice and easy interface with which to configure SQL Server 2000's tools!

Debugging Stored Procedures

I have performed many tasks in numerous different roles, and one of the most frustrating has been debugging stored procedures. But no more! The ability to debug stored procedures as though we were debugging any development platform code is part of one of the enhancements to SQL Server 2000's Query Analyzer. We can insert break points, step into, step over, and so forth. This is wonderful for those of us who have tried to monitor what is happening in a stored procedure.

Previously we could do this with SQL Server 7.0 and Visual InterDev, but there was a lot of overhead in setting it up. With the new debugging tools, all we do is right-click and select Debug. How simple is that?

We have the standard debugging windows as well. We can get the values of variables from the Watch window and view the procedures that have been called and not completed in the Callstack window. This makes it easy to migrate from a development environment to using SQL Server 2000. So you Access developers out there must be getting really excited by now!

The new debugging screen in Query Analyzer looks similar to that shown in Figure 14.10.

14

Figure 14.10

The new Debugging screen in Query Analyzer.

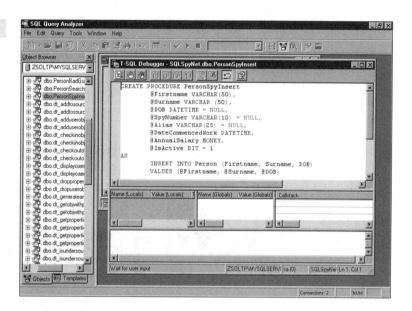

  Note

So far this feature is only available for stored procedures, but I am sure that in the future you might find Microsoft has enabled debugging of views and functions as well as compiled queries. However, this is only my view, and as far as I know it is not yet a reality.

What? No More Room?

Although we spent some time on administration in Chapter 11, "Administering Spy Net," one of the trouble spots a DBA must keep an eye on is conserving a computer's most precious resources, memory and disk space.

If we have several databases on one server, we can find that we run out of disk space, and if that happens, our databases will fail.

Of course, in Spy Net's fictional scenario, that could mean World War III! But in the real world, running out of space can still cause serious problems, especially in mission-critical databases such as utilities or emergency response systems. In this section, we look at the causes of resource failure and several ways to avoid down time, including managing file and log size.

How Memory Affects Database Transactions

The memory-deprived databases will fail because tempdb is where most of the changes that you make to your data are performed before they are committed to disk. If you have enough RAM available, SQL Server 2000 will put as much of your database as it can up into RAM. After all, it is much faster to read from RAM than to scan a disk for the information. However, if RAM is a short commodity or you have concerns about the amount of disk space your database is eating, relax, because we have even have control over that.

When you are in Enterprise Manager you have the option to view how much space your data files for your database are allocated and how much is used. To see this information, simply click the SQLSpyNet (or any other) database within Enterprise Manager, and you will see a screen similar to Figure 14.11.

Figure 14.11

Space allocated to and used by the data files for the SQLSpyNet database.

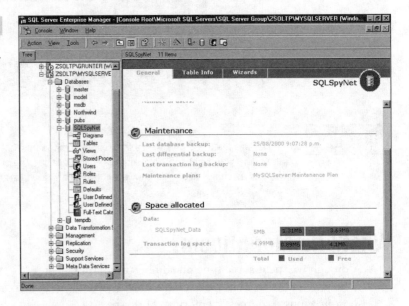

If you do not see the Web page view for the SQLSpyNet database, click the database (within Enterprise Manager), and then select View from the toolbar menu item. Select the TaskPad item from the menu, as shown in Figure 14.12.

Figure 14.12

How to change the way SQL Server Enterprise Manager looks.

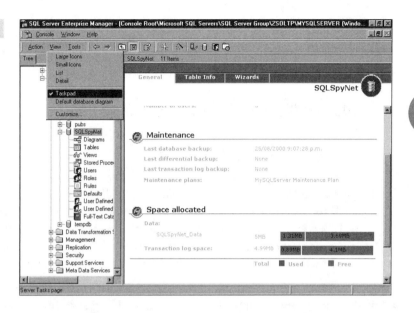

14

Let's take a look now at shrinking our data files to save space.

Shrinking Your Data Files to Reduce the Database

When we are talking about shrinking our data files we are not actually referring to the process of compacting them like a zip program would.

If we shrink our data files, we remove unused data pages. For example, if we had a table that had five data pages on which it stored the data, and we deleted two pages worth of the data, although our table would have only three pages that actually stored data, SQL Server 2000 still would have five pages allocated to the table.

When we shrink the data files, we just get rid of the extra two pages that the table was using. This does, however, have restrictions, but I think you get the idea.

Note

You cannot shrink an *entire* database smaller than the size it was when it was created. For example, our SQLSpyNet database started out as 5MB. If it grows to 25MB, we cannot shrink the database to 3MB.

What do we do when our data files are too large? Although we cannot shrink an *entire* database smaller than its original size, we can shrink our data files smaller than their original allocation sizes. We must do this by shrinking each data file individually by using the DBCC SHRINKFILE Transact-SQL statement. This allows us to reallocate how much space the given data file is allowed to use.

Altering the Size of the Transaction Log Files

Shrinking a transaction log is a little different from shrinking a data file. The main difference is when the process occurs.

When a data file is shrunk, the task is performed almost immediately, whereas with a transaction log it is not. The log file is marked, so SQL Server 2000 knows that it needs to be shrunk later on. When the transaction log is truncated or backed up, SQL Server 2000 will attempt to shrink the log to the size that has been specified. However, if *active* sections are on the end of the log, it will not be shrunk until the active sections are moved to the beginning of the transaction log.

An *active* portion (section) of the log cannot be truncated. It is used to recover the database to any point in time, so all incomplete transactions must be able to be identified so they can be rolled back. It is always present within the database so if the server fails, the database can be recovered when the server restarts.

Active transactions that have not yet been either committed or rolled back are marked as being incomplete transactions. For definition of these terms refer to the "Making Transactions Pass the ACID Test" section in Chapter 8.

Some DBAs cause the active sections of the log to be moved (in quiet databases) to the beginning of the log by filling the log up with dummy transactions.

What defines a section of the transaction log as active? Transaction logs are made up of smaller logs. These smaller logs are referred to as *Virtual logs*.

Virtual logs make up the transaction log. They mark which transactions are active and, when the active transactions are committed or rolled back, the virtual logs are then freed to allow new active transactions to be written. After SQL Server 2000 has written to a virtual log, it will move on to the next virtual log, whether the previous one is free or not. Only when the end of the log file is reached is the beginning used again. However, if the log is totally full (full of active transactions) the log size is increased.

For example, we have a log file of 200MB on our database; this potentially could be made up of five virtual logs each 40MB in size.

14

> You set the size of the transaction log and the data files when you first create your database. Refer to Chapter 3. However, you can change the size of the logs at any time by going into the properties of the database through Enterprise Manager and changing the size of the log file within the properties window, as we did in Chapter 3. Alternatively you could run the Transact-SQL ALTER DATABASE statement. Refer to Books Online for more information on the statement.

When a virtual log contains no further active transactions in the database, the log is truncated or marked for shrinking, and the space can then be reallocated to further transactions.

Truncating the Transaction Log

Truncating the transaction log allows us to reallocate the space that we have on the transaction log after there are no further active transactions. In our SQLSpyNet database we set this to happen for us automatically, but in a production system this is not something that we would normally do. Check out Chapter 10.

We truncate the log in our development database because it is not mission critical that we have a point-in-time recovery plan. For the data we are using, it is perfectly okay to restore to last night's backup rather than have the extra overhead of backing up our transaction logs every 10 minutes.

> You cannot back up your database or transaction log when you are shrinking the data files or transaction log. And conversely you cannot shrink the files while performing a backup.

> You actually truncate the transaction log when you perform either a full database backup or back up the transaction log. SQL Server 2000 automatically truncates the log for you. Refer to Chapter 10 to see how to perform a database backup.

Keeping the Faith with Fail-Over Clustering

If we can't manage memory or if we simply outgrow our resources, it's time to consider adding new servers to help share the load and keep our single server from failing if something goes wrong. *Clustering* is the ability to add a group of SQL Servers together to support each other.

A cluster allows us to scale our applications indefinitely because when resources get a little low, we just add another server. Partitioning tables and distributed views, which are covered in Chapter 15, "Exploring SQL Server 2000 on Your Own," mean we can split tables across several servers and then view them as though they are a single table or view.

In a cluster, we can have many nodes (these are servers), but what happens when one of these nodes fails? This is where fail-over clustering support comes in. This is a process that defines what happens when one of the servers fails. This can be a little like load balancing. When one server fails the others take over the load that the server had. This makes scheduled maintenance a walk in the park!

In SQL Server 2000, clustering is easy to set up and support and is an improvement over SQL Server 7.0. In the setup of SQL Server 2000 you can configure clustering right from the CD by selecting the Virtual Server option from the installation wizard. However, you must install the Microsoft Cluster Service (MSCS) to select the Virtual Server option. Check Appendix B for information on customizing your installation and setting this option.

So clustering allows us to achieve high availability of our applications. If a server fails, we have another to take over. This means that although our response time might slow, our application databases will still be there!

Summary

Boy we are really ripping through the chapters now; another one down, and another step closer to completing our knowledge of SQL Server 2000 and the ease with which it supports application development.

In this chapter we took a further look at the tools of SQL Server 2000, but from a slightly different slant: using the tools to solve common problems (such as an error) that can occur within any application development.

The capability of the tools to find and locate problems for you easily and quickly just makes SQL Server 2000 an all-around great RDBMS.

Next Steps

In the next chapter we are going to move away from application development and talk about ways you can explore some of the cool new features of SQL Server 2000. We also explore how to use Books Online, the ultimate development resource for SQL Server DBAs and developers.

So let's get into it!

Exploring SQL Server 2000 on Your Own

This is one of the chapters that I was looking forward to writing the most. It gives me a chance to rave about some of the cool new functionality in SQL Server 2000. Plus, I can show you some of the things that are not totally relevant to our application but that you definitely will want to know as you continue developing and maintaining SQL Server.

Although the enhancements to the new version have not been as drastic as they were between SQL Server 7.0 and SQL Server 6.5, many cool features have surfaced in SQL Server 2000.

In this chapter we'll look at some of the wizards that make your work easier and ways to handle multiple instances of SQL Server 2000 and multiple servers with the same database. Whatever avenue you do explore with SQL Server 2000, you can look up more information. Let's take a look now at the documentation that SQL Server 2000 provides so you can find out more about DTS (so you can figure out how to solve the little DTS challenge I gave you in Chapter 13's "Checking the Results of the Import" section).

Using Online Resources to Explore SQL Server 2000

What type of documentation is on SQL Server 2000? The question really should be "What kind of documentation *isn't* available for SQL Server 2000?"

Microsoft has worked hard to ensure that plenty of documentation is available on time and when you need it!

Books Online ships with SQL Server 2000. This is for SQL Server 2000, earlier versions (where appropriate), and related technologies documentation, such as ADO and SQL DMO. It is very comprehensive and can help you with almost everything you need to know about the different aspects of SQL Server 2000.

For example, if you are a little unsure of the syntax of a CREATE TABLE statement, you can check it out in Books Online. If you need to get an overview of Analysis Services, you can get all the information you need in Books Online.

Where do I find Books Online? There are two ways that you can get to Books Online.

- The first way is through the Start menu. There is a Books Online icon in the SQL Server 2000 program group, as shown in Figure 15.1

Figure 15.1

Where to find Books Online within the SQL Server 2000 program group.

- The second way is with the F1 key within Enterprise Manager, Query Analyzer, or any of the other SQL Server 2000 tools. Usually, this help is context sensitive. If you have the table designer open in Enterprise Manager and press F1, Books Online will open with information relevant to the table designer.

Search and Retrieval Tips for Books Online

How do I get the most relevant information from Books Online? Books Online provides the same three basic ways as other Microsoft Help files when you want to locate information. You're most likely familiar with the Contents, Index, and Search tabs. In this section, I show you some hints for honing your searches.

Books Online has a great search engine, but you need to learn how to search well, a little like with the search engines on the Net. For example, if you want to search on Analysis Services, you will locate more hits if you enter the keywords `Analysis Services` than you will if you enter `"Analysis Services"` inside quotation marks. Why? The first search gets all the topics that contain the words "Analysis" and "Services." The second search gets all the topics that have the words "Analysis Services" together.

15

 Note Use quotation marks wisely because you could limit your search far more than you intended to.

Like this book, Books Online has some basic font standards that apply to make navigation much easier.

- `Monospace`—This indicates code samples, error messages, and text that is displayed.
- `UPPERCASE`—Key Transact-SQL words, for example `CREATE PROCEDURE`.
- *`Italic`*—This shows you where to enter your names for variables, tables and so forth, for example `CREATE TABLE` *`tablename`*.
- **`Bold`**—Used for stored procedures names, variable type names, table names, and so forth, and indicates that the word needs to be typed *exactly* as shown. If you were looking at `sp_help` it would be bolded, similar to **`sp_help`**.

SQL Server 2000 Books Online also has navigation standards that will help you get the most out of the books.

- Glossary of terms—Contains keywords and brief descriptions of the keywords.
- Expanding text—This is indicated with a plus (+) icon next to the text. Click the plus icon to expand the text and view further help.
- Related topics—This is indicated with an icon in the top right of the topic. Click the icon to view the related topics.
- Hyperlinks—This will navigate you to related topics within Books Online or to external Web sites that will provide help on the topic. This will be noted by colored, underlined text.
- Home page—SQL Server 2000 Books Online is browser based and has standard browser features including a Home button, Forward, Back, Previous, Next, and so forth.

- Favorites—Books Online has a Favorites folder, similar to that in Internet Explorer. If you regularly require help on a topic, you can add it your Favorites by clicking the Favorites folder, and then clicking Add, as shown in Figure 15.2.

Figure 15.2

Adding a topic to the Favorites folder within Books Online.

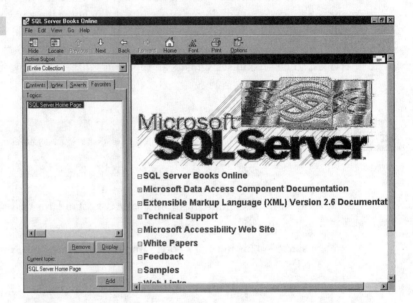

Although Books Online is very comprehensive and can seem a little daunting, one of the best ways to get information out is to use the context-sensitive help functionality.

If you are importing data from an Excel spreadsheet within the Import and Export Data Wizard, click the Help button or press F1. Books Online will then bring up help related to the subject of importing data via DTS.

Finding Help on the Web

Occasionally you can come across problems that you cannot solve with Books Online alone. Microsoft has recognized this and has provided developers and DBAs alike with other major documentation features.

- Microsoft Developer Network (MSDN)—This is almost the be-all and end-all of developer resources. Although this is subscription based, you can find most of the information online, http://msdn.microsoft.com, and it is free! MSDN contains code samples on many different topics including VB, VBScript, Visual C++, SQL Server, ADO—you name it, it's there!

- Microsoft TechNet (MSTN) —This is more of a technical resource and will help you find workarounds to known bugs and common problems. Like MSDN, it is also subscription based, but is available on the Web for free at `http://www.microsoft.com/technet`. This resource will answer most of those common questions for you.

- Microsoft's SQL Server site— This site contains all sorts of useful information, including excerpts from developer books, professional advice, best practices, online conferences, and so forth. You can find it at `http://www.microsoft.com/sql`.

- PASS—This is the Professional Association for SQL Server. This site contains many helpful hints from DBAs, developers, and so forth. The organization is a not-for-profit group that wants to advocate SQL Server as a development platform. You can find PASS at `http://www.sqlpass.org`.

- There are also numerous newsgroups that have regular discussions on SQL Server topics.

Remember that these groups, books, and online resources have been set up to help *you*. Make sure you use them, or we will lose them!

You will not be an ineffectual DBA if you have to look up something in Books Online. There's nothing worse than a new DBA who keeps pestering more senior DBAs because she does not use the tools that are available to her to answer simple questions. So research first, and then ask.

However, if you are struggling with a problem, do not struggle on and on before asking for help. Most DBAs will enjoy taking a moment out of their day to help you; after all, they know what it was like to start from scratch. An old saying I heard once that I keep in the back of my mind most times when I ask a question is

"It is better to look like a fool for a moment than remain a fool for a lifetime."

We have now had a quick look at getting help on a topic when you need it most. Let's take a look at some of the future enhancements we could build into our application.

Seeing Double (or Triple, or...)

The more you do as a DBA or developer, the more you realize how much "more" really means. Sometimes, you'll end up juggling many instances of SQL Server (all versions), many machines, and more data in more locations. Now, to help us keep everything straight and in sync, we can take advantage of these new and cool features.

Running Multiple Instances on One Machine

The introduction of SQL Server 2000 enables us to have multiple instances of SQL Server running on a single machine. In the past we only had one instance of SQL Server, which in SQL Server 2000 is called the Default instance. Now we can have as many named instances as we want. Microsoft has tested up to 15 named instances and one default instance! I am sure that is more than enough for most peoples' needs.

So why multi-instance support? In the past when we had very small client databases with separate security settings we were required to have several servers so that we could configure each one differently. This became a very expensive overhead for application providers.

With multi-instance support, each instance of SQL Server 2000 is totally separate, so it is like having multiple servers. They are totally configurable without causing the changes implemented on one to affect another.

Each instance shares only two things, the client tools and Microsoft Data Access Components (MDAC). These include Query Analyzer, Enterprise Manager, and Profiler. Be a little careful if you upgrade MDAC because it will affect each instance on the server.

How did Microsoft achieve this new miracle? In the Registry (see Figure 15.3), SQL Server 2000 will create a new entry for each instance, and on the local file system everything will be installed under the folder name MSSQL$InstanceName. The dollar sign ($) allows us to have separate folders for each instance.

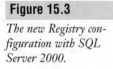

Figure 15.3

The new Registry configuration with SQL Server 2000.

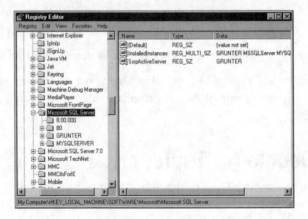

Is there anything else to watch out for? Because each instance is a fully working copy of SQL Server 2000, you can find that disk space is filled up quickly if you have several instances installed.

Also, SQL Server 2000 will use as much memory as is available on your machine. But it does enable memory sharing by default, so for example you have 128MB of RAM and SQL Server 2000 has a hold on all the available free RAM, it will relinquish RAM as need to other applications.

15

SQL Server 2000 normally uses as much memory as it can, but if another application wants some, SQL Server 2000 will release the amount of memory that the next process needs.

If you have multiple instances of SQL Server 2000 installed, each instance will try to take as much memory as it can. When the first instance releases memory to the next application (in this case SQL Server 2000), it will not realize that it is another copy of SQL Server 2000 requesting the memory. Currently there is no sharing of memory space between SQL Server 2000 instances.

Finally, because it can be resource intensive, Microsoft does not recommend installing too many instances of SQL Server 2000 on one machine. In fact, if you have very high performance transactional databases, keep them on separate servers. The resources will not be shared, thus improving performance.

This feature was really only introduced to cater to developers moving an application to testing, or a smaller database server being freed up to allow a bigger server to be moved into its own environment.

You have to admit; this is a pretty cool new feature, especially when we are developing applications that require different settings on each server.

Using Multiple Collation

In the past with SQL Server, once we had set the collation setting for a server, each and every one of our databases would have to use those settings.

If you need to know what collation settings are, refer to Appendix B, "Installation Tips for SQL Server 2000," where we installed SQL Server 2000.

But now that has all changed. With SQL Server 2000 we can specify a collation setting for not only the server, but for each database as well. But wait—there's more! Not only can we specify the collation setting for the database, but we can also specify the collation setting for each column in our tables. This gives us a greater range of flexibility when we have international data feed in. We can get extended character support for Japanese, Arabic, and virtually any data character.

Because we have different collation settings we can also have different sort orders, case sensitivity, and so on. Talk about flexibility!

Keeping Multiple Database Applications in Sync with Replication

Replication is a powerful feature of SQL Server 2000 that allows you to keep more than one database (in fact a whole enterprise of databases) in sync. This means that half of your users can be updating a database in Siberia, and the other half in Dunedin.

The changes that users make can be replicated across to the other database, allowing the users in Siberia to see the changes that the users in Dunedin make, and vice versa! This type of replication is known as *two-way replication*. The data is pushed from one server to another and in both directions.

One-way replication is where local databases send their data through to a central database. The central database receives the data but does not push any information back.

Since the introduction of SQL Server 2000, we can now do some really cool things when it comes to replication.

SQL Server 2000 is available in a CE version for Windows CE-compatible handhelds. This allows staff out in the field to enter real-time information into their Windows CE devices, save the data, and when they get back to the office, have it replicate to a central server. Talk about cool!

But with the new .Net platform initiative that Microsoft is driving, we have even greater flexibility than this. We can actually build our own interfaces for Windows CE using VB, C#, C++, and so on. So a custom interface that the users are familiar with can be put in the palm of their hands. And with new products like the Compaq iPAQ we can even have nice colored screens. The next wave of computing is here!

Leveraging Enhancements to Improve Development

SQL Server 2000 offers several ways to streamline development and improve data integrity. This section shows you some cool things you can do with Query Analyzer and other development tricks you can use.

Using Cascading Declarative Referential Integrity (Cascading DRI)

When we first created our database we used the database-diagramming tool to create some of the relationships between our tables. When we created the relationships, we had the option to implement Cascading DRI, as shown in Figure 15.4. Although we neglected to take it up, it is perhaps one new feature of SQL Server 2000 that will excite those who have had to write complex triggers in the past to perform this functionality.

DRI are the foreign key constraints that we implement between tables to ensure that relationships enforce the integrity of our data. DRI helps make sure that when an UPDATE is performed, existing data is not violated by the data change. DRI can be supplemented by defining triggers on tables, custom defaults, and so on. We took a look at DRI in Chapter 3's "Creating Relationships" section.

Figure 15.4

The new declarative referential integrity within SQL Server 2000.

Cascading DRI allows us to delete child rows out of a table when the parent row is deleted. In relational databases it is not possible to delete the parent row before the child row. In the past we had to write complex triggers and stored procedures to perform this functionality. Now SQL Server 2000 can do this!

This doesn't just apply to deletes, but also to updates. If the primary key of a column changes (and it shouldn't, it really shouldn't), we can replicate this through the database. The change will propagate through the database making the change for us.

All those Access programmers out there will have no problem migrating to SQL Server 2000 now!

Mimicking Built-In Functions with User-Defined Functions

User-defined functions (UDFs) rock! We have already created one in Chapter 6's "Tweaking Dates from Around the Globe" section. UDFs allow us to create compliant units of Transact-SQL that can return either a *scalar value* or a *table*.

 A *scalar value* returns a single value (as our UDF did) of the type we specify in the CREATE FUNCTION statement.

 A *table* returns a table of results. It leverages the new data type (which we discuss soon). From this type of function we can return a similar concept to a recordset.

We supply one or more parameters to our UDF. These are of any data type except the new TABLE data type, timestamp, or Cursor. We can use these functions in a SELECT statement, in a WHERE clause, and so forth. They can be used as we would use any of the built-in SQL Server 2000 functions.

Our UDF functions can be bound to a table so that the table structure cannot be changed unless the UDF is dropped. Within the UDF we can also reference other SQL Server 2000 built-in functions. This allows us to get access to the server name, version of SQL Server, and so on. In my opinion this is one of the greatest features of SQL Server 2000.

Coding with Three New Data Types

Three new data types come with SQL Server 2000.

- SQL_Variant—This is a special data type that allows any type of data type to be stored, except SQL_Variant, ntext, text, and timestamp. Because it is not strongly typed, we can have softer data structures that allow many different bits of information to be stored.

- BigInt—This is an 8-byte integer. This came around for some of the very large databases (VLDB), with more than 2 billion rows of data. SQL Server 2000 now supports TINYINT, SMALLINT, INT, and BIGINT.

- TABLE—This is perhaps one of the coolest new data types. It allows us to create temporary tables as a data type, but these do not remain in scope like a temporary table, so you do not have to specifically drop them once finished.

These new data types allow greater flexibility in designing and implementing our applications. We can have softer, more fluid structures with the SQL_Variant data type.

Our tables can contain billions of rows with the BIGINT data type, and with the new data type of TABLE we can have temporary tables that are only for the current user rather than being more global and persistent.

Getting More from Query Analyzer

The new Object Browser in Query Analyzer is one of the most noticeable changes in the latest version of SQL Server 2000, as shown in Figure 15.5.

Figure 15.5

The new Object Browser in Query Analyzer.

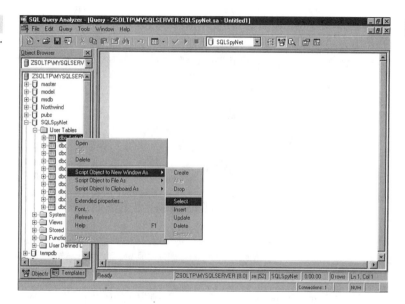

This allows us to navigate our way through the server. We can look at the databases, tables, views, and stored procedures, but it doesn't stop there; we can also have the object scripted to the window as drop, creates, selects, and so on. For example, we right-click on a table and select Script Object to New Window As, Select. This creates the basic outline of a SELECT statement and from there we can fill in the gaps. This is really programming by example.

The Object Browser is not only for such things as user-defined tables and stored procedures. From within the Object Browser we can select built-in SQL Server 2000 functions. This gives us a list of the parameters that the functions expect, as well as their data types, and it also gives us the return type that the functions will return to us. This will save you time having to refer to Books Online to find the data types that a specific function returns.

The Object Browser also allows us to store templates. Some predefined templates come with the installation of SQL Server 2000, but more than that, we can create our own. This will allow us to create a structured outline that we want all of our developers to follow when they create a stored procedure, view, and so on. We can fully implement standards into our database development.

The Object Search screen (another new feature) enables us to enter search criteria (for example, a table name), and SQL Server 2000 will search through the databases to find a match. This makes finding stored procedures within a database that has hundreds of stored procedures very simple, as shown in Figure 15.6.

Figure 15.6

The new Object Search screen in Query Analyzer.

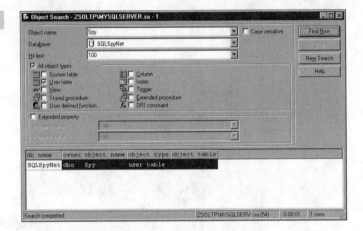

The new grid control in Query Analyzer enables multiple results to be returned to the one window. In earlier versions you would have a new result window for each set of results returned. Although this is a little enhancement, it means a lot for ease of use.

The Customize screen in Query Analyzer enables us to create shortcuts to the most commonly used Transact-SQL statements. For example, Alt+F1 will execute the `sp_help` stored procedure. The Customize screen is under Tools, Customize and looks similar to that shown in Figure 15.7.

Scripting Database Objects

The ability to script database objects is a wonderful mechanism for DBAs. For example, if we have two sites running, development and production, whenever we make a *structural* change in development we need to replicate that change to the production site. We can't use the Copy Database Wizard because we do not want to lose the data that we have in the production database. Scripting the database objects allows us to bring the structural changes across without affecting the data in our production database.

Figure 15.7

The Customize screen in Query Analyzer.

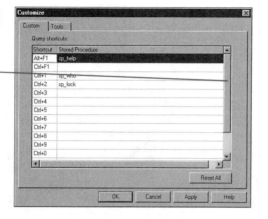

Let's try scripting one of our stored procedures. Open Enterprise Manager and navigate to the Stored Procedures folder. Find the `PersonSpyInsert` stored procedure. Right-click the stored procedure, select All Tasks, and then Generate SQL Script, as shown in Figure 15.8.

Figure 15.8

The Generate SQL Script option is in Enterprise Manager.

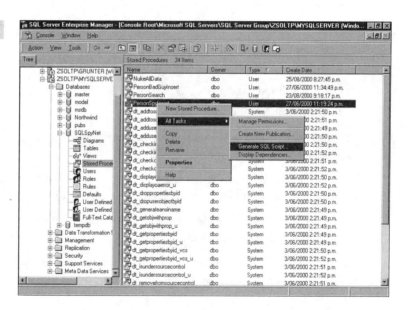

This will launch a screen that allows us to specify the different options that we need when creating a script. The screen will look similar to that shown in Figure 15.9.

Figure 15.9

The Generate SQL Scripts screen.

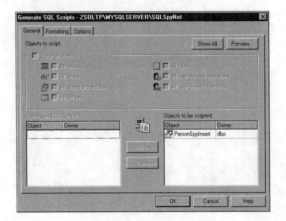

With this screen we can actually script our *whole* database. We can generate SQL Scripts for

- Tables
- Views
- Stored procedures
- Defaults
- Rules
- User-defined data types
- User-defined functions

On the Formatting tab we can specify the format for our scripts, including whether to create DROP statements for each object.

The Option tab allows us to specify whether the permissions on the object(s) come across when the object is scripted. We can also script our database users.

On the General tab we can preview the script before we save it to disk, allowing us to verify that the script looks as it should.

When we save the file, it is saved with a .sql file extension. This file can be viewed in Notepad because it is only a text file. The Web and SQL Server 2000 are cool, aren't they?

Scripting gives a lot of flexibility when migrating our changes from a development site to a live site. I am sure that you will make good use of this feature.

Using AFTER and INSTEAD OF Triggers

We looked at triggers in Chapter 5, "Viewing Data and Automating Updates with DDL." Let's take a look at them again, except this time from the angle of what's new and cool?

Earlier versions of SQL Server have supported triggers for quite a long while. But in this new version of SQL Server we see some enhancements to the way triggers fire and behave. The best thing is that we have even more control over our triggers.

SQL Server 2000 supports the following two types of triggers:

- AFTER triggers—These triggers fire after an event has occurred. For example, our trigger that we defined on the Spy table in Chapter 5 is an AFTER trigger. The trigger fires *after* the data has been inserted into the table. These triggers cannot be placed on a view. We are also allowed to specify multiple AFTER triggers on a table for a defined event (INSERT, UPDATE, or DELETE). We can then set the order in which those triggers fire.

- INSTEAD OF (BEFORE) triggers—These are the new addition to SQL Server 2000. With INSTEAD OF triggers, we capture an event before it is processed. An INSERT into our Spy table captures the data *before* the data is inserted into the table. We can then manipulate the data, execute stored procedures, and so on. These new triggers can be defined on views.

What does this mean for us? With the new enhancements we can move our business rules to SQL Server without having to get our user interface (in a two-tier model) to capture the rules. So if business rules change, we only need to modify them in one place.

Looking at Distributed Views

A distributed view is a cool new feature that allows us to *horizontally partition* a table across several servers.

Horizontally partitioning means to break up a table horizontally. For example, if we have a 10,000-row table and 10 servers, we place 1,000 rows on the first server, 1,000 on the second, 1,000 on the third, and so on.

How do we achieve this? We place rows 1–1,000 on the first server, 1,001–2,000 on the second server, and so on. To enforce this we use CHECK CONSTRAINTS to limit the value that a column can hold.

After the data has been partitioned we can create a view that links all the servers together as though we were looking at a single table. What's so cool about that? When we place a restriction on the view, for example all rows less than 5,000, SQL Server 2000 will use the CHECK CONSTRAINTS of the servers to decide which servers to query for the data. So servers 5–10 will be excluded from the query immediately. This saves querying servers for data for no apparent reason.

Now isn't that cool? This type of flexibility allows us to support the largest corporate environments or the busiest Web sites. In the future if we find that we need more resources, we just add another server. Talk about scalable!

Creating Enhanced Indexes

Indexes, like triggers, have always been a part of SQL Server but now we have even more features that we can take advantage of when creating indexes.

One of the biggest changes is allowing us to have an index on a computed column. A computed column is the answer from a sum. For example, consider a column called SumOfAandB. If the underlying value for this column was columnA + columnB, in the past we couldn't reference this column quickly. However, we can now use an index on this column. Instead of SQL Server 2000 having to compute the column every time we reference it, it can draw the results from the index, making data retrieval wickedly faster!

So what else has changed with indexes? We can now specify indexes not only on computed columns, but also on views! This gives us views that are very fast. But SQL Server 2000 goes one step ahead of this. If you have an index defined on a view and you retrieve data from one of the base tables, SQL Server 2000 will use the index defined on the view to get the data back quickly. Now isn't that cool!

We can specify what order to build the index in, either ascending or descending. This stores the data on disk in the order specified, making retrieval very efficient. So if we have a column (say the Firstname column in Person) that we normally retrieve in ascending order, by using a sort, we can specify an index on the Firstname column, thus preventing a sort when we retrieve the data. This will dramatically speed up your queries.

When creating indexes, we can also specify that the index be created in tempDB. This gets SQL Server 2000 to sort the rows in tempDB, before creating the index. Although this increases the amount of disk initially used to create an index, it allows indexes to build quickly and efficiently, especially if tempDB is on another disk.

Leveraging XML Support

This is probably one of the most talked about new enhancements in SQL Server 2000. We have all heard the hype and seen the big push by companies to get on the XML bandwagon, but Microsoft is certainly one of the leaders in this field.

The SQL Server 2000 relational database engine has support for XML and allows us to retrieve our results from a query in a specified XML format. We can query the database as normal with SELECT statements, and by specifying the new FOR XML clause at the end of the SELECT statement we can retrieve results in a XML format. Nice, huh?

Let's take a quick look at an example. Enter the code in Listing 15.1 into Query Analyzer.

Listing 15.1   Performing a SELECT Using XML as the Output

```
SELECT Firstname, Surname, DOB FROM Person WHERE PersonID = 1 FOR XML AUTO
```

This will return the results in an XML format, as shown in Figure 15.10.

Figure 15.10

The new FOR XML AUTO *option that you can specify on a* SELECT *statement in SQL Server 2000.*

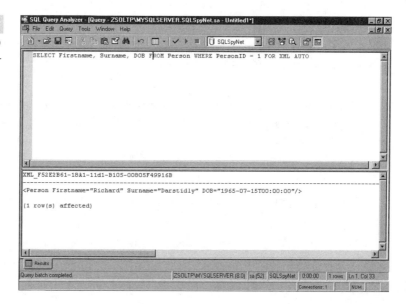

But SQL Server 2000 does not stop here. If you are running Windows 2000 you can configure Internet Information Server (IIS) to allow you to query the database directly through a URL (universal resource locator).

The configuration is easy to perform and set up because SQL Server 2000 comes with a tool called Configure SQL XML Support in IIS, as shown in Figure 15.11. This is a simple and easy-to-use interface designed to help you to perform this task.

There has been some confusion about security. If you can query the database with a browser, this exposes all of your data. But you have full control over the configuration of the XPath Queries. You can specify the account that everyone uses when they perform queries against the database.

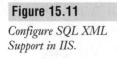

Figure 15.11

Configure SQL XML Support in IIS.

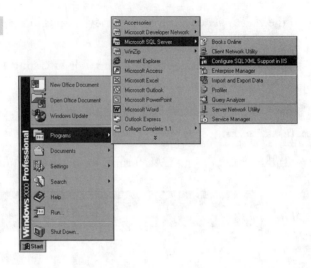

What type of queries can a user perform? Currently there is support for the SELECT and EXECUTE statements within the XPath query, but there is an add-on (XML Updategrams) that allows you to perform most of the Transact-SQL statements that you can in Query Analyzer, including UPDATE, INSERT, and DELETE as well as DROP and CREATE statements.

Why would you want to do this? Well this gives us complete control of our server no matter where in the world we are!

We can write clever stored procedures that can perform all our administration tasks. Then we call the stored procedures from our browser at home, and violà, our maintenance is done, without having to leave the couch. Bring it on!

Using the New Wizards in SQL Server 2000

SQL Server 2000 introduces the Copy Database Wizard and an enhanced version of the Index Tuning Wizard. Let's take a look at both of these wizards, starting with the Index Tuning Wizard.

Tuning Indexes

The Index Tuning Wizard will assess your workload and give you suggestions for creating optimal indexes and statistics for your databases. The wizard can be launched from within Enterprise Manager by selecting Tools, Wizards. In the Select Wizard dialog, expand the Management list and choose Index Tuning Wizard, as shown in Figure 15.12. This will launch a screen similar to that shown in Figure 15.13.

Figure 15.12

*Expanding the
Management wizards
list to find the Index
Tuning Wizard.*

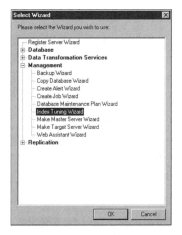

15

Figure 15.13

*The enhanced Index
Tuning Wizard in
Enterprise Manager.*

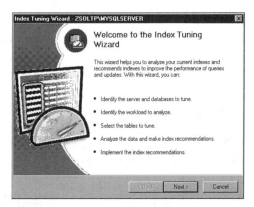

A *workload* is a saved Transact-SQL script or trace from Profiler. The wizard will analyze the scripts and make suggestions for increasing the performance of the query.

Why use a wizard? I thought this is what a DBA is for? You are right! But the wizard allows us to decide on performance enhancements without having an exhaustive understanding of the intricacies between the data structures. The wizard will make recommendations for placing indexes on a workload by using the Query Optimizer to analyze the queries that you supply in the workload. It also assesses the impact on the database by placing an index on the table, view, or query and analyzes the use of the index based on the workload that you supply.

It will also recommend what you can do to enhance small queries that perform badly. Like most things in SQL Server 2000, you can change the recommendations to suit your own needs with some advanced options. Nice, isn't it?

Copying Databases

The next wizard we will take a look at is the Copy Database Wizard. This wizard allows you to move databases from one server to another or between instances of SQL Server 2000 on one machine, and provides you with an easy way to upgrade SQL Server 7.0 databases to SQL Server 2000. This wizard does it all! (Well not quite, but you get the picture.)

You can launch the Copy Database Wizard from Enterprise Manager by selecting Tools, Wizards, and then expanding the Management list and selecting Copy Database Wizard (refer to Figure 15.12). This will launch a screen similar to that shown in Figure 15.14.

Figure 15.14

The new Copy Database Wizard in SQL Server 2000.

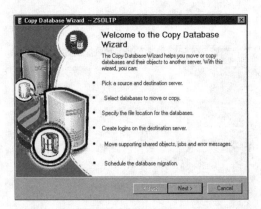

I hear you say, "I can do this through a backup and restore operation." Well that's true, but when you do a backup and restore, although you get the whole database, you do not get everything that goes with that database, for example, any SQL Server 2000 logins or scheduled jobs.

With the Copy Database Wizard you get the lot. It really is just a case of point and shoot! You can even schedule the time that the process is going to take place, allowing for quiet periods on the server. This is especially useful if the database is very large.

As you can imagine, this makes migrating development databases to a live server a simple process. Now there are no more complex scripts to get all of the dependent objects on the database to replicate across to the new server, just a nice, simple process.

Improving Security

As you move into a multi-user environment, security, user, and resource management will become key to the performance and integrity of your application. Some of these security features are available on Windows 2000 only.

Understanding Kerberos and Security Delegation

Unfortunately, we cannot take advantage of these new enhancements. We are not running Windows 2000—maybe that's a good reason to upgrade.

 Delegation is the ability to hand over a task to someone else. The same principle applies to SQL Server 2000. When we have the ability to connect to multiple servers, we can pass the user's credentials on from one server to another, as they were when the user first logged in.

So for example James logs into our SPYNET domain, (SPYNET\James) and connects to our first instance of SQL Server 2000, which then connects to another server. The second server knows James's connection information, including the domain from where he came.

How does it work? For delegation to work, the servers must be running on Windows 2000 and have *Kerberos* support running on the machine. The servers must also be using the new Active Directory features of Windows 2000. A number of configuration options need to be specified when setting this up, and you can find these options on MSDN.

 Kerberos is a security protocol defined by an Internet standards document RFC 1510. Kerberos uses security tokens as they were defined in Internet standards document RFC 1964.

What other security enhancements do we have with SQL Server 2000? One of the newest security enhancements we have is password security on database backups.

Using Password Security on Database Backups

We took a brief look at this when we discussed the maintenance of our database in Chapter 10, "Ensuring Data Availability". Password protecting our backups prevents others from easily copying the backup files and restoring them. Although the passwords and the backup sets are *not* encrypted, they do supply some level of security that we did not have in the past.

The other thing to note is that although the backup set cannot be restored without a password, the contents of the backup set can still be overwritten.

If your data is important, do not rely only on the password protection of the backup set. You need to take more rigorous methods to secure your important data, including, but not limited to

- Authenticating your users through Windows NT if possible
- Not giving just anybody the ability to perform database backups
- Keeping the server in a locked room

You can take many other measures to secure your data. If in doubt, get a specialist in to help.

Using C2 Auditing

We also took a look at C2 auditing earlier, in Chapter 9. SQL Server 2000 fully supports C2 auditing and has C2 accreditation. You can find out more on the Radium Web site

```
http://www.radium.ncsc.mil/tpep/epl/entries/TTAP-CSC-EPL-00-001.html
```

C2 auditing is a set of security rules that have been defined by the U.S. Department of Defense. As you can imagine, these rules are very stringent and capture virtually everything that an instance of SQL Server 2000 is doing!

We discussed this earlier, but the following are some of the highlights:

- Auditing is key to SQL Server 2000. If auditing fails, the service is stopped.
- Use SQL Profiler to capture the audited events.
- All security changes (GRANT, REVOKE, DENY, password changes) are audited.
- Server performance can be affected by auditing.

There are lesser levels of auditing that we can use, and you can configure these as you want.

To review what we discussed earlier, see Chapter 9, "Implementing Security in Spy Net."

Summary

Wow, that was some of the most fun I've had writing the book. It is great being able to come to grips with new software, and SQL Server 2000 has not let me down.

The new features of SQL Server 2000 build on the versatility and functionality of the existing features of SQL Server 7.0, and only offer us better performance, reliability, and scalability.

Although I have covered several of the new features of SQL Server 2000, please do not think of this as a definitive list. I have not even touched on several new features, including

- Full-text search enhancements
- Text in data row
- Log shipping (though we did touch on this in our replication overview)
- Enhancements to replication
- Enhancements to Data Transformation Services

This doesn't even begin to cover the list that of items that I haven't covered!

I believe the enhancements that I did cover are the ones that will affect your day-to-day work the most dramatically at first. As you become more familiar with SQL Server 2000 I am sure that you will find ways to achieve tasks by taking advantage of new features that I haven't even thought of.

We also took a look at Books Online. This is a great resource that you should use extensively when researching and expanding your knowledge. I find that Books Online is one of the best resources available on SQL Server, but it assumes that you already understand some of the more basic components of SQL Server.

And that, ladies and gentleman, is it from me. It has been a wonderful experience being able to deliver a book on SQL Server 2000, and I would like you to continue your interest with the software. So my advice to you is get into it! Have fun, but just remember, don't play on a live system!

In this appendix

- *Installing Personal Web Server*
- *Configuring PWS*

Setting Up Your PC as a Web Server

To finish the development of our Spy Net application, we must install a Web server of some sort onto our machines. We must set up our machine as a Web server so that we can leverage the deployment of the interface we built in Chapter 12, "Designing a Front End to Support Our SQLSpyNet Database." The installation of Personal Web Server (PWS) for Windows 98 is covered in this appendix.

Configuring a PC as a Web server is really pretty easy. You need to have a copy of PWS, which should be on your Windows 98 CD-ROM, or you can download the software for free from Microsoft's Web site.

```
http://www.microsoft.com/msdownload/ntoptionpack/askwiz.asp
```

 Note

If you're running Windows NT, these sites can get you started in setting up a Web server on your machine:

- Installation guideline for Windows NT 4.0 option pack:

    ```
    http://msdn.microsoft.com/library/periodic/period98/
    ewn98b1.htm
    ```

- Recommended installation information from MS about IIS 4.0 (for Win NT):

    ```
    http://support.microsoft.com/support/iis/install/install_
    iis4.asp?RLD=71
    ```

After you have a copy of the setup files, just follow these simple steps, and we will be away laughing!

The installation of PWS that we will cover is for the Standard Installation. Although I covered both the Typical and Custom installation options for SQL Server 2000, I will only cover the Typical installation for PWS. After all, the entire book is about SQL Server 2000, not Web development!

When you are ready, double-click the Setup.exe icon.

If the setup Windows screen does not automatically start when you insert your CD-ROM, you can browse through the CD to find the file. The Setup.exe file for PWS can be found under *x*:\add-ons\pws\setup.exe, where x is your CD-ROM drive.

When the install program launches you will see a screen similar to that shown in Figure A.1.

Figure A.1

The initial install screen for PWS.

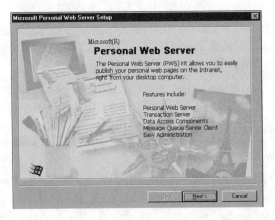

Like most install programs, the first screen is a little limited, and all you can do is either exit or continue. So let's continue. Click the Next button. This will give you the license agreement screen as shown in Figure A.2.

Figure A.2

The license agreement screen for PWS.

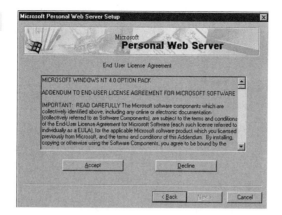

After you have accepted the license agreement, you will be presented with a screen similar to that shown in Figure A.3.

Figure A.3

Installation options available for PWS.

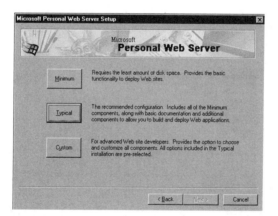

This screen allows us to choose the installation option that we want to perform. As I said, though, we will only cover the Typical installation. Click the Typical button to bring up the screen that allows us to configure where on the file system our Web site will be located, as shown in Figure A.4.

 Note

> When our site goes live, we will want to configure our Web site to be located on another section of our file system. This is mainly for security reasons because a hacker will try to look under `x:\Inetpub\wwwroot` first.

Figure A.4

Selecting where our Web files will be located for PWS.

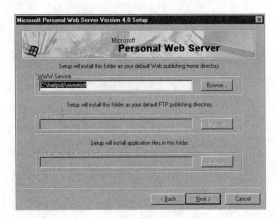

Although the default is not optimal for live systems, it is fine for our development; so just let PWS go to the default directory. Click the Next button and we will really be on our way.

This will begin the installation program, and you will see a screen similar to that shown in Figure A.5.

Figure A.5

Installation progress for PWS.

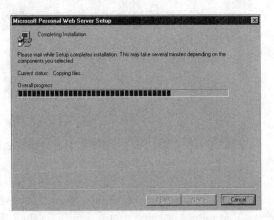

After the installation has finished, you might have to reboot your machine. If the setup program prompts you for this, allow your machine to reboot. While your PC is rebooting let's take a look at some of the programs that PWS will install.

- PWS Manager—A GUI that allows you to configure your Web service.
- FrontPage server extensions—Special file extensions that allow you to connect to a Web server and edit the Web pages that the server has.

- Microsoft Data Access Components (MDAC)—These are the data access core components for SQL Server 2000 and allow for data communication between many disparate sources.

- Documentation—Help files and other documents that will help you get started.

EXCURSION

FrontPage Server Extensions and How They Fit In

Notice the name *FrontPage*? This is not the same FrontPage we use to author our Web pages. FrontPage server extensions are special extensions that exist on a Web server and allow us to connect to the Web server and to edit the pages on the server.

There is much more to FrontPage server extensions than this, but this gives you a brief idea of the function they perform.

A

Your PC should have rebooted by now, so let's take a look at how we check that our site is running and ready to go.

You will find the program for configuring PWS (Personal Web Manager) within your Start menu, under Microsoft Personal Web Server, similar to how it is shown in Figure A.6.

Figure A.6

Where to find PWS in the Start menu.

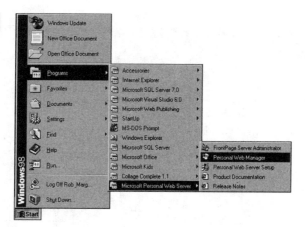

After you have launched PWS from the Start menu you will see a screen similar to that shown in Figure A.7.

 Note

You might get the Tips screen at startup. If you are interested you can read some of these tips and gain some valuable insight into PWS.

Figure A.7

The PWS Manager and configuration component.

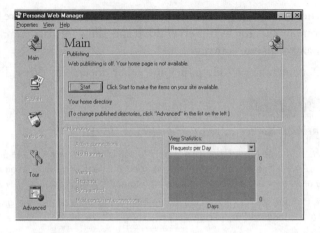

The main configuration screen contains a Start/Stop toggle button. For example, if the Web service is running, the button will be a Stop button and vice versa. If the button is in the Start state, click the button, and voilá your machine has become a Web server! To check out your default home page, open a browser window and type your Web server name in the browser window, for example `http://grunter`.

You should see a screen similar to that shown in Figure A.8.

Figure A.8

The default home page for your Web server.

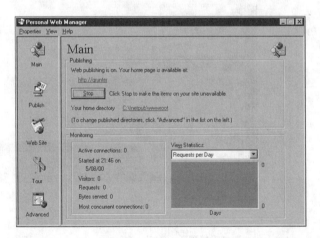

The home page you see is for your Web server, it is not for SQLSpyNet on the Web. To see how to set up SQLSpyNet as a Web site (called SpyNet), check out Chapter 12, "Designing a Front End to Support Our SQLSpyNet Database."

There we have it! Not only a SQL Server, but now your machine is also a Web Server!

In case you are wondering, you do not need to be connected to the Internet to have your machine act as a Web server. With the configuration that we have, it is known as an intranet site rather than an Internet site.

 An *Internet site* is a site that is public and available for the whole world to see, for example http://www.quepublishing.com.

 An *intranet site*, conversely, is a protected site that restricts access. Most companies have an intranet for keeping staff updated with up and coming events, for example. Our SpyNet Web site is an intranet. A characteristic of an intranet is that all the machines reside on a Local Area Network (LAN), meaning they are physically close to each other.

 An *extranet* is similar in concept to an intranet; that is, it's protected from the general public, but it is on a Wide Area Network (WAN). This means that a company like Spy Net can have a shared site even though one office is in Boston and another is in London. Extranets can be extended to allow suppliers, customers, and privileged clients to gain access to the company's extranet through an Internet site that has some very secure access permissions surrounding it.

Because our machine does not have to be connected to the Net, you can just view the Web pages without having to dial up your Internet service provider (ISP). You now have your very own Web Server, SQL Server, and LAN! Maybe you will even become a network engineer!

There we go; you should now go back to Chapter 12 and complete the installation of SpyNet for the Web. And get your Web development career started as well as becoming a DBA.

A

Installing and Configuring SQL Server 2000

This guide is adapted from the SQL Server 2000 CD. Within this appendix, you will find the most relevant way to configure SQL Server 2000 for our requirements. Just remember it is not the only way, but it is the best for us!

This appendix is full of steps and figures that show you exactly what you need to know when performing the installation.

Note that this installation of SQL Server 2000 was performed on a standalone PC—in other words, it was not connected or configured for network access. If your machine is connected to a network or has network drivers installed and configured, your screens might look a little different from those shown.

For this installation guide, I assume you have these three things:

- All the minimum software requirements installed. If you're not sure about the details, see the "System Requirements" section of the Introduction.

- A copy of SQL Server 2000 Personal Edition. This is the version of SQL Server 2000 that we use to develop the SQL Spy Net application. Or, you can use the evaluation version from the CD accompanying this book. If you have the Standard Edition or are working on a network, by all means proceed with your version, but just be aware that you'll encounter some variations in the screens.

- You also should have the Windows 98 or other Windows version installation disk handy (just in case).

> Most of the options in this installation guide will be the same for SQL Server 2000 Personal Edition on Windows 98, 2000, or NT without major differences in the screens. However, where there is a difference I have noted it for you. Isn't that nice?

I suggest that you back up any important files you have on your machine to ensure that, if the installation turns "pear-shaped," you can recover. These installations usually do not have a lot of user interaction, but it still pays to be careful.

> As I point out throughout this installation, I have already installed at least one *instance* of SQL Server on my machine. You can follow these steps with or without an existing instance of SQL Server or a previous version currently installed. I point out the differences as we go along, but the process is still the same.

[ic:geek]A SQL Server *instance* is an installation of SQL Server on your machine. This can be any version of SQL Server, but if it is prior to SQL Server 2000 your named instance will be Default. Named instances allow us to have multiple installations of SQL Server on our machines (a new feature) that all behave like separate machines.

So, now that we're ready to go, let's begin.

Selecting the Type of Installation

Pop the SQL Server 2000 CD into your CD-ROM drive. The install application should start automatically, but if it doesn't, locate the Autorun.exe on the root of the CD, and double-click to start the installation.

After the install application starts, you see a display screen similar to that shown in Figure B.1.

Figure B.1

The initial install screen for SQL Server 2000.

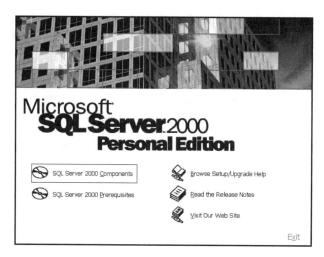

Five options are available at this stage.

One option, the SQL Server 2000 Prerequisites option, is where you install the pre-requisites (Common Controls Library updates) for Windows 95 (if you are installing *Connectivity only*).

> *Connectivity only* allows a client PC running Windows 95 to talk to SQL Server 2000. It *does not* install any of the management tools used to configure SQL Server 2000. This is mainly used so that custom applications written for Windows 95 can establish a connection to SQL Server 2000.

One other option, the Browse Setup/Upgrade Help option, offers help on installa-tion for your given operating system and the installation options available to certain platforms.

To continue with this installation, select the SQL Server 2000 Components option. You see a screen similar to the previous one, but with fewer options. This screen enables you to install the database engine and support services for SQL Server 2000 (see Figure B.2) .

- Analysis Services is the replacement installation for the former Online Analytical Processing (OLAP) Component in SQL Server 7.0. Analysis services enables the development of OLAP Services and data-mining components.

- English Query is the installation option for a further SQL Server 2000 service. English Query enables users to model English-like statements to the database—to retrieve information rather than form SQL statements.

Figure B.2

Install the Database Engine for the Personal Edition of SQL Server 2000.

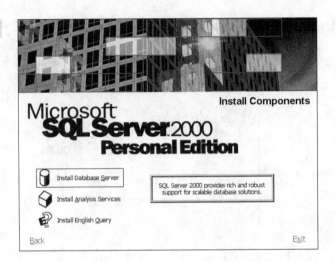

Don't worry too much about these services; they are a little surplus to our requirements, so we won't need to touch on them for our application. However, you can find out more about these services by browsing through the help supplied with the Installation Wizard (see Figure B.1).

To begin the installation of SQL Server 2000 Personal Edition, select the Install Database Server option. You should see a screen similar to that shown in Figure B.3.

Figure B.3

Launching the Installation Wizard for SQL Server 2000 Personal Edition.

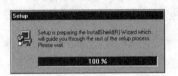

This launches the Installation Wizard (and might take a couple moments). The steps required to perform the installation are discussed next.

Installing the Application Following the Step-By-Step Wizard

The first screen (Welcome) of the wizard appears in Figure B.4. What you can do here is definitely limited. If you are sure you want to continue with the installation, click Next.

Figure B.4

The Welcome screen of the Installation Wizard for SQL Server 2000.

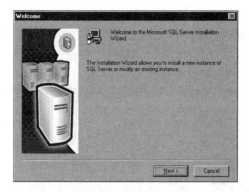

The second screen (Computer Name) looks similar to that shown in Figure B.5.

 Note   If this installation were being performed for a network installation, the screen would let you choose other options. If you are connected to a network, please be sure you choose the Local Computer option. Click Next to proceed with the installation.

B

Figure B.5

Select the computer on which you want to install SQL Server 2000.

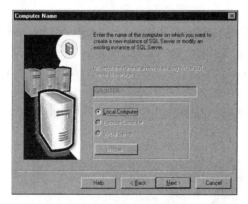

The third screen you see (Installation Selection) is similar to that shown in Figure B.6.

After you have completed this installation, if you want to modify the installation or remove it, you can select the Upgrade, Remove, or Add Components to an Existing Instance of SQL Server option.

Under the Advanced Options, you can choose from the following:

- **Record an Unattended .ISS file**—This option enables you to create a setup file for unattended installation; in other words, no user interaction.

- **Registry Rebuild**—This option is for fixing corrupted Registry information for your installation of SQL Server 2000.
- **Maintain a Virtual Server for Fail-over Clustering (if your previous installation supports it)**—This option enables you to make changes to existing cluster installations, such as changing a name or adding and removing nodes. If your previous installation does not support it, this option will be grayed out.

Figure B.6

The Installation Selection screen of the Installation Wizard for SQL Server 2000.

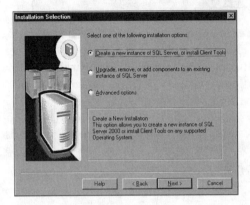

However, we are going to install a new instance of SQL Server 2000 Personal Edition. Select this option and click Next.

The next screen of the wizard (User Information) is similar to that shown in Figure B.7. This screen captures the user information with which you want to register the installation. Enter your name and, if relevant, company information into the boxes provided. Click Next.

Figure B.7

The User Information screen of the Installation Wizard for SQL Server 2000.

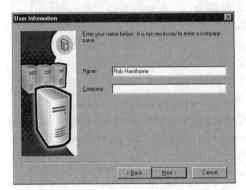

You then see the Software License Agreement and an amendment to the End User License Agreement (EULA). You must select Yes to continue with the installation (see Figure B.8).

Figure B.8

The Software License Agreement for the installation of SQL Server 2000.

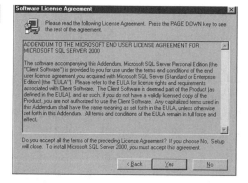

The next screen you see (Installation Definition) in the Installation Wizard looks similar to that shown in Figure B.9.

B

Figure B.9

The Installation Definition screen of the Installation Wizard for SQL Server 2000.

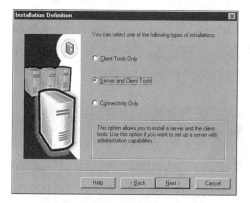

The following options are available:

- **Client Tools Only**—Use this option if you want to install only the tools necessary to connect to an existing server, and if you want to have the option of selecting individual components.

- **Server and Client Tools**—This is the installation option we require. It enables you to set up a server with administrative resources and gives you access to the full range of installation options.

- **Connectivity Only**—Use this when you want to connect to an existing server but do not want the option of selecting the components you install. The

Connectivity Only option installs just the files needed for client applications to make a connection to the server. For example, the MDAC (Microsoft Data Access) drivers are updated so that you can use ODBC to connect to SQL Server 2000. Don't worry if you do not fully understand this yet; we will take a closer look when we talk about front-end applications.

To continue with our installation, select the Server and Client Tools option and click Next.

The next screen (Instance Name) enables you to specify the instance name of the SQL Server you want to install (see Figure B.10). In the installation I perform here, I call my installation of SQL Server 2000 MYSQLSERVER. However, you do not have to use this name; you can use any name you want, as long as the name follows a few rules (discussed in the following list).

The Default check box on the screen enables the installation to proceed with the default instance name for the service under which SQL Server 2000 runs.

Note If the Default check box is not enabled (as in Figure B.10) then an instance of SQL Server is already installed on your machine. This could be an instance of SQL 6.5, 7.0, or 2000. As you can see with my installation, I cannot select the Default check box because I already have another version of SQL Server installed on my machine.

Figure B.10

The Default check box is not available for this installation of SQL Server 2000.

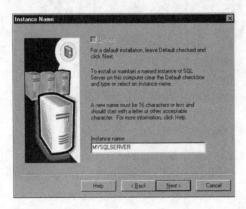

The instance name must follow some rules, and these are listed here. These rules are from the SQL Server Setup Help provided with the CD for installation.

- An instance name is not case sensitive.
- An instance name cannot be the terms `Default` or `MSSQLServer`.

- Instance names are limited to 16 characters.

- The first character in the instance name must be a letter, an ampersand, an underscore, or a number sign (#). Acceptable letters are those defined by the Unicode Standard 2.0, which includes Latin characters a–z and A–Z, in addition to letter characters from other languages.

Subsequent characters can be the following:

- Letters as defined in the Unicode Standard 2.0.

- Decimal numbers from either Basic Latin or other national scripts.

- The $, #, or _ symbols.

- Embedded spaces or special characters are not allowed in instance names, neither are the backslash (/), comma (,), colon (:), or @ sign.

Only characters that are valid in the current Microsoft Windows code page can be used in instance names in SQL Server 2000. If a Unicode character that is not supported under the current code page is used, an error occurs.

B

Even if the Default check box is available, do not select the Default option. Deselect the box and enter an instance name (preferably the same one I used). Why? Well, a new and key component that SQL Server 2000 now supports is the ability to have multiple instances of SQL Server 2000 running on your machine. Besides, it suits our needs very well.

If you decide to install the Default instance now, you might notice that some of the screens are a little different than in this guide.

EXCURSION

An Instance, an Instance, My Kingdom for an Instance

In past versions of SQL Server it was only possible to have one instance (now called Default) installed on your PC. This meant that if you had development and testing needs while running a production database, you would need two machines with SQL Server installed. Well, no more!

With SQL Server 2000 you can have multiple instances of the relational database management system (RDBMS) installed, in conjunction with a previous version installed (as in my machine's configuration). Each instance is a separate program, so each one "owns" its own little piece of the PC, including memory and hard-drive space.

As with all things, you can have too much of a good thing. Microsoft recommends that you not install more than 16 named instances (the number of named instances they have tested, including the Default) on any one machine, and in fact only install one instance if that is all you require. But hey, it's nice to know we can have more if we want!

 Note   If you do not install the Default instance of SQL Server 2000 now, you can install it at any time later.

Click Next after you have typed in an instance name. If you try to click Next before supplying an instance name, and the Default check box is not selected, an error message is displayed telling you that you must enter an instance name.

The next wizard screen (Setup Type, shown in Figure B.11) enables you to select the type of installation you want to perform. The following options are available:

- **Typical**—This is the recommended installation for most users. It installs all SQL Server's tools and add-ons except the Code Samples. For the Development Tools installation, it installs the Debugging tool only. This installation will be fine for the setup requirements necessary in the book.

- **Minimum**—This installs the core components required for SQL Server 2000 to run. This is especially effective if you have limited disk space.

- **Custom**—This enables you to select the tools and add-ons you want SQL Server 2000 to install on your machine. This option enables you to modify Windows and SQL Server 2000's collation settings. Collation settings relate to the character set you are using and the sort order. You should choose this option only if you are absolutely sure of the installation configuration you require.

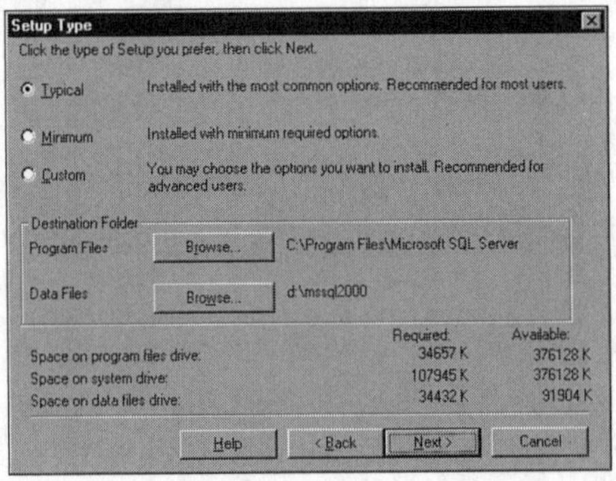

Figure B.11

The Setup Type screen of the Installation Wizard for SQL Server 2000.

The Browse buttons on this screen enable you to specify where you want SQL Server 2000 to store its data and program files. This is useful if you have disk space issues on the machine to which you are deploying. If you don't, the default settings will be fine.

 Note

For our installation select the Typical option. However, if you have specific needs to change the collation settings or want the add-ons installed, you can choose the Custom setting. Don't worry, I cover how to perform a custom installation in the section "What Happens If I Select the Custom Install Option?"

After you select the Typical option and click Next, you see the screen shown in Figure B.12.

Figure B.12

The Authentication Mode screen of the Installation Wizard for SQL Server 2000.

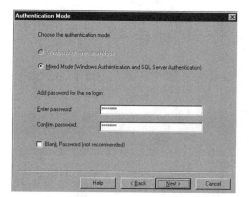

This screen (Authentication Mode) enables you to set the user account password for the SQL Server 2000 System Administrator (sa). Make sure you enter a password you will not easily forget and that others will not be able to guess too easily.

 Warning

Be sure you will remember your password, or keep it in a safe place, for the System Administrator account. If you forget your password, unfortunately you will have to uninstall and then reinstall your instance of SQL Server 2000.

Note

If you are connected to a network or running a Windows 2000 or NT operating system, you might be presented with the option Windows Authentication Mode. This means that the account that the SQL Service will use to gain access to the instance of SQL Server 2000 is the currently logged-on user account. If this option is available, choose the Mixed Mode option. This enables you to connect as sa to SQL Server, as well as connect through your NT network (if connected). More on security in Chapter 9, "Implementing Security in Spy Net."

After you click Next, the screen (Start Copying Files) shown in Figure B.13 is the last chance you have to go back and change installation options or to quit before the installation takes place.

Figure B.13

Start copying files or go back and change your options for the installation of SQL Server 2000.

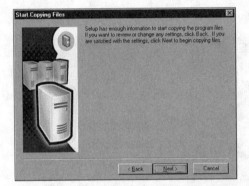

Click Next to begin the installation of SQL Server 2000 with the options you selected.

From here, you might as well go and get a cup of coffee. The install process copies several (hundreds it seems!) files onto your PC from the CD. Your screen during the installation process might look similar to Figure B.14.

When it's complete (the better part of 15 minutes on my Pentium 75), allow your PC to be restarted by the installation program (if required); then click Finish to complete the installation of SQL Server 2000 (Setup Complete, see Figure B.15). See, wasn't that painless?

Figure B.14

Files being copied during the installation process of SQL Server 2000.

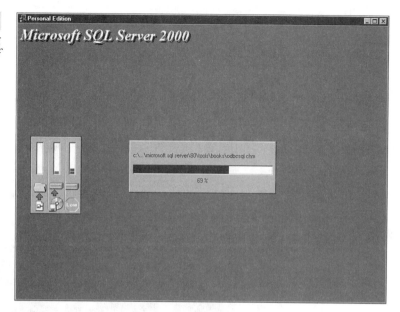

Figure B.15

The final screen of the Installation Wizard for SQL Server 2000.

What Happens If I Select the Custom Install Option?

If you select the Custom option for the installation, I assume you either want everything you possibly can get or you have a specific need to alter the collation settings for your installation. The Custom installation option gives you more steps than if you had selected the Typical installation option.

The first extra screen you see is the Select Components screen (shown in Figure B.16). This enables you to select or remove components that are either not covered by the Typical installation (such as code samples and add-ons) or that you do not require in your installation.

Figure B.16

Select the components you require for your installation of SQL Server 2000.

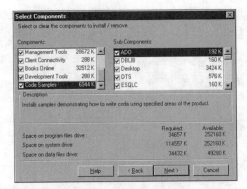

 Warning

Be careful removing components from the installation. If you remove the wrong component—a required component—the installation will fail, and you will have to repeat the whole process again.

Within this screen you can add the code samples that ship with SQL Server 2000 to help you when developing client applications to talk to your database. This option is sneakily hidden right at the bottom of the list box on the left. To select it, click the check box (as shown in Figure B.16).

After you're satisfied with the components you have selected, click Next to proceed with the installation.

The next screen you see is the Authentication Mode screen (see Figure B.17).

Figure B.17

The Authentication Mode screen of the Installation Wizard for SQL Server 2000.

This screen enables you to set the user account password for the SQL Server 2000 System Administrator (sa). Make sure you enter a password you will not easily forget and that others will not be able to guess too easily.

Be sure you will remember your password, or keep it in a safe place, for the System Administrator account. If you forget your password, unfortunately you will have to uninstall and then reinstall the instance of SQL Server 2000.

If you are connected to a network or running a Windows 2000 or NT operating system, you might be presented with the option Windows Authentication Mode. This means that the SQL Service will use the currently logged-on user account to gain access to the instance of SQL Server 2000. If this option is available, choose the Mixed Mode option. This enables you to connect as sa to SQL Server, as well as connect through your NT network (if connected). More on security in Chapter 9.

The next screen you see is the Collation Settings screen (see Figure B.18).

Figure B.18

The collation options screen of the Custom install option for SQL Server 2000.

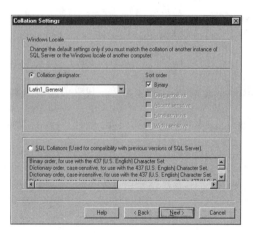

This is where things begin to get interesting. If you need to talk to another instance of SQL Server that has a different Windows *locale* or collation setting from your machine, you must adjust the setting to that of the instance of SQL Server you want to connect to. The instance can be running on a remote machine or on your PC. For our requirements, we do not need to do this, but if the need grabs you...

The *locale* refers to the way the characters on your computer are displayed and stored. The locale is set for your machine when the operating system is installed. Various countries and languages use different locale settings to enable the unique characters of their languages to be displayed. For example, the U.S. English character set uses the Latin1_General locale.

If you are connecting to a computer that uses a locale setting different from your computer, when data is sent, the receiving computer must interpret the information into its own locale. This can cause data to transfer very slowly, especially when there are large amounts of information. If the sending computer has characters that are not in the receiving computer's locale set (an extended character set), the data will be lost.

The next setting you must ensure is correct is the Sort Order option. The following options enable different combinations of sort orders:

- **Binary**—The fastest sort order, it is always case sensitive. This means that lowercase will always come before uppercase. For example, "m" will always appear before "M." If Binary is selected, the Accent and Case sensitive sort order options are grayed out.

- **Case sensitive**—Forces SQL Server 2000 to evaluate the case of the character. Lowercase will always come before uppercase. For example, "a" will always appear before "A." If this option is not selected, SQL Server 2000 considers "a" and "A" to be equal.

- **Accent sensitive**—Forces SQL Server 2000 to evaluate accented and unaccented characters. For example, "a" will not be equivalent to "à." Like case sensitive, if Accent sensitive is not selected, SQL Server 2000 considers the accented and unaccented characters to be equal.

- **Kana sensitive**—Forces SQL Server 2000 to evaluate the difference between the two Japanese character sets (Hiragana and Katakana). If Kana sensitive is not selected, SQL Server 2000 considers the Hiragana and Katakana character sets to be equal.

- **Width sensitive**—Forces SQL Server 2000 to evaluate the difference between a single-byte (half-width) character and its corresponding double-byte (full-width) character. If Width sensitive is not selected, SQL Server 2000 considers the single-byte and double-byte characters to be equal.

Note Because of the way character data is sorted on a computer, Binary sort ordering might not sort by the same rules as a dictionary sort order for any given language. So, people who speak the language might see results in an order different from the way they expect them to be.

I suggest that you specify the Binary Sort order option for your installation, but only if you do not need to specify that the Collation Setting be compatible with earlier versions of SQL Server (keep reading). Although this sometimes might not sort in the order you expect, it is much faster, and performance is an essential ingredient of a good database.

The final option in this screen is the SQL Collations option. As the screen specifies, this option is used for compatibility with previous versions of SQL Server, including versions 7.0, 6.5, and earlier. Select this option only if the installation will communicate with installations of earlier versions (not required for our SQL Spy Net application).

However, one of the cool new features of SQL Server 2000 is the collation support at a database level. In previous versions of SQL Server, after the collation setting was set, you couldn't change it without reinstalling. But with SQL Server 2000, you can have your server set to Windows collation, but when you create a database, you can set its collation setting to SQL collation. This takes away the mind-reading capabilities you used to need when performing your installations. Now that's cool!

When you are happy with the settings, click Next. The next screen (Network Libraries) you see is similar to the one shown in Figure B.19.

Figure B.19

Configuring the Network Libraries for a custom installation.

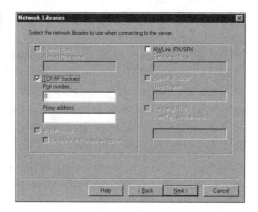

This screen relates to the Network Libraries you want to install for SQL Server 2000 to communicate between *client* and *server*. For a more thorough discussion of how client/server architecture fits in with these options, see Chapter 12, "Designing a Front End to Support Our SQLSpyNet Database."

The *Network Libraries* are the communication protocols that SQL Server 2000 uses to communicate on various networks. The protocols enable SQL Server 2000 to communicate by allowing *packets* to travel between the SQL Service and the PCs with which it is communicating.

 Packets are small bits of data grouped together to be sent as one item. This is analogous to putting an invoice and an advertising flyer in an envelope and forwarding the package to your customer.

A SQL Server 2000 installation can listen on a Network Library only if it has been configured. If multiple network libraries are configured, SQL Server 2000 can listen to all libraries that are configured.

The following options are available for configuring SQL Server 2000's communication protocols:

- **Named Pipes**—This option is used for configuring installation on an NT 4.0 or a Windows 2000 operating system only. Windows 95 or 98 do not support this protocol.

- **TCP/IP Sockets**—By default, this is the Network Library that all configurations of SQL Server 2000 use on the operating system on which it is deployed.

- **Multi-Protocol**—This protocol is used when you want to combine the network protocols that your organization might have. For example, it is tested and supported for TCP/IP, NWLink, IPX/SPX, and Named Pipes. It enables the use of Windows Authentication on all protocols supported by the Windows NT Remote Procedure Call (RPC) functionality.

- **NWLink IPX/SPX**—This protocol is used when you are deploying SQL Server 2000 on a Novell Network. This enables the Novell SPX client computers to connect and communicate with SQL Server 2000.

- **AppleTalk ADSP**—This protocol is used when you want Apple Macintosh client computers to connect and communicate with SQL Server 2000 using AppleTalk rather than having to use TCP/IP.

- **Banyan VINES**—This is another network protocol that is similar to the well-known Novel and NT networks. This communication protocol is specifically for the VINES Network.

If you install a named instance (as we have), the Multi-Protocol, AppleTalk, and Banyan VINES protocols will not be available options for you to select.

The following protocols have not been enhanced by Microsoft and still run at the same level of functionality as they did for SQL Server version 7.0:

- AppleTalk ADSP

- Banyan VINES

According to the documentation, these will not be enhanced, and Microsoft plans to drop them in future releases. These protocols are not supported for named instance installations.

For our installation, select TCP/IP Sockets.

EXCURSION

Picking the Right Port

As you can see in my installation, the port number I have is zero. Why? Well, SQL Server usually communicates on port number 1433 (the Internet Assigned Number Authority [IANA] has assigned this number specifically for SQL Server). I already have an instance of SQL Server installed on my machine, so I cannot use 1433 because another instance of SQL Server will have that port tied up. By leaving the port set to zero, SQL Server 2000 dynamically assigns the port number for me (allowing multiple instances to exist on my machine).

If this is the first installation of any version of SQL Server on your machine, you will see that the port has the default number 1433. If this is the case, leave it as is.

However, if you are like me and have had previous installations of SQL Server (no matter what version), your port number will default to 0 (zero) and the proxy address box will be blank. Accept this default.

You should specify a port number only if you want SQL Server 2000 to "listen" on a port other than the default (1433) instance. However, on a PC with more than one named instance of SQL Server 2000 installed, the port number is not allocated until the named instance is running. If you specify a particular port number for a named instance, SQL Server 2000 uses that number instead. If you specify to use a different port number, make sure it is a free port!

This completes the additional information for the Custom installation option. If you now revert back to the install guide, going to the step that allows SQL Server 2000 to Start Copying Files and follow on from there, you should be ready to roll.

Checking the Installation's Success

Congratulations, and well done! Your installation of SQL Server 2000 and the management tools is now complete.

The following section shows you how to find SQL Server 2000 in your Start menu and how to check whether your installation of SQL Server 2000 is running on your machine.

After your PC has restarted (if required), you might find SQL Server 2000 in your Start menu under Programs, Microsoft SQL Server (as shown in Figure B.20).

Figure B.20

Where to find SQL Server in the Start menu group.

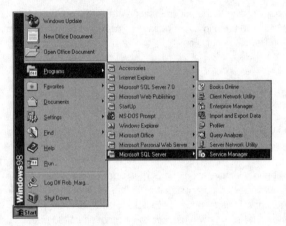

Within the SQL Server Start menu group, you will find the configuration and management tools for SQL Server 2000. To check that the installation is running correctly on your PC, select the Service Manager utility. This looks similar to the screen shown in Figure B.21.

Figure B.21

The Service Manager Utility for SQL Server 2000.

Under the Server drop-down box, you can see the instances of SQL Server 2000 that are installed on your machine. The instance name you created will be in the list, probably prefixed by your computer's name, such as *machinename\instancename*.

Select the instance you want to start. Then, select the service (the SQL Server service) you want to have running.

Click the green triangle if it is not grayed out. This starts the SQL Service on your machine. Select the Auto-Start Service When OS Starts check box. This ensures that the SQL Service starts when your PC boots up.

If the green triangle is grayed out, the SQL Service is already running on your machine. You need to stop the Service by clicking the Stop button, and then restart the service by clicking the green triangle.

Next, ensure the Auto-Start Service When OS Starts option is selected. The stopping and starting of the SQL Service ensures the service starts correctly each time your PC restarts.

And that concludes our installation guide for SQL Server 2000 on a Windows 98 PC. Pretty simple, wasn't it? Now that you have installed SQL Server 2000, you must go through a few "hoops" to set some of the options you'll need when you make your first connection.

Configuring SQL Server 2000

As already mentioned, SQL Server 2000 has an intuitive and friendly user interface that enables you to find your way through the application quickly and easily. And now is your chance to find out! I am going to introduce you to the main application in the SQL Server 2000 suite, the Enterprise Manager.

Within Enterprise Manager we are going to connect to the instance of SQL Server 2000 that we installed earlier. So I hope you remembered what you set your sa account password to!

1. Fire up SQL Server 2000 Enterprise Manager by selecting the icon from the group in the Start menu (see Figure B.22).

2. When the application first starts you will be presented with the Enterprise Management console application similar to that shown in Figure B.23.

If you've gotten this far, you are ready to establish a connection to SQL Server 2000 and begin getting our application development underway.

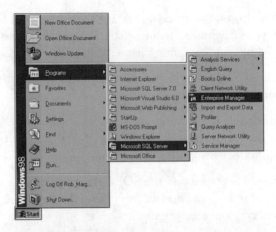

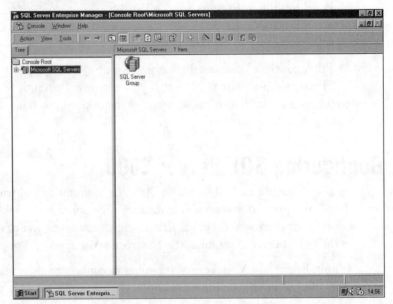

Connecting to SQL Server 2000 for the First Time

I don't know about you guys, but when this part happens, it gets kind of exciting. Why? Well, this signifies that we are on our way to developing our first ever, real-life application in SQL Server 2000. Now doesn't that just light your fire? Ahh well, we aren't all excited by the same things, and I guess the world would be a bit of a boring place to be if we were. Anyway let's get on with it!

1. To start the connection process to SQL Server 2000, click the plus sign next to the Microsoft SQL Servers icon at the top of the tree-view control. This is located just under the Console Root folder (refer to Figure B.23).

This will expand the tree-view control to contain a new item called SQL Server Group. If you do not see this icon, right-click the SQL Servers icon and select the New SQL Server Group command from the list, as shown in Figure B.24.

Figure B.24

The new SQL Server Group command within Enterprise Manager.

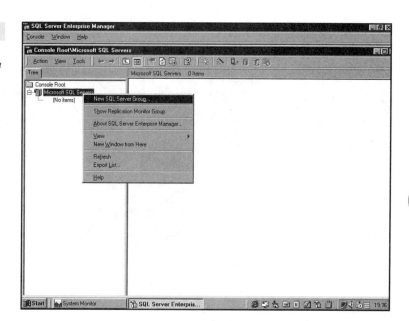

2. Fill in the SQL Server Group name that you want to appear here, as shown in Figure B.25. I've called my group SQL Server Group, but you can name yours something different.

Figure B.25

The SQL Server Groups registration dialog within Enterprise Manager.

Setting up a SQL Server group enables us to specify that either a single instance of SQL Server 2000 or a cluster of SQL Server 2000 instances can belong to the group. This is especially useful when you have multiple servers (or instances) running different versions of SQL Server. You can have a SQL Server 2000 group and a SQL Server 7.0 group. This allows you to group together similar applications.

After you have created the group in which your instance is going to reside, you must create an actual connection to the instance of SQL Server 2000 that you have installed. There are two ways of doing this (aren't there always?). I will show you the manual connection way first (my preferred way) and then the wizard approach.

1. Right-click the SQL Server Group and select New SQL Server Registration (see Figure B.26).

Figure B.26

The New SQL Server Registration command within Enterprise Manager.

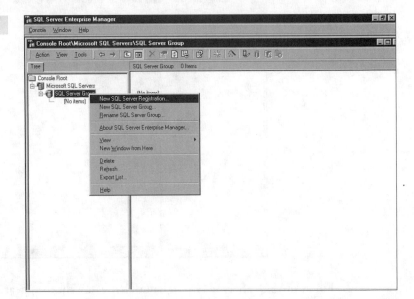

2. This will more than likely launch a Register SQL Server Wizard screen, which appears in Figure B.27. However, if the wizard screen does not appear, proceed to step 3.

Figure B.27

The Register SQL Server Wizard within Enterprise Manager.

To continue with the manual connection, click the From Now On, I Want to Perform This Task Without Using a Wizard box, and then click Next. You will be presented with a screen similar to that shown in Figure B.28. If you want to use the wizard to make your connection to SQL Server 2000, do not check the box and click the Next button. For more instructions, go to the "Using a Wizard to Connect to SQL Server 2000" section later in this appendix.

Figure B.28

SQL Server registration dialog box within Enterprise Manager.

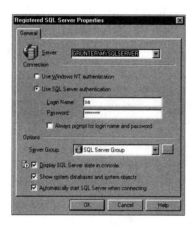

3. This screen enables you to manually set up the connection information needed for your client computer to talk to SQL Server 2000.

4. The first option box enables you to type in or select from the list your SQL Server installation name. If it does not appear in the list, just type the name in the box. This is in the format Servername\InstanceName.

5. Next you need to supply the credentials you will use to connect to SQL Server 2000. Enter the username sa and the password that you assigned sa during the installation. Leave this blank if you did not assign sa a password.

 Note

If you have forgotten your sa password you are in big trouble, mister! Seriously though, you will have to uninstall the instance of SQL Server 2000 that you have installed, and then re-install a new instance. It is a real pain, but I bet you'll never forget your password again!

6. If you select the Always Prompt for Login Name and Password option, SQL Server 2000 will pop up a login dialog for you whenever you try to connect. This will prevent others who use your machine from getting into your SQL Server 2000 instance, unless they know your username and password.

If your machine is secure do not select this option.

7. Now you need to assign your connection a SQL Server group to belong to. Select the group name that you created earlier. If you do not see your group name, click the ellipsis (...) button and retype the group name. Make sure if you do this that you select it to be a top-level group (this means it sits at the top of the tree-view control rather than under another group name). This action will re-create the group for you.

The last three option boxes have to do with the way SQL Server 2000 looks and behaves when you connect.

- Display SQL Server State In Console—This enables you to turn service polling on or off.

- Show System Databases and System Objects—SQL Server uses some system objects (tempDB, Master, and so on) similar to Windows. This option enables you to see these objects in the tree-view control.

- Automatically Start SQL Server When Connecting—This option specifies that if SQL Server 2000 is not running (the service has stopped), the service will be automatically restarted when you connect.

I suggest that you leave all three of these options selected unless you have a specific reason for changing any of them.

When you click OK, Enterprise Manager will try to establish a connection to SQL Server 2000. When it has succeeded (this can take a couple of seconds or a couple of minutes depending on your machine), you are ready to start browsing around SQL Server 2000. Your screen will look similar to Figure B.29.

Figure B.29

Enterprise Manager connected to SQL Server 2000.

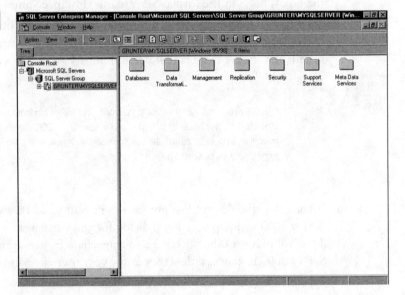

Note

If you receive an error, first check the username and password you supplied, then check the ServerName\InstanceName combination. If the problem is neither of these, refer to SQL Server 2000's Books Online. It will provide you with an invaluable resource for troubleshooting installations. Alternatively, you could visit Microsoft's Web site and go to either `http://msdn.microsoft.com/` or `http://www.microsoft.com/technet/` (these addresses were current at time of writing). These online resources will become invaluable to you as your career progresses, and best of all, the information is free!

8. Finally, click the little plus icon next to the ServerName\InstanceName icon. This will expand the tree-view control, and you will be able to see all the databases and other associated objects. See Figure B.30 for how the screen should look.

Figure B.30

Enterprise Manager expanded with database objects shown.

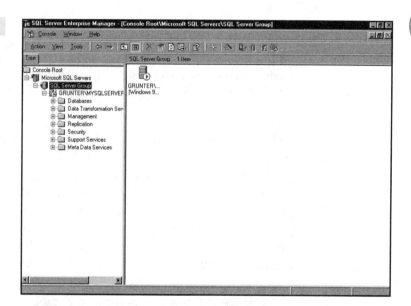

That's it, you're finished! The next section describes how to connect using the wizard provided by SQL Server 2000, but you just successfully did all the connection information you need. Well done, and congratulations! You have received an A+ for your second assignment.

Using a Wizard to Connect to SQL Server 2000

Okay, so you would like to use the built-in SQL Server 2000 wizard to make a connection to SQL Server 2000. After completing the first screen in the wizard (as previously discussed), you will be presented with a screen similar to that shown in Figure B.31.

Figure B.31

The second screen in the registration wizard for Enterprise Manager.

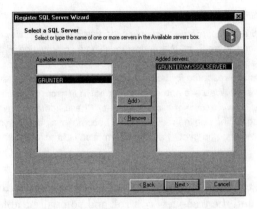

1. If you do not see your server and instance names in the Available Servers box you can type them in. This will be in the format ServerName\InstanceName.

To get the name of the server, launch the SQL Service Manager application (in the SQL Server Start menu group). This will have all the instance names in the format you need in the drop-down box. You can then copy the name and paste it into the wizard screen.

After you have supplied the server name, click the Add button. The server name will appear in the Added Servers box. Click Next.

2. As shown in Figure B.32, this screen enables you to set the type of authentication that Enterprise Manager will use to connect to SQL Server 2000. Select The SQL Server Login Information option. If you are connected to a network you might be able to select the The Windows NT Account Information option, but we are designing our application to use SQL Server 2000 security, so the first option should be selected.

Figure B.32

The security screen in the registration wizard for Enterprise Manager.

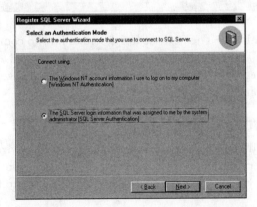

3. Click next. As shown in Figure B.33, the next screen enables you to enter the login name and password that you will use to connect to SQL Server 2000. Enter sa in the Login Name box and the password that you set for sa when you installed the instance of SQL Server 2000. If you didn't set a password, leave this option blank.

If you have forgotten your sa password you are in big trouble, mister! Seriously though, you will have to uninstall the instance of SQL Server 2000 that you have installed, and then re-install a new instance. It is a real pain, but I bet you'll never forget your password again!

Figure B.33

The password details for the sa screen in the registration wizard for Enterprise Manager.

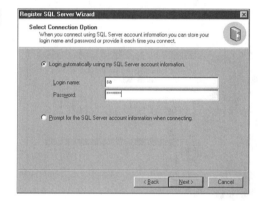

The second option, Prompt for the SQL Server Login Information When Connecting, means whenever you try to connect to SQL Server 2000 using any of the management tools, you will be asked for your login name and password. This is very good on a shared machine where you would like to restrict the access that other users have. However, do not select this option if your machine is secure. Click Next.

4. This screen, as shown in Figure B.34, enables you to choose the SQL Server group to which your registration information will belong. Select your group that you created earlier from the drop-down list.

If you do not see your group, select the Create a New Top-Level SQL Server Group option, and type the group name you would like the group to be called. This will re-create a group for you. Click Nxext.

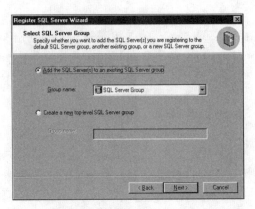

5. The final screen, shown in Figure B.35, confirms the ServerName\InstanceName you have selected.

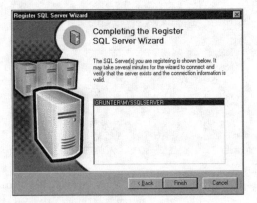

If you want to make any modifications, click the back button. Click Finish when you're happy with your options.

6. You will see a screen similar to that shown in Figure B.36. This shows Enterprise Manager's progress with the connection information.

When the process has run you can return to step 4 in the previous section, and as Shakespeare once said, "Read on, McDuff!"

How Does It All Work?

If you did the custom install (if not, refer to the notes in the first half of this appendix), you might remember setting some properties and values for the network libraries. These network libraries enable us to make connections to SQL Server 2000.

Because we are running SQL Server 2000 on Windows 98 and we are not connected to a network, we must use the TCP/IP connection protocol. For us to connect to SQL Server 2000 there must be matching protocols on both the client and the server. SQL Server 2000 installs these both for you by default, eliminating some of the connection issues you could face if manually configuring them.

Installed with SQL Server 2000 are two tools that help you configure the protocols used to connect to the server: the Server Network utility and the Client Network utility. The Server Network utility is used to configure the protocols that SQL Server 2000 will listen on for client requests. And conversely, the Client Network utility is used to configure the network libraries that the client will use to talk to SQL Server 2000.

The TCP/IP protocol is all that is supported by a Windows 98 installation. This makes it very easy for us to configure and talk to SQL Server 2000.

When we established a connection to SQL Server 2000 through the Enterprise Manager we were acting as the client computer. We were making a request to SQL Server 2000, and it responded by allowing us to make the connection, so we could say SQL Server 2000 was listening for our request and responded on demand.

I know it seems a little strange that the computer you are using is both a server and a client at the same time, but there are many roles in life where the server becomes the client. For example, in a shopkeeper scenario, the server is the person behind the counter, and you are the client making requests. However, when the shopkeeper (server) places an order with his suppliers, he then becomes a client.

All right, I know the overview is brief, but you will learn more about the concepts of client/server architecture as we progress through the book. So let's get back to our SQL Spy Net application.

You are now ready to rock, so stop sitting there and get on with the book already!

Where to Go from Here

Well guys, it saddens me a little, but also excites me, that we are finally on the last segment of the book. This has been a great project for me, and I hope that you have enjoyed yourself along the way as well. You see, we Kiwis are not that bad!

In this appendix we will check out some of the opportunities available to you with your newfound knowledge. We will also look at some ways that you can further your knowledge through study and certification.

As you should have guessed by now, the role of a DBA is very versatile. As a DBA, you know that when you go to work each day you will have the opportunity to partake in something new, whether that is fixing a client's database because something has gone wrong or finding a new way of making your day-to-day tasks easier.

If a sense of adventure is the sort of job fulfillment you are looking for then a DBA role is probably for you. Besides which, good DBAs can be very hard to find, so you can almost set your own salary! Great, isn't it?

SQL Server DBAs are in demand within many organizations around the world. I list some sites that are able to help you in your job searching, but please know that I have no affiliation with any of these sites. They just seemed to have the most SQL Server DBA jobs available at the time of this writing.

One of the greatest things about the IT industry is that you do not need to have any formal qualifications, unlike lawyers or accountants. Instead, experience, self-teaching, and a desire to get ahead are all that you need.

Please do not get me wrong. If you get the chance to go to university to gain a degree or diploma, do it! Although university is theoretical in base, the knowledge you gain will enable you to learn many concepts that can be quite hard to teach yourself, such as

- Relational theory
- Software (or System) Development Life Cycle (SDLC)
- Effective database design
- Disk space storage and enhancement
- Multiuser environments including locks and transactions

However, regardless of whether you have formal qualifications, Microsoft offers a range of recognized qualifications that will enhance your career opportunities. These qualifications are made up of several certifications.

Let's take a look at these certifications now.

Microsoft Certification

Microsoft offers a range of exams that lead to certification.

As you can imagine, these exams are based around Microsoft technologies. But more than that, they also include some of Microsoft's development philosophies, such as the Microsoft Solution Framework (MSF), which is generally about the roles that each person plays in application development, as well as the iterations (cycles) that an application will go through in its lifetime.

You can take exams on virtually every Microsoft product available, including, but not limited to

- Visual Basic
- SQL Server
- Windows 2000 Professional
- Windows 2000 Server
- Office 2000

and hundreds of others! So whatever you are good at, Microsoft has an exam for you to try to see how good you really are.

What are the different types of certification and what is required for each? Five basic qualifications are available in the technical arena.

You can become accredited with many other Microsoft certifications, such as MOUS, but I only cover the basic development ones.

Microsoft has a site dedicated to its training and development. At the end of each certification listing, I give information on how to find more about that certification, but the basic URL is the same:

`http//www.microsoft.com/mcp/`

Let's take a look at the certifications offered at Microsoft.

How to Become a Microsoft-Certified Professional (MCP)

This is the first credential that you can gain and is easy to become accredited in. All that is required is that you take and pass *one* of the Microsoft technical exams. Sounds easy, right? Well it is.

Microsoft has designed the exams to challenge you, but you should have no problem passing as long as you put in a little effort before taking the exam.

The exams are based on many areas of expertise and include development (Visual Basic, Visual C++, and so forth), BackOffice (Windows 2000 Professional and Server), Internet (TCP/IP), Site Builder (Visual InterDev, FrontPage), and a host of others.

So where do I go to get more information? You can find the requirements for the MCP credential by selecting MCP from the menu on the left side of the Certification home page.

Two other MCP certification add-ons are also available within the MCP credential.

- MCP + Site Building—This certification is based on a choice of two specialized Microsoft exams that form the Site building requirements. After you have taken two of these exams you will have gained not only MCP + Site Building, but also MCP. How easy is that?

- MCP + Internet—This is like the MCP + Site Building certification except that you need to take three exams based on Internet requirements. Like the MCP + Site Building, upon completion you have not only MCP + Internet, but also MCP.

To find out more about these two certifications, select MCP + Internet or MCP + Site Builder from the menu on the left side of the Certification home page.

How to Become a Microsoft-Certified Solution Developer (MCSD)

The MCSD certification requirements are higher than those required by the MCP status. This certification requires you to take four exams based on application development and deployment. Three of the exams are mandatory for the certification, but of those three you can have some choices in which exams you take. For example, you can select either a Visual C++ or Visual Basic desktop exam for one of your required exams.

The fourth exam that you take is known as an elective, and you can choose from a very large list of exams that will help you gain accreditation, including SQL Server.

To find out more information, select the MCSD menu item from the left side of the Certification home page.

There are no additional certifications within the MCSD certification. However, after you have gained one exam from the MCSD list you will have your MCP status. This makes it very easy to become qualified.

How to Become a Microsoft-Certified Systems Engineer (MCSE)

The MCSE certification is probably the toughest of all the certification requirements in the Microsoft curriculum. Seven; yes that's right, seven exams are required to pass the MCSE certification.

 **Note**

The guide I provide here is for the Windows 2000 track. This is the most up-to-date certification track because most of the NT 3.51 exams will be phased out shortly, and the NT 4.0 ones won't be far behind.

Of those seven, four are mandatory, and you do not really have too much choice about the exams you take. The fifth exam allows you to choose from two possibilities. Luckily, exams six and seven are elective exams, and like the MCSD certification, allow you to choose from a large list of possibilities.

To get more information on the MCSE certifications, select MCSE from the menu on the Certification home page.

Like the other certifications, the completion of one exam will allow you to gain MCP status while you work toward your MCSE.

One other certification is within the MCSE certification, and that is MCSE + Internet. If you are brave enough to take on this challenge you will need to take and pass *nine* exams, seven of which are core exams, and two of which are electives.

To find out more, select the MCSE + Internet menu item from the left side of the Certification home page.

A big task to ask of anybody, right? No, not really. With the right study and discipline you should be able to gain MCSE + Internet within 6–12 months, as well as work full time!

How to Become a Microsoft-Certified Database Administrator (MCDBA)

I purposely left this for last because it is the most relevant certification to the book!

The MCDBA certification requires taking and passing *five* exams.

> Like the MCSE guide, I am basing the MCDBA certification guide on the Windows 2000 track.

Four of these exams are core examinations and offer you little choice in which ones you take. The final exam is, as you guessed, an elective examination and comes from a long list of exams. As with the other certifications, you gain MCP status on passing any one of the exams that are part of the requirements.

The coolest thing is that around December 2000 the new SQL Server 2000 exams will be released! To see more information, select the MCDBA menu item from the left side of the Certification home page.

That is the basic list of certifications that are available, but how do you go about planning which exams to take for which certifications?

How to Plan for Microsoft Certification

Because many certifications have similar examination requirements, when you pass one exam for certification, it can actually count toward another certification! This is similar to a university where the concept of cross-crediting your papers is available.

Before you take an exam you should plan which exams have the maximum cross-credit capability. You need to analyze the requirements for each certification, both core and elective exams, and find the exams that will give you the maximum benefit.

> Do not choose exams that give you the greatest cross-creditability but might exclude you from taking those that interest you. You need to find a balance between gaining certification and career advances.

You do not have to apply to Microsoft to get more than one certification; this is given automatically when you have enough exams to fulfill the requirements of each certification.

One of the most common questions is, "How do I know when I am ready to take an exam?" Unfortunately, the real answer is whenever you feel as though you are. Some study guides can help you assess your capabilities, and we will look at those shortly, but it really is up to you.

Having said that, though, if you take an exam and do not pass it, it is really not that big of a deal. It might be recorded that you did not pass the exam the first time, but even if it is, after you have the accreditation and someone else does not, who cares?

You must remember that there are many different parts to each of Microsoft's tools, and it is almost impossible to know every one of them well. But you are tested on them, so try to become as familiar with each part of a product as you can. For example, in SQL Server try to get to know Enterprise Manager, Query Analyzer, Profiler, Client/Server network utilities, and so forth.

The next part of the certification track is to check out what study guides are available.

Study Guides

Probably the most common way to study for an exam is by getting hands-on experience with the product.

On each exam, Microsoft has some basic requirements stipulated for the exam, including how much experience you should have with the product or tool being tested. Besides this though, Microsoft provides downloadable practice exams that enable you to experience the exams before you take them.

 The downloadable exams are practice exams only. They are designed to allow you to get a grip on the concept of what it is like to take an electronic exam. The results you get are not indicative of the results you will get on the actual exam.

Microsoft also has Microsoft Press books and study guides available, which can help you in your preparation for exams. These can be ordered directly from Microsoft or from one of their agents.

However, Microsoft is not the only company that can help you out when preparing for study. Numerous other companies such as Transcender (http://www.transcender.com) have exams available that mimic the real Microsoft exams.

Transcender offers two types of exam simulation software, TranscenderCert and TranscenderFlash. TranscenderCert is a tool for actually simulating the real exam, and TranscenderFlash is a review tool that offers topic-related questions in flash-card format.

Many Web sites can assist you in gaining certification by providing hints and tips on different exams.

So my final piece of advice on exams is: Do not be afraid! Have a go! Even if you do not pass, you will have given it a good shot, and you will be better prepared for next time!

Job Opportunities

This is probably one of the bits you have been really waiting for! Where can you use the newfound knowledge you have gained?

As stated earlier, good SQL Server DBAs are hard to find. If you really know your stuff, you are worth your weight in gold. But how do you get to that stage? Unfortunately, everybody has to start at the bottom. To get your foot in the door with a company you must show drive, determination, and a willingness to learn.

 **Note** I do not profess to be a guidance counselor or an employment consultant. For real professional advice, seek professional help.

After you have a job as a junior DBA, you will probably perform many mundane tasks such as data conversion from legacy systems and maintenance of existing systems. Do not let these tasks scare you away from what you want to do! Without the knowledge gained from the very mundane tasks, you cannot effectively analyze a server and pinpoint potential problems. Without learning about data structures you cannot effectively design a new application.

Finally, many Web sites can help you in your quest to find a job that has SQL Server as a main component.

Many sites offer free online training, so check this out before signing up with any one employment consultant.

Some tips for finding the right job for you!

Go indirect: Let the recruiters help you do the searching. Find a place to post your resume or post it with a reputable recruiter. You can find recruiters who handle the types of jobs you are interested in by going to a large site such as Monster. Then when you find a similar job posting, contact that recruiter. Beware, though, and don't undersell yourself to the recruiter.

Go direct: Look at the Web sites of companies you like and check out their jobs. Most companies have several jobs available on their Web sites, attracting people from many disciplines.

Create your own Web site: Heck, if you can do all that's in this book, you could really show off your skills by creating your own SQL Server 2000 application for a Web site. Or at least have your own site available with all your information for any prospective employer to view.

If you need further help in getting your career off the ground, get in touch with a local IT employment agency; heaps of them are available in this day and age. They might be able to recommend some steps for you to take to get that job you really want!

A Thank You to You, the Reader

Because this is the last section in the book, I thought I would offer you my kindest regards for taking the time to read the book.

I realize that I have only scratched the surface of SQL Server 2000, but I do hope that the information I have provided has been everything that you need to get your first SQL Server 2000 application off the ground and really humming.

Once again, my students, I thank you for being patient and putting up with my warped sense of humor.

I look forward to gracing your coffee tables in the future with yet another book, maybe even on another version of SQL Server! However it probably won't be too soon. I was once told that writing a book is like giving birth to your thoughts. If this is true then the labor has been long and hard!

Anyway, take the chance now to reflect a little on what we have achieved, and if you feel the need, go back to page one and start again.

Thank you, your gracious teacher, Rob Hawthorne.

Index

X-Z

Other Related Titles

Special Edition Using SQL
Rafe Colburn
ISBN: 0-7897-1974-6
$39.99 U.S./$59.95 CAN

Companion CD-ROM Installation Information

SQL Server 2000 120-Day Enterprise Evaluation Edition

System Requirements:

- PC with an Intel or compatible pentium 166 MHz or higher processor
- Microsoft Windows NT Server 4.0 with Service Pack 5 or later, Windows NT Server 4.0 Enterprise Edition with Service Pack 5 or later, Windows 2000 Server, Windows 2000 Advanced Server, or Windows 2000 Datacenter Server operating system
- Minimum of 64MB of RAM (128MB or more recommended)

Hard-disk space required:

- 95–270MB for database server; approximately 250MB for typical installation
- 50MB minimum for Analysis Services; 130MB for typical installation
- 80MB for Microsoft English Query (supported on Windows 2000 operating system but not logo certified)
- Microsoft Internet Explorer 5.0 or later
- CD-ROM drive
- VGA or higher resolution monitor
- Microsoft Mouse or compatible pointing device

NOTICE